JOHNNY CLEGG

Critical reflections on his music and influence

JOHNNY CLEGG

Critical reflections on his music and influence

Edited by
MICHAEL DREWETT AND LUCILLA SPINI

WITS UNIVERSITY PRESS

Published in South Africa by:
Wits University Press
1 Jan Smuts Avenue
Johannesburg 2001

www.witspress.co.za

Compilation © Michael Drewett and Lucilla Spini 2025
Chapters © Individual contributors 2025
Images © Copyright holders
Cover photograph © Marguerite de Villiers Coetzee 2017
Lyrics and music of Johnny Clegg's songs are reproduced courtesy of Scatterlings Pty Ltd and the Clegg Family. All lyrics and music © Scatterlings Pty Ltd.

First published 2025

http://dx.doi.org.10.18772/22025109643

978-1-77614-964-3 (Paperback)
978-1-77614-965-0 (Hardback)
978-1-77614-966-7 (Web PDF)
978-1-77614-967-4 (EPUB)

All rights reserved. No part of this publication may be reproduced, stored in a retrieval system, or transmitted in any form or by any means, electronic, mechanical, photocopying, recording or otherwise, without the written permission of the publisher, except in accordance with the provisions of the Copyright Act, Act 98 of 1978.

All images remain the property of the copyright holders. The publishers gratefully acknowledge the publishers, institutions and individuals referenced in captions for the use of images. Every effort has been made to locate the original copyright holders of the images reproduced here; please contact Wits University Press in case of any omissions or errors.

This publication is peer reviewed following international best practice standards for academic and scholarly books.

Project manager: Alison Paulin
Copyeditor: Karen Press
Proofreader: Alison Paulin
Indexer: Margaret Ramsay
Cover design: Hybrid Creative
Typeset in 11 point Minion Pro

This book is dedicated to the memory of Jonathan (Johnny) Clegg.

CONTENTS

LIST OF ILLUSTRATIONS		ix
PREFACE		xiii
ACKNOWLEDGEMENTS		xv
Chapter 1	Critical Reflections on the Music and Influence of Johnny Clegg *Michael Drewett and Lucilla Spini*	1
PART 1:	**JOHNNY CLEGG'S ENGAGEMENT WITH LIFE IN SOUTH AFRICA**	
Chapter 2	The Unheard Live Recordings of Johnny Clegg: Listening to Clegg's Early Performances within the Context of Alternative Popular Music in South Africa *Lizabé Lambrechts and Pakama Ncume*	19
Chapter 3	'Woza Moya Omuhle': Johnny Clegg and Sipho Mchunu's Unifying Cross-Cultural Brotherhood *Andrew Grant Innes*	41
Chapter 4	Johnny Clegg as Interlocutor of African Culture: A Thematic Analysis of a Selection of His Songs *Martina Viljoen*	61
Chapter 5	Johnny Clegg and the Poetry and Politics of Migrant Labour *Richard Pithouse*	83
Chapter 6	The Praise Names of Johnny Clegg *Sipho Mchunu and Andrew Grant Innes*	113
PART 2:	**GLOBAL RECEPTION**	
Chapter 7	Johnny Clegg and the Cultural Boycott in the United Kingdom *Michael Drewett*	125
Chapter 8	Johnny Clegg: *Le Zoulou Blanc* in France *Lucilla Spini*	147

| Chapter 9 | Lost or Misconstrued: Johnny Clegg in Hollywood
Chris Letcher | 169 |
| Chapter 10 | Digging for Some Words: Johnny Clegg's Academic Experiences in North America
Lucilla Spini and Andrew J. Friedland | 183 |

PART 3:	**TRANSITIONS IN JOHNNY CLEGG'S MUSIC AND LIFE**	
Chapter 11	From Juluka to Savuka: Johnny Clegg's Changing Compositional Practices *Caleb Mutch*	209
Chapter 12	What We Don't See: The Afterlives of '*Asimbonanga*' *Nicol Hammond*	229
Chapter 13	Clegg Is Cancelled? Johnny Clegg and Questions of Zulu Cultural Appropriation *Brett Houston-Lock*	249
Chapter 14	King of Time: A Lament for Johnny Clegg *Marguerite de Villiers Coetzee*	269

| CONTRIBUTORS | 307 |
| INDEX | 313 |

LIST OF ILLUSTRATIONS

CHAPTER 2

Figure 2.1	Johnny Clegg and Sipho Mchunu in the Market Café, 16 January 1977.	20
Figure 2.2	'Free People's Concert', University of the Witwatersrand, Johannesburg, 1972.	27
Figure 2.3	Johnny Clegg, Sipho Mchunu and Wa Madhlebe dancers, Wits University 'Free People's Concert', 1972.	28

CHAPTER 3

Figure 3.1	Inside the Mchunu main roundhouse in Magobhe, Makhabeleni, KwaZulu-Natal, where the *Ukwamukelwa Ekhaya* ceremony was conducted.	51
Figure 3.2	*Amabutho* (warriors) gathered at the *Ukulandwa Kongasekho* ceremony for Johnny Clegg in the *isibaya*, Magobhe, Makhabeleni, KwaZulu-Natal, 8 February 2020.	53
Figure 3.3	*Amabutho* (warriors) gathered at the *Ukulandwa Kongasekho* ceremony for Johnny Clegg in the *isibaya*, Magobhe, Makhabeleni, KwaZulu-Natal, 8 February 2020.	53

CHAPTER 6

Figure 6.1	The authors together with Bafazana Qoma and Charlie Mzila at the launch of Johnny Clegg's book, *Scatterling of Africa: My Early Years*, Johannesburg, 29 September 2021.	114

CHAPTER 8

Figure 8.1	Johnny Clegg and Renaud Séchan in South Africa in 1987.	150
Figure 8.2	Johnny Clegg and Claude Six backstage, July 1989.	152

CHAPTER 9

Figure 9.1	The wave form showing the structure of the album version of 'Scatterlings of Africa' compared with the edited remix used in the film.	174
Figure 9.2	Transcription by the author of the first verse of 'Cruel, Crazy, Beautiful World', used in the film *Career Opportunities*.	177

CHAPTER 10

Figure 10.1	Johnny Clegg receives an honorary doctorate of humane letters from the president of Dartmouth University, Jim Yong Kim, on 10 June 2012.	193
Figure 10.2	The Dartmouth undergraduate class with Terry Tempest Williams, Johnny Clegg, Andrew Friedland, 13 April 2014.	194

CHAPTER 11

Figure 11.1	Two metrical interpretations of the opening of Juluka's and Savuka's versions of *'Siyayilanda'*.	211
Figure 11.2	Two interpretations of the drums in Savuka's *'Siyayilanda'*.	212
Figure 11.3a	The lead-in and start of the chorus of 'Scatterlings of Africa', Juluka and Savuka versions.	216
Figure 11.3b	The continuation of the chorus of 'Scatterlings of Africa', Juluka and Savuka versions.	217
Figure 11.4	Bass and lead vocals of 'I Call Your Name', beginning of each type of section.	221

CHAPTER 14

Figure 14.1	Johnny Clegg at The Teatro, Montecasino, Johannesburg, 15 July 2016.	270
Figure 14.2	Jesse Clegg's debut concert at The Venue, Melrose Arch, Johannesburg, 2 May 2009.	273
Figure 14.3	Guest appearance by Arno Carstens at Jesse Clegg's debut concert at The Venue, Melrose Arch, Johannesburg, 2 May 2009.	273
Figure 14.4	Jesse Clegg at the 'Joburg Day' festival held on Riversands Farm, Fourways, 17 October 2009.	274
Figure 14.5	Johnny Clegg at the 'Joburg Day' festival held on Riversands Farm, Fourways, 17 October 2009.	275
Figure 14.6	Johnny Clegg and Sipho Mchunu backstage at Kirstenbosch National Botanical Garden, Cape Town, 29 March 2015.	276
Figure 14.7	Johnny Clegg at the Walter Sisulu National Botanical Garden, Johannesburg, 30 August 2015.	277
Figure 14.8	Johnny Clegg shakes hands with an audience member and fan who recognised him at a dance event outside Jeppe Hostel in central Johannesburg, 7 December 2014.	277

List of illustrations

Figure 14.9	Prior to posing for a photograph together, a leader at Denver Men's Hostel in Johannesburg playfully comments on how Johnny Clegg's face has changed over the years, 13 November 2016.	278
Figure 14.10	Jesse Clegg joins Johnny Clegg on stage at the first of the 'Final Journey Tour' concerts at Cape Town's Grand West Casino, 30 June 2017.	279
Figure 14.11	Sipho Mchunu and Johnny Clegg perform together at the second 'Final Journey Tour' concert at Cape Town's Grand West Casino, 1 July 2017.	279
Figure 14.12	Various artists on stage take a bow at the end of Johnny Clegg's public memorial service held in Sandton, Johannesburg, 26 July 2019.	287
Figure 14.13	Sipho Mchunu speaks at the public memorial service held for Johnny Clegg in Sandton, Johannesburg, 26 July 2019.	288
Figure 14.14	Johnny Clegg is joined on stage by his sons Jesse and Jaron and Sipho Mchunu at the end of the 'Final Journey Tour' performance in Cape Town, 30 June 2017.	289
Figure 14.15	Johnny Clegg's sons, Jesse and Jaron, speak at a tribute held by Johnny Clegg's former dance teammates at Jules Park in central Johannesburg, near Jeppe Hostel, 1 September 2019.	289
Figure 14.16	Dancers perform a tribute for Johnny Clegg at Jules Park in central Johannesburg, near Jeppe Hostel, 1 September 2019.	290
Figure 14.17	Bafazana Qoma, Johnny Clegg's long-time friend, who organised and participated in the tribute to Clegg held at Jules Park in central Johannesburg, near Jeppe Hostel, 1 September 2019.	290
Figure 14.18	Johnny Clegg's sons, Jesse and Jaron, speak at the Tribute Show at Emmarentia Botanical Gardens, Johannesburg, 17 July 2022.	292
Figure 14.19	Former band members Andy Innes (of Savuka) and Sipho Mchunu (of Juluka) perform together at Johnny Clegg's Tribute Show at Emmarentia Botanical Gardens, Johannesburg, 17 July 2022.	293
Figure 14.20	Jesse Clegg performs 'Cruel, Crazy, Beautiful World' while home videos of him and his father are displayed on a screen behind him at The Teatro, Montecasino, Johannesburg, 25 November 2023.	294
Figure 14.21	Nicholas Petricca of Walk the Moon performs with Jesse Clegg at his 'Songs and Memories' gig at Montecasino in Johannesburg, 25 November 2023.	295
Figure 14.22	The first photograph the author took of Johnny Clegg, at the Joburg Day festival in September 2006.	296
Figure 14.23	The last photograph the author took of Johnny Clegg, at the 'Final Journey Tour' performance in Cape Town's Grand West Casino, 1 July 2017.	296

PREFACE

On behalf of the Clegg family, we're honoured to introduce this collection of reflections on Johnny's life and music. Each contributor, many of whom were his friends and collaborators, brings heartfelt insight into how Johnny Clegg's songs bridged cultures, challenged injustice and celebrated our shared humanity. We thank Wits University Press, Michael Drewett, Lucilla Spini and every writer who gave their time and passion to this project. May these pages remind you of the joy, resilience and unity his music and life continue to inspire.

—*Jenny, Jaron and Jesse Clegg*

ACKNOWLEDGEMENTS

This book was inspired by the strong influence that Johnny Clegg had on our lives and academic interests. It has been made possible thanks to the authors of the chapters, who have contributed their time, knowledge and enthusiasm in addressing many different dimensions of Clegg's life, activism and artistic production. In addition, we would like to thank all those who have contributed material, clarifications and photographs towards the account of Johnny Clegg provided here.

Lyrics from Johnny Clegg's songs are reproduced courtesy of Scatterlings Pty Ltd and the Clegg Family; we express sincere gratitude for this generous permission. All lyrics & music © Scatterlings Pty Ltd.

We would like to convey special thanks to Hilton Rosenthal for having been a great resource person throughout all the phases of the development of this book.

Many thanks are due to Wits University Press for dedication and support in the production of the book. We are grateful to Karen Press for her thoughtful work on the manuscript.

Finally, we would like to thank Johnny Clegg for providing inspiration through his many areas of engagement. This book is dedicated to his memory and the ongoing impact of his life's work.

CHAPTER

1

Critical Reflections on the Music and Influence of Johnny Clegg

Michael Drewett and Lucilla Spini

And so he walked in the fashion of his lands
Until at last he cried out
Can anybody hear me, hear me, hear the song in my heart
There's a song to be sung that can heal these broken men
Let us sing and we'll walk through the dark
Hand in hand, hand in hand

—Juluka, 'Africa', *Universal Men*, 1979

REMEMBERING JOHNNY CLEGG

Johnny Clegg (1953–2019) was a singer, songwriter, dancer, anthropologist, ethnomusicologist, lecturer, storyteller, cultural ambassador, anti-apartheid activist, musical and cultural activist; he was an *igxagxa* (cultural vagabond), the white Zulu, a French Knight, *Skeyi jikel'eshobeni*,[1] a University of the Witwatersrand alumnus, an inspiration, a public intellectual, a universal man, an Officer of the Order of the British Empire (OBE), the quintessential South African, a global citizen, a national treasure, a great heart and, of course, a Scatterling of Africa. These are just some of the many titles, labels and expressions that have been used to describe Clegg's diversity of talents and interests, his polycultural persona, his life achievements, as well as his impact on the musical, cultural and political landscape of South Africa and beyond.

Clegg was born in Lancashire, United Kingdom (UK), to an English father and a Rhodesian mother. As a child he lived in the UK, Southern Rhodesia (now Zimbabwe), Zambia and South Africa. In 1964, at the age of 11, South Africa became his permanent home. Music was always a central part of his life, given that his mother, Muriel Braudo, was a cabaret jazz singer. In fact, at a young age Clegg started to learn classical guitar. This training began his musical journey, in part enabling the young Clegg to discern the interesting and captivating Zulu guitar sounds that he heard Charlie Mzila perform one day, near the local corner store.[2]

Mzila went on to introduce Clegg to Zulu street guitar playing and war dancing. He also introduced him to the world of the migrant Zulu workers in Johannesburg, and to Zulu culture and language more broadly.[3] In this context, Clegg found a sense of belonging and community, established his identity as a young man, and forged many friendships that would last a lifetime. Among these were friendships with Bafazane Qoma (referred to in the song 'Bullets for Bafazane' on Juluka's 1983 album *Work for All*), Dudu Ndlovu Zulu (a member of Savuka) and, of course, Sipho Mchunu, with whom he performed and recorded in the 1970s, first as Jonathan and Sipho and then as Juluka, despite all the restrictions imposed by the apartheid government at that time.[4] In those years, Clegg completed an honours degree in anthropology at the University of the Witwatersrand and embarked on a master's degree which he never completed. He lectured in anthropology for four years, also presenting and publishing academic papers with a particular focus on Zulu music, dance and culture. He also became a political activist, working with his academic mentor, Dr David Webster.

Despite police harassment and selective broadcast censorship on apartheid state radio, the early Juluka became relatively successful in South Africa. This was in part down to the role played by the producer Hilton Rosenthal, who believed in, encouraged and produced them. Their song 'Africa', from their debut album, *Universal Men*, was the second South African song to reach number one on the semi-independent Transkei-based *Capital Radio*.[5]

In 1981 their song '*Impi*' ('War', from the album *African Litany*) received wider airplay and broadened Juluka's fan base in South Africa.[6] In 1982 their song 'Scatterlings of Africa' (from the album *Scatterlings*) continued their success in South Africa and also attracted the attention of overseas record companies.[7] This validation induced Clegg to ask his head of department for a sabbatical in order to attempt a professional music career. However, the sabbatical request turned out to be a resignation.[8] His musical career went on to span several decades, in which he developed different crossover music styles, performing with different bands. Apart from greatest hits compilations and live albums, he released eight studio albums with Juluka, four studio albums with Johnny Clegg & Savuka, and five solo albums.[9] His music was also used in South African and overseas films. His final contribution was an autobiography, *Scatterling of Africa: My Early Years* (published posthumously in 2021), which covered his early years prior to forming Savuka.

Both Juluka's and Savuka's successes occurred within the context of apartheid restrictions as well as national and international anti-apartheid struggles, including the academic and cultural boycotts of South Africa. Clegg consequently became increasingly involved in South African cultural politics. He was instrumental in the formation and leadership of the South African Musicians' Alliance, actively participated in United Nations (UN) symposia on the academic and cultural boycotts, fostered dialogue among different communities and languages in South Africa, and educated his audiences abroad to become aware of the impact of apartheid on South Africans.

Throughout his career, Clegg addressed South African and international political, geopolitical and socio-cultural issues in his songs, storytelling, talks and interviews. He reached out to a diverse fan base both in South Africa and internationally – particularly in Europe, North America, New Zealand and Australia. A growing group of fans have self-identified as 'Scatterlings', developing a sense of community stemming from Clegg's song 'Scatterlings of Africa' – a song that was present in most of the encore sections of his shows, reinforcing a sense of belonging to the human family.

He was acknowledged locally and internationally through a series of awards.[10] In 1991 the French government appointed him a *Chevalier de l'Ordre des Arts et des Lettres* ('Knight of French Arts and Letters'); in 2007 the University of the Witwatersrand awarded him an honorary doctorate in music; in 2011 he received an honorary doctorate of law from the City University of New York; in 2012 the South African government awarded him the Order of Ikhamanga, Silver (OIS), the highest honour that can be bestowed on a South African citizen; in 2012 he received an honorary doctorate of humane letters from Dartmouth College, United States of America; in 2013 the University of KwaZulu-Natal awarded him an honorary doctorate in music; in 2015 he was honoured with an OBE; and in 2018 the Durban University of Technology awarded him an honorary doctorate of philosophy in visual and performing arts, alongside his Juluka bandmate Sipho Mchunu.

Clegg's musical recordings, his relentless touring, his engagement with humanitarian, cultural, environmental and political issues, and all his awards reflect his importance as a South African musician and citizen. This book explores many of the multifaceted and intertwined aspects of his life and influence. It is a project that was particularly enabled by the cross-disciplinary collective of contributors with backgrounds in sociology, anthropology, environmental science and sustainability, performing arts, music composition and performance, musicology, archival and library science, ethnomusicology, journalism, photography and media, futurology, as well as in music production and the music industry. In contrast to a traditional biography, the book eschews a linear narrative approach. Instead, the authors have homed in on specific aspects of Clegg's life and work that intrigue them, resulting in a collection of thematic explorations that offer insights into various dimensions of his life and music, with certain songs and events emerging as particularly pivotal and discussions of these recurring across different chapters.

The book does not aim to cover every significant facet of Clegg's life and career. Rather, it serves as a continuation of discussions and analyses spread across journals, books, newspapers and magazines over several decades; and as a book project, it constitutes an initial foray into understanding the complexities of his music and legacy. Hopefully there will be more books to follow.

The book is structured in three parts, each focusing on a key theme: Clegg's engagement with life in South Africa, the global reception of his music, and transitions in his music, life and legacy. While these sections provide a framework for exploring Clegg's multifaceted journey, they also intersect and overlap, encouraging readers to contemplate his life, music and legacy from different perspectives.

JOHNNY CLEGG'S ENGAGEMENT WITH LIFE IN SOUTH AFRICA

The first part of this book covers Clegg's music career from his early solo career to his partnership with Sipho Mchunu and the formation of Juluka. There are occasionally references to his time with Savuka, although this period is dealt with in more detail in the second and third parts.

In chapter 2, Lizabé Lambrechts and Pakama Ncume provide a fascinating look at Clegg's formative years, both as a solo performer and alongside Sipho Mchunu, delving into his various appearances on the early Johannesburg folk circuit, at the 'Free People's Concerts' and at the Market Theatre Café. They explore the Hidden Years Music Archive, the culmination of David Marks' life work, in which he recorded a plethora of live concerts both sonically and photographically. Spanning the early 1970s to 1978, this chapter offers a rich tapestry of Clegg's evolution as a musician, tracing his journey from tentative beginnings to becoming a more seasoned artist.

Marks' comprehensive recordings afford a rare glimpse into the complete concert experience, capturing not only the music but also the interactions between musicians and audiences. Through skilful storytelling, Lambrechts and Ncume paint a vivid portrait of Clegg and Mchunu's emergence, particularly highlighting Clegg's growth in confidence and prowess on stage. Importantly, the authors contextualise these performances within the tumultuous landscape of apartheid South Africa and the burgeoning alternative music scene. The necessity for Clegg and Mchunu, as a white–Zulu duo, to seek out venues accommodating multiracial audiences underscored the restrictive realities of the era. Thus, this chapter offers a glimpse into a marginalised music scene wherein performers like Clegg and Mchunu navigated a precarious path, melding their respective cultural backgrounds through the mediums of language, attire, dance and music.

Andrew Grant Innes also focuses on the cultural and political significance of the relationship between Clegg and Mchunu, in chapter 3. He explores the transformative cross-cultural bond forged by their friendship and artistic collaboration. Examining their relationship through the lens of hindsight, he illuminates how their friendship, camaraderie and mutual passion for music manifested as both intentional and incidental disruptions over time. Central to his narrative is the enduring bond between Clegg and Mchunu, which persisted even beyond Juluka's dissolution. Against the backdrop of apartheid's oppressive grip, characterised by laws such as the Group Areas Act (No. 41 of 1950) and the pass laws that placed restrictions on where black South Africans could live, work and socialise with white people, Innes underscores the existential and material challenges faced by Mchunu during that era. He delves into the intricate dynamics of their collaboration, elucidating how Clegg and Mchunu navigated the complexities of race, class and the urban–rural divide to craft a mesmerising fusion. Their journey offers valuable insights into potential avenues for reconciliation in South Africa's ongoing quest for a shared sense of identity and purpose across diverse backgrounds. Clegg and Mchunu's relationship serves as poignant reminder of the possibility of unity and understanding amidst a history marred by division and discord.

Similarly to Andrew Grant Innes, Martina Viljoen notes in chapter 4 that Clegg's groundbreaking musical collaborations and humanistic lyrics constituted a challenge to the separateness and racial injustices of apartheid. Clegg's songs captured a profound sense of humanism and solidarity with the marginalised. In response, the apartheid state arrested, harassed and monitored him, and some of his songs were banned from airplay on state-controlled radio.

Drawing on his background in anthropology, Clegg crafted a musical identity that celebrated diversity and interconnectedness. His use of multiple languages and cultural influences facilitated a cross-cultural dialogue, weaving together a narrative of struggle and hope. Viljoen analyses four of Clegg's songs, 'Scatterlings of Africa', *'Asimbonanga'* ('We Have Not Seen

Him'), 'Talk to the People' and 'One (Hu)'Man One Vote', elucidating his role as a cultural intermediary and dissenting voice.[11] Viljoen argues that Clegg pioneered a genre-defying sound that transcended borders, embodying the spirit of resistance and resilience.

While Richard Pithouse also recognises the importance of Clegg and Mchunu's interracial synergy, both culturally and politically, he contends in chapter 5 that the impact of Clegg's life and work transcends mere racial collaboration. Central to his analysis is Clegg's immersion in the everyday experiences of migrant labour, giving rise to a remarkable body of work which often underscored the plight of workers, particularly those ensnared within the perilous web of migrant labour. Hence, Clegg's artistic contributions were deeply entwined with issues of class, in addition to and intersecting with race. Pithouse retraces Clegg's narrative with a focus on his connections with labour concerns. This encompasses his formative encounters with workers in migrant labour hostels, his advocacy for workers' rights as a student, his affiliations with trade unions, and the poignant commentary woven into his poetic lyrics.

From the outset Clegg and Mchunu recorded songs that espoused themes pertinent to workers' struggles. The early Jonathan and Sipho single *Woza Friday* (Come Friday) was a worker's love song for the weekend, but it was on their first album, *Universal Men*, that they fully engaged with the theme of migrant labour.[12] The album implicitly offers a Marxist understanding that labour is the source of wealth, and that labourers from the rural periphery, sustained in part by rural homesteads, built the country's wealth. On Juluka's subsequent albums, the theme of migrant labour and the plight of workers remains a recurrent theme. Whether in 'African Sky Blue' on the *African Litany* album, or 'Baba Nango' from the *Work for All* album, Clegg and Mchunu consistently draw attention to the struggles and aspirations of workers.[13]

The transition to Savuka heralded a more international focus, albeit with intermittent references to migrant labour such as in 'The Crossing' on the *Heat, Dust and Dreams* album.[14] In the post-Juluka period, Clegg was elevated to the status of an icon of post-apartheid, multicultural collaboration. However, Pithouse cautions against oversimplifying Clegg's oeuvre as merely a harbinger of racial inclusivity within the middle classes while overlooking his deep empathy for migrant workers, as captured in many of Juluka's most powerful and enduring songs.

As Clegg's fellow musicians, Mchunu and Innes provide an in-depth discussion of Clegg's praise names, a significant aspect of his Zulu identity, in chapter 6. They explain that Zulu oral traditions form an important part of the broader tapestry of South African Nguni-language oral traditions, encompassing languages like isiXhosa, isiZulu, siSwati and isiNdebele. Societies such as amaZulu without a written literary tradition rely heavily on oral histories (*amabali* or *amahubo*) and poetic narrative (*izibongo*) to preserve the rich tapestry of historical events and the personas of individuals. Within Zulu culture, the bestowal of praise names upon individuals extends to various categories, largely depending on the status of groups and individuals. While names for clans and royalty may exude admiration, those crafted for individuals may not consistently carry flattering connotations. Zulu *izibongo* encapsulate concise narratives of one's life, weaving together achievements and traits as well as quirks and flaws, often using metaphor and simile, and delivered with a dash of humour by the *imbongi* (praise poet). In the oral tradition, these names serve as living chronicles, highlighting pivotal moments that define an individual's journey, thereby offering listeners a window into their essence. Mchunu and Innes record the praise names of Clegg, offering translations alongside glimpses into the events and characters captured within these epithets. They thereby illuminate Clegg's transformative encounters with Zulu culture. His praise names, in both their unabridged form and the abbreviated 'Skeyi', remained a constant presence throughout his life, resonating in various settings from his nuptials to Zulu dance gatherings, traditional festivities in Zulu communities to spirited dances in hostels, up until the very end at his graveside.

GLOBAL RECEPTION

The second part of this book focuses on Clegg's entrance onto the international stage. International interest in Juluka's music grew in around 1983 with the release of their *Scatterlings* album and the *Scatterlings of Africa* single.[15]

At this point Clegg and Mchunu became full-time musicians, with overseas success being crucial to a sustained and reliable music career.

In chapter 7, Michael Drewett focuses on Clegg's experiences navigating the cultural boycott as it was imposed in the UK. Since Clegg had British citizenship he joined the British Musicians' Union (BMU), believing this would make it easier for him to perform in the UK and appear on British television. The chapter focuses on Clegg's attempts to do so in the 1980s, with both Juluka and Savuka. Despite initial success with international releases like 'Scatterlings of Africa', Juluka faced resistance from the BMU and the Anti-Apartheid Movement, which led to confrontations over work permits and television appearances. These challenges continued after the formation of Savuka, as Clegg advocated a selective boycott to allow artists aligned with the anti-apartheid struggle to perform internationally. Clegg's expulsion from the BMU, and his later exclusion from the Nelson Mandela 70th birthday tribute concert at Wembley Stadium, highlighted the complexities of the boycott as administered in the UK. Despite these obstacles, Clegg persisted in his musical career in that country, eventually returning many times without issue after Mandela's release in 1990.

In chapter 8, Lucilla Spini explores Clegg's experience in France, which commenced in the early 1980s alongside the initial release of Juluka's records in that country and grew with the huge success there of Johnny Clegg & Savuka. Her narrative unfolds against the backdrop of an era marked by burgeoning enthusiasm for world music and the growth of anti-apartheid action across Europe. She begins by highlighting the launch platform of the 'Festival Jazz et Musiques Métisses' in Angoulême in 1986 (a key world music festival where Clegg would perform many more times). Concurrently, she traces the pivotal role of Claude Six's management, which led to Clegg's introduction to the well-known French singer/songwriter Renaud. Renaud became a supporter of Clegg throughout his life.

The chapter accentuates how France provided a welcoming stage for Clegg, who was affectionately referred to by the French public as '*Le Zoulou Blanc*' – 'The White Zulu'. Clegg's fame traversed many sectors of French society, including anti-apartheid activists, members of government such as Michel Rocard, then the prime minister of France, and celebrities within the artistic realm. Clegg's success included sold-out concerts, chart-topping record sales, and a variety of prizes and awards, including the prestigious *Chevalier de l'Ordre des Arts et des Lettres* conferred by the French government in 1991. Spini also explores Clegg's interest in French culture – an interest which motivated him to learn French and to add some French to his songs.

Chris Letcher examines another facet of Johnny Clegg's ascent to international recognition in chapter 9: the incorporation of his music into the cinematic landscape of Hollywood. Letcher posits that an incongruity exists between the visual narratives depicted in the films and the essence encapsulated within Clegg's context-specific songwriting. The chapter focuses in detail on two examples: Savuka's 'Scatterlings of Africa' in Barry Levinson's *Rain Man* (1988) and 'Cruel, Crazy, Beautiful World' in John Hughes' *Career Opportunities* (1991).

Letcher provides a close analysis by considering the precise position of each song in the films and analysing the particular excerpts used. For Letcher, while it comes as no surprise that Hollywood filmmakers might display indifference towards a song's lyrical or musical essence and its socio-political backdrop, the incorporation of Clegg's music into mainstream Hollywood cinema unveils broader insights. By scrutinising the music's placement, we can discern the evolving landscape of post-*Graceland* cinematic practices and aesthetics alongside the evolving perceptions of Clegg's music within a Western context. Letcher contends that, while the glossy, polished pop production techniques of the two songs undoubtedly facilitated broader exposure for Clegg through the selection of these songs as part of film soundtracks, their positioning within the films may have simultaneously obscured the music's deeper essence and resonance. Nevertheless, he concludes, 'there is also something pleasingly ungovernable about their presence on these soundtracks'.

In chapter 10, Lucilla Spini and Andrew J. Friedland provide an account of Clegg's academic experiences in North America, with a focus on the United States of America (US). The chapter is situated within the context of Clegg's academic training as an anthropologist and lecturer in South Africa. Although his formal academic career in South Africa ended when he began pursuing a professional career in music, over the years he engaged with academia in North America. This engagement can be traced back to the early to mid-1980s, when he delivered lectures at the City University of New York's Hunter College, notably in Dr Larry Shore's class on the music industry, and to his involvement in UN symposia during the 1990s concerned with cultural and academic boycotts. However, it was in the 2000s that his academic involvement in the USA truly flourished. This was facilitated by the reception of honorary degrees, including an honorary doctorate of law degree from the City University of New York School of Law in 2011 and an honorary doctorate in humane letters at Dartmouth in 2012. Clegg's contributions extended beyond ceremonial awards, as he was frequently invited to give guest lectures such as those at Berklee College of Music and the prestigious Montgomery Fellowships at Dartmouth in 2014. These recognitions by US academia mirrored similar accolades bestowed upon Clegg by South African academic institutions, including the University of the Witwatersrand, the University of KwaZulu-Natal and the Durban University of Technology.

Spini and Friedland conclude their chapter by focusing on Clegg's Montgomery lecture at Dartmouth in 2014. They consider his 'creative nonfiction' style of lecturing, whereby he framed his academic lectures as 'conversations': a form of dialogue that transcended traditional academic confines, extending to concert stages worldwide, and symbolising a unique fusion of scholarly discourse with his musical knowledge.

TRANSITIONS IN CLEGG'S MUSIC AND LIFE

The final part of this book focuses on transitions in Clegg's music and life. He always embraced change as he searched for new musical ideas, a Zulu identity, a post-apartheid society and so on. This section considers transitions in his musical style from Juluka to Savuka, the changing meaning of one of his songs, contestations over the meaning of his 'Zuluness', and ultimately that final transition: from life to death.

Caleb Mutch begins this section by considering Clegg's changing compositional practices from Juluka to Savuka in chapter 11. Mutch notes that Clegg's formation of Savuka was a pivotal point in his musical career.

While Juluka primarily delved into the fusion of Zulu and Western folk styles, Savuka took a different trajectory, embracing a stronger influence of rock music and a diverse range of world music traditions. However, Mutch argues that the evolution of Clegg's recordings between his earlier works and the Savuka period runs deeper than previously appreciated, as evidenced by the analysis of three of his compositions. He carefully examines the changes Clegg made to the only two of his Juluka-era songs which he went on to record with Savuka: '*Siyayilanda*' ('We Are Fetching It') and 'Scatterlings of Africa', showing how the songs were altered towards a more Western rock aesthetic.[16] He follows this with an analysis of Savuka's 'I Call Your Name', which sees Clegg further exploring South African musical traditions.[17] The song exhibits a nuanced reinterpretation of 1970s-era mbaqanga music. Through his analysis of the three songs, Mutch illuminates Clegg's artistic evolution and prompts a reconsideration of the fundamental elements shaping his compositions.

Whereas Mutch considers Clegg's shifting styles from Juluka to Savuka, in chapter 12 Nicol Hammond considers the changing meaning of Johnny Clegg & Savuka's song '*Asimbonanga*' (1986) over time.[18] She argues that '*Asimbonanga*' not only resonated deeply with audiences when they first heard it in the mid- to late 1980s, but continued to captivate listeners after Mandela's release from prison in 1990. As South Africa transitioned into the post-apartheid era, the song underwent a significant evolution. What was once a mournful protest anthem gradually transformed into a hopeful celebration of the openness and potential of a new South African society. Clegg himself acknowledged that the song came to symbolise the journey towards a new South Africa, still in the process of realising its potential.

Hammond argues that the enduring significance of Clegg's music, particularly his protest songs, lies in its remarkable capacity to adapt and resonate with shifting political landscapes. The chapter focuses on the multifaceted resonances of '*Asimbonanga*', tracing its journey from its mid-1970s origins as a Zulu maskanda protest song against Chief Kaiser Matanzima, the leader of the Transkei Bantustan, to its mid-1980s reinvention and release as a protest against the imprisonment of Nelson Mandela during the late apartheid era, to its iconic performances alongside Nelson Mandela in 1999 and subsequent renditions by the Soweto Gospel Choir in 2013 and Karen Zoid in 2015. Hammond explores the anthemic qualities of the song, dissecting its musical features and examining the nuanced changes introduced through these performances and covers. Each rendition serves to illuminate, and sometimes obscure, the evolving meanings of '*Asimbonanga*' within different performance contexts, offering insights into the dynamic relationship between music, politics and cultural identity.

In chapter 13, Brett Houston-Lock explores Clegg's deep connection with Zulu culture, a relationship that has sparked debates and criticisms regarding cultural appropriation, with some critics accusing Clegg of exploiting Zulu culture for financial gain. Houston-Lock traces these arguments back to a North American perspective on race relations. These viewpoints have gained traction globally, shaping discussion on racism worldwide through the lens of ideas originating in the USA. Houston-Lock contends that thoughtless adoption of dominant foreign cultural narratives can inflict real harm on countries grappling with their own complex histories and racial dynamics. Concerns about cultural appropriation, originally rooted in North American contexts, have now permeated South African discourse, impacting discussion surrounding Clegg's legacy and potentially undermining his and his musical partner Sipho Mchunu's efforts to foster a truly non-racial, post-apartheid identity for South Africans. Through various examples, Houston-Lock demonstrates that the cultural appropriation argument overlooks the cultural milieu in which Clegg and Mchunu operated.

Politically, Clegg's immersion in Zulu culture represented a brave stance against apartheid-era essentialism, challenging the government's racial and cultural segregation. His embrace of Zulu culture mirrored the natural exchange and evolution of cultures throughout human history. Houston-Lock argues that defending Clegg against accusations of cultural appropriation is unnecessary, advocating instead for a rejection of the imposition of North American frameworks, particularly when applied erroneously to South Africa.

In a very fitting closing chapter, Marguerite de Villiers Coetzee considers Clegg's life in relation to time in chapter 14. She notes that death, that unavoidable certainty of life, is also a realm of profound illusion and imagination. Anthropologists have, for generations, scrutinised the myriad ways in which cultures grapple with dying, grieving and memorialisation. Yet, she asks, what of the death, mourning and memory of an anthropologist?

Coetzee suggests that one way of exploring Clegg's symbolic imagination and his methods of place-making is to search for clues to the spatio-temporal basis of his music. Her aim is to interpret the intricate interplay between the passage and preservation of time, and the delicate balance between physical absence and ephemeral presence, as informed by the Zulu philosophies and cultural sensibilities that shaped Clegg's world view, value system, artistic expression and sense of identity. The chapter is divided into three parts: the first unpacks how Clegg confronted his own death, the second considers how he dealt with the death of others, and the third reviews how others have processed his death. Throughout the chapter, Coetzee refers to Clegg's lyrics and corresponding moments in his life, concluding with a lamentation that celebrates 'the magical, paradoxical and untranslatable enigma that is Johnny Clegg' (chapter 14 in this volume).

NOTES

1   That is, 'the peg of the yoke that holds the neck of the ox that transforms itself into a dancing tail' (Johnny Clegg, *Scatterling of Africa: My Early Years* [Johannesburg: Pan Macmillan, 2021], 192). See also chapter 6 in this book by Sipho Mchunu and Andrew Grant Innes.
2   Clegg, *Scatterling*, 67–68.
3   Clegg, *Scatterling*, 67–77.
4   Juluka, *Work for All* (album, Johannesburg: MINC, MINC – (L) 1070, 1983).
5   Juluka, 'Africa', on *Universal Men* (album, Johannesburg: Gramophone Records Co./CBS Records, CBS – DNW 2429, 1979).
6   Juluka, '*Impi*', on *African Litany* (album, Johannesburg: MINC, MINC – (L) 1020, 1981).
7   Juluka, 'Scatterlings of Africa', on *Scatterlings* (album, Johannesburg: MINC, MINC – (L) 1040, 1982).
8   Clegg, *Scatterling*, 289.
9   Details of these albums are given in the discography at the end of this chapter. More comprehensive discographies for Clegg are available at Rhythm Safari, *Rhythm Safari Website*, accessed 12 December 2024, https://www.rhythmsafari.com.au, and Daniel Pontreau and Fabrice Feitussi, *In My African Dream Website*, accessed 31 December 2024, http://inmyafricandream.free.fr/index.htm.
10 See the official Johnny Clegg website, www.johnnyclegg.com, for information about these awards.
11 Juluka, 'Scatterlings of Africa', on *Scatterlings*; Johnny Clegg & Savuka, 'Scatterlings of Africa', on *Third World Child* (album, Sandton: EMI, EMCJ (D) – 2407331, 1987); Johnny Clegg & Savuka, '*Asimbonanga*', on *Third World Child*; Johnny Clegg & Savuka,

'Talk to the People', on *Shadow Man* (Sandton: EMI, EMCJ (D) – 7904111, 1988); Johnny Clegg & Savuka, 'One (Hu)'Man One Vote', on *Cruel, Crazy, Beautiful World* (Sandton: EMI, EMCJ (E) – 7934461, 1989).

12 Jonathan and Sipho, *Woza Friday* (single, Johannesburg: EMI Brigadiers/Jamloti, JM139, 1977); Juluka, *Universal Men*.
13 Juluka, 'African Sky Blue', on *African Litany*; Juluka, 'Baba Nango', on *Work for All* (Johannesburg: MINC, MINC – (L) 1070, 1983).
14 Johnny Clegg & Savuka, 'The Crossing', on *Heat, Dust and Dreams* (album, Sandton: EMI, CDEMCJ (WF) 5499, 1993).
15 Juluka, *Scatterlings*; Juluka, *Scatterlings of Africa* (single, Johannesburg: MINC, MINC – MC 92, 1982).
16 Johnny Clegg & Savuka, 'Siyayilanda', on *Shadow Man*; Johnny Clegg & Savuka, 'Scatterlings of Africa', on *Third World Child*.
17 Johnny Clegg & Savuka, 'I Call Your Name', on *Shadow Man*.
18 Johnny Clegg & Savuka, 'Asimbonanga', on *Third World Child* (album, Sandton: EMI, EMCJ (D) – 2407331, 1987).

REFERENCES

Clegg, Johnny. *Johnny Clegg Official Website*. Accessed 31 December 2024. www.johnnyclegg.com.
Clegg, Johnny. *Scatterling of Africa: My Early Years*. Johannesburg: Pan MacMillan, 2021.
Parliament of South Africa. *Group Areas Act (No. 41 of 1950)*. Cape Town: Parliament of South Africa, 1950.
Pontreau, Daniel and Fabrice Feitussi. *In My African Dream Website*. Accessed 31 December 2024. http://inmyafricandream.free.fr/index.htm.
Rhythm Safari. *Rhythm Safari Website*. Accessed 12 December 2024. https://www.rhythm-safari.com.au.

DISCOGRAPHY

Singles

Jonathan and Sipho. *Woza Friday*. Single. Johannesburg: EMI Brigadiers/Jamloti, JM139, 1977.
Juluka. *Scatterlings of Africa*. Single. Johannesburg: MINC, MINC – MC 92, 1982.

Studio albums as Juluka

Juluka. *African Litany*. Album. Johannesburg: MINC, MINC – (L) 1020, 1981.
Juluka. *Crocodile Love*. Album. International: HR BV Music/One World Music/CNR Music, 3032202, 1997.
Juluka. *The International Tracks*. Album. Johannesburg: MINC, MINC(O) 1098, 1984.
Juluka. *Musa Ukungilandela*. Album. Johannesburg: MINC, MINC(E) 1100, 1984.
Juluka. *Scatterlings*. Album. Johannesburg: MINC, MINC – (L) 1040, 1982.
Juluka. *Ubuhle Bemvelo*. Album. Johannesburg: MINC, MINC – (E) 1030, 1982.
Juluka. *Universal Men*. Album. Johannesburg: Gramophone Records Co./CBS Records, CBS – DNW 2429, 1979.
Juluka. *Work for All*. Album. Johannesburg: MINC, MINC – (L) 1070, 1983.

Studio albums as Johnny Clegg

Clegg, Johnny. *Human*. Album. Paris: EMI Music France, 5099991179132 0, 2010.
Clegg, Johnny. *King of Time*. Album. Johannesburg: Universal Music, UMGCD 145, 2017.
Clegg, Johnny. *New World Survivor*. Album. Pretoria: Value Music, CDVM (WFL) 45, 2002.
Clegg, Johnny. *One Life*. Album. Johannesburg,: Sting Music, STIDCD 106, 2006.
Clegg, Johnny. *Third World Child*. Album. Johannesburg: MINC, MINC (L) – 1140, 1985.

Studio albums as Johnny Clegg & Savuka

Johnny Clegg & Savuka. *Cruel, Crazy, Beautiful World*. Album. Sandton: EMI, EMCJ (E) – 7934461, 1989.
Johnny Clegg & Savuka. *Heat, Dust and Dreams*. Album. Sandton: EMI, CDEMCJ (WF) 5499, 1993.
Johnny Clegg & Savuka. *Shadow Man*. Album. Sandton: EMI, EMCJ (D) – 7904111, 1988.
Johnny Clegg & Savuka. *Third World Child*. Album. Sandton: EMI, EMCJ (D) – 2407331, 1987.

PART 1: JOHNNY CLEGG'S ENGAGEMENT WITH LIFE IN SOUTH AFRICA

CHAPTER

2

The Unheard Live Recordings of Johnny Clegg: Listening to Clegg's Early Performances within the Context of Alternative Popular Music in South Africa

Lizabé Lambrechts and Pakama Ncume

Sometimes archives surprise us, opening moments in time through which histories, artists and communities can be rediscovered and reimagined. One such moment was listening to Johnny Clegg and Sipho Mchunu's performance in the Market Café (figure 2.1) while it was being digitised in 2019 as part of a digitisation project of the Hidden Years Music Archive.[1] Clear and crisp, Clegg's voice accompanied by Mchunu drew us into the small and intimate café venue and transported us back to 16 January 1977.

This tape forms part of a collection of sonic and visual material that provides traces of Clegg developing his musical style and onstage persona as a performer from the late 1960s to the late 1970s. The collection includes photographs, posters, programmes, newspaper clippings, demo tapes and live concert recordings documenting his performances at festivals and coffee clubs as a solo musician, as well as his collaborative work. The material also locates Clegg within the counterculture and alternative popular music community of the 1970s in Johannesburg, a context rarely discussed in relation to his musical development. Clegg, as a solo artist

Figure 2.1: Johnny Clegg and Sipho Mchunu in the Market Café, 16 January 1977. Photograph by David Marks. Hidden Years Music Archive, Documentation Centre for Music, Stellenbosch University.

or performing with Mchunu, regularly played at concerts with musicians such as Paul Clingman, Colin Shamley, Keith Blundell, David Marks and Edi Niederlander, as well as with groups such as Malombo and Freedom's Children. Some of these concerts, such as 'Tribal Blues' (1971) and the 'Free People's Concerts' (1972–1990), included line-ups with musicians from different racial, class and ethnocultural backgrounds performing in a wide array of genres ranging from township jazz to urban folk, from traditional African and Indian spiritual music to country, Celtic and rock music. They marked moments of convergences where alternative lifestyles, beliefs and political ideals could be expressed that challenged the apartheid ideologies and policies of the time.

This archival material was collected, recorded and preserved by David Marks, the director of the 3rd Ear Music Company, an independent record label in South Africa. Marks' intention with the recordings was to keep the ambience of the live performances. He therefore recorded not only the songs, but also the humorous moments and stories shared by musicians between songs, and the audience's interactions including laughter, applause and comments. The result of Marks' recording style is a unique record of live performances wherein Clegg's explanations of songs, stories, instructions and the dances he performed on stage can be heard. Largely unheard and unseen for the past 50 years, these recordings are preserved in the Hidden Years Music Archive, one of the largest popular music archives in South Africa. It was established by Marks to preserve the material he collected during his career in the music industry. In 2013 he donated the collection to Stellenbosch University, where it has continued to expand with the addition of new collections.[2]

This chapter will focus on six events that are representative of Clegg's early musical career in the Hidden Years Music Archive, namely the 'National Folk Festival' in 1970, 'Tribal Blues' in 1971, the early 'Free People's Concerts' of 1972 and 1975, and Clegg's performances in the Market Café in 1977 and 1978.

FIRST ENCOUNTERS AND THE DEVELOPMENT OF CLEGG'S MUSICAL STYLE ON THE FOLK MUSIC SCENE

Jonathan Clegg was born on 7 June 1953 in England and spent his early years in Rhodesia (now Zimbabwe) before moving to Johannesburg in 1964 with his mother, Muriel, a cabaret and jazz singer.[3] As a teenager in Johannesburg, Clegg immersed himself in Zulu culture, visiting hostels designated for black migrant workers. Here he joined a dance troupe from Msinga as an apprentice dancer and learned to sing and dance.[4] Clegg's early encounters with the musician Charles Mzila in 1967 when he was 14, and with gardener and maskandi musician Sipho Mchunu when he was 16, were significant moments in his life that shaped his knowledge of the isiZulu language as well as the maskanda guitar and dance styles of the Zulu people.[5] While Mchunu taught Clegg about Zulu culture, including stick fighting (which later became a feature in their early performances),[6] he also received weekly cultural lessons from Credo Mutwa, a traditional healer, storyteller and keeper of African wisdom who shared his deep knowledge of culture, history and spirituality with Clegg.[7]

In 1968, Mutwa was booked by David Marks to perform at The Troubadour, one of the first folk clubs in South Africa.[8] Mutwa suggested to Marks that Clegg, then 15 years old, open his concert with a couple of songs.[9] Clegg soon became a favourite on the folk music scene, and in 1970 Clegg and Mchunu played one of their first public concerts at a soirée organised by Des and Dawn Lindberg. These concerts were held every Sunday night at the Lindbergs' house and became a well-known institution on the Johannesburg music scene.[10]

By the 1970s, folk music, or more specifically English singer-songwriters writing and performing original compositions, was a burgeoning scene in South Africa, with music concerts, folk festivals and clubs across the country. Clegg writes that the musicians on this scene 'wanted me to be part of that world because what I was playing was essentially indigenous folk music – that's what maskanda is'.[11]

The 1970 'National Folk Song Festival, Old Routes & New Directions' was organised by the South African Folk Music Association from 20 to 26 July in the Sandton Civic Theatre, Johannesburg. The festival, while featuring a variety of folk music and musicians, focused on original South African compositions.[12] The line-up included Mel Miller, Johnny Clegg, Andy Dillon, Brian Bebbington, Clem Tholet and Edi Niederlander, among others.[13] On a live recording of the performances of 23–24 July, we can hear, among the well-trodden folk songs and covers such as 'If I Had a Hammer' and 'Scarborough Fair', the original mbira-playing and storytelling of Andy Dillon, Edi Niederlander's blues-rock, Colin Shamley's song 'Judy Marigold', and a young Johnny Clegg walking on to the stage. Opening with a short maskanda riff, he introduces his first song, 'Apollo 11', in a thin and nervous voice, stammering over some of the words: 'When Apollo 11 went on it..s historic journey to the moon, a television..set was installed at the City Ha..a..ll foyer, and um, hundreds of Bantu were watching the..this journey and there happened to be a..a Zulu folk singer amongst them and he sort-of gave a running commentary. It went something like this'.[14]

The moment Clegg starts singing his timidity disappears, and he repeats every isiZulu line in English for the audience to follow:

> *Ndiyakhweza phezulu, ndiyakhwez' enyangeni*
> I can see the moon, I can see the sky

> *Phezulu, nyangeni*
> *Ndayibamba phezulu, ndayibamb' enyangeni*
> I can touch the moon, I can touch it
> *Sayibamba phezulu, sayibamb'enyangeni*
> *Phezulu, nyangeni*
> *Sayibamba phezulu, sayibamb'uApollo*
> Apollo has caught the moon.[15]

While he performs this maskanda song at a much slower tempo than one would expect, exemplifying the technical difficulties of this guitar style, Clegg has mastered the fluidity of the two parts on the guitar and of his singing in his second song, 'City of Gold'. In this song, he introduces the story of a man who must go to the city to make money after his cattle and goats are not accepted as barter any more. Similarly to what he does in the first song, Clegg first sings each line in isiZulu before translating the song for the audience:

> *Siqed' ukuhamba manje yebaba*
> We have just left
> *Thina siy' eGoli yebaba*
> We are leaving for Johannesburg
> *Ngizokhumbul' ekhaya kumama*
> I will miss home, my mother's place
> *Apho iinkomo zidl' entabeni*
> Where the cattle graze in the mountains.[16]

In his autobiography, *Scatterling of Africa: My Early Years,* Clegg writes about his growing unease with the folk music scene during this early period in his career:

> In a way, I was a cultural exotic moment for people. I didn't resent it, but it made me feel inauthentic, in some kind of way, by being there. I was speaking Zulu and learning the language, and trying to learn the rules of composition, and trying to increase my repertoire. But I

> was not an interloper or a curious onlooker. I did not see myself as exotic ... I was part of it and it was part of me. I was in the hostels. I was singing. I was dancing. The migrant community was where I felt at home.[17]

This sense of being ill at ease, feeling like a spectacle or something exotic, comes across in his timid voice and performance during the folk festival, especially when he is talking. This is markedly different from his performance in 'Tribal Blues: A South African Music Concert' on 11–12 August 1971. This concert, organised by Marks under the auspices of 3rd Ear Music in collaboration with the National Union of South African Students, was the first major concert in which Clegg and Mchunu appeared together.[18] The concert was held in the Wits Great Hall at the University of the Witwatersrand (Wits). The Great Hall was one of the few venues in Johannesburg where a multiracial audience could get together to watch the same show, because it was located on private property and the university therefore had some say in what happened on its grounds.[19]

The concert programme included Clegg, then 19 years old and a first-year student at Wits, Mchunu, then 21 years old, and their Wa Madhlebe dance group made up of 18 men from Mchunu's home district, Makhabaleni in Kwazulu-Natal. Their performance was followed by Count Wellington Judge with Denis Mpale (trumpet), Barney Rachabane (alto sax), 'Bugs' Congco (pianist), Nelson Magwaza (drummer) and Ernest Mohle (bass). After the interval Malombo performed with Julian Bahula (congos and mbira), Abe Cindi (flute) and Lucky Ranku (guitar). They were joined on stage for the final act by Ramsay Mackay (bass), Kenny Henson (electric guitar), Colin Pratley (drummer) and Brian Davidson (singer) to perform excerpts from *Orang-Outang*, a musical written by Mackay.

The live recording opens with Clegg, Mchunu and the group performing '*Izibongo*', Zulu popular praises.[20] Thomas Pooley writes that in these praises the performers 'articulate the experiences, genealogy and heritage of their orators', and that they are full of idioms and codes that will be 'intelligible only to those familiar with the context'.[21] Due to the placement of the performers on stage in relation to the microphones, we cannot clearly distinguish what is being sung, but recognise that they are praising people and mentioning clan names.[22] We then hear Clegg's searing voice initiating the song: '*Kwakhal' ingane kwaZulu kwaze kwasa*' ('Enduring Cries of Zulu Children').[23] The group joins in the chorus singing and dancing. After the audience applause a muted discussion takes place between Clegg and Mchunu, wherein Mchunu alerts Clegg to his broken bead pieces, their panting offering evidence of the vigour of their dancing.

This is followed by two maskanda walking songs, '*Hawu Wena Ngane, Tshitshi Lami*' ('Hey Child, My Maiden, What Are You Doing'), a song where Mchunu sings about a broken relationship, followed by Clegg's performance of '*Igundwani*' ('The Mouse'). These two songs are very short, and while Mchunu displays his proficiency with the finger-picking style gaining popularity at that time, Clegg plays in a style reminiscent of earlier solo maskanda songs with a strumming sound.

After these songs, Clegg and Mchunu sing '*Sizobashaya ngenduku*' ('We'll Fight Them with Sticks'). They are joined by the dancers in *ngoma* dancing, clapping and whistling, with Clegg's voice lifting out calling them to action:[24]

> Call: '*Uthini?*' ('What are you saying?')
> Response: '*Awujiki, kusho inkunz'emdaka awujiki*' ('You don't retreat, said the black bull, you don't retreat').[25]

This flows into a choral song reminiscent of a wedding song, '*Hawu hawu, lomhlaba ungakuwe, YeMakobongela sizothini na*' ('The Land Has Been Taken, Makobongela, What Are We Going To Do?'). While singing they dance off the stage and we can hear the audience's applause.[26]

In the songs for 'Tribal Blues', there is a freedom of performance in Clegg that is turned inwards towards the performers themselves, and not towards the audience, their tastes or their understanding. There is minimal outward interaction and translation. Instead, this concert creates the impression that Clegg is on stage as part of a ceremony or a gathering, joining the group as one would at a homestead. While steeped in Zulu culture and tradition, one can hear in this freedom the development of Clegg and Mchunu's sound, musical collaboration and identities.[27]

They are finding their sound in a culturally rich and diverse musical landscape and line-up wherein the realities faced by these musicians, while vastly different, can be shared. For example, Count Wellington Judge, who performs after Clegg and Mchunu, walks on stage laughing tersely into the microphone. His continued laughter eventually gets the audience to laugh with him, and then he says: 'I am laughing on the outside but crying on the inside'. His pianist, 'Bugs', had been picked up the previous night by the police when he was boarding a bus because he forgot his pass. 'I got no pianist tonight, because he's inside, he is playing the blues in a cell.'[28] The line-up further includes workers in Johannesburg hotels, flats, construction sites and gardens, and professional musicians including established jazz musicians Mpale and Rachabane, who are both performing with Dollar Brand (later Abdullah Ibrahim) at this time.[29] In addition, the closing act of Orang-Outang makes visible collaborations across genre and race, with African jazz from Malombo and progressive rock from Freedom's Children and Abstract Truth.[30]

Shows with line-ups such as these were highly irregular in apartheid South Africa, where venues, audiences and amenities were almost always segregated according to race. But however strict the laws and regulations were on paper, these concerts still took place, as 'Tribal Blues' shows, and the networks that formed between the musicians extended to other events: for example, the 'Free People's Concerts', day-long multiracial events hosted on the Wits University campus.

CLEGG AS PERFORMER ON THE ALTERNATIVE POPULAR MUSIC SCENE

The 'Free People's Concerts' were conceptualised by Marks and Tony Campbell in 1970 as events to 'provide a platform for local musicians of all races to play before a multi-racial audience'.[31] The purpose was 'to get people together to experience alternative South African music in a free environment irrespective of race'.[32] The early concerts were organised under the auspices of 3rd Ear Music and the South African Folk Music Association, drawing crowds of up to 5 000 people (figure 2.2).[33] The line-up featured a wide array of musicians performing across a wide spectrum of genres

Figure 2.2: 'Free People's Concert', University of the Witwatersrand, Johannesburg, 1972. Photograph by Tony Campbell. Hidden Years Music Archive, Documentation Centre for Music, Stellenbosch University.

ranging from folk, country and western, Indian ragas and Irish jigs to blues, township jazz and, in the 1980s, also rock, reggae and punk.[34]

On Sunday, 12 March 1972, Clegg and Mchunu appeared at their first 'Free People's Concert' with their *indlamu* dance group, Wa Madhlebe.[35] Unfortunately, there is no recording of their first performance, but photographs show that they performed many dance routines (see figure 2.3).

The first recording of them performing at a 'Free People's Concert' was on 16 February 1974 where they sang three walking songs to an exuberant crowd. Clegg describes the first song, *'Emadlozini'* ('In the Place of the Ancestors') as a lament from a man who lost both his parents and is now calling to the ancestors to protect the family from any misfortunes.[36] After the storytelling, Clegg sings in isiZulu without translation for the audience:

> *Oobaba sebengibikile emadlozini bandla*
> *Angisenalutho*
> *Angisenababa, anginesamamalo*
> *Kudlala amavolontiya, amagwal' ankosi.*[37]

Figure 2.3: Johnny Clegg, Sipho Mchunu and Wa Madhlebe dancers, Wits University 'Free People's Concert', 1972. Photograph by Frank Black. Hidden Years Music Archive, Documentation Centre for Music, Stellenbosch University.

(My fathers have announced me to the ancestors
I own nothing/ I am an orphan
I have lost my father; I have lost my mother
The home is deserted.)[38]

This song expresses Zulu cultural traditions, exploring the universal themes of death and loss in the context of Zulu beliefs about their ancestors. In a later performance of the song at the Market Café in 1977 (figure 2.1), Clegg explains that the song is written in the style of a walking song and is very repetitive, pointing out that 'the orthodox Zulu feel that if a song is not repetitive, it has no virility, it has no strength, it has no *joie de vivre*'.[39] After each song, cheers and applause from the audience attest to the growing popularity of Clegg and Mchunu at these events.

In the line-up with Clegg and Mchunu were folk singers Clem Tholet, Paul Clingman, Colin Shamley, Mike Dickman and Edi Niederlander, mbaqanga group Amagugu and the Intuthuko Brothers, afro-funk group The Beaters (later known as Harari), light rock group El Socrates, and Sage playing Irish jigs. These line-ups were a mix of genres, races and languages, and musicians were increasingly incorporating political commentary into their songs through singing about the events they witnessed around them in apartheid South Africa. Lizabé Lambrechts and Schalk van der Merwe point out that the 'Free People's Concerts' formed part of the counterculture and alternative music movements of South Africa,[40] and provided the platform through which 'alternative lifestyles, sexualities and spiritualities could be shared and lived'.[41] As a young student at Wits, Clegg moved within these networks, describing the years he spent as a student at the university as a 'heady and inspiring time' with proactive student politics speaking out against the apartheid government.[42] The yearly 'Free People's Concerts' played a role, albeit small, in activating students politically, and Glenn Moss points out that these concerts 'offered a sense of what a different society could be or what a different "normal" could be'.[43] Through their performances, musicians at these concerts communicated between and within cultural enclaves that had historically sought to keep them apart.[44]

Through these networks, Clegg also formed a lasting friendship with musician Paul Clingman, who saw Clegg and Mchunu perform at the 1972 'Free People's Concert'.[45] Clingman, born in 1950, was 23 at the time and he and the 20-year-old Clegg spent hours together making music. Clegg was then still mostly performing maskanda songs, and Clingman, singing in the style of Bob Dylan,[46] learned to perfect a finger-picking style that 'took everything off to a new level'; he remembers increasingly seeing 'an opportunity to define a South African way of making music'.[47] Clingman started experimenting with mixing 'black traditional sounds with Western folk/pop rock' and became one of the first musicians in the genre later defined as crossover music.[48] Clingman, Clegg and Mchunu regularly performed together, and in 1977 Clingman released his second album, *Father to the Child*, with Clegg and Mchunu performing as backing musicians.[49] This album, with songs such as '*Amabaca*',[50] 'Dingaan's Day' and 'Valley of a Thousand Hills', was banned from airplay by the South African Broadcasting Corporation because it mixed English and isiZulu languages.[51] Soon thereafter, Clegg and Mchunu released their second single, *Woza Friday* (Come Friday) (1977), which was similarly banned from radio airplay for mixing languages.[52]

Clegg describes this song as a 'crossover piece, using Western folk-picking style, Western melody and Zulu lyrics'.[53] Early acoustic performances of *Woza Friday* are reminiscent of the 1976 finger-picking style of Clingman, but with a much more distinct maskanda-inspired timbre, as heard during the performance at the Market Café in 1977.

DEFINING THEIR UNIQUE SOUND: CLEGG AND MCHUNU AT THE MARKET CAFÉ

In 1976, Mannie Manim and Barney Simon opened the Market Theatre in the former Indian Fruit Market in Braamfontein, Johannesburg. David Marks and his wife, Frances Marks, joined them in opening the Market Café, a small and intimate venue with a seating capacity of 50 people.[54] As a marketplace, the building was zoned as an industrial site, meaning that it was not racially designated.[55] This loophole, although not foolproof, made it possible for the theatre and café to host multiracial productions.[56]

Marks installed a small recording studio at the back of the venue and used it to record the live concerts.[57] Some of these concerts were released as singles on the Market Café label by Marks, for example the Elastic Head Band performing in 1977. This studio set-up, in combination with the small venue, had a significant impact on the recording quality of the tapes of the Market Café concerts now available in the Hidden Years Music Archive. Marks' sonic control of the space can be heard in the finer details of the recordings, such as the overtones clearly audible during Clegg's performance on the Zulu umhube bow (originally a Xhosa mouthbow instrument, umrhubhe) during his first concert in the café on 16 January 1977.[58]

This concert is markedly different from the others discussed so far. Clegg and Mchunu come across as confident and at ease, both spontaneously making jokes that create an easy rapport between them and the small audience. We also hear distinctive moments of the sound that will become synonymous with Juluka, the group formed by Clegg and Mchunu in 1979. The recording opens with Clegg correcting Marks' pronunciation of Mchunu's surname, then greeting the audience in English. Before he can continue, Mchunu interrupts him by greeting the audience in isiZulu and then mimicking an elaborate British English accent: 'Good mo[w]ning, and [g]how are you?'⁵⁹ Both serious and light-hearted, this exchange sets the tone for the rest of the concert wherein Clegg uses the songs, humour and storytelling to teach the audience about Zulu culture and life experiences in apartheid South Africa.

They open the concert with a walking song, '*Thula 'Mtanami, Umama Uzokuphathel' Amaswiti*' ('Hush My Child, Mother Will Bring You Sweets'). The lullaby, composed by Mchunu, deals with the socio-economic inequalities of South Africa, migrant workers, and the responsibility that women have to endure while their husbands are away at work. After '*Emadlozini*' ('The Place of the Ancestors'), they perform '*Inkunzi Ayihlabi Ngokumisa*' ('Don't Judge a Bull by His Horns'). Clegg introduces the song through an elaborate story wherein he explains the importance of bulls in Zulu culture. The song, he explains, is adapted from a Zulu idiom, and teaches us that victory is not determined by the size of a bull's horns, but by the mind.⁶⁰ In a later interview Clegg explained that the song 'symbolises the victory of the underdog over his oppressor'.⁶¹ While sharing the story on stage, Clegg lightens the mood by humorously recounting the fight between a little bull and a bull with 'magnificent horns':

> It is a little bull, it is like a bulldog ... the little bull just steps down and looks ... and the other one pulls at the ground and boom! It starts charging ... as he starts charging ... the little bull collects this big, huge big massive oncoming bull ... and he takes it ... the huge bull hanging over the little bull's horns ... the little bull walks around parading [Clegg parades around mimicking the little bull to the audience's laughter] ... and the old man says '*kade ngisho, inkunzi ayihlabi ngokumisa*' (I have always said this, a bull doesn't stab with his horns, it stabs with its head).⁶²

In this song, Clegg performs on an umhube. He explains that he made this instrument and adapted it by placing a violin string on a hollowed-out piece of bamboo that served as the bow, to get a better sound. Mchunu plays the guitar and sings, while Clegg's mouthbow playing follows the melodic and rhythmic patterns of Mchunu's guitar-picking.

In contrast to previous songs composed by Clegg, performed mostly in isiZulu and then translated into English for the audience, '*Unkosi Bomvu*' ('The Red King') and 'Gambling Africa' have been written by Clegg in isiZulu and English, with both languages working together to establish the narrative arc of each song. 'Gambling Africa', later to become 'Africa' on Juluka's first album, *Universal Men* (1979), is performed as a slow, acoustic lullaby with a guitar riff of single extended notes between verses played over guitar-strumming that is more reminiscent of the crossover music Clegg shaped with Paul Clingman than of maskanda.[63]

After intermission, Clegg and Mchunu demonstrate a stick fight for the audience, with Clegg teaching the audience about the objects used in stick fighting, *isikhwili* (attacking stick), *ubhoko* (defending stick) and *ihawu* (defending shield).[64] Clegg and Mchunu enact a mock battle to establish who is the dominant warrior when facing the enemy, or to establish 'the bull' among the herd during factional fights. He explains that this performance teaches *ukuqina* (how to be strong). The strength is not simply physical, but requires mental agility to overcome the many obstacles faced in life. Stick fighting not only provides Zulu men with skill but also builds courage, something they believe distinguishes them as notorious warriors.[65] Clegg fully immerses himself in the performance and he can be heard breathing heavily at the end of the staged fight. The audience loves it, laughing along.

After the stick fight, Clegg discusses the patriarchal system in Zulu culture, wherein some parents still hold on to the traditional beliefs that only sons can inherit and look after their fathers' wealth and that children should not be sent to school. Clegg and Mchunu then perform '*Ndaze Ndalusa Amanxiwa*' ('Men, I'm Now Watching the Ruins – the Decay of the Old Order'). This song will also be performed during their last concert in the Market Café on 5 May 1978.

The song is sung in English, and at the 1978 performance Clegg emphasises that it is a 'multilevel song' about a mad woman, darkness, a loss of home and traditions, and those who stay behind to guard the traditions and homelands for those 'who forget and are about to return'. He introduces the song by telling a story of how Inkatha members are convincing traditional Zulu cattle herders to send their children to school, and how the man, while watching his son leave for school, looks into the future upon the decay of his traditions and the old order.⁶⁶

The song is based on a maskanda-like repetitive rhythmic pattern, and Clegg points out that it is written on a semi-tonal scale called the 'scale of old men'.⁶⁷ The harmonies and melody are comparable to folk songs composed by his contemporaries on the English folk music scene and are sung without the grittiness that characterises Clegg's voice in his performances of maskanda songs. Similarly, in 'Deliwe', a song about a man who falls in love with a woman and tries to persuade her to come back with him to his homeland, we hear Clegg and Mchunu combining maskanda cyclical patterns and rhythms with English folk harmonies and singing styles. During their performances at the café, we hear Clegg and Mchunu coming into their own sound while sharing and performing Zulu culture and traditions through storytelling and the enactment of stick fighting. The new sound and identity they are developing by 'choosing different musical collaborations, sounds and identities' has taken shape and is beginning to come into focus.⁶⁸

In the concert of 1978, they perform songs like '*Asimbonanga*' ('We Have Not Seen Him'), '*Wesab' inganono*' ('Afraid of the Cannon'), 'Mamkhize's Brew', '*Thula 'Mtanami*', 'Africa' and 'Deliwe'.⁶⁹ The last three songs were reworked from acoustic versions and released on Juluka's first album, *Universal Men*. The album included a diverse group of musicians, among them Sipho Gumede (bass), Gilbert Mathews (drums), Paul Petersen (electric guitar), Robbie Jansen (flute, saxophone), Mervyn Africa (keyboards, synthesiser) and Colin Pratley (African drums); together with Clegg and Mchunu they created a musical synthesis that blended maskanda guitar, folk music, African jazz, rock and kwela to produce a unique South African sound.⁷⁰

CONCLUSION

In an interview with Marguerite de Villiers Coetzee, Clegg revealed that his 'career began as a project embedded in celebrating a traditional system of music' and that 'it has now shifted into a more globalised project of looking for new ways to cross over'.⁷¹ Listening to Clegg's early live performances from 1970 to 1978 reveals this shift in sound and identity from performing traditional Zulu maskanda music to a sound that encompasses his broader life-world and the cultural diversity of South Africa. Through listening to Clegg's development from a young man of 18 years in 1970 to a confident 26-year-old performer in 1978, we can hear how he honed his stage presence with Mchunu and crafted his artistic identity through storytelling, serious reflections on Zulu culture and tradition, humour and entertainment.

From the first recording we have of Clegg performing at the 'National Folk Festival', though self-conscious and reticent on stage he displayed an acute awareness of the socio-political context in which he was performing. His songs resonated with themes of migrancy, inequality, traditions and apartheid's impact on those traditions and family values. At the same time, in 'Tribal Blues', he displayed a deep knowledge and understanding of Zulu culture, embodying its spirituality, idioms, customs, dances and stories. In doing so, he cultivated a musical universe wherein his distinctive style and sensibility could develop and grow. Clegg's receptiveness to the nuances of being a maskandi musician, coupled with his ability to translate these nuances into captivating performances, established his role as a facilitator who educated and transported audiences into the life-world of Zulu people. His grasp of Zulu aesthetics transcended the superficial, and allowed him to develop a 'true polycultural identity' deeply embedded in Zulu culture, both philosophically and spiritually.[72]

In the postscript to Clegg's autobiography, his family acknowledges the importance he placed on his early years, how he realised 'that so much of who he was and how he understood the world came out of this early period of his life when he first encountered Zulu culture'.[73] Listening to Clegg's live music performances with Mchunu during his formative years expands the discourse on his first encounters with Zulu culture, allowing us to experience the various facets, identities and sounds that would lead to the becoming of one of South Africa's most iconic duos.

NOTES

1. The Hidden Years Music Archive is preserved at the Documentation Centre for Music, Stellenbosch University. The digitisation project and broader research initiatives were funded by the Volkswagen Stiftung under the direction of Lizabé Lambrechts (2013–2022) and supported by the Andrew W. Mellon Foundation (2018–2021) through a grant held by Stephanus Muller of the Africa Open Institute for Music, Research and Innovation.

   The names 'Market Theatre Café', 'Market Café', and 'Café' were used interchangeably in the archival and published sources. For the purposes of this chapter, the standardised form 'Market Café' will be used throughout.
2. For more information see Lizabé Lambrechts, 'Letting the Tape Run: The Creation and Preservation of the Hidden Years Music Archive', *South African Journal of Cultural History* 32, no. 2 (2018): 1–23, and https://hiddenyearsmusicarchive.co.za.
3. Thomas M. Pooley, 'Sikeyi: In Memoriam – Johnny Clegg (1953–2019)', *Muziki: Journal of Music Research in Africa* 17, no. 1 (2020): 131.
4. Pooley, 'Sikeyi', 131.
5. Johnny Clegg, *Scatterling of Africa: My Early Years* (Johannesburg: Pan Macmillan, 2021), 67, 102. We use 'maskanda' to refer to the music and 'maskandi' to refer to a maskanda musician.
6. Clegg, *Scatterling*, 179–188.
7. David Marks, interview with Lizabé Lambrechts, 3 August 2020. See also Adrian English, 'White Boy Leads Zulu Warriors', newspaper unknown, 12 August 1971, 21 (digitised newspaper clippings, Hidden Years Music Archive, hy-dm-clegg-1971-001.pdf).
8. The Troubadour was opened in 1964 by Des Lindberg and Keith Blundell as the first dedicated venue for folk music in Doornfontein, Johannesburg. See Lizabé Lambrechts and Jeremy Taylor, 'They Called Me the "Ag Pleez Deddy" Man': On the (Be)longing of Jeremy Taylor', *SAMUS: South African Music Studies* 39, no.1 (2019): 78.
9. Ian Lawrence, then manager of The Troubadour, was on tour in Zimbabwe with Richie Morris. He asked David Marks and Neil McCallum to manage the venue while away on tour. Marks, interview with Lizabé Lambrechts, 3 August 2020.
10. Des and Dawn Lindberg, *Every Day Is an Opening Night: Our Journey Together* (Johannesburg: Jacana Media, 2021), 194–219.
11. Clegg, *Scatterling*, 279–280.
12. Staff Reporter, 'Local Emphasis', *Rand Daily Mail*, 30 June 1970.
13. 'National Folk Festival', 23–24 July 1970 (digitised reel-to-reel tape, Hidden Years Music Archive, hymap-dm-reel-miller-clegg-1970-001 and hymap-dm-reel-folk-festival-1970-002).
14. 'National Folk Festival', 23–24 July 1970. Transcribed by the authors.
15. 'National Folk Festival', 23–24 July 1970. Transcribed by the authors.
16. 'National Folk Festival', 23–24 July 1970. Transcribed by the authors.
17. Clegg, *Scatterling*, 280.
18. 'Tribal Blues Concert Programme' (digitised programme, Hidden Years Music Archive, hymap-dm-prog-tribal-blues-a-south-african-music-concert-1971-08-11-1971-08-12).
19. Lizabé Lambrechts and Schalk van der Merwe, 'Ghosts of the Popular: The Hidden Years Music Archive and the Interstices of South African Popular Music History', *Journal of Popular Culture* 53, no. 6 (2020): 1324. See also David Marks, 'The Township

Blues Crews & A Farm Boys Rock – A Theory!' *3rd Ear Music*, accessed 7 May 2025, https://3rdearmusic.com/hyarchive/hyarchive/malombo.

20 We would like to thank Kathryn Olsen for her generous comments on these songs, performing styles and meanings.

21 Thomas Pooley, 'Umaskandi Izibongo: Semantic, Prosodic and Musical Dimensions of Voice in Zulu Popular Praises', *African Music: Journal of the International Library of African Music* 10, no. 2 (2016): 7.

22 Identified by Pakama Ncume from 'Tribal Blues: A South African Music Concert', 11–12 August 1971 (digitised reel-to-reel tape, Hidden Years Music Archive, hymap-dm-tribal-blues-1971-002.mp3). Recording made on the first night, 11 August 1971.

23 'Tribal Blues', 11–12 August 1971.

24 For more information about *ngoma* dancing, consult the work of Kathryn Olsen, *Music and Social Change in South Africa: Maskanda Past and Present* (Philadelphia: Temple University Press, 2014). Clegg's deep knowledge and understanding of Zulu dance is also reflected in his publications during the 1980s on *ngoma* dance and stick-fighting. See for example Johnny Clegg, 'The Music of Zulu Immigrant Workers in Johannesburg: A Focus on Concertina and Guitar', in *Papers Presented at the Symposium on Ethnomusicology, Music Department, Rhodes University, Grahamstown, 10–11 October 1980*, edited by Andrew Tracey (Grahamstown: International Library of African Music, 1981), 2–21; Johnny Clegg, 'Towards an Understanding of African Dance: The Zulu Isishameni Style', in *Papers Presented at the Second Symposium on Ethnomusicology, Music Department, Rhodes University, Grahamstown, 24–26 September 1981*, edited by Andrew Tracey (Grahamstown: International Library of African Music, 1982), 8–14.

25 'Tribal Blues', 11–12 August 1971, transcribed and translated by Pakama Ncume. Various scholars have written on these chants called *izaga*. Godshero Nkonzoyakhe Donda, for example, writes about the chant that is recited in this performance, pointing out that it is a battle cry in a call and response format. This proverb encourages the troops to face the enemy. See Godshero N. Donda, 'Ucwaningo Olunzulu Ngesakhiwo Nobumqoka Bamahubo Nezaga Zesizulu' (PhD diss., University of KwaZulu-Natal, 1999).

26 'Tribal Blues', 11–12 August 1971. During their performance on the second night, the group danced with so much vigour that they caused approximately R10 000 worth of damage to the stage. (See Untitled article, *Rand Daily Mail*, 8 January 1977 [newspaper clippings, Hidden Years Music Archive]).

27 Clegg, *Scatterling*, 279.

28 'Tribal Blues', 11–12 August 1971.

29 'Tribal Blues Concert Programme'.

30 Lambrechts and Van der Merwe, 'Ghosts of the Popular', 1324.

31 '4000 of All Races at Wits Music Festival,' *The Star*, 13 March 1972 (newspaper clippings, Hidden Years Music Archive).

32 '4000 of All Races at Wits Music Festival'.

33 See 'Around & About: Free People's Concert', *Time Out*, March 1972; 'Aid from Musical Marathon', *The Star* (Johannesburg), 9 March 1972 (newspaper clippings, Hidden Years Music Archive).

34 Clegg performed at the 'Free People's Concerts' from 1972 until the last concert in 1990.

35 *Indlamu* is a late-nineteenth century Zulu dance style. See Christopher Ballantine, 'A Brief History of South African Popular Music', *Popular Music* 8, no. 3 (1989): 305–310.

36. 'Free People's Concert', 16 February 1974 (digitised reel-to-reel tape, Hidden Years Music Archive, hymap-dm-reel-free-peoples-concert-1974-001).
37. 'Free People's Concert', 16 February 1974; transcribed by Pakama Ncume.
38. Translation by Pakama Ncume.
39. Johnny Clegg and Sipho Mchunu, 'Market Café, 16 January 1977' (digitised reel-to-reel tape, Hidden Years Music Archive, hymap-dm-reel-clegg-mchunu-1977-001); transcribed by the authors.
40. Lambrechts and Van der Merwe, 'Ghosts of the Popular', 1318.
41. Pakama Ncume, 'Being Public: Musicians and the Market Theatre Café, 1976–1980' (master's thesis, Stellenbosch University, 2023), 133.
42. Clegg, *Scatterling*, 211.
43. Glenn Moss quoted in Heather Dugmore, 'The Day That People Felt Free', *Wits Review*, October 2017, accessed 10 July 2025, https://issuu.com/witsalumnirelations/docs/witsreview_october_2017_issuu/s/109865.
44. See also Ingrid Bianca Byerly, 'Mirror, Mediator, and Prophet: The Music Indaba of Late Apartheid South Africa', *Ethnomusicology* 42, no. 1 (1998): 8.
45. Paul Clingman, interview with Lizabé Lambrechts, 30 July 2020.
46. See for example Clingman's first album, *Morning on the Line* (Johannesburg: The Record and Tape Co., RTL.4022, 1973).
47. Clingman, interview with Lizabé Lambrechts, 30 July 2020.
48. Helen Lunn, 'Hippies, Radicals and Sounds of Silence: Cultural Dialectics at two South African Universities, 1966–1976' (PhD diss., University of Kwazulu-Natal, 2010), 140.
49. Paul Clingman, *Father to the Child* (album, Johannesburg: Stanyan Africa, 3 EE 7000, 1977).
50. '*Amabaca*' is the spelling of the title on the album. The correct spelling of this isiZulu word is '*AmaBhaca*'.
51. Paul Clingman, interview with Lizabé Lambrechts, 30 July 2020.
52. Their first single, *Uthi Angizule* (He Tells Me Not to Stray), was released in 1976. *Woza Friday* was initially banned from airplay on Radio Bantu and Radio Zulu because of the mixing of English and isiZulu lyrics, which went against the government's broader agenda of cultural segregation and its supposed 'promotion' of racial and linguistic purity. See Johnny Clegg and Michael Drewett, 'Why Don't You Sing About the Leaves and the Dreams? Reflecting on Music Censorship in Apartheid South Africa', in *Popular Music Censorship in Africa*, ed. Martin Cloonan and Michael Drewett (London: Routledge, 2016), 128.
53. Clegg, *Scatterling*, 283.
54. Lambrechts, 'Letting the Tape Run', 11. See also Ncume, 'Being Public'.
55. J. Brooks Spector, 'Dreams of Rebuilding the Old Market', in *The Market Theatre: 40 Years of Storytelling 1976–2016*, edited by The Market Theatre Foundation (Johannesburg: DesLink Media, 2016), 52. See also Carlos Amato, 'Joburg's Market Theatre Turns 40', *Cape Times*, 12 June 2016, accessed 28 March 2025, https://www.timeslive.co.za/sunday-times/lifestyle/2016-06-12-joburgs-market-theatre-turns-40/.
56. The theatre was not completely free from the restrictions of petty apartheid. For example, an inspection of the theatre's racially mixed toilet facilities and change rooms was carried out by the Group Areas Board in 1977. See Pat Schwartz, *The Best of Company: The Story of Johannesburg's Market Theatre* (Johannesburg: A.D. Donker, 1988), 83.
57. Marks, interview with Lizabé Lambrechts, 24 April 2017.

58 Johnny Clegg and Sipho Mchunu, Market Café, 16 January 1977 (digitised reel-to-reel tape, Hidden Years Music Archive, hymap-dm-reel-clegg-mchunu-1977-001). The umrhubhe is a musical bow instrument often made with a brass wire. It is played by rubbing the string with a reed or scraped stick, using the mouth as a resonator. It is common among the amaXhosa, amaZulu and amaMpondo people. See Dave Dargie, 'The Xhosa Umrhubhe Mouthbow: An Extraordinary Musical Instrument', *African Music: Journal of the International Library of African Music* 9, no. 1 (2011): 33–55.
59 Johnny Clegg and Sipho Mchunu, Market Café, 16 January 1977.
60 Johnny Clegg and Sipho Mchunu, Market Café, 16 January 1977.
61 Jeremy Marre and Hannah Charlton, *Beats of the Heart: Popular Music of the World* (New York: Pantheon Books, 1985), 39.
62 Johnny Clegg and Sipho Mchunu, Market Café, 16 January 1977; transcribed by the authors.
63 Clegg's comments audible on the recording, Johnny Clegg and Sipho Mchunu, Market Café, 16 January 1977; Juluka, *Universal Men* (Johannesburg: Gramophone Records Co. / CBS Records, DNW 2429, 1979).
64 Johnny Clegg and Sipho Mchunu, Market Café, 16 January 1977.
65 See also Marie-Heleen Coetzee, 'Playing Sticks: An Exploration of Zulu Stick Fighting as Performance', *South African Theatre Journal* 14, no. 1 (2000): 97–113.
66 Johnny Clegg and Sipho Mchunu, 'Market Café, 7 May 1978' (digitised reel-to-reel tape, Hidden Years Music Archive, hymap-dm-reel-clegg-mchunu-1978-001); transcribed by the authors.
67 Clegg's comments, audible on the recording. Johnny Clegg and Sipho Mchunu, Market Café, 16 January 1977.
68 Clegg, *Scatterling*, 279.
69 The earlier version of '*Asimbonanga*' performed in 1978 refers to the former prime minister of Transkei, Chief Kaiser Daliwonga Matanzima, while the 1986–87 version was a tribute to Nelson Mandela, who was imprisoned at the time. Both versions have the same lyrics, except for the two different names. The name change echoes a broader socio-political shift in South Africa from the homeland leadership to a yearning for democratic governance.
70 See also Pooley, 'Umaskandi Izibongo', 132.
71 Marguerite de Villers, 'Johnny Clegg: A Shadow Man', *Anthropology Southern Africa* 39, no. 1 (2016): 63.
72 Lucilla Spini and Andrew Grant Innes, 'Johnny Clegg: A Polycultural Anthropologist On Stage for Social Justice', *International Journal of Anthropology* 37, no.1–2 (2022): 78.
73 Clegg, *Scatterling*, 325–326.

REFERENCES

'4000 of all Races at Wits Music Festival'. *The Star*, 13 March 1972. Newspaper clippings. Hidden Years Music Archive, Documentation Centre for Music, Stellenbosch University.

'Aid from Musical Marathon'. *The Star*, 9 March 1972. Newspaper clippings. Hidden Years Music Archive, Documentation Centre for Music, Stellenbosch University.

Amato, Carlos. 'Joburg's Market Theatre Turns 40'. *Cape Times*, 12 June 2016. Accessed 28 March 2025. https://www.timeslive.co.za/sunday-times/lifestyle/2016-06-12-joburgs-market-theatre-turns-40/.

'Around & About: Free People's Concert'. *Time Out*, March 1972. Newspaper clippings. Hidden Years Music Archive, Documentation Centre for Music, Stellenbosch University.

Ballantine, Christopher. 'A Brief History of South African Popular Music'. *Popular Music* 8, no. 3 (1989): 305–310.

Byerly, Ingrid Bianca. 'Mirror, Mediator, and Prophet: The Music Indaba of Late Apartheid South Africa'. *Ethnomusicology* 42, no. 1 (1998): 1–44.

Clegg, Johnny. 'The Music of Zulu Immigrant Workers in Johannesburg: A Focus on Concertina and Guitar'. In *Papers Presented at the Symposium on Ethnomusicology, Music Department, Rhodes University, Grahamstown, 10–11 October 1980*, edited by Andrew Tracey, 2–21. Grahamstown: International Library of African Music, Rhodes University, 1981.

Clegg, Johnny. *Scatterling of Africa: My Early Years*. Johannesburg: Pan Macmillan, 2021.

Clegg, Johnny. 'Towards an Understanding of African Dance: The Zulu Isishameni Style'. In *Papers Presented at the Second Symposium on Ethnomusicology, Music Department, Rhodes University, Grahamstown, 24–26 September 1981*, edited by Andrew Tracey, 8–14. Grahamstown: International Library of African Music, Rhodes University, 1982.

Clegg, Johnny and Michael Drewett. 'Why Don't You Sing About the Leaves and the Dreams? Reflecting on Music Censorship in Apartheid South Africa'. In *Popular Music Censorship in Africa*, edited by Martin Cloonan and Michael Drewett, 127–135. London: Routledge, 2016.

Clegg, Johnny and Sipho Mchunu. 'Market Café, 16 January 1977'. Digitised reel-to-reel tape, hymap-dm-reel-clegg-mchunu-1977-001. Hidden Years Music Archive, Documentation Centre for Music, Stellenbosch University.

Clegg, Johnny and Sipho Mchunu. 'Market Café, 7 May 1978'. Digitised reel-to-reel tape, hymap-dm-reel-clegg-mchunu-1978-001. Hidden Years Music Archive, Documentation Centre for Music, Stellenbosch University.

Coetzee, Marie-Heleen. 'Playing Sticks: An Exploration of Zulu Stick Fighting as Performance'. *South African Theatre Journal* 14, no. 1 (2000): 97–113.

Dargie, Dave. 'The Xhosa Umrhubhe Mouthbow: An Extraordinary Musical Instrument'. *African Music: Journal of the International Library of African Music* 9, no. 1 (2011): 33–55.

De Villers, Marguerite. 'Johnny Clegg: A Shadow Man'. *Anthropology Southern Africa* 39, no. 1 (2016): 58–63.

Donda, Godshero N. 'Ucwaningo Olunzulu Ngesakhiwo Nobumqoka Bamahubo Nezaga Zesizulu'. PhD diss., University of KwaZulu-Natal, 1999.

Dugmore, Heather. 'The Day That People Felt Free'. *Wits Review*, October 2017. Accessed 10 July 2025, https://issuu.com/witsalumnirelations/docs/witsreview_october_2017_issuu/s/109865.

English, Adrian. 'White Boy Leads Zulu Warriors'. Newspaper unknown, 12 August 1971. Digitised newspaper clipping, hy-dm-clegg-1971-001.pdf. Hidden Years Music Archive, Documentation Centre for Music, Stellenbosch University.

'Free People's Concert', 16 February 1974. Digitised reel-to-reel tape, hymap-dm-reel-freepeoples-concert-1974-001. Hidden Years Music Archive, Documentation Centre for Music, Stellenbosch University.

Lambrechts, Lizabé. 'Letting the Tape Run: The Creation and Preservation of the Hidden Years Music Archive'. *South African Journal of Cultural History* 32, no. 2 (2018): 1–23.

Lambrechts, Lizabé and Jeremy Taylor. 'They Called Me the "Ag Pleez Deddy" Man': On the (Be)longing of Jeremy Taylor'. *SAMUS: South African Music Studies* 39, no. 1 (2019): 44–86.

Lambrechts, Lizabé and Schalk van der Merwe. 'Ghosts of the Popular: The Hidden Years Music Archive and the Interstices of South African Popular Music History'. *Journal of Popular Culture* 53, no. 6 (2020): 1316–1334.

Lindberg, Des and Dawn Lindberg. *Every Day Is an Opening Night: Our Journey Together*. Johannesburg: Jacana Media, 2021.

Lunn, Helen. 'Hippies, Radicals and the Sounds of Silence: Cultural Dialectics at Two South African Universities 1966–1976'. PhD diss., University of KwaZulu-Natal, 2010.

Marks, David. 'The Township Blues Crews & A Farm Boys Rock – A Theory!' *3rd Ear Music*. Accessed 7 May 2025. https://3rdearmusic.com/hyarchive/hyarchive/malombo.

Marre, Jeremy and Hannah Charlton. *Beats of the Heart: Popular Music of the World*. New York: Pantheon Books, 1985.

'National Folk Festival', 23–24 July 1970. Digitised reel-to-reel tapes, hymap-dm-reel-miller-clegg-1970-001 and hymap-dm-reel-folk-festival-1970-002. Hidden Years Music Archive, Documentation Centre for Music, Stellenbosch University.

Ncume, Pakama. 'Being Public: Musicians and the Market Theatre Café, 1976–1980'. Master's thesis, Stellenbosch University, 2023.

Olsen, Kathryn. *Music and Social Change in South Africa: Maskanda Past and Present*. Philadelphia: Temple University Press, 2014.

Pooley, Thomas M. 'Sikeyi: In Memoriam – Johnny Clegg (1953–2019)'. *Muziki: Journal of Music Research in Africa* 17, no.1 (2020): 131–136.

Pooley, Thomas M. 'Umaskandi Izibongo: Semantic, Prosodic and Musical Dimensions of Voice in Zulu Popular Praises'. *African Music: Journal of the International Library of African Music* 10, no. 2 (2016): 7–34.

Schwartz, Pat. *The Best of Company: The Story of Johannesburg's Market Theatre*. Johannesburg: A.D. Donker, 1988.

Spector, J. Brooks. 'Dreams of Rebuilding the Old Market'. In *The Market Theatre: 40 Years of Storytelling, 1976–2016*, edited by The Market Theatre Foundation, 52–53. Johannesburg: DesLink Media, 2016.

Spini, Lucilla and Andrew Grant Innes. 'Johnny Clegg: A Polycultural Anthropologist On Stage for Social Justice'. *International Journal of Anthropology* 37, no. 1–2 (2022): 75–94.

Staff Reporter. 'Local Emphasis'. *Rand Daily Mail*, 30 June 1970. Newspaper clippings. Hidden Years Music Archive, Documentation Centre for Music, Stellenbosch University.

'Tribal Blues: A South African Music Concert', 11–12 August 1971. Digitised reel-to-reel tape, hymap-dm-tribal-blues-1971-002.mp3. Hidden Years Music Archive, Documentation Centre for Music, Stellenbosch University.

'Tribal Blues Concert Programme'. Digitised programme, hymap-dm-prog-tribal-blues-a south-african-music-concert-1971-08-11-1971-08-12. Hidden Years Music Archive, Documentation Centre for Music, Stellenbosch University

Untitled article. *Rand Daily Mail*, 8 January 1977. Newspaper clippings. Hidden Years Music Archive, Documentation Centre for Music, Stellenbosch University.

DISCOGRAPHY

Clingman, Paul. *Father to the Child*. Album. Johannesburg: Stanyan Africa, 3 EE 7000, 1977.

Clingman, Paul. *Morning on the Line*. Album. Johannesburg: The Record and Tape Co., RTL.4022, 1973.

Juluka. *Universal Men*. Album. Johannesburg: Gramophone Records Co./CBS Records, DNW 2429, 1979.

CHAPTER

3

'Woza Moya Omuhle': Johnny Clegg and Sipho Mchunu's Unifying Cross-Cultural Brotherhood

Andrew Grant Innes

A few weeks after the winter solstice, on the afternoon of Wednesday, 17 July 2019, roughly an hour before sunset, the sound of a voice chanting in isiZulu rang out across the Jewish section of Westpark Cemetery in Johannesburg.

A small group of fewer than 30 mourners was gathered alongside a freshly dug mound of dark soil near the perimeter wall of the graveyard.[1] The late afternoon sun filtered almost horizontally through the poplar trees, illuminating the fine dust and clods of earth next to a roughly hewn plain pine box holding the remains of Jonathan Paul Clegg, OBE, OIS. This rudimentary container was fitting for the life of passionate pragmatism, devoid of airs and graces, that had been lived by the deceased.

Beginning with a drawn-out wail and occasionally cracking with emotion, this voice called the Zulu praise names (*izibongo*) of Johnny Clegg: '*Hawu! Umfowethu! Skeyi jikel'eshobeni ...*'[2] These were the words of Sipho Mchunu, honouring his deceased musical partner of some 50 years' standing. Those 50 years had seen the pair witness the subjugation of a populace, the fall of a system, and the birth of the rainbow nation – an event they had envisaged, anticipated and fought for.

As Sipho's poignant eulogy ended, the males among the assembled mourners took turns using a shovel to deposit earth on the surface of the coffin, which had been lowered into the freshly dug grave. At this point, Johnny's sons Jesse and Jaron recited the *Kaddish*, the Aramaic prayer for the dead, in the presence of the rabbi who was conducting the funeral proceedings: '*Yitgadal v'yitkadash sh'mei raba b'alma di-v'ra; chirutei, v'yamlich malchutei b'chayeichon; uvyomeichon uvchayei d'chol beit yisrael, ba'agala; uvizman kariv, v'im'ru: amen*' ('Magnified and sanctified is the great name of God throughout the world, which was created according to Divine will. May the rule of peace be established speedily in our time, unto us and unto the entire household of Israel. And let us say: Amen.').[3]

Here were people gathered from two communities, separated by faith, history, geography and ideology, each with their own long history of violent oppression, both claiming Johnny as their own with no hint of dissonance understood or implied in his belonging to both groups.

This was representative of Johnny's lived reality, his multicultural or 'polycultural' spirit and his search for unity and meaning through the shared human condition.[4] He had striven throughout his life to reconcile and balance his constantly changing inner construct of a multicultural identity. This identity wound its course between numerous competing yet synergistic social realities – a uniquely and typically South African identity.[5] This presents an interesting opportunity to look at how Johnny and Sipho's bond came about, and what we can take from this relationship and its development. It is relevant to think of this in terms of how society in South Africa came into being and how it functions today across cultures. This chapter investigates that bond and its impact on the forces that defined their environment in the context of norms governing art and music at the time.

HEGEMONY, CULTURE AND POWER

Sipho Mchunu and Johnny Clegg's first encounter was not a likely occurrence. They came from entirely different worlds in late 1960s South Africa.

These worlds had been defined, developed and perpetuated in paradigms of power with deep roots stretching back to the early eighteenth century. These were multilayered paradigms, built with intention and purpose to undermine and neuter one set of socio-cultural systems to the advantage of another.[6] This is 'hegemony', and hegemony is maintained through a conflation of culture and power.

There are obvious indications of the effects of hegemony in South African society, such as the unwritten requirement of fluency in English to achieve socio-economic advancement.[7] However, hegemony also manifests its power in more subtle ways. All forms of culture in a hegemony are part of a network of power relations, and this power is evident when viewed in context.[8] It is in power positioned against an idea or a way of life to enable its antithesis that hegemony becomes operational. Hegemony is rarely detected in the civilised, surface-level dance of the system in motion. The hegemonic system weaves an illusion of symmetry and refined calm through the machinations of its fields and apparatus.[9] For any nascent hegemony of domination, culture is the first and last battleground. Every juxtaposition – of civilisation and barbarism, refinement and crassness, religion and superstition – is a lever of power, pulled or pushed to create tactical advantages in an overarching strategy of socio-economic domination.[10] If we look at the relative budgets allocated to vernacular broadcast media as opposed to English- and Afrikaans-language media under apartheid, we see the drivers and effects of hegemony in promoting certain forms of art and culture over others in South Africa.[11] Beyond the budgetary considerations, this divided system of African-language broadcasting was designed to promote and reify subcultural and linguistic separation. This hegemony, alongside the overdetermination effect of centuries of war, dispossession, proselytisation, racism and ethnocentrism, painted the reality of the world Sipho and Johnny inhabited when they first met in Johannesburg in 1969.

The apartheid government in South Africa had deployed a carefully constructed system of racial and cultural segregation. Accompanying legislation such as the Group Areas Act (No. 41 of 1950) and the Prohibition of Mixed Marriages Act (No. 55 of 1949), alongside the homelands policy, enforced this division.¹² The word 'segregation' is important here. In a model of acculturation, when groups or individuals reduce their relationship with society while maintaining their heritage culture, this is called 'separation'.¹³ In apartheid South Africa, with its pseudo-liberal policy of 'separate development', the element of force was a catalyst in the acculturation process.¹⁴ When this occurs, 'separation' comes to be termed 'segregation'.¹⁵ In South Africa's case, we cannot refer to this as a voluntary strategy (as originally envisaged for acculturating immigrant populations), as the acculturation process towards the dominant culture at the time was one that posited the national majority as the acculturating group, doing so under extreme duress. The acculturation process of subordinate classes modifying their cultural orientation to align with the symbolically dominant culture is a necessary feature of hegemony. However, cultural diffusion can move in more than one direction, where the proximity of cultures to one another results in two-way exchanges – precisely what occurred between Johnny and Sipho.

A MEETING OF MINDS

Sipho recalls that, as a migrant labourer, he had obtained regular employment in Houghton, an affluent suburb of Johannesburg, working in the garden of a large home in that suburb in 1969.¹⁶ It was during the course of that year that he met Johnny through mutual acquaintances and began teaching him Zulu guitar styles. Sipho introduced Johnny to the space of the migrant labour hostels and the forms of cultural expression that existed in those places. Johnny had been attracted to the different forms of Zulu dance, and became adept in the *Mzansi*, *Shameni* and *Bhaca* styles, which he learned at Sipho's home in Makhabeleni and in the hostels.¹⁷

The two formed a strong bond and developed their art during their early collaborations, with the support of well-known folk duo Des and Dawn Lindberg (performing at soirées at the couple's home in Yeoville) and mining magnate Harry Oppenheimer (taking part in performances at his Brenthurst estate). These performance opportunities were key to the development and dissemination of their music, as they could not perform together in public due to apartheid-era laws. Sipho describes this:

> We had a huge problem with the police and ... Des and Dawn helped us a lot. They helped put us on the map – got us in the newspapers. At that time, we couldn't even put food on the table. They invited us to play at their home in Yeoville ... There were these boys from Nkandla of the Shange clan. They worked at Oppenheimer's place. I introduced Johnny to them and every Christmas we would go and perform traditional [songs and] dances [at Brenthurst].[18]

Johnny and Sipho's meeting would ultimately present a direct challenge to the brutal system of apartheid that categorised and oppressed groups of people on the basis of race.[19] The system had sought through its mechanisms to perpetuate the colonial demonisation of African beliefs, and to marginalise African culture and its struggle voices that had pushed for balance in the system, or alternatively for its destruction.

Some voices have accused Clegg of cultural appropriation and pursuing African culture for a profit motive (see chapter 13 of this book by Brett Houston-Lock for more detail about these accusations), but Sipho speaks to the authenticity of their relationship:

> He was my age and then I was a man giving him my culture ... Johnny helped me a lot. We learned how to live with each other – he [saw] the truth of my life and he liked it ... I also [saw] the truth of his life and I liked it. We sensed one another. In my life I could sense him, and he also knew how to sense me.
>
> [Despite initial communication difficulties] we sensed one another – in the eyes. Eyes – they speak louder than anything ... the feeling, [your sense of someone], is more important. Life is about sensing things. We grew up to sense one another. We understood one another.[20]

CENSORSHIP, POWER AND RESISTANCE

Johnny frequently used detailed anecdotes on stage to introduce songs during the course of his shows. He often told the story of how he had met with Yvonne Huskisson, who was the head of *Radio Zulu* at the time (known today as *Ukhozi FM*), when Johnny and Sipho's first single, *Woza Friday* (Come Friday), was released in 1977, under the duo name 'Jonathan and Sipho'. At the meeting, according to Johnny, Huskisson informed him that *Woza Friday* had been censored due to a violation of the language purity rule. The fact that there were English words interspersed among the isiZulu lyrics (for example: '*Woza* Friday my sweetie') was what had triggered the violation. Another objection was the patois slang introduced in the lyrics (for example: '... Friday my *dali* [darling]').[21] At the time, Johnny related, he had pointed out to her: 'But that's how people speak. They mix languages and use slang'. This apparently aggravated the matter further rather than settling it, with Huskisson telling Johnny in 'no uncertain terms' that the song would not be broadcast on *Radio Zulu*. At this point in the tale, Johnny would conclude with a broad smile that the song went on to become a smash hit on *Radio Sotho*, effectively launching the live performance career of Juluka. *Radio Sotho* was broadcast in Sesotho – a language not mutually intelligible with isiZulu. He referred to this as a 'particularly South African ironic twist'. He had always enjoyed the humorous philosophical absurdity of these kinds of situations. Johnny relates some of this in his autobiographical work, *Scatterling of Africa: My Early Years*, and in an interview with Michael Drewett.[22]

Johnny and Sipho were being censored because of their practice of mixing languages and violating a rule based on classic cultural divergence theory (the idea that cultures are stable and maintain their core characteristics when interacting with other cultures).[23] On another level, they were essentially being singled out by parts of the apartheid apparatus for finding synergy in the unification of opposites. They had gone against the stream and created new art that sat outside the realm of possible imaginings in apartheid South Africa. The culture-power construct was designed and maintained to both deride and prevent these very possibilities.

Art and music are as much weapons as rifles and bullets are when considering the 'war of position' waged by the forces at play in a hegemonic system.[24] Johnny and Sipho, in their own way, initiated a form of countercultural resistance against the National Party government (see chapter 4 by Martina Viljoen and chapter 5 by Richard Pithouse in this book for more on this). Johnny mentioned in interviews later in life that when culture is weaponised, it can be problematic, as all knowledge has an agenda – citing Jürgen Habermas' work *Knowledge and Human Interests* in an interview with *Higher Education Today*.[25] While Juluka's music was not initially designed to be a form of countercultural resistance, their hybrid art came to present a direct challenge to the systematic marginalisation, disruption and destruction of indigenous culture practised by the apartheid state.[26] The lyrical content of Juluka's early songs focused mainly on Zulu culture and social issues such as the life challenges of migrant labourers, as can be seen in this extract from 'African Sky Blue': 'The warrior's now a worker and his war is underground ... when the smoking rock face murmurs, he always dreams of you, African Sky Blue ...'[27]

However, Johnny and Sipho also began using metaphor to embed veiled messages of resistance in their art. A good example of this in their early work is the haunting isiZulu ballad performed with voice, guitar and umhube bow, '*Inkunzi ayihlabi ngokumisa*' ('Don't Judge a Bull by Its Horns') from the *Universal Men* album:[28]

> *Yiyo le nkunzi, yiyo emaqobotshana bandla, ayihlabi ngokumisa*[29]
> *Zish'inkunzi, emaqobotshana, ayihlabi ngokumisa*
>
> (This is the small bull, don't judge it by its horns
> they say this bull, this small bull, should not be judged by its horns)[30]

The lyrics describe a bull that seems to be less powerful but can still win a fight through its ability and does not reveal its true power until it strikes.

By the time Juluka released their final album in the first phase of their career, the lyrics had taken on a stronger and more blatant tone in addressing the apartheid state, as we hear in '*Akanaki Nokunaka*' ('They Don't Care'):

> *Akanaki nokunaka, hawu bheku-G.G.*
> *Umuzi kababa, wawuthela efusini*
>
> (They don't care, just look at these police
> they threw my father's home onto a rubbish heap)[31]

They had also become more vocal in describing a possible future where, contrary to the dictates of apartheid, South Africans could be united, as in '*Woza Moya*' ('Come Spirit'):

> *Woza moya omuhle*
> *Sibambane ngezandla sibe munye*
>
> (Come beautiful spirit
> let us hold one another's hands and become one)[32]

A WATERSHED MOMENT

The '*Woza Moya*' lyrics are from the *Musa Ukungilandela* ('Don't Follow Me') album released in 1984. In the same year a very different album was released – *Stand Your Ground*.[33] *Stand Your Ground* was released into international markets containing four new songs with English lyrics (sung by Johnny) and hard-hitting electro bass and keyboard instrumentation with pop/rock rhythm section feels. These songs were designed to align with contemporary international chart-topping songs, and were forerunners of the Johnny Clegg solo and Savuka sounds which were to follow. The album departed significantly in musical feel and lyrical content from the former Juluka releases. Caleb Mutch explores some of the differences between Juluka and Savuka's musical styles in chapter 11 in this book.

It is feasible that this change in direction was a consequence of what Pierre Bourdieu calls 'symbolic domination', where art that aligned with the

Western ideal of the time, with just enough exoticisation of African culture, had stronger financial prospects.[34] The direct relationship between shifting the cultural position of Juluka into a kind of cultural Overton window of acceptable art forms for Western audiences and the accompanying potential profit bolsters this assertion.

The following year, after serving out a one-year notice period, Sipho left Juluka, effectively disbanding the entity. The change in musical direction described above coincided with the end of Juluka. This possible explanation for how Juluka came to a fork in the road is suggested by the content of two articles. A 1984 article in the *Washington Post* had this to say about *Stand Your Ground*: 'Singing in English and emphasizing musical patterns similar to the West's melodic song form, Juluka should be accessible to average Americans in a way that Bob Marley was and King Sunny Adé isn't ... Juluka does not play traditional Zulu music anymore, but Clegg and Mchunu have created a hybrid music with sure roots in Zulu and new branches stretching out to the rest of the world'.[35] In a subsequent interview with *Bona* magazine, Sipho said, in relation to new music he was developing for his own solo projects, 'I'm going for traditional music ... the real African message, deep from the roots of our tradition'.[36]

The situation raises interesting questions, because the two positions on either side of what appear to have been diverging strategies for Juluka's continued existence were both valid. Sipho was a Zulu traditionalist who wanted to create Zulu art that promoted his culture and communicated Zulu ideas in a musical paradigm. Those responsible for monetising the music clearly saw potential in a hybrid art form which married the Zulu musical idiom and contemporary Western styles in a manner that would propel the group to international fame and fortune. This much is clear from the fact that there was a deal on the table with Columbia in the USA with an advance of US$150 000 due upon signing.[37] A cynical view of this might ascribe the shift to hybrid art as being driven purely by a profit motive, but there was an accompanying opportunity to spread a message of anti-apartheid resistance and equality to a wider, global audience. This proposed opportunity is precisely what followed in the Savuka years.

A detailed analysis of this period in Clegg's career is beyond the scope of this chapter, but the chapters in this collection by Richard Pithouse,

Lucilla Spini and Chris Letcher cover the period comprehensively. In an interview, Sipho makes it clear that his departure was not driven by differing approaches to the musical output, but rather by a need to return home after the death of his parents to consolidate his homestead. This was his preordained duty as the appointed custodian of Zulu culture among his siblings:

> When I left the band, it was to come back to my place to organise myself, because my home was empty with nobody here. My mother and father had passed away ... I told Johnny I needed to go back and re-establish my home ... Johnny said, 'I understand. I know what you're thinking, but to do all these things that you're thinking about, you have to make money.'
>
> ... But my heart was saying, 'who's going to help me to follow my dream?' ... I said to Johnny – 'I want to follow my dream for my home. You can give me 10 million, 1 million, [it won't make a difference] I'm talking about *ikhaya lami* [my home].'
>
> ... That was my point. These were the shoes my father [left me]. I didn't go to school ... my father said everybody could go to school except [me]. He told me I would stay at home. I cried seeing all my brothers and my sisters going to school, dressing nicely ... and at the end he said, 'go fetch my bull there, on the mountain' ... You know, all those mountains there [pointing outside], I know them – I have walked them with my feet ... my father knew what he was talking about. And he did sense my life [purpose]. I'm the one he appointed to [preserve] the family.[38]

ZULU SPIRIT

Sipho's homestead is surrounded by steep mountains, which circle this enduring social fortress of Zulu culture in the valley of Makhabeleni on the banks of the Tugela River. Life is lived here in terms of a core Zulu philosophy and practice. Many of the daily rituals, ways of life, and their symbolic and

'Woza Moya Omuhle'

Figure 3.1: Inside the Mchunu main roundhouse in Magobhe, Makhabeleni, KwaZulu-Natal, where the *Ukwamukelwa Ekhaya* ceremony was conducted. Photograph © Andrew Innes 2023.

ethical underpinnings are conducted as they have been for hundreds of years in rural Zulu society. Sipho and his family have modernised much of the infrastructure. However, despite some evidence of twenty-first-century technological additions, the ethos of life and how it is lived there remains rooted in core Zulu traditions and belief systems.

In the middle of Sipho's large property is the *isibaya* ('kraal') where the cattle spend their nights – a circular enclosure roughly 50 metres in diameter with walls made of long thin wooden poles. Johnny was inducted into the Chunu clan in an *Ukwamukelwa Ekhaya* ancestral ceremony in Makhabeleni in 1970 in the main roundhouse built on the eastern side of the *isibaya* (figure 3.1).[39] This is a structure with an open-plan architectural design that can easily accommodate 30 people. During the ceremony he was presented to the Mchunu ancestors as a new member of the family, accompanied by the ritual sacrifice of a goat. He wore an *isiphandla* made from the goat's skin in the months following the ceremony. The *isiphandla* is cut in bracelet form from the skin of the animal at the time of sacrifice and is stretched over the hand of the recipient onto the wrist while it is still fresh and pliable. It dries rapidly and must remain on the recipient's arm until it falls off. This is an act of appeasement of the ancestors, and it is considered extremely bad form (and bad luck) to cut the *isiphandla* from your wrist before it falls.[40]

The *isibaya* is the gravitational centre of the traditional Zulu homestead, its beating heart. The cattle in the enclosure represent the wealth and strength of the homestead, and all buildings on the property surround this structure. The *isibaya* and the herd inhabiting the structure are also central to the spirituality of the homestead. This key relationship led Johnny and Sipho to name their musical union Juluka, meaning 'sweat', which was also the name of Sipho's bull at the time. It was in this enclosure that the *Ukulandwa Kongasekho* ('To Fetch the Departed') ceremony was conducted for the spirit of Johnny Clegg in February of 2020 (figure 3.2 and figure 3.3). This was his Zulu spiritual crossing.[41] Sipho explains in more detail:

> Johnny and I spoke [and promised each other] that – 'my brother – If I die before you, you will do my ceremony'. I also said that if he should go first, I would do his ceremony. I performed his first *Ukwamukelwa Ekhaya* here at home because he was a member of the family ... the second one we did at home ... Me and him and all these people with his two children. They are the truth of my life – these boys. So, when he passed away, I performed the ceremony here. Before I could perform the ceremony, I had to go and tell my ancestors at Mchunu's house, we welcome him – you welcome the white man to our family – he belongs to our family from now on. He will be in our family forever. That's why we did it at home. Because we are doing it for the family member we lost. We had to let the ancestors know that our brother died. Now we must bring him home.[42]

Johnny had been acknowledged with several formal recognitions as a member of the Zulu community. He was formally initiated into the *iNala* ('Abundance') Zulu age regiment.[43] Zulu age regiments are groups of *ontanga*

'Woza Moya Omuhle'

Figure 3.2 and Figure 3.3: *Amabutho* (warriors) gathered at the *Ukulandwa Kongasekho* ceremony for Johnny Clegg in the *isibaya*, Magobhe, Makhabeleni, KwaZulu-Natal, 8 February 2020. Photographs © Andrew Innes 2020.

(people of a similar age) who are conscripted into military regiments, and each age grouping is given a name and presented to the royal house.[44] Johnny's *iNala* regiment was inducted by King Goodwill Zwelithini.[45] A famous age regiment, the *iNgobamakhosi* ('Benders of Kings') who were central in the Zulu victory over the British forces at Isandlwana,[46] is mentioned in the Juluka song '*Impi*' ('War'): 'Hopeless battalion destined to die / Broken by

53

the Benders of Kings'.[47] The *amabutho* (warriors in an age regiment) who were Johnny's age mates assembled at the *isibaya* to honour him and witness the *Ukulandwa* ceremony.[48] Carrying their traditional weapons, they sang the chants of their regiment, which Johnny had sung with them upon his initiation some four decades previously and at subsequent gatherings.

SIYAWELA – WE ARE CROSSING

The apartheid state came to an end in 1994, nine years after the dissolution of Juluka, through a set of circumstances and interventions that are beyond the scope of this chapter, but 'economic apartheid' (the entrenched racial capitalism that underpinned apartheid) persists.[49] Large sections of South African society still experience the continuing effects of overdetermination in the culture–power confluence. Attitudes and norms entrenched by the colonial powers which the apartheid state subsequently reinforced have been hard for South Africans to unlearn. Despite race being a political and social construct, everything was about race during the colonial and apartheid periods.[50] We have a deeply ingrained cultural memory of race being a determinant of multiple outcomes in people's lives. Many things in South Africa are still frequently determined by race, and our post-apartheid government continues to use racial classifications to assess population trends and affect restitution.[51] We use the same labels to attempt to correct the mistakes of the past, but the labels should not be mistaken for the only valid map of the fault lines in our society. It is convenient to assess our environment in terms of simplistic typologies, even where weak correlations are revealed. We keep making the same mistakes moving forward. Where heritage ethnicities are shoehorned into the false construct of 'race', we would be well advised to remember that race is not class and race is not culture.

If we look to the weapon that was used to create the rift, the self-perpetuating culture–power construct, we see that while race was the primary determinant of suffering under apartheid, the culture–power overdetermination effect has since become more nuanced. It relates to the digital divide, to skills and education, to socio-economic class and marginalised people in a set of cultural systems that have a lower ascribed and perceived value in the hegemonic view of society. These people and cultural systems are the majority in South Africa, which situates our bipolar reality as 'islands of prosperity in a sea of poverty'.[52]

These islands and the cultures surrounding them are bound to concepts that Johnny interrogated with his activism and his music, and bring us back to the example of Johnny and Sipho. How did they find ways to mitigate the compounded effect of the culture–power relationship, and what lessons can contemporary South African society learn from them? They crossed boundaries and broke down walls. They joined forces and created art that had value in the world. Every time '*Impi*' plays to announce the national rugby team in a stadium, each time their isiZulu-English hybrid radio hits ascend on the national charts, the boundaries of the culture–power hegemony are pushed back a little and a shared South African cultural identity inches forward into the social space. They learned one another's cultures and they wrote a story that crafted an extended metaphor of collective human victory over darkness and separation. In Sipho's words, they *sensed* one another.

Ironically, this echoes the former motto of the South African coat of arms: '*Ex Unitate Vires*' ('From Unity, Strength'), which has been repurposed for the current South African coat of arms as '!ke e: |xarra |ke' ('Unity Through Diversity' in the |Xam language, the original language of the aboriginal San people of the Western Cape region).

People don't always know exactly what it is about Johnny Clegg's music and his story that moves them, but it is probably this: the faintly glimmering possibility of a win-win ending to a tragedy.

ACKNOWLEDGEMENTS

With thanks to Sandile Ngidi for his initial inputs, to Zinhle Ndaba for assistance with translations and transcription, and to Sipho Mchunu and Bafazana Qoma for their time and thoughts.

NOTES

1. The author and Sipho Mchunu were present at the funeral ceremony.
2. Sipho Mchunu, interview with the author, Makhabeleni, 28 November 2023. The interview was conducted in isiZulu and English; Zinhle Ndaba assisted in checking the author's transcription and translation of Mchunu's isiZulu responses, and in translating some sections of the interview. See chapter 6 in this book by Sipho Mchunu and Andrew Grant Innes for the full list of praise names recited.
3. Sharon Memorial Park, 'The Mourner's Kaddish', accessed 21 November 2023, https://sharonmemorial.com/customs-and-traditions/the-mourners-kaddish/.
4. See for example David Coplan, *In Township Tonight! South Africa's Black City Music and Theatre* (Cape Town: Jacana, 2007), 258; Lucilla Spini and Andrew Grant Innes, 'Johnny Clegg: A Polycultural Anthropologist on Stage for Social Justice', *International Journal of Anthropology* 37, no. 1–2 (2022): 75–94, https://doi.org/10.14673/IJA2022121089.
5. Personal observation by the author, who worked as a guitarist and music director in Clegg's bands for 27 years (from 1992 to 2019).
6. See for example Frantz Fanon, *The Wretched of the Earth*, trans. Constance Farrington (New York: Grove Press, 2002), 236.
7. See Neville Alexander, 'The Impact of the Hegemony of English on Access to and Quality of Education with Special Reference to South Africa', in *Language and Poverty*, ed. Wayne Harbert et al. (Bristol: Multilingual Matters, 2008), 54, https://doi.org/10.21832/9781847691200-006.
8. Pierre Bourdieu, *The Field of Cultural Production: Essays on Art and Literature*, ed. Randal Johnson (New York: Columbia University Press, 1993).
9. Bourdieu, *Cultural Production*; Michel Foucault and Colin Gordon, *Power/Knowledge: Selected Interviews and Other Writings, 1972–1977* (New York: Pantheon Books, 1980).
10. See Bourdieu, *Cultural Production*, 34, 139.
11. See for example Sanele Justice Gamede, 'Public Participation in the South African Broadcasting Corporation (SABC) Radio Stations: A Case Study of Ukhozi FM and SAfm' (PhD thesis, University of KwaZulu-Natal, 2020), 26.
12. Johnny Clegg, *Scatterling of Africa: My Early Years* (Johannesburg: Pan Macmillan, 2021), 130.
13. J.W. Berry et al., 'Acculturation Attitudes in Plural Societies', *Applied Psychology* 38, no. 2 (1989): 185–206, https://doi.org/10.1111/j.1464-0597.1989.tb01208.x.
14. See Clegg, *Scatterling*, 130.
15. Berry et al., 'Acculturation Attitudes'.
16. Mchunu, interview with the author.
17. Mchunu, interview with the author.
18. Mchunu, interview with the author.
19. See Coplan, *In Township Tonight!*, 242.
20. Mchunu, interview with the author.
21. Jonathan and Sipho, *Woza Friday* (single, Johannesburg: EMI Brigadiers/Jamloti, JM139, 1997).
22. Clegg, *Scatterling*, 282–284; Johnny Clegg and Michael Drewett, 'Why Don't You Sing about the Leaves and the Dreams? Reflecting on Music Censorship in Apartheid South Africa', in *Popular Music Censorship in Africa*, ed. Martin Cloonan and Michael Drewett, 127–136 (London: Ashgate, 2006), accessed 28 March 2025,

https://www.academia.edu/39866997/Why_Don_t_You_Sing_about_the_Leaves_and_the_Dreams_Reflecting_on_Music_Censorship_in_Apartheid_South_Africa.

23   See David A. Ralston, 'The Crossvergence Perspective: Reflections and Projections', *Journal of International Business Studies* 39, no. 1 (January 2008): 29, https://doi.org/10.1057/palgrave.jibs.8400333.
24   Antonio Gramsci, *Selections from the Prison Notebooks of Antonio Gramsci*, ed. Quentin Hoare and Geoffrey Nowell Smith (London: Lawrence & Wishart, 2012), 237.
25   Jürgen Habermas, *Knowledge and Human Interests*, ed. Jeremy J. Shapiro (Boston: Polity Press, 1994); Steven Roy Goodman, 'Johnny Clegg, Musician and Anthropologist', interview by Steven Roy Goodman, *Higher Education Today*, 8 April 2014, accessed 28 March 2025, https://www.youtube.com/watch?v=zh4ox9DPV4Q.
26   Mchunu, interview with the author; Fanon, *Wretched of the Earth*, 236–238.
27   Juluka, 'African Sky Blue', on *African Litany* (album, Johannesburg: MINC, MINC – (L) 1020, 1981).
28   The isiZulu '*umhube*' spelling (Clement Martyn Doke et al., eds, *English–Zulu, Zulu–English Dictionary*, 1st combined edition [Johannesburg: Witwatersrand University Press, 1990], 346) appears to be a transliteration of the isiXhosa bow spelling '*umrubhe*'. The two bows differ in that the Zulu bow is made from two parts – a resonator chamber of bamboo together with a curved branch inserted into the end of the bamboo resonator and a string (originally gut, but frequently a wire or viola string in later times) tensioned between the two, whereas the Xhosa bow is fashioned from a single piece of wood and the string. Both bows are played with a dowel or horsehair playing bow (as is the case with a violin), the player's mouth making the bow whistle with melodic overtones. See Clegg building and playing a bow for the author's album recording at Andy Innes, 'Mouthbow Clegg', YouTube video, 02:09, accessed 28 March 2025, https://www.youtube.com/watch?v=KtgCZGDISxg.
29   Translator's note: literally '*Ayihlabi ngakumisa*' in formal isiZulu.
30   Juluka, '*Inkunzi Ayihlabi Ngokumisa*', on *Universal Men* (album, Johannesburg: Gramophone Records Co./CBS Records, DNW 2429, 1979).
31   Juluka, '*Akanaki Nokunaka*', on *Musa Ukungilandela* (album, Johannesburg: Rhythm Safari/HR Music, MINC(E) 1100, 1984). 'G.G.' refers to the GG (government garage) numberplate suffix on police vehicles that patrolled the townships during the apartheid era.
32   Juluka, '*Woza Moya*', on *Work for All* (album, Johannesburg: MINC / HR Music, MINC – (L) 1070, 1983).
33   Juluka, *Stand Your Ground* (album, Burbank, CA: Warner Bros Records, 925 155-1, 1984).
34   David Swartz, *Culture and Power: The Sociology of Pierre Bourdieu* (Chicago: University of Chicago Press, 1997); see also Edward W. Said, *Orientalism* (New York: Vintage Books, 1979).
35   Geoffrey Himes, 'Juluka: Zulu for the Masses', *Washington Post*, 2 November 1984, accessed 28 March 2025, https://www.washingtonpost.com/archive/lifestyle/1984/11/02/juluka-zulu-for-the-masses/f5c7733b-1908-4234-8919-eb697ce614e8/.
36   Amos Mngoma, 'Juluka's Sipho on Comeback Trail', *Bona*, December 1988, accessed 28 March 2025, https://3rdearmusic.com/reissue/siphomchunu.
37   Clegg, *Scatterling*, 292.

38. Mchunu, interview with the author. Translator's note: this is not uncommon in large Zulu families, where one child will be appointed as cultural custodian while others will be educated and obtain employment.
39. Mchunu, interview with the author; Clegg, *Scatterling*, 174–177. The literal meaning of '*Ukwamukelwa Ekhaya*' is 'to be welcomed to the home/homestead' – a ritual confirming integration into the family and spiritual acceptance by the ancestors.
40. The author completed the same induction ceremony in the same room in the summer of 1999.
41. Nikita Coetzee, 'Johnny Clegg Honoured with Traditional Zulu Crossing Ceremony', *News24*, 26 February 2020, accessed 28 March 2025, https://www.news24.com/life/watch-johnny-clegg-honoured-with-traditional-zulu-crossing-ceremony-20200226. See more on the rituals and beliefs associated with these events in chapter 14 of this book by Marguerite de Villiers Coetzee.
42. Mchunu, interview with the author.
43. Bafazana Qoma, interview with the author, 23 November 2023.
44. Renier H. van der Merwe and Innocent Pikirayi, 'The Organisation and Layout of Zulu Military Homesteads (*Amakhanda*)', *Azania: Archaeological Research in Africa* 54, no. 1 (2019): 3–5, https://doi.org/10.1080/0067270X.2018.1540218.
45. Johnny Clegg, personal communication with the author.
46. Donald R. Morris, *The Washing of the Spears: A History of the Rise of the Zulu Nation under Shaka and its Fall in the Zulu War of 1879* (New York: Da Capo Press, 1998), 369.
47. Juluka, 'Impi', on *African Litany*.
48. In isiZulu '*amabutho*' is used interchangeably for 'warriors' and 'regiments', as is the singular form 'ibutho'.
49. Aroop Chatterjee, Léo Czajka and Amory Gethin, 'Wealth Inequality in South Africa, 1993–2017', *World Bank Economic Review* 36, no. 1 (2022): 19–36, https://doi.org/10.1093/wber/lhab012.
50. See for example Stuart Hall, *Essential Essays, Volume 2: Identity and Diaspora*, ed. David Morley (Duke University Press, 2018), 109, https://doi.org/10.2307/j.ctv11smnnj; Jonathan Jansen and Cyrill Walters, eds, *Fault Lines: A Primer on Race, Science and Society* (African Sun Media, 2020), https://doi.org/10.18820/9781928480495.
51. Statistics South Africa, *Census 2022 Statistical Release* (Pretoria: Statistics South Africa, 10 October 2023); Commission for Employment Equity, *23rd Commission for Employment Equity Annual Report 2022-2023* (Pretoria: Commission for Employment Equity, 2023).
52. Thabisile Phumo, 'DAC Webinar – The Role of Business Leaders in Meeting Basic Needs in Africa', YouTube video, 1:26:13 (Dunning Africa Centre, Henley Business School, Africa Campus, 20 September 2023), accessed 28 March 2025, https://youtu.be/3xdOssxnHPA.

REFERENCES

Alexander, Neville. 'The Impact of the Hegemony of English on Access to and Quality of Education with Special Reference to South Africa'. In *Language and Poverty*, edited by Wayne Harbert, Sally McConnell-Ginet, Amanda Miller and John Whitman, 53–66. Bristol: Multilingual Matters, 2008. https://doi.org/10.21832/9781847691200-006.

Berry, John W., Uichol Kim, S. Power, M. Young and M. Bujaki. 'Acculturation Attitudes in Plural Societies'. *Applied Psychology* 38, no. 2 (1989): 185–206. https://doi.org/10.1111/j.1464-0597.1989.tb01208.x.

Bourdieu, Pierre. *The Field of Cultural Production: Essays on Art and Literature*. Edited by Randal Johnson. New York: Columbia University Press, 1993.

Chatterjee, Aroop, Léo Czajka and Amory Gethin. 'Wealth Inequality in South Africa, 1993–2017'. *World Bank Economic Review* 36, no. 1 (2022): 19–36. https://doi.org/10.1093/wber/lhab012.

Clegg, Johnny. *Scatterling of Africa: My Early Years*. Johannesburg: Pan Macmillan, 2021.

Clegg, Johnny and Michael Drewett. 'Why Don't You Sing about the Leaves and the Dreams? Reflecting on Music Censorship in Apartheid South Africa'. In *Popular Music Censorship in Africa*, edited by Martin Cloonan and Michael Drewett, 127–136. London: Ashgate, 2006. Accessed 28 March 2025. https://www.academia.edu/39866997/Why_Don_t_You_Sing_about_the_Leaves_and_the_Dreams_Reflecting_on_Music_Censorship_in_Apartheid_South_Africa

Coetzee, Nikita. 'Johnny Clegg Honoured with Traditional Zulu Crossing Ceremony'. *News24*, 26 February 2020. Accessed 28 March 2025. https://www.news24.com/life/watch-johnny-clegg-honoured-with-traditional-zulu-crossing-ceremony-20200226.

Commission for Employment Equity. *23rd Commission for Employment Equity Annual Report 2022–2023*. Pretoria: Commission for Employment Equity, 2023.

Coplan, David. *In Township Tonight! South Africa's Black City Music and Theatre*. Cape Town: Jacana, 2007.

Doke, Clement Martyn, D.M. Malcolm, J.M.A. Sikakana and B.W. Vilakazi, eds. *English–Zulu, Zulu–English Dictionary*. 1st combined edition. Johannesburg: Witwatersrand University Press, 1990.

Fanon, Frantz. *The Wretched of the Earth*. Translated by Constance Farrington. New York: Grove Press, 2002.

Foucault, Michel and Colin Gordon. *Power/Knowledge: Selected Interviews and Other Writings, 1972–1977*. New York: Pantheon Books, 1980.

Gamede, Sanele Justice. 'Public Participation in the South African Broadcasting Corporation (SABC) Radio Stations: A Case Study of Ukhozi FM and Safm'. PhD thesis, University of KwaZulu-Natal, 2020.

Goodman, Steven Roy. 'Johnny Clegg, Musician and Anthropologist'. Interview by Steven Roy Goodman. *Higher Education Today*, 8 April 2014. YouTube video, 29:52. Accessed 28 March 2025. https://www.youtube.com/watch?v=zh4ox9DPV4Q.

Gramsci, Antonio. *Selections from the Prison Notebooks of Antonio Gramsci*. Edited by Quentin Hoare and Geoffrey Nowell Smith. London: Lawrence & Wishart, 2012.

Habermas, Jürgen. *Knowledge and Human Interests*. Edited by Jeremy J. Shapiro. Boston: Polity Press, 1994.

Hall, Stuart. *Essential Essays, Volume 2: Identity and Diaspora*. Edited by David Morley. Duke University Press, 2018. https://doi.org/10.2307/j.ctv11smnnj.

Himes, Geoffrey. 'Juluka: Zulu for the Masses'. *Washington Post*, 2 November 1984. Accessed 28 March 2025. https://www.washingtonpost.com/archive/lifestyle/1984/11/02/juluka-zulu-for-the-masses/f5c7733b-1908-4234-8919-eb697ce614e8/.

Innes, Andy. 'Mouthbow Clegg'. YouTube video, 02:09. Accessed 28 March 2025, https://www.youtube.com/watch?v=KtgCZGDISxg.

Jansen, Jonathan and Cyrill Walters, eds. *Fault Lines: A Primer on Race, Science and Society*. African Sun Media, 2020. https://doi.org/10.18820/9781928480495.

Mngoma, Amos. 'Juluka's Sipho On Comeback Trail'. *Bona*, December 1988. Accessed 28 March 2025. https://3rdearmusic.com/reissue/siphomchunu.

Morris, Donald R. *The Washing of the Spears: A History of the Rise of the Zulu Nation under Shaka and its Fall in the Zulu War of 1879*. New York: Da Capo Press, 1998.

Parliament of South Africa. *Group Areas Act (No. 41 of 1950)*. Cape Town: Parliament of South Africa, 1950.

Parliament of South Africa. *Prohibition of Mixed Marriages Act (No. 55 of 1949)*. Cape Town: Parliament of South Africa, 1949.

Phumo, Thabisile. 'DAC Webinar – The Role of Business Leaders in Meeting Basic Needs in Africa'. Presented at the Dunning Africa Centre, Henley Business School, Africa Campus, 20 September 2023. Accessed 28 March 2025, https://youtu.be/3xdOssxnHPA.

Ralston, David A. 'The Crossvergence Perspective: Reflections and Projections'. *Journal of International Business Studies* 39, no. 1 (January 2008): 27–40. https://doi.org/10.1057/palgrave.jibs.8400333.

Said, Edward W. *Orientalism*. New York: Vintage Books, 1979.

Sharon Memorial Park. 'The Mourner's Kaddish'. Sharon Memorial Park. Accessed 21 November 2023. https://sharonmemorial.com/customs-and-traditions/the-mourners-kaddish/.

Spini, Lucilla and Andrew Grant Innes. 'Johnny Clegg: A Polycultural Anthropologist on Stage for Social Justice'. *International Journal of Anthropology* 37, no. 1–2 (2022): 75–94. https://doi.org/10.14673/IJA2022121089.

Statistics South Africa. *Census 2022 Statistical Release*. Pretoria: Statistics South Africa, 10 October 2023.

Swartz, David. *Culture and Power: The Sociology of Pierre Bourdieu*. Chicago: University of Chicago Press, 1997.

Van der Merwe, Renier H. and Innocent Pikirayi. 'The Organisation and Layout of Zulu Military Homesteads (*Amakhanda*)'. *Azania: Archaeological Research in Africa* 54, no. 1 (2019): 75–93. https://doi.org/10.1080/0067270X.2018.1540218.

DISCOGRAPHY

Jonathan and Sipho. *Woza Friday*. Single. Johannesburg: EMI Brigadiers/Jamloti, JM139, 1997.

Juluka. *African Litany*. Album. Johannesburg: MINC, MINC – (L) 1020, 1981.

Juluka. *Musa Ukungilandela*. Album. Johannesburg: Rhythm Safari/HR Music, MINC(E) 1100, 1984.

Juluka. *Stand Your Ground*. Album. Burbank, CA: Warner Bros Records, 925 155-1, 1984.

Juluka. *Work for All*. Album. Johannesburg: MINC/HR Music, MINC – (L) 1070, 1983.

Juluka. *Universal Men*. Album. Johannesburg: Gramophone Records Co./CBS Records, DNW 2429, 1979.

CHAPTER 4

Johnny Clegg as Interlocutor of African Culture: A Thematic Analysis of a Selection of His Songs

Martina Viljoen

As an intellectual, poet, musician, dancer and politically committed artist, Johnny Clegg was a unique figure in the history of South African popular music. His innovative, ethnically integrated musical collaborations, informed by his training as an anthropologist, constituted a powerful statement against apartheid. Richard Pithouse posits that Clegg's lyrics, consistently grounded in a deeply humanistic aspiration for justice and profound empathy for the oppressed, echo the work of Chilean poet-diplomat Pablo Neruda.[1] Neruda's life-long commitment to a political cause could be cited as a point of comparison, as could his reflection on 'philosophical and whimsical questions about the present and future of humanity'.[2] However, it is Neruda's early work, described by Manuel Duran and Roberto Echevarría as 'vigorous, poignant and direct, yet subtle and very original in its imagery and metaphors' to which Clegg's lyrics most clearly convey resemblance, and which serves in this chapter as the inspiration for a thematic analysis of ideas central to the songs considered.[3]

During the apartheid era Clegg was arrested, harassed and spied upon by the Special Branch of the South African Police, and the state-controlled

South African Broadcasting Corporation censorship board banned some of his songs.[4] Yet most of the songs by Juluka (meaning 'Sweat' in isiZulu) and Savuka ('We Have Risen' in isiZulu) were allegorical, not overtly political. It may be argued that, ultimately, Clegg was an artist whose music convincingly symbolised representations of cultural fusion. Still, undeniably, his work speaks of a defiant and explicit identification with those who suffered most under South Africa's racist regime. After apartheid ended in 1994, Clegg remained a musical activist, advocating for various humanitarian causes, including HIV/Aids and tuberculosis awareness.

Clegg's academic training in anthropology formed part of the basis of his celebrated polycultural artistic identity and his unique crossover style. Kathryn Olsen's account of his research on maskanda, for instance, shows how his work aids recognition of the value of cultural differences in South Africa and of music's ability to challenge prejudiced assumptions about race, gender and other forms of social inequality.[5] More recently Lucilla Spini and Andrew Grant Innes have argued that Clegg utilised anthropology as a living tool for achieving social cohesion and an empathetic understanding of the human condition, notably that of the oppressed.[6] Thomas Pooley upholds the view that 'a bridging of distances real and imagined ... came to define Clegg's songcraft'.[7] The multilayered, multilingual lyrics of his music – performed in English, isiZulu, Afrikaans and French – suggest dialogue among different communities. This was achieved by a vibrant overlay of voices, visually enhanced by dazzling Zulu warrior dancing, which resulted in Clegg being given the nickname 'the White Zulu' ('*Le Zoulou Blanc*' – a name first used by Christophe Nick of the French magazine *Actuel* in the 1980s to describe Clegg to a European/French audience; see also chapter 8 by Lucilla Spini in this book).[8] As a teller of stories Clegg drew on a rich construction of indigenous narratives that highlighted racial divisions, yet also spoke of a democratically conceived future. Stylistically, his music fused Zulu music with Irish, Scottish and English folk traditions and popular genres such as rock, jazz, blues, reggae, funk and township jive. On the album *Third World Child* high-tech, electronic soundscapes were also featured; as a whole, 'a polyglot musical imagery that at its best possessed a raw vitality'.[9]

Against a background of cultural hybridity and political advocacy, this chapter aims to trace recurring themes in Clegg's music as represented in a selection of his songs that, either implicitly or explicitly, refer to repression and hardship under apartheid. These are 'Scatterlings of Africa' on the albums *Scatterlings* (1982) and *Third World Child* (1987), '*Asimbonanga*' ('We Have Not Seen Him', on *Third World Child*, 1987), 'Talk to the People' (on *Shadow Man*, 1988) and 'One (Hu)'Man One Vote' (on *Cruel Crazy Beautiful World*, 1989).[10] Celebrated both locally and internationally, these songs encompass explicit reference to racial segregation and discriminatory pass laws ('Scatterlings of Africa'), the imprisonment of Nelson Mandela and the elimination of other struggle martyrs ('*Asimbonanga*') and violent resistance ('Talk to the People' and 'One (Hu)'Man One Vote'). Yet, simultaneously, each song highlights a yearning for reconciliation and shared dialogue, inferring Clegg's spiritual and political vision for a new South Africa.

My analysis draws on a method of thematic analysis proposed by Albert Mills, Gabrielle Durepos and Elden Wiebe.[11] The method offers an approach to textual analysis that involves 'identifying themes or patterns of cultural meaning; coding and clarifying data ... according to themes; and interpreting the resulting thematic structures by seeking commonalities, relationships, ... patterns, theoretical constructs, or explanatory principles'.[12]

As an overarching interpretative strategy, I follow David McDonald who, drawing on Judith Butler's idea of performativity, emphasises the performativity of subversive artistic expression, thereby underlining its dynamic, culturally and politically contingent nature.[13] Such a point of departure is relevant to Clegg's musical output in that the social structures and processes by which this output was shaped were situated within discursive fields that were marked by directly conflicting ways of constructing subjectivity. In this sense, Clegg's work may be conjured as an individualist subjectivity, constantly (re-)interpreted through his unique artistic agency, which included his powerful bodily and non-verbal identification with Zulu culture, and his voice, including his use of isiZulu and English language. For this reason, apart from the lyrics cited in this chapter, my analysis also considers performances by Juluka and Savuka that are available on the internet.

THE IMPACT OF CLEGG'S MUSIC

Music is an important channel for political communication and agent of political socialisation, challenging the status quo either with explicit messages, such as protest songs, or in more restrained, covert ways – as is mostly the case in Clegg's recordings and performances, where the mere existence of a multiracial group during the apartheid era spoke of resistance. For this reason, governments often seek to censure and control those musicians whose work is perceived to contest the objectives of the state – as, again, was the case with Clegg and his fellow musicians.[14] John Street maintains that the very fact that regimes make the effort to censor popular culture is 'the best proof that it is nothing trivial'.[15] For Anne Schumann, popular songs masking covert content have the potential to be far more dangerous to authorities than outright protest songs.[16] Citing the example of the apartheid regime in South Africa, Eric Hobsbawm observes that the role of artists was imperative: 'In the absence of real politics and a free press, practitioners of the arts were the only ones who spoke for what their people … thought and felt'.[17] In this sense the importance of Clegg's contribution can hardly be overstated.

Clegg's music continues to speak through allegory. Yet, during the apartheid era its subversive nature could be understood as a destabilisation of the social status quo. Apart from politically covert, and in some cases overt, allusions in his lyrics, this was demonstrated by his cross-cultural artistic practices, including his fusing of tongues, the incorporation of Zulu musical and dance styles and Zulu traditional attire into his performances, or, later in his career, the wearing of bold African-inspired prints. These acts of opposition may be understood as reinscribing practices rooted within an individualist aesthetic of resistance.

As David Coplan states, Clegg was 'the most visible avatar of the phenomenon of "cross-over", a hybrid musical movement that crossed the deeply ingrained divisions of race, class and age during the 1980s'.[18] For Muff Anderson, of all the crossover bands in South Africa, Juluka 'most successfully transcended cultural barriers and black/white barriers to create a unique South African sound'.[19] In Pooley's view, Clegg and Juluka mixed the dynamics of race, language and ethnicity 'in ways that repudiated segregation. This syncretism was a transgression that angered authorities'.[20] For these reasons, Pooley describes Clegg as 'a being taut between worlds, a shadow man dancing into the light'.[21]

A THEMATIC READING OF A SELECTION OF CLEGG'S SONGS

'Scatterlings of Africa'

'Scatterlings of Africa', performed by Juluka, was first released on the 1982 album *Scatterlings*.[22] The song, later reinterpreted by Juluka's successor band Savuka on the album *Third World Child* (1987) which had its main launch in France, became hugely popular.[23] The music comprises an energetic fusion of late 1960s English folk, African rhythms and 1980s commercialised synth-pop, with allusions to maskanda and mbaqanga to which Clegg and Sipho Mchunu, on the official music video issued together with the 1987 re-release of the song, deliver vigorous *ngoma* dance moves.[24] Despite the upbeat nature of the soundtrack, Timothy Taylor finds that it contains musical elements underscoring the sombre theme of the lyrics. He notes the use of a 4/4 meter subsiding into a 7/4 meter, which, for him, subverts the idea of a regular downbeat, while, similarly, alterations between major and minor tonalities undermine 'fixed views of identity and social position'.[25] Such subtle signification may, for many listeners, go unnoticed – including for members of regulatory boards. From this it may be concluded that the spirited dynamics of the soundtrack, apart from providing a fitting soundscape for displaying Clegg's and Mchunu's robust dance moves, served to mask the critical impetus of the lyrics.

Yet, through more easily perceptible musical elements, 'Scatterlings of Africa' speaks of resistance. Louise Meintjes observes that the song is influenced by *ngoma* dance and its associated music, as seen, for example, in the repeated cycle of isiZulu vocables present in the introduction.[26] Therefore, though 'Scatterlings of Africa' is sung mainly in English, within the song's multilayered soundscape a transgressive mixing of cultural symbolism is evident.

Alan Cowell maintains that Clegg's poetic verse in 'Scatterlings of Africa' relates 'the myriad dislocations of South African society'.[27] Though some phrases celebrate the glorious African landscape ('Copper sun sinking low'; 'a journey to the stars') these phrases may conceal ambiguous meanings. The idea of a sunset may point to an implied darkness and danger. This is underlined by the allusion to fugitives seeking refuge in the night, which infers the inhumanity of racial segregation and discriminatory pass laws. Moreover, though Clegg's 'journey to the stars' invokes images of a stellar African sky, the very next phrase implies the loss of personal and collective dreams: 'Far below we leave forever / Dreams of what we were'.

The chorus illustrates that the 'Scatterlings of Africa' are, indeed, uprooted, as they make their way to Phelamanga – a made-up word inferring a mythical destination: 'a place where truth begins'.[28] In referring to 'Ancient bones from Olduvai / Echoes of the very first cry', the lyrics further obscure direct mention of apartheid South Africa. Rather, the allusion to the Olduvai Gorge in Tanzania, one of the most important paleoanthropological localities in the world, seems to suggest that not only African peoples are scatterlings, searching for truth on their 'journey to the stars', but that this endeavour may also be true for humanity as a whole – a further concealment of critical content.[29] Similarly, Spini suggests a broader, humanitarian understanding of the term 'scatterlings', which she describes as 'a very broad and dynamic category which defines all human beings by incorporating space, time, mobility and diversity as well as common origin'.[30]

In terms of allegory, the most poignant aspect of 'Scatterlings of Africa' is, perhaps, the underlying idea of a spiritual and political journey, and the search for truth and authenticity for which the fugitives have 'a burning hunger' in their hearts. Clegg's identification with the uprooted and the disowned is strongly emphasised ('I love the scatterlings of Africa / Each and every one' and 'we are the scatterlings of Africa / Both you and I').[31] Likewise, Juluka's intense, bodily engagement in the video rendition of the song represents no incidental act of cultural resourcefulness or virtuosity, but rather a physical demonstration of values unique to these musicians which, at the time, held considerable personal risk. Figuratively, this physical demonstration of identification could be understood as performativity of 'the journey' and of belonging.

'Asimbonanga'

Although Clegg and his fellow musicians acted against apartheid, they never used the word 'apartheid' in their lyrics.[32] Yet, a few of his songs were written in direct response to political events. One such example is 'Asimbonanga', recorded by Savuka on the album *Third World Child* (1987). The song, also called '*Asimbonanga* (Mandela)', was first released as a 12-inch single in 1986, and then included on the 1987 album.[33] In a radio interview with Renee Montagne, Clegg explained that the song, the title of which could be translated as 'We Have Not Seen Him', came to him one morning when he awoke to the sound of gunshots.[34] While contemplating who could 'cross the dirty waters of South African politics', the name that occurred to him was Mandela, who at that stage had been imprisoned on Robben Island since 1962.[35] Thus, the lyrics of '*Asimbonanga*' alluded to Mandela's absence from society, also mentioning the anti-apartheid activists Steve Biko, Victoria Mxenge and Neil Aggett by name. Biko and Aggett died in police detention; Mxenge was gunned down in 1985 in front of her children outside her home in Umlazi by four men who were thought to be part of a government 'death squad'.[36] As Judith February writes, speaking the names of these slain activists in a song 'at a time when even breathing [them] meant transgression ... became for many a small act of defiance'.[37] It could thus have been predicted that, on its release, '*Asimbonanga*' would be banned from radio broadcast in South Africa.

In contrast to 'Scatterlings of Africa', '*Asimbonanga*', described by Coplan as a haunting tribute to Mandela, is a lamentation, mixing English verses with isiZulu choruses sung in the close-harmony vocal style of *isicathamiya*.[38] The restrained instrumental backing, consisting mainly of electric guitars and percussion, lends the song the effect of a slow township jive.[39] Video recordings of performances of the song show it being delivered with great simplicity and sincerity, so that all emphasis shifts to its anthem-like character and all-important words.

As in 'Scatterlings of Africa', the lyrics of '*Asimbonanga*' are suggestive of a journey and a futuristic vision – this time, the 'long road to freedom' suggested in the song's closing phrase ('when will we arrive at our destination').[40] Though Mandela has been removed from society, as if by prophetic foresight Clegg imagines him as the leader who will 'close the distance between you and me'. Yet despondency prevails. Apart from citing the names of prominent slain anti-apartheid activists, referring also to 'the [unknown] place where [our brother] died', the lyrics suggest the isolation and hardship of Mandela's imprisonment ('Oh the sea is cold and the sky is grey / Look across the island into the bay'). While freedom is momentarily suggested ('A seagull wings across the sea'), this image simultaneously speaks of solitude and 'silence', which in this song becomes a metaphor for political estrangement and for the voices of those who had been violently quieted forever.

The symbolic act of identification with Mandela and other martyrs of apartheid is 'performed' by way of multilayering (Clegg's solo line as set against the close-harmony vocal accompaniment, underlined by minimalist instrumental backing) and the sombre tone of the song. Yet it is notable that the lyrics, while acknowledging isolation, hardship and even death, also speak of a deep longing for reconciliation and the possibility of shared dialogue. Still, while by no means a traditional protest song, '*Asimbonanga*' carries an explicit political message, and later 'became something of an anthem for the [Mass Democratic Movement]'s umbrella organisation, the United Democratic Front'.[41]

'Apartheid isn't just something outside,' Clegg said of the song, 'it's something that divides you from a greater whole. For me, Mandela was a link pin toward wholeness. He held the key to bringing together different groups, to bringing unity. Not a cynical political unity, but a psychic, spiritual, intellectual, cultural unity. Because apartheid fragments all those levels'.[42]

'Talk to the People'

As part of the album *Shadow Man*, released by Savuka in 1988, 'Talk to the People' is another of Clegg's songs that contains a political, anti-apartheid message. The lyrics are mainly in English, while the chorus with its backing vocals is sung in isiZulu. As in many of Clegg's songs, the music is influenced by 1980s pop music, mixed with elements of township jive, maskanda and a percussive guitar sound.

For Pooley, the image of the 'shadow man' is illustrative of Clegg's 'liminal self'; of a being strained between different worlds.[43] Indeed, in 'Talk to the People', Clegg figures as the interlocutor who observes suffering and injustice – but, simultaneously, follows the dream of a united South Africa. This is evident in the 'prayer' with which the song ends: 'God hear the children / God save the country / God hear the people / God bless the dreams they dream at night'. While in the first verse 'snapshots' of everyday apartheid scenes seem innocent enough, the question posed by the chorus ('Answer, Mister / This way, how will we arrive?') confronts the listener with South Africa's political complexity. Though the idea of a journey is foregrounded ('how will we arrive … Walk through the country') and the image of a dream of freedom and healing ('Do you know the dreams they dream at night … Only you, only you can free me / Only you can breathe life into the land / Touch me with your healing hand'), the lyrics of the second verse take on a more sinister meaning. Here, Clegg refers to violent black resistance ('A shipment of A.K.s on the underground'); to black-on-black violence, which was, supposedly, provoked by white authorities ('A throw of dice on a Soweto train / A waiting knife if you should win the game'); and to the gross human rights violations of the so-called Special Branch of the South African security forces ('A human rights lawyer with a torture claim / A union activist never ever seen again'). However, Clegg still foregrounds the idea of shared dialogue as part of the dream and a solution to the country's woes ('*Phendula wemadoda*' ['Give the answer / Talk to me']).

'One (Hu)'Man One Vote'

'One (Hu)'Man One Vote', released by Savuka on the album *Cruel Crazy Beautiful World* (1989), is, within the context of Clegg's creative output, perhaps his most direct, most ardent chronicle of the violence and treachery of apartheid. The song was written in honour of David Webster, an anti-apartheid activist and a mentor and friend of Clegg, lecturing in anthropology at the University of the Witwatersrand in Johannesburg at the time of his death. Webster was assassinated by apartheid security forces on

1 May 1989.⁴⁴ This came as an immense shock to Clegg: 'I felt like I'd been axed, like a cleaver had come into my brain':

> I was seized once again by this ... paralysis, an impotence, a real fright. In a death like this, you realize the contingency of history, the reality of existing in chaos. We have a superficial web of order we place over things. This smashed my web.
>
> I had a sense of hopelessness. I felt paralyzed. Desperate. There were these two opposing factions — the securocrats and the young black militants — neither of whom gave any quarter. There's always been a hidden, invisible middle ground in South Africa of connections between people and cultures. That was being incinerated. Music was the most effective way I could work out my feelings. It was a way of trying to understand what I was experiencing.⁴⁵

Clegg's response in the lyrics of 'One (Hu)'Man One Vote' refers to violent uprising:

> *Bayeza abafana bancane wema*
> *Bayeza abafana bancane wema*
> *Baphethe iqwasha, baphethe ibazooka*
> *Bathi 'Sangena savuma thina,*
> *Lapha abazange bengena abazali bethu*
> *Nabadala, bayasikhalela thina ngoba asina voti'*

> (The young boys are coming
> the young boys are coming
> They carry homemade weapons and a bazooka
> They say 'We have agreed to enter a place
> that has never been entered before
> by our parents or our ancestors
> and they cry for us, for we do not have the right to vote')

Thus, in this song Clegg's lyrics are suggestive of 'war', referring to the abuse of human rights and exclusion on ethnic grounds under the apartheid regime. In mentioning a universal history of political uprising in the West ('Ten thousand years of marching through a veil of tears'), again, allegorically, the lyrics allude to the idea of a journey – this time towards an ideal, just world (South Africa); a world, however, seized not by way of passive resistance, but by active confrontation.[46] The final verse is evocative of a spiritual call – perhaps to the ancestors – and, again, the dream of a new future is encountered ('On a visible but distant shore – a new image of man').

The musical setting of 'One (Hu)'Man One Vote' represents some of Clegg's most brilliant work. While the introduction contains elements of African call and response, African drumming and vocal interjections, from the outset the song is characterised by an aggressive pop-rock rhythm and Clegg's high-pitched style of singing; jazz-style trumpeting adds texture and 'swing' to the song. Savuka's usual instrumental setting is expanded to incorporate extra backing instruments, including the already mentioned trumpets, saxophones, electronic percussion, electronic keyboards and extra backing vocals. What results is a vigorous, multilayered musical soundscape against which the grim lyrics are set. The words 'fast forward', spoken in the introduction, suggest the possible fulfilment of Clegg's implied 'journey' and 'dream'.[47]

CLEGG'S RESISTANCE IN ACTION

Thematically within the selected songs, concepts of displacement and repression in the lyrics of 'Scatterlings of Africa' represent a covert anti-apartheid expression, whereas '*Asimbonanga*' reveals more overt sentiments of resistance, especially in Clegg's naming of prominent struggle icons. 'Talk to the People' refers to violence and the transgressions of the Special Branch of the South African Police, while 'One (Hu)'Man, One Vote' contains explicit references to violent uprising. Juluka's and Savuka's very existence was perceived as a threat by the apartheid government, resulting in some of Clegg's music being banned from the airwaves. The songs discussed here thus integrated musical and cultural collaboration in a way that represents resistance to apartheid.

The theme of allegory encompasses Clegg's unique, figurative approach to storytelling. In 'Scatterlings of Africa' the idea of dislocation is central to the narrative. Though the lyrics contain no explicit reference to apartheid, the idea that all people on earth come from Africa opposes the idea of racism espoused by apartheid ideologues. Simultaneously, a subtle application of musical materials suggests a subversive meaning in the song. While ambiguous political meaning is concealed by Juluka's intense, bodily engagement in the video rendition of the song, this physical demonstration of identification was understood as a confirmation of identification and belonging.

'*Asimbonanga*' speaks of 'silence' – a metaphor for political estrangement, for the voices of those who had been silenced by way of violent political intervention and the lack of conciliatory dialogue. Yet in this song, Clegg's sincere yearning for reconciliation and shared dialogue is strongly highlighted – as is also the case in 'Talk to the People' and the more provocative 'One (Hu)'Man, One Vote'. As a prominent recurring theme, it unites and underwrites the themes of 'the journey' and 'the dream', inferring Clegg's spiritual and political vision for a new South Africa.

Clegg's strong desire to identify with those impacted most negatively by apartheid affirms the intertwinement of the personal and the political, seen in each of the songs as an expression of political resistance and a testimony to his humanist advocacy. Like Neruda, his poetic vision was never static, and adapted according to the realities he encountered. Yet, as observed in this chapter, political resistance, integrated artistic collaboration and cultural fusion, allegory, the journey and the dream are themes consistently appearing in the songs discussed.

Of Neruda, Federico García Lorca said that he was 'closer to blood than to ink'.[48] In a symbolic sense this may be true also of Clegg. For, like Neruda, his work was constantly shaped by a deep commitment to a futuristic dream and a profound, all-encompassing love for the land and its people.

CLEGG'S WORK AS PERFORMATIVE SUBVERSION

Earlier in this chapter I argued, following McDonald, that Clegg's work may be construed as performative, subversive artistic expression, thereby underlining its dynamic, culturally and politically contingent nature.[49] From this perspective, Clegg's music reflects his individualist subjectivity, as he constantly interpreted political events by way of his unique artistic agency.

My readings of emblematic songs presented in this chapter highlight my position that Clegg's most 'performative' act of insubordination was his 'doing' of identification; an undertaking illuminated most clearly in ritualised, aestheticised moments of public performance. In McDonald's interpretation of Judith Butler's thought, such moments, however ephemeral and located within a specific time and space, may be understood as a powerful 'performativity of belonging'.[50] This means that belonging is based in specific processes and performances of identification – as are realised in Clegg's music.

However, from the perspective of Butler's thought, the idea of performativity also holds deeper 'political' consequences. For her, the idea that performative speech acts accomplish something beyond mere semantic and syntactical meaning is a crucial aspect of her thought, and one that is relevant to my interpretation as offered in this chapter. She employs the idea of performativity to understand the myriad ways in which identities (or gendered bodies, according to her focus) are produced and performed amidst fields of social and political consequence.[51] Within contexts of domination and disempowerment, this means that performative acts may have consequences beyond the creation of linguistic meaning, in the sense that they can mediate and 'perform' fundamental aspects of what it means to resist. Simply put, the implication is that, for Butler, an act is performative if it produces material effects.

Clegg's attraction to and performance of powerful Zulu masculinity constitutes a specific gendered performative act. In an interview with Anastacia Tsioulcas he explained that Zulu men taught him 'what it meant to be a man': 'The body was coded and wired – hard-wired – to carry messages about masculinity which were pretty powerful for an adolescent boy'.[52] He observed furthermore that 'they knew something about being a man, which they could communicate physically in the way that they danced and carried themselves. And I wanted to be able to do the same thing. Basically, I wanted to become a Zulu warrior. And in a very deep sense, it offered me an African identity. It was like a homecoming for me'.[53]

Such a perception of an African identity goes against the subservient role that apartheid authorities ascribed to black men. From such a perspective,

Clegg's performance of Zulu identity, as a reinscribing practice embedded within systems of meaning, values and aesthetics, took on a material meaning. As a performative act of resistance, it reached beyond symbolic forms of liberation to 'demonstrate' opposition to the complex workings of dominant forms of political power. This implies that Clegg's strategic utilisation of the constitutive modalities of music, poetic verse and dance could, indeed, be seen as 'performative resistance' in the sense that it was of consequence in the 'real' world. Regarding '*Asimbonanga*', for instance, February testifies to the way this song informed Clegg's fans about the state of South African politics at the time:

> 'Who has the words to close the distance between you and me?' the song went on to ask. Then many of us knew as we sang along to this haunting melody that our country was in deep trouble, the 'mutually hurting stalemate' tearing us apart and the nightly news spewing forth propaganda about 'terrorists' and 'communists'. Clegg was reminding us all that we could not say 'we did not know'.[54]

In agreement with this view, McDonald argues that popular culture may 'speak for the masses' so that expressive media become 'constitutive fields where the political and ideational [are] not only expressed but given materiality'.[55] Within such performative realms, he maintains, artists may declare what they dare not say and do publicly on the streets or in the media.[56] In relation to Clegg and his fellow musicians, it may be said that his songs opened social spaces for dialogue where images, ideas and dreams could be reconfigured into imaginings of a new South African reality. Similarly, his 'enactment' of solidarity confronted positions of displacement and disownment, so that, as Pooley remarks, he bridged the distances that separated South Africa's diverse communities in powerful ways.[57] Importantly, Clegg's identification was, to a considerable degree, bodily and non-verbal, including his use of isiZulu and English language, and of his voice, through which he demonstrated that resistance can be expressive of specific subjectivities and cultural practices that can disrupt and dislodge the oppressive securities of hegemonic rule.

It can thus be concluded that Clegg's anthropology did not end at observation or theorisation, but resulted in a hybridised art that actively challenged apartheid's cultural and racial essentialism.[58] For him, this did not only amount to a way of 'coding reality' to 'make sense of the views, systems and practices that place boundaries around identities and practices'.[59] Rather, it was his lifelong resolve to 'facilitate a communication, understanding and celebration of everyone's endeavor … We take out of this a deep understanding of what it is to be human'.[60]

Thus, as Chris Webb concludes, Clegg's personal and musical journey was a pursuit of 'a humanist universal culture, refusing the narrow boundaries of racial and cultural essentialism … It was an attempt at using anthropology as performative practice, to not only decode and interpret but to communicate common hopes and struggles'.[61]

Citing the lyrics of '*Asimbonanga*', February potently underlines what was perhaps Clegg's most powerful, most 'performative' contribution as an artist: 'But in these words, there was also the freedom Clegg seemed to display – a glimpse of a new way of being, of seeing our country and speaking truth to power. This was a South Africa where we could cross the distances because if he could, we all could, surely? Simplistic-sounding perhaps but real because Clegg himself lived his truth'.[62]

THE TIMELESSNESS OF CLEGG'S MUSIC

It should be conceded that Clegg 'was of a particular time'.[63] Yet his songs transcended the period of fraught South African history of which he was a part. Even decades after its initial release and subsequent reinterpretation, 'Scatterlings of Africa' is treasured as an anthem by African people globally – and, indeed, by 'scatterlings' of all nations. Moreover, the word 'scatterlings' has taken on special symbolic meaning as it features in different academic and literary contexts that trace the history and heritage of the African continent, such as Rešoketšwe Manenzhe's *Scatterlings*, or Eve Hemmings' *Scatterlings – A Tapestry of Afri-Expat Tales*.[64] Likewise, '*Asimbonanga*' has become a symbol and identification marker of Clegg, especially in Europe, as is evident from the reuse of the word in Italy by the young Italian singer Leo Gassman.[65]

Clegg's idea of 'one (hu)'man, one vote' remains relevant today. As he stated in an interview with Jenni Baxter, he believed that all South Africans should have the same human rights, 'the same idea about how to deal with each other on a social, political and cultural level. But that can only come about if we all share the same vision of what mankind is and what mankind means'.[66] Even before the dawn of democracy in South Africa, he espoused the idea of coalition politics: 'I believe the notion of one "man", one vote will take place in a decentralized political structure. Here, unlike in Zimbabwe, we have enough groups to make multi-party democracy and one man, one vote a viable political alternative'.[67]

In a world scarred by wars of territorial control, Clegg's statement as quoted by Baxter takes on special relevance: 'We need a new image – a global human being belonging to a single planetary civilization'.[68] The sentiment underlying this 'declaration' makes clear that Clegg's acts of performative resistance and his sheer humanity, in Pooley's words, 'transcended not only the dichotomies of race and ethnicity that have for so long shaped the South African condition', but also showed his striving toward the betterment of humanity on planet Earth.[69]

ACKNOWLEDGEMENTS

I would like to acknowledge Lucilla Spini and Michael Drewett's input into this chapter.

NOTES

1. Richard Pithouse, 'Johnny Clegg: Rebel, Intellectual, Musician', *Mail & Guardian*, 18 July 2019, accessed 30 March 2025, https://mg.co.za/article/2019-07-18-johnny-clegg-rebel-intellectual-musician/.
2. Manuel E. Duran and Roberto González Echevarría, 'Pablo Neruda: Chilean Poet', *Encyclopedia Britannica*, accessed 30 March 2025, https://www.britannica.com/biography/Pablo-Neruda.
3. Duran and Echevarría, 'Pablo Neruda'. See Pithouse's reference in Chapter 5 of this book to a line from Neruda's poem 'The Watersong Ends' echoed in Clegg's 'Universal Men' on his solo album *New World Survivor* (Pretoria: Value Music, CDVM (WFL) 45, 2002).
4. Johnny Clegg and Michael Drewett, 'Why Don't You Sing about the Leaves and the Dreams? Reflecting on Music Censorship in Apartheid South Africa', in *Popular*

Music Censorship in Africa, eds Martin Cloonan and Michael Drewett (London: Routledge, 2016), 130ff. See also chapter 7 in this book by Michael Drewett.
5   Kathryn Olsen, *Music and Social Change in South Africa: Maskanda Past and Present* (Philadelphia: Temple University Press, 2014), 22ff.
6   Lucilla Spini and Andrew Grant Innes, 'Johnny Clegg: A Polycultural Anthropologist on Stage for Social Justice', *International Journal of Anthropology* 37, no. 1–2 (2022): 75–94.
7   Thomas M. Pooley, 'Sikeyi: In Memoriam – Johnny Clegg (1953–2019)', *Muziki: Journal of Music Research in Africa* 17, no. 1 (2021): 132.
8   Bev Mortimer, 'Johnny Clegg Talks about the Years of "Le Zoulou Blanc"', *St Francis Chronicle*, 11 November 2012, accessed 30 March 2025, https://stfrancischronicle.com/2012/11/11/johnny-clegg-talks-about-the-years-of-le-zoulou-blanc/.
9   Pooley, 'Sikeyi', 132; Johnny Clegg & Savuka, *Third World Child* (album, Sandton: EMI, EMCJ (D), 2407331, 1987).
10 Juluka, 'Scatterlings of Africa', on *Scatterlings* (album, Johannesburg: MINC, MINC – (L) 1040, 1982); Johnny Clegg & Savuka, 'Scatterlings of Africa', on *Third World Child*; Johnny Clegg & Savuka, 'Asimbonanga', on *Third World Child*; Johnny Clegg & Savuka, 'Talk to the People', on *Shadow Man* (album, Sandton: EMI, EMCJ (D) – 7904111, 1988); Johnny Clegg & Savuka, 'One (Hu)'Man One Vote', on *Cruel Crazy Beautiful World* (album, Sandton: EMI, EMCJ (E) – 7934461, 1989).
11 Albert J. Mills, Gabrielle Durepos and Elden Wiebe, *Encyclopedia of Case Study Research*, vols I and II (Thousand Oaks: Sage, 2010).
12 Mills et al., *Case Study Research*, 926.
13 David McDonald, *My Voice Is My Weapon: Music, Nationalism and the Poetics of Palestinian Resistance* (Durham, NC: Duke University Press, 2013).
14 Clegg and Drewett, 'Why Don't You Sing', 130ff.
15 John Street, 'The Politics of Popular Culture', in *The Blackwell Companion to Political Sociology*, eds Kate Nash and Alan Scott (Oxford: Blackwell Publishing, 2001), 303.
16 Anne Schumann, 'The Beat that Beat Apartheid: The Role of Music in the Resistance Against Apartheid in South Africa'. *Stichproben: Vienna Journal of African Studies* 8, no. 14 (2008): 19.
17 Eric Hobsbawm, *Age of Extremes: The Short Twentieth Century 1914–1991* (London: Abacus, 1995), 506.
18 David Coplan, 'Black Popular Music in South Africa', in *The Concise Garland Encyclopedia of World Music*, vol. 1 (London: Routledge, 2013), 122.
19 Muff Anderson, *Music in the Mix: The Story of South African Popular Music* (Johannesburg: Ravan Press, 2001), 160.
20 Pooley, 'Sikeyi', 133.
21 Pooley, 'Sikeyi', 131.
22 All lyrics quoted in this chapter derive from the website johnnyclegg.com, where they may be accessed in full.
23 Anastasia Tsioulcas, 'Johnny Clegg, A Uniting Voice Against Apartheid, Dies At 66', *National Public Radio*, 16 July 2019, accessed 30 March 2025, https://www.npr.org/2019/07/16/738065415/johnny-clegg-a-uniting-voice-against-apartheid-dies.
24 Johnny Clegg & Savuka, 'Johnny Clegg and Savuka – Scatterlings of Africa (1987)', YouTube video, 03:48, accessed 27 April 2025, https://www.youtube.com/watch?v=qnYtcH4YS44.
25 Timothy Taylor, *Global Pop: World Music, World Markets* (London: Routledge, 2014), 218ff.

26 Louise Meintjes, *Dust of the Zulu: Ngoma Aesthetics After Apartheid* (Durham, NC: Duke University Press, 2017), 160ff.
27 Alan Cowell, 'Johnny Clegg, South African Singer Who Battled Apartheid With Music, Is Dead At 66', *The New York Times*, 16 July 2019, accessed 30 March 2025, https://www.nytimes.com/2019/07/16/arts/music/johnny-clegg-dead.html#.
28 See Phelamanga, 'Building Lasting Relationships', accessed 7 May 2025, https://phelamanga.co.za/2023/09/12/whats-in-a-name/.
29 Ignatio de la Torre and Rafael Mora, 'The Transition to the Acheulean in East Africa: An Assessment of Paradigms and Evidence from Olduvai Gorge (Tanzania)', *Journal of Archaeological Method and Theory* 21 (2014): 781–823.
30 Lucilla Spini, *Of Scatterlings and Stakeholders: Diversity, Inclusion and Transnational Governance for Sustainable Development* (Florence: Pontecorboli Editore, 2020), 9–10.
31 This identification is also evident in the title of Clegg's posthumously published book, *Scatterling of Africa: My Early Years* (Johannesburg: Pan MacMillan, 2021).
32 Judith February, 'Johnny Clegg Wasn't "Begging to be Black". He Simply Was', *Daily Maverick*, 17 July 2019, accessed 30 March 2025, https://www.dailymaverick.co.za/opinionista/2019-07-17-johnny-clegg-wasnt-begging-to-be-black-he-simply-was/.
33 Johnny Clegg & Savuka, *Asimbonanga* (single, Johannesburg: MINC, 12XMC(P) 4054016, 1986).
34 Renee Montagne, 'Songwriter Clegg on Mandela, South Africans' "Bridge"', *National Public Radio*, 6 December 2013, accessed 30 March 2025, https://www.npr.org/2013/12/06/249236653/songwriter-clegg-on-mandela-south-africans-bridge.
35 Montagne, 'Songwriter Clegg'. Famously, a 1999 video clip of *'Asimbonanga'* being performed at a concert in Frankfurt shows Mandela joining the musicians on stage and performing his customary jive to the music (February, 'Johnny Clegg'). See Johnny Clegg & Savuka, 'Johnny Clegg (With Nelson Mandela) - Asimbonanga - 1999 Fran', YouTube video, 06:12, accessed 28 April 2025, https://www.youtube.com/watch?v=BGS7SpI7obY.
36 Pooley, 'Sikeyi', 134. Mxenge's husband, Griffiths Mxenge, had already been killed by security police agents in Umlazi in 1981. See South African History Online, 'Griffiths Mlungisi Mxenge', 25 April 2012, accessed 30 March 2025, https://www.sahistory.org.za/people/griffiths-mlungisi-mxenge.
37 February, 'Johnny Clegg'. Peter Gabriel's song 'Biko', originally from Gabriel's eponymous third album, was also inspired by Steve Biko's death in police custody in 1977. The song was re-released in November 1987 to coincide with the release of the anti-apartheid film *Cry Freedom*, directed by Richard Attenborough (USA: Universal Pictures, 1987). See Petergabriel.com, 'Biko: Re-release', accessed 30 March 2025, https://petergabriel.com/release/biko-1987/.
38 David Coplan, 'God Rock Africa: Thoughts on Politics in Popular Black Performance in South Africa', *African Studies* 64, no. 1 (2005): 13.
39 Coplan, 'Black Popular Music', 122.
40 As the title of Nelson Mandela's autobiography, *Long Walk to Freedom* (London: Abacus, 1994), this expression has become iconic as a description of the struggle against apartheid.
41 Jakobus M. Vorster, 'The Possible Contribution of Civil Society in the Moral Edification of South African Society: The Example of the "United Democratic Front" and the "Treatment Action Campaign" (1983–2014)'. *HTS Theological Studies* 71, no. 3 (2015): 1–8, accessed 30 March 2025, http://www.scielo.org.za/pdf/hts/v71n3/03.pdf; Coplan, 'God Rock Africa', 13.

The Mass Democratic Movement was a section of the liberation movement during the late apartheid period of the 1980s. The United Democratic Front (UDF) was a popular front that had as its goal a 'non-racial, united South Africa'.

For an exposition on the origins of *Asimbonanga* as a Zulu maskanda song and its more recent rendition by the Soweto Gospel Choir, as well as use of its chorus by the Afrikaans singers Snotkop and Karen Zoid, see chapter 12 in this book by Nicol Hammond.

42 Clegg quoted in Samuel G. Freedman, 'Johnny Clegg's War on Apartheid', *Rolling Stone*, 19 July 2019, accessed 30 March 2025, https://www.rollingstone.com/music/music-features/johnny-clegg-south-africa-apartheid-samuel-freedman-860888/
43 Pooley, 'Sikeyi', 131.
44 Freedman, 'Johnny Clegg's War'. Webster had encouraged Clegg to specialise in anthropology; later Clegg became a junior lecturer in the field. As an activist Webster had been a founding member of the UDF.
45 Freedman, 'Johnny Clegg's War'.
46 In the original music video released together with the song, in addition to images of protest against apartheid, images of the Berlin Wall and student protests in China, among others, are shown, lending the song a global perspective. See Johnny Clegg & Savuka, 'One Man One Vote', YouTube video, 04:18, accessed 28 April 2025, https://www.youtube.com/watch?v=DPP3wo1F3r4.
47 It is ironic that the idea of 'one man, one vote' seems to perpetuate the gender stereotype of male dominance. However, the bracketed '(Hu)'man' of the song's title signifies gender-inclusive language.
48 Lorca quoted in René de Costa, *The Poetry of Pablo Neruda* (Cambridge, MA: Harvard University Press, 2009), 74.
49 McDonald, *My Voice Is My Weapon*.
50 McDonald, *My Voice Is My Weapon*, 23.
51 Judith Butler, *Bodies That Matter: On the Discursive Limits of 'Sex'* (London: Routledge, 1993): 2ff.
52 Tsioulcas, 'Johnny Clegg'.
53 Tsioulcas, 'Johnny Clegg'.
54 February, 'Johnny Clegg'.
55 McDonald, *My Voice Is My Weapon*, 31.
56 McDonald, *My Voice Is My Weapon*, 32.
57 Pooley, 'Sikeyi'.
58 Chris Webb, 'Apartheid, Anthropology and Johnny Clegg', *Africa Is a Country*, 19 July 2019, accessed 30 March 2025, https://africasacountry.com/2019/07/apartheid-anthropology-and-johnny-clegg.
59 Marguerite de Villiers, 'Johnny Clegg: A Shadow Man', *Anthropology Southern Africa* 39, no. 1 (2016): 60.
60 De Villiers, 'Johnny Clegg', 60.
61 Webb, 'Apartheid, Anthropology and Johnny Clegg'.
62 February, 'Johnny Clegg'.
63 February, 'Johnny Clegg'.
64 Rešoketšwe Manenzhe, *Scatterlings* (Johannesburg: Jacana Media, 2020); Eve Hemmings, *Scatterlings: A Tapestry of Afri-Expat Tales* (Bloomington: Xlibris Corporation, 2013).
65 Sky.it, 'Cosa significa Asimbonanga, la traduzione della citazione nella canzone di Leo Gassmann', accessed 30 March 2025, https://tg24.sky.it/spettacolo/musica/2020/02/07/asimbonanga-traduzione. See also chapter 12 in this book by Nicol Hammond.

66 Clegg quoted in Jenni F. Baxter, 'Johnny Clegg: Earth Man', *TALK*, May 1990, accessed 28 April 2025, https://www.thecelebrityinterviews.com/johnny-clegg-interview/.
67 Baxter, 'Johnny Clegg'.
68 Baxter, 'Johnny Clegg'.
69 Pooley, 'Sikeyi', 131.

REFERENCES

Anderson, Muff. *Music in the Mix: The Story of South African Popular Music*. Johannesburg: Ravan Press, 2001.

Attenborough, Richard, dir. *Cry Freedom*. Film. USA: Universal Pictures, 1987.

Baxter, Jenni F. 'Johnny Clegg: Earth Man'. *TALK*, May 1990. Accessed 28 April 2025. https://www.thecelebrityinterviews.com/johnny-clegg-interview/.

Butler, Judith. *Bodies That Matter: On the Discursive Limits of 'Sex'*. London: Routledge, 1993.

Clegg, Johnny. *Scatterling of Africa: My Early Years*. Johannesburg: Pan MacMillan South Africa, 2021.

Clegg, Johnny and Michael Drewett. 'Why Don't You Sing about the Leaves and the Dreams? Reflecting on Music Censorship in Apartheid South Africa'. In *Popular Music Censorship in Africa*, edited by Martin Cloonan and Michael Drewett, 127–136. London: Routledge, 2016.

Coplan, David. 'Black Popular Music in South Africa'. In *The Concise Garland Encyclopedia of World Music*, vol. 1, 110–122. London: Routledge, 2013.

Coplan, David. 'God Rock Africa: Thoughts on Politics in Popular Black Performance in South Africa'. *African Studies* 64, no. 1 (2005): 9–27.

Cowell, Alan. 'Johnny Clegg, South African Singer Who Battled Apartheid With Music, Is Dead At 66'. *The New York Times*, 16 July 2019. Accessed 30 March 2025, https://www.nytimes.com/2019/07/16/arts/music/johnny-clegg-dead.html#.

De Costa, René. *The Poetry of Pablo Neruna*. Cambridge, MA: Harvard University Press, 2009.

De la Torre, Ignatio and Rafael Mora. 'The Transition to the Acheulean in East Africa: An Assessment of Paradigms and Evidence from Olduvai Gorge (Tanzania)'. *Journal of Archaeological Method and Theory* 21 (2014): 781–823.

De Villiers, Marguerite. 'Johnny Clegg: A Shadow Man'. *Anthropology Southern Africa* 39, no. 1 (2016): 58–63.

Duran, Manual E. and Roberto González Echevarría. 'Pablo Neruda: Chilean Poet'. In *Encyclopedia Britannica*. Accessed 30 March 2025. https://www.britannica.com/biography/Pablo-Neruda.

February, Judith. 'Johnny Clegg Wasn't "Begging to be Black". He Simply Was'. *Daily Maverick*, 17 July 2019. Accessed 30 March 2025. https://www.dailymaverick.co.za/opinionista/2019-07-17-johnny-clegg-wasnt-begging-to-be-black-he-simply-was/

Freedman, Samuel G. 'Johnny Clegg's War on Apartheid'. *Rolling Stone*, 19 July 2019. Accessed 30 March 2025. https://www.rollingstone.com/music/music-features/johnny-clegg-south-africa-Apartheid-samuel-freedman-860888/.

Hemmings, Eve. *Scatterlings: A Tapestry of Afri-Expat Tales*. Bloomington: Xlibris Corporation, 2013.

Hobsbawm, Eric. *Age of Extremes: The Short Twentieth Century 1914–1991*. London: Abacus, 1995.

Johnny Clegg & Savuka. 'Johnny Clegg and Savuka – Scatterlings of Africa (1987)'. YouTube video, 03:48. Accessed 27 April 2025. https://www.youtube.com/watch?v=qnYtcH4YS44.

Johnny Clegg & Savuka. 'Johnny Clegg (With Nelson Mandela) - Asimbonanga - 1999 Fran'. YouTube video, 06:12. Accessed 28 April 2025. https://www.youtube.com/watch?v=BGS7SpI7obY.
Johnny Clegg & Savuka. 'One Man One Vote'. YouTube video, 04:18. Accessed 28 April 2025. https://www.youtube.com/watch?v=DPP3wo1F3r4.
Mandela, Nelson. *Long Walk to Freedom*. London: Abacus, 1994.
Manenzhe, Rešoketšwe. *Scatterlings*. Johannesburg: Jacana Media, 2020.
McDonald, David A. *My Voice Is My Weapon: Music, Nationalism and the Poetics of Palestinian Resistance*. Durham, NC: Duke University Press, 2013.
Meintjes, Louise. *Dust of the Zulu: Ngoma Aesthetics After Apartheid*. Durham, NC: Duke University Press, 2017.
Mills, Albert J., Gabrielle Durepos and Elden Wiebe. *Encyclopedia of Case Study Research*, vols I and II. Thousand Oaks: Sage, 2010.
Montagne, Renee. 'Songwriter Clegg on Mandela, South Africans' "Bridge"'. *National Public Radio*, 6 December 2013. Accessed 30 March 2025. https://www.npr.org/2013/12/06/249236653/songwriter-clegg-on-mandela-south-africans-bridge.
Mortimer, Bev. 'Johnny Clegg Talks about the Years of "Le Zoulou Blanc"'. *St Francis Chronicle*, 11 November 2012. Accessed 30 March 2025. https://stfrancischronicle.com/2012/11/11/johnny-clegg-talks-about-the-years-of-le-zoulou-blanc/.
Olsen, Kathryn. *Music and Social Change in South Africa: Maskanda Past and Present*. Philadelphia: Temple University Press, 2014.
Petergabriel.com. 'Biko: Re-release'. Accessed 30 March 2025. https://petergabriel.com/release/biko-1987/.
Phelamanga. 'Building Lasting Relationships'. Accessed 7 May 2025., https://phelamanga.co.za/2023/09/12/whats-in-a-name/.
Pithouse, Richard. 'Johnny Clegg: Rebel, Intellectual, Musician'. *Mail & Guardian*, 18 July 2019. Accessed 30 March 2025. https://mg.co.za/article/2019-07-18-johnny-clegg-rebel-intellectual-musician/.
Pooley, Thomas M. 'Sikeyi: In Memoriam – Johnny Clegg (1953–2019)'. *Muziki: Journal of Music Research in Africa* 17, no. 1 (2021): 131–136.
Schumann, Anne. 'The Beat that Beat Apartheid: The Role of Music in the Resistance Against Apartheid in South Africa'. *Stichproben: Vienna Journal of African Studies* 8, no. 14 (2008): 17–39.
Sky.it. 'Cosa significa Asimbonanga, la traduzione della citazione nella canzone di Leo Gassmann'. Accessed 30 March 2025. https://tg24.sky.it/spettacolo/musica/2020/02/07/asimbonanga-traduzione.
South African History Online. 'Griffiths Mlungisi Mxenge'. *South African History Online*, 25 April 2012. Accessed 30 March 2025. https://www.sahistory.org.za/people/griffiths-mlungisi-mxenge.
Spini, Lucilla. *Of Scatterlings and Stakeholders: Diversity, Inclusion and Transnational Governance for Sustainable Development*. Florence: Pontecorboli Editore, 2020.
Spini, Lucilla and Andrew Grant Innes. 'Johnny Clegg: A Polycultural Anthropologist on Stage for Social Justice'. *International Journal of Anthropology* 37, no. 1–2 (2022): 75–94.
Street, John. 'The Politics of Popular Culture'. In *The Blackwell Companion to Political Sociology*, edited by Kate Nash and Alan Scott, 302–311. Oxford: Blackwell Publishing, 2001.
Taylor, Timothy. *Global Pop: World Music, World Markets*. London: Routledge, 2014.
Tsioulcas, Anastasia. 2019. 'Johnny Clegg, A Uniting Voice Against Apartheid, Dies At 66'. *National Public Radio*, 16 July 2019. Accessed 30 March 2025. https://www.npr.org/2019/07/16/738065415/johnny-clegg-a-uniting-voice-against-Apartheid-dies.

Vorster, Jakobus M. 'The Possible Contribution of Civil Society in the Moral Edification of South African Society: The Example of the "United Democratic Front" and the "Treatment Action Campaign" (1983–2014)'. *HTS Theological Studies* 71, no. 3 (2015): 1–8. Accessed 30 March 2025. http://www.scielo.org.za/pdf/hts/v71n3/03.pdf.

Webb, Chris. 'Apartheid, Anthropology and Johnny Clegg'. *Africa Is a Country*, 19 July 2019. Accessed 30 March 2025. https://africasacountry.com/2019/07/Apartheid-anthropology-and-johnny-clegg.

DISCOGRAPHY

Clegg, Johnny. *New World Survivor*. Album. Pretoria: Value Music, CDVM (WFL) 45, 2002.

Johnny Clegg & Savuka. *Asimbonanga*. Single. Johannesburg: MINC, 12XMC(P) 4054016, 1986.

Johnny Clegg & Savuka. *Cruel Crazy Beautiful World*. Album. Sandton: EMI, EMCJ (E) – 7934461, 1989.

Johnny Clegg & Savuka. *Shadow Man*. Album. Sandton: EMI, EMCJ (D) – 7904111, 1988.

Johnny Clegg & Savuka. *Third World Child*. Album. Sandton: EMI, EMCJ (D) – 2407331, 1987.

Juluka. *Scatterlings*. Album. Johannesburg: MINC, MINC – (L) 1040, 1982.

CHAPTER

5

Johnny Clegg and the Poetry and Politics of Migrant Labour

Richard Pithouse

When apartheid ended Jonathan Clegg was, like many other former dissidents, incorporated into the new order as a respected establishment figure. The same was true of his art. After his death in July 2019, he was canonised as a patron saint of 'racial harmony'. Terms like 'unity', 'human rights', 'peace' and 'tolerance' were regularly used in obituaries, as were the claims that his music 'united South Africans' and 'promoted racial healing'.

There was a strong sense that Clegg's 'message' (a word that was relentlessly used) prefigured (implicitly middle class) black and white people happily sharing a post-racial reality. This was taken to include his most artistically successful period in the Juluka years from 1979 to 1984, as well as his unevenly but nonetheless most explicitly politically militant period from the release of 'Asimbonanga' ('We Have Not Seen Him') as a single during the state of emergency in 1986 to the *Heat, Dust and Dreams* album, released in 1993 during the violent interregnum between the unbanning of the liberation movement and the advent of electoral democracy.[1]

The rainbow-washing of Clegg was both a mainstream and an academic exercise. The obituary for Clegg in *Africa Is a Country*, an online publication for hip university-trained intellectuals, argued that 'the real threat that

Clegg and Juluka posed to apartheid was the free and open association of black and white artists' that 'allowed many South Africans to glimpse a post-apartheid future in which opportunity, friendship and culture would not be narrowly defined by race or ethnicity'.[2]

Clegg's refusal to conform to the laws and norms of a violently segregated society was significant, and frequently met with state repression, including arrests and the shutting down of performances. Nonetheless, reducing the meaning of Clegg to this aspect of his life and art erases both his participation in the life-world of migrant workers and the way in which the Juluka period produced a remarkable body of work, much of which was focused on labour, and particularly migrant labour. His personal transgressions and artistic achievements were mediated through class as much as race.

A notable exception to the overwhelming erasure of the centrality of migrant workers to Clegg's achievements as an artist came from the trade unions. Both the major trade union federations in the country, the Congress of South African Trade Unions and the South African Federation of Trade Unions, issued statements on Clegg's death, making very clear points about his support for workers' struggles. A statement issued by the general secretary of the National Union of Metalworkers of South Africa, the largest union in the country, said that 'Clegg, always a modest and kind man, never spoke publicly about his activism and quiet behind the scenes support for the workers' movement. He was a close friend of Neil Aggett, the doctor and trade unionist who died in detention in 1982, performed to audiences of workers in hostels and union halls, and often translated materials into Zulu for trade union publications'.[3]

Clegg first met Sipho Mchunu, who would become his partner in Juluka, in Johannesburg in 1969. They were teenagers, drawn together by a shared passion for maskanda, a syncretic form of Zulu folk music often, but not always, featuring a picking guitar style. It was predominantly performed by men and, at the time, often associated with migrant workers. Clegg had begun to participate in the life-world of migrant workers, many but not all of them Zulu, in 1967 at the age of 14 after meeting Charlie Mzila, who agreed to teach him maskanda guitar.[4] This was not only an encounter between a white teenager and a black man, it was also an encounter between a middle class white teenager and a working class black man, a migrant worker employed as a caretaker in a block of flats reserved for white people.

In interviews, Clegg was always reluctant to ascribe this movement into the life-world of migrant workers to politics, often commenting that politics found him. In his incomplete and fragmentary autobiography, his account of his formation as a teenager is a story of a search for masculine belonging and identity that centres participation in *ngoma* dance (forms of martial dance collectively performed by men). His autobiography tells a story of a boy without a father finding masculine affirmation and connection via the dance. 'In many ways,' he wrote, 'the dance and its brotherhood was a male parent to me.'[5]

When Clegg became a student at the University of the Witwatersrand (Wits) in 1971, Mchunu was working as a gardener for a white family. Their shared experience of friendship and playing maskanda in informal street competitions was clearly profound, but as young men their lives were calibrated to move along very different trajectories.

Clegg had been seriously alienated from white society in his high school years. As a result, he struggled with school despite his sparkling intelligence. But at university he began to encounter radical white teachers and peers, enabling a productive connection between the two worlds that he inhabited, with both activism and theory enabling that connection.

He had arrived on a campus in political ferment. Young people around the world had been electrified by the global youth rebellion of 1968, with the uprising in Paris in May of that year being particularly influential on campuses in many countries. That uprising was marked by workers and students entering each other's life-worlds and collaborating politically. Kristin Ross writes that it was animated by 'flight from social determinations, with displacements that took people outside of their location in society with a disjunction, that is, between political subjectivity and the social group'. She stresses that it was 'a shattering of social identity that allowed politics to take place'.[6] Jean-Paul Sartre was the philosopher of the moment, and ideas of radical freedom, including the possibility of what he called 'mutation' at the level of being, were in the air. Frantz Fanon, a philosopher who was also taken up in this moment, insisted that the human 'is motion towards the world' and placed the idea of mutation at the centre of his work.[7] His biographer, Alice Cherki, wrote that 'the project of being exclusively identified with one's origins was at odds with Fanon's conception of what it meant to be a free subject'.[8] All this is in striking contrast to the current fashion for ideas of ontological fixity including, in some cases, the view that transgressing some of the social categories into which we are born is inherently dubious.

The youth rebellion on campuses across the world took two forms in South Africa. One was the Black Consciousness Movement, which first began to take form in 1968. The other was the encounter between students and workers following the Durban strikes in 1973. The Black Consciousness Movement and the movement of students, often but not always white, into the nascent trade union movement were not wholly separate projects. Steve Biko, the leading figure in the Black Consciousness Movement, introduced the ideas of the Brazilian intellectual Paulo Freire to South African radicals, and Freire's thinking about forms of praxis grounded in mutuality, inspired to a significant degree by Fanon, became very influential among the university-trained intellectuals in and around the unions.[9] The idea of what Fanon had called a 'mutual current of enlightenment and enrichment' between university trained intellectuals and oppressed people was central to Freire's thinking, as was, in Freire's phrase, 'the affirmation of men and women as persons' being both a mode of struggle and a key goal of struggle.[10] This commitment to humanism, and to openness and reciprocity between people consigned to different social locations by oppressive systems, shaped much of the art and politics of the period.

Clegg was swiftly plugged into the vibrant progressive milieu at Wits, which included a good number of brilliant intellectuals. He and Mchunu performed at the first 'Free People's Concert' at Wits in 1971, a project of radical students. David Webster, an anthropologist who would be assassinated in 1989, had a particularly significant influence on Clegg.

When black workers struck in Durban in January 1973, productive encounters between workers and students played an important catalytic role in the development of the black trade union movement. In September that year, 11 miners were murdered by the police at the Western Deep

Levels mine outside Johannesburg. Following the example set in Durban, students – led by Steven Friedman, who went on to play an important role in the trade union movement – began to engage the emerging labour movement. Clegg was among them, and his work included translation of the materials put out by the unions with the support of radical students, and connecting students and workers. Friedman recalls that 'quite a few of us joined because we had read texts and were into an intellectual and political project. For Johnny this wasn't an intellectual project, it was about people'.[11] Nonetheless, the turn to unions and the theoretical questions posed around labour issues by many of the most gifted of that generation of academics and students gave Clegg a powerful set of tools to make sense of the lived experience of migrant labour from within his immersion in that lived experience.

In 1976, the year that Clegg completed his Bachelor of Arts degree, an uprising in Soweto led by school children was met by a massacre perpetrated by the South African security forces. This was the year in which Clegg and Mchunu first began to record music. Two seven-inch singles were released that year. The first contained a song credited to Clegg and another to Mchunu, without a name being used for the duo or either track being billed as a single. *Sengikhumbula Emakhabe Leni* was credited to Clegg. It should have been spelt '*Sengikhumbula eMakhabeleni*', which means 'I Miss eMakhabeleni'; eMakhabeleni is Mchunu's village near Greytown in KwaZulu-Natal. '*Baba Ungadlali Ngomama*' ('Father Don't Play with Mother') was credited to Mchunu.[12] The second single was *Uthi Angizule*, which should have been '*Guthi Angizule*' (I Feel Like Wandering), which came out under the name 'Jonathan Clegg & Sipho Mchunu'.[13] In 1977 two other singles, '*Ngasala Obala*' ('Left in the Open', figuratively meaning left exposed to everyone) and then an early version of *Woza Friday* (Come Friday) which would be re-recorded five years later, were released under the name 'Jonathan & Sipho'.[14] In the same year, Clegg and Mchunu both appeared on *Father to the Child,* the 1977 album by the folk singer Paul Clingman.[15] A performance of a song, '*Ngwaka Nyambe Nkonyane*' (possibly a contraction of '*Ngi ngo wakwa Nyambe Nkonyane*' and translated on the track listing as 'I Am from the Nyane Clan'), also recorded that year, appears on the live album *South Africa: Cologne Zulu Festival* recorded in 1981 and released in 1992.[16]

The first two singles are extremely rare, and there are no versions of them available online. The third, which can occasionally be found at the price of a few thousand rands, is a maskanda song about desertion by a father and a search for marriage. *Woza Friday*, which has a pop inflection in parts, has a sense of both a lament for life squandered in low-paid work and joy at the prospect of the coming weekend. Clegg often spoke of how the song emerged from his experience of working on a chicken farm with migrant workers from Malawi. It became a hit, and was certified gold in 1978.[17]

Clegg and Mchunu's work on the Clingman album anticipated some of what was to come with the first two Juluka albums, *Universal Men* (1979) and *African Litany* (1981).[18] In the delicate and beautiful track 'Sweet Rivers', English and isiZulu lyrics are mixed and there is confluence between maskanda and the Euro-American folk music that had been central to dissident youth cultures in the West since the 1960s. But although the Clingman album included a song on the 1976 uprising, composed by Clingman, none of the work by Clegg and Mchunu on that album engaged the political drama of the moment.

The live recording '*Ngwaka Nyambe Nkonyane*' is credited as a traditional composition and is centred on the mouthbow. The lyrics are not easily discernible. The rest of the *South Africa: Cologne Zulu Festival* album includes ten tracks by Ladysmith Black Mambazo and another eight by Clegg and Mchunu, credited to Duo Juluka, all recorded in 1981 but sounding very much like the music performed and recorded in the period before the release of the debut Juluka album in 1979. They are beautiful maskanda songs, delicate and gentle in their expression, and largely centring on rural themes, although there is a song sending greetings from KwaMashu, in Durban, after arriving in the city by train. This is the music of migrant workers, much of it about nostalgia for home.

A recording of a performance by Clegg and Mchunu at the Market Theatre in Johannesburg in 1978, which has never been released or made available online, includes a version of '*Asimbonanga*' in which the person who is not seen is Kaizer Matanzima, the leader of the Transkei Bantustan.[19]

Here many of the same lyrics that would later celebrate Mandela disparage his nephew Matanzima, who was widely viewed as a collaborator with apartheid.

It is possible that Clegg performed other directly political songs at the time, but his recorded music would first take an openly dissident form, aligned to the mass insurrection of the time, with the release of a new version of *Asimbonanga* as a single in 1986.[20] While the song was now about Nelson Mandela, it also referenced three people who had been murdered by the state: Biko, Aggett and the United Democratic Front (UDF)-aligned lawyer Victoria Mxenge. Although it was, following the release of Mandela, later incorporated into the rainbow nation ideology, it was a profoundly dissident and brave statement at the time. Many people who first heard *Asimbonanga* at the moment of its release recall, with absolute clarity, both the circumstances under which they heard the song and the physical sensation of its electric power.

The debut Juluka album, *Universal Men*, released in October 1979, stands as one of the great contributions to South African music and a work of global import. It came out of an open-ended collaborative studio process that included some of the country's best musicians, including the jazz musicians Sipho Gumede, Mervyn Africa and Robbie Jansen, as well as the rock musician Colin Pratley. Its producer, Hilton Rosenthal, recalls that he gave the musicians the time and space 'to experiment and be spontaneous'.[21] In 2000 Clegg recalled that 'the whole project was, musically, completely new. No one had done this before – we were flying a kite and hoping to be struck by lightning'.[22]

In musical terms the album is wholly unique, bringing forms of African music, jazz and Western folk together in a way that goes beyond braiding different sounds together and enables something new. Jansen played a large role in creating the album's distinctive and warm timbre. His flute and saxophone rising over maskanda guitar do not sound like sonic collage, nor does the mouthbow sensitively played by Clegg on the final track. It all sounds like it comes from one coherent creative impulse. The same is true of the cohesiveness of the parts of the work that are in isiZulu and English, as well as of the compositions by Clegg and Mchunu.

Clegg and Mchunu appear on the cover of the album, looking reflective in a photograph taken on a mine dump. The name of the band is at the top left corner, engraved on a gold bar. Its shimmering glitz clashes, pointedly, with the more organic colours of the sky, the rocks and the clothes worn by the two men, which include *izimbadada* (car tyre shoes associated with migrant workers, and with impoverished rural people elsewhere in the global south).[23] The message is clear: Johannesburg's wealth and glamour are built not just on gold but also on the labour of the men, the migrant labourers, who mined that gold.

Universal Men has a sustained thematic focus on migrant labour, and implicitly brings in Marxist understandings of how labour is the source of wealth, and an understanding that labourers from the rural periphery, sustained in part by rural homesteads, built the modern cities. It is never didactic, though. On the contrary, the poetic quality of the work is superb, arguably unmatched in any South African music in English. The work is lyrical and carries a quality close to myth, with the characters in the songs taking on an archetypal dimension. Migrant workers are placed in the context of a specific history and culture, one in which they recall the lost power of their people that has shackled them to migrant labour while they dream of the hills, the murmurs of the rivers, their cattle and children at home. It often has the quality of lament, and has none of the masculine energy that Clegg had sought out in *ngoma* dance, something in which Mchunu also excelled.

An allusion on the title track to a line from a poem by Pablo Neruda gives some indication of Clegg's interest in poetry.[24] Clegg has been anthologised as a poet, but has not been fully recognised for the poetic power of his early work. Consider these lines from 'Deliwe' (a woman's name, meaning to leave something or someone behind, to disown or forsake) on *Universal Men*, in which a man is singing to a woman:

> The bees are buzzing in your honey mouth
> And I have drawn the water from your well
> The deep rushing down while the night birds call
> And the waters wash me on the inside[25]

The citation for the honorary doctorate awarded to Clegg at Wits in 2007 declared that he had written 'lyrics of outstanding literary quality'.[26] Alain Badiou understands the literary genre of the poem 'as dictation of being' and, when done well, it offers a particularly potent discursive tool to resist dehumanisation, something that, in the ideology of oppression, always includes the flattening out or even annihilation of being.[27]

In a 2000 interview about *Universal Men*, Clegg spoke at some length about a book he had been reading while composing the lyrics: *A Seventh Man* by John Berger, with photographs by Jean Mohr.[28] Published in 1975, it is a deeply empathetic account of migrant labour in Europe, centring on the themes of departure, work and return, and showing that people often considered peripheral and out of time to modern Europe are, in fact, central to it. These themes are at the heart of *Universal Men*, with lines from the title track bringing the wider work into clear focus: 'I have undone this distance / so many times before / That it seems as if this life of mine / is trapped between two shores'.[29]

Discussing the relation of *A Seventh Man* to the album, Clegg said:

> *Universal Men* is about bridging two worlds. Going and coming. While the worker is en route, on a bus or a train, he is given the time to look over the distances, geographic and otherwise, in his life. Migrant labourers, in Africa, Europe, everywhere, are like universal joints. They are this incredible human resource who are just sucked up by the capitalist system and used anywhere. The system makes no concessions and so the workers have to create a whole new universe of meaning.[30]

Three songs on the album, 'Sky People', 'Universal Men' and 'Old Eyes', all fully or partially composed by Clegg, offer narratives in which migrant worker characters are presented with a deep empathy that, going beyond Berger's work, sensitively place the characters in a cultural context. 'Old Eyes' is about homecoming. Clegg explained that, for the migrant labourer, 'homecoming is everything – you're carrying presents and it's the moment when you reveal yourself to your community as a successful person. You become a source of abundance; it's an elevated and life giving moment in the migrant universe. There is redemption. All the degradation and alienation which you've endured is redeemed and transformed into a hugely meaningful event when you arrive home'.

But in this song, the longed-for redemption is out of reach – shattered between the anvil and hammer of apartheid. The returning worker finds that he is the 'only one to witness my homecoming' and reflects that

> When I left that mountain land so gold and green
> I was a sturdy 16 years
> The work was hard and the wage was low
> And the seasons passed me by one by one
> And I dreamed Maria you would wait for my return
> We'd build a home upon the rock beneath the smiling sun

He finds an old man who remembers him from his youth, who tells him that

> Son I'll be old until I die now
> And then I will join our people in the sky
> I am not the one to ask why our people have been scattered in the wind
> You've got old eyes – *amehlo madala* ['old eyes'] – you've seen much too much for one so young[31]

'*Unkosibomvu*' ('The Red King'), composed by Clegg and Mchunu, and 'Africa', composed by Clegg, speak to the cosmology of Zulu migrant workers. In Mchunu's tenderly performed composition, '*Thula 'Mtanami*' ('Hush Child'), the song's protagonist tells a child that their mother will return with care and sweets. '*Inkunzi Ayihlabi Ngokumisa*', another co-composition, this time organised around the mouthbow rather than the guitar, draws from folklore as Mchunu sings an exquisite and almost mournful allegory of power. Clegg translated the title as meaning literally 'A bull doesn't stab by means of the way in which its horns have grown' and metaphorically carrying the meaning, in the form of a proverb, of 'don't judge a bull by its horns'.[32] Some have read the allegory – a bull with smaller horns being able to defeat a rival with larger horns – in political terms.

A version of this track had been released earlier, in January 1979, on the now classic compilation album *Rhythm Of Resistance – Music Of Black South Africa*.[33] Accompanied by a documentary of the same name that was directly linked to the anti-apartheid struggle, and used photographs by Peter Magubane taken from an exhibition funded by the African National Congress (ANC)-aligned International Defence and Aid Fund, it ran a high risk of being seen as ANC-linked by the apartheid state. The album itself was not a collection of directly political songs. Other artists featured included Malombo, Ladysmith Black Mambazo, and the Mahotella Queens, with eight of the ten tracks produced by Mike Howlett, a well-known Australian producer working in London.

In a remarkable poem included in *A Seventh Man,* Berger speaks of a city 'milling with invisible survivors'.[34] The book is written and photographed in fidelity to the principle that 'equality ... is the recognition of being ... The principle of equality is the revolutionary principle ... because it asserts that all men [sic] are equally whole'.[35] There is no revolutionary sloganeering on *Universal Men*, but it is suffused with the recognition of being, of an equal wholeness at the level of being.

Aside from an allegorical line about a force of some sort in the north – 'But in the North the thunderclouds would judge you' from 'Deliwe' – there is no reference on *Universal Men* to politics as collective action, whether via the new trade union movement or the Soweto revolt, and no direct reference to the imminent independence of Zimbabwe, although two lines that originally declared 'The drums of Zimbabwe speak / they roll across the great divide' were changed, in the studio, to 'The drums of Zambezi speak' to avoid the risk of censorship.[36] The politics of the work lie in the profound way in which it humanises the people Berger had said are rendered as non-human, or at least invisible as human, within the social systems that rely on migrant labour.

The second Juluka album, *African Litany*, was released in March 1981. Although it is entirely sonically coherent, and a solid follow-up to the debut album, it is not as tightly thematically focused as *Universal Men*. It builds on the unique sound developed in *Universal Men*, and includes a good number of remarkable songs, including the under-recognised 'Thandiwe' (a woman's name meaning 'beloved') which has a fabulous groove. 'Heart of the Dancer' recounts Clegg's early encounter with *ngoma* dance, the dance of 'the powerful people ambushed by history'. 'Mama Shabalala', a song about a repeatedly displaced elderly woman seeking a home in Weenen County in what was then rural Natal, has the sort of narrative character that fits well with songs like 'Deliwe' and 'Old Eyes' on *Universal Men*. It is also a sensitive and empathetic portrayal of a female character in a body of work that is primarily concerned with the experiences of men.

In 'Impi' ('War'), a song charged with all the martial, masculine energy of the dance, he takes on the Battle of Isandlwana of 1879 in which Zulu regiments defeated the invading British forces.

There is a strong strand in white consciousness, in South Africa and in Britain, that can simultaneously affirm Zulu military prowess and remain committed to white supremacy, via the colonial trope of martial races deemed simultaneously strong and courageous on the one hand and pre-modern on the other. Clegg intended the song to be an affirmation of a direct confrontation with colonial power, and while many listeners heard it in this way, and still do, there was, and perhaps still is, a current of white appreciation for the song that has colonial overtones.

'African Sky Blue', a standout track that follows '*Impi*', begins with a delicate maskanda *izihlabo* (opening flourish) and links colonial conquest to labour:

> The warrior is now a worker and his war is underground
> With cordite in the darkness, he milks the bleeding veins of gold
> When the smoking rockface murmurs, he always thinks of you
> African sky blue, will you see him through?[37]

Here the tone is more reflective than the martial theme in '*Impi*'. The military glories of the past are presented as having transformed into a workers' struggle, and the future seems uncertain.

'High Country' speaks to a generalised colonial condition – 'In the backstreets, in the poor towns I hear a thunder which cannot roll' – and then to settler paranoia:

> Someone's been at the liquor cabinet
> She's sure someone's been wearing her shoes
> All around her chaos and anarchy
> Light and reason overthrown
> I'm sure she says, they will attack the embassy[38]

Ubuhle Bemvelo ('The Beauty of Nature'), released in November 1981, is quite different from the first two Juluka albums.[39] It is a collection of old and new songs sung in isiZulu, including compositions from the time when Clegg and Mchunu were an acoustic duo, and is animated by an overt, and entirely successful, pop sensibility often driven by mbaqanga or township jive sensibilities. Like much popular music in the palette from which the album draws, the songs generally offer vignettes from ordinary working class life that paint everyday emotions and experiences, rather than an attempt directly to engage class or, for that matter, race.

Although not composed as an album, it is certainly coherent and sounds like an album. It includes the now standard version of a classic South African popular song, '*Woza* Friday' ('Come Friday'), Juluka's first hit, and '*Umfazi Omdala*' ('Old Woman'), a staple of Clegg's live sets for the rest of his performing career. '*Woza* Friday' is a worker's song:

> *Webaba, kunzima kulomhlaba*
> *Webaba, lo msebenzi ubhokile*
> *Webaba, nemali ayingeni*
> *Engathi leli veki lingaphela*
> *Ngithi woza, woza* Friday, my darling
>
> (Oh father, it is difficult in this world
> Oh father, there is a lot of work

> Oh father, money does not come in
> I wish this week would end
> I say come, come Friday, my darling)[40]

Its tone is very different from classic songs about alienated labour, such as Tracy Chapman's 'Fast Car' or Bruce Springsteen's 'Factory'.[41] This version carries more joy than the original, enough to make the arrival of Friday, rather than the low-paid work that precedes it, feel like the real point.

Scatterlings was released in September 1982.[42] It has often been overshadowed by the success of the title track, which endures as a classic, but it is a superb album with powerfully honed lyrics, a compelling rock influence on some songs, excellent use of brass, and on some tracks a more masculinist sensibility than the bulk of the previous work. There are a number of songs here, such as *'iJwanasibeki'* ('Johannesburg'), 'Spirit Is the Journey' and 'Simple Things', that belong in the South African canon.

In an interview given in the year after the album's release, Clegg explained that the album was crafted with the explicit intention of enabling it to succeed elsewhere in the world.[43] This was achieved with the title track, which charted in the United Kingdom in February, after which *Impi*, released as a single in the UK, charted in August.[44] It's often the case that a desire to build a bigger audience compromises the artistic integrity of music, but this album, while very different in terms of its sound to Juluka's earlier work, is wholly successful as art.

There's a significant existential strand in the work centred on the value of life and a resolve to live it intensely. *Scatterlings* presents a vision of an African-derived humanity expressed in universal terms but, of course, intensely relevant to apartheid South Africa. *'iJwanasibeki'* is, like 'African Sky Blue', a song about men working as miners, but far more masculinist than that song in the sonic tone of its presentation.

> Blow whistle blow
> Down you go alive
> The cage is falling
> Like a comet in the night

Beads of sweat glisten
In the underground light
Smoulder boulder
Rock reeks fumes
Songs of the outlands
Change colour when shift is due
And you've grown a little older
Seen bone blown smoking blue![45]

One song, 'Digging for Some Words', has two lines – the first in Clegg's recorded work – that move away from political allegory, often not specifically tied to South Africa, and into concrete politics. The reference is to the war in Angola:

Seven seasoned soldiers have been summoned from Saigon
A craven walkie talkie puts their bloodshot armour on
Some drink beer milk, some drink kinky-kola
Sheep dogs live in Outeniqua
Gun dogs in Angola
Flames lick the corners of each hungry horseman's smile
They have locusts in their scabbards and deserts in their eyes
Passing through the air they leave a sea of fetid rumours
As they ride across the skyline on a secret trail of lies[46]

'Two Humans on the Run' and *Siyayilanda* ('We Are Fetching It' – figuratively meaning we are seizing the future) have no explicit political meaning but were read politically by thoughtful listeners. In concert Clegg often introduced *Siyayilanda* by explaining that it was for Neil Aggett, the doctor and trade unionist murdered while being tortured by the police in February 1982. He and Clegg had been friends, and Aggett's funeral became a major step towards the unity of the black trade union movement when a range of previously divided unions came out in solidarity.

In a number of interviews at this time, Clegg explained that engaging political themes via, in a phrase used in one interview, 'metaphor, oblique references' was necessary to avoid repression.[47] But songs were often given an explicitly political framing during live performances, and Juluka concerts were clearly experienced as dissident spaces.

Work for All came out in November 1983 with a trade union slogan as its title and images of workers on the cover.[48] Rosenthal, who produced all the Juluka albums and much of Clegg's work after Juluka, recalls that the title track was directly inspired by Clegg's work with trade unions.[49] The UDF had been formed in August that year and mass struggle had moved out of workplaces and into communities. Clegg, who had strong connections to the UDF, was carried into more explicit militancy by this rising tide. Mchunu recalls that 'John was very strong in politics at that time, you could really hear it in his songs'.[50]

Work for All is the Juluka album with the strongest claim to equalling the achievement of *Universal Men*. As with tracks like '*iJwanesbeki*' on the *Scatterlings* album, there are songs here in which the form of masculinity developed in the dance is strongly present. 'December African Rain', a love song sung from the perspective of a dying protagonist, richly deserves its standing as a classic. 'Bullets for Bafazane' is about the violence of migrant life, and there is a set of songs that explore aspects of rural life, one of which, 'Baba Nango', returns to the theme of the migrant labourer returning home:

> I'm travelling light, I'm going to Baba Nango
> I'm leaving tonight, I'm going to Baba Nango
> I'm leaving my crying behind, I'm going to Baba Nango
> And when my people see me they will say
> '*Halala*! It's the child of the hungry earth'[51]

The End Conscription Campaign, which opposed the conscription of young white men into the apartheid army to fight in the townships and the escalating 'border war' in Angola, had been formed in October 1983. Men who refused conscription were jailed. 'Gunship Ghetto' engages this with some degree of directness: 'Border Order / Prison Warder … Paper holder holds a soldier / Not yet born to be / But six months older, he'll be much bolder / See things he's never seen'.[52]

'*Mana Lapho*' ('Stand There', figuratively meaning stand your ground) is a powerful freedom song:

Voices in the air of those gone before sing
Mana Lapho (Stand your ground)
There's nowhere to hide which side you stand on
Mana Lapho (Stand your ground)
The time is drawing near, can you hear
Can you hear a long sung song of freedom?
Bana manga we 'ndoda bathu iculo lethu sedifile
(They tell lies oh man for they say our song of freedom is dead)
Mana nans' indaba isho ngefreedom
(Stand for here is a matter and it speaks of freedom)[53]

'Work for All' is another song about workers and labour. In 1983 urban unemployment was beginning its escalation into the contemporary crisis, and the song, organised around the phrase '*Sifun'umsebenzi*' ('We want work') presents the unemployed as political protagonists: 'Hear them sing in the streets now / Hear the sound of marching feet now'.

Its chorus declares:

> *Sifun'umsebenzi* – work for all – we need to work to be
> *Sifun'umsebenzi* – work for all – there's a jobless army in the streets
> *Sifun'umsebenzi* – work for all – in a wage, a hidden war[54]

Once again martial ideas appear in the context of work.

But it is in 'Mdantsane' that Clegg's lyrics bring Juluka into the band's most concrete engagement with struggle and repression. On 4 August 1983 a bus boycott in Mdantsane, a township outside East London, was met with murderous repression by the police at the cost of 11 lives, with 36 people injured. The song directly references 'I'm Explaining a Few Things', a well-known anti-fascist poem by Neruda, placing the massacre in Mdantsane in a wider context of anti-fascism. Clegg's lyrics are:

> Why don't you sing about the African moon?
> Why don't you sing about the leaves and the dreams?
> Why don't you sing about the rain and the birds?
> 'Cause mister I've seen

> Mud coloured dusty blood
> Bare feet on a burning bus
> Mud coloured dusty blood
> Broken teeth and a rifle butt
> On the road to Mdantsane[55]

Neruda's lines are:

> And you will ask: why doesn't his poetry
> speak of dreams and leaves
> and the great volcanoes of his native land?
>
> Come and see the blood in the streets.
> Come and see
> the blood in the streets.
> Come and see the blood
> in the streets![56]

In 1984 a compilation album released for European and North American markets, an EP (extended play), and a new studio album for South African audiences were released. The compilation album, titled *Stand Your Ground*, included six songs from *Work for All*, a track, '*Umbaqanga* Music', previously released on an international release of *Scatterlings*, and three new songs.[57] '*Umbaqanga* Music' and 'Fever', one of the three new songs, were both reworked versions of the melodies of earlier isiZulu songs given English lyrics unrelated to the original isiZulu lyrics. The new material was all musically solid but wholly non-political work with pop-style lyrics designed with the aim of achieving international success. '*Umbaqanga* Music', a surprisingly overlooked track, has a particularly well-developed pop sensibility. *Stand Your Ground* sounds coherent, in sonic terms, as an album rather than a compilation, but did not achieve the hoped for international breakthrough.

The EP, *International Tracks*, included the four songs from *Stand Your Ground* that had not been previously released in South Africa, and dance mixes of 'Fever' and a track titled 'Kilimanjaro' – a first, and successful, foray into music for club dance floors.⁵⁸ It was striking that – although released in the year after the launch of the UDF, with which Clegg as a personality and Juluka as a band came to be associated, and during a growing urban insurrection – it did not contain a single political gesture in its lyrics.

The new studio album, *Musa Ukungilandela* ('Don't Follow Me'), was sung entirely in isiZulu and, like *Ubuhle Bemvelo*, carried strong mbaqanga and township jive influences.⁵⁹ It is a consistently strong album, but largely remembered for '*Ibhola Lethu*' ('Our Ball' – meaning football), a propulsive take on the experience of following football. Mchunu rates 'Zodwa', the second track on the album, as among his favourite Juluka songs.⁶⁰

'Fever' and 'Kilimanjaro', the two singles from *International Tracks*, did well with white audiences on radio and in clubs in South Africa, while *Musa Ukungilandela*, which had produced a single that won an appreciative black audience, was wholly invisible to all but highly committed white Juluka fans. Steven van Zandt, the original lead guitarist in Bruce Springsteen's E Street Band who, in 1985, put together a large group of globally famous musicians to perform his anti-apartheid song 'Sun City', called it 'one of the great albums of all time'.⁶¹ The songs generally deal with experiences from everyday life from a perspective that is not explicitly political, but '*Akanaki Nokunaka*' is a striking exception, dealing directly with forced removals at the hands of 'GG', the white government.

> *Mabangiyeke mina sengidelile*
> *Kahle 'mfowethu kodwa yini?*
> *Ubani ongasula izinyembezi*
> *Ezawela phansi esigodini sakithi?*
> *Saswela amandla ngalelolanga?*
> *Mhla saphela isigodi sakithi*
>
> *Akanaki nokunaka*
> *Hawu bheke uG.G*
> *Umuzi kababa*
> *Wawuthela efusini*
> *Wabona ukuthi ngiswela amandla*

(Let them leave me alone, I have had enough
My brother, what is going on?
Who can wipe away the tears
That fell in our district?
We had no power on that day
The day our district fell

He doesn't care
Just look at GG
My father's homestead
He removes and pours it out into a wasteland
He saw I had no strength left to resist)[62]

'*Izinhlobo Nezinhlobo Zabantu*' ('Types and Types of People', meaning many kinds of people) is the only song in the entire Juluka catalogue with lyrics that directly conform to the idea that the band sang songs 'promoting racial harmony'. Its concluding lines are '*Siyafana ngempela uma sibekesisana / Noma abanye bedidwa 'amabala*' ('When we really look at each other we are all the same / Although others are confused by the different colours'). But, of course, few of the writers presenting Clegg's legacy in these terms would have understood the song (and the album did not come with liner notes or a lyric sheet). Many would not have heard the song at all. It is a marginal track on an album with a largely isiZulu-speaking working class audience.

When Juluka split up in 1985 the reasons for the breakup of the band were not personal or political. Mchunu recalls that all the time on the road made it very difficult to meet his familial and other obligations at his rural homestead.[63] But if the split had not happened in that year the band would have faced an extremely difficult political situation. The first state of emergency was declared by the government in July 1985, and this was also the year in which the conflict between Inkatha and the UDF began to escalate into what people were starting to call a war. Inkatha, backed by the apartheid state and organised as an ethnic Zulu project, was violently opposed to the popular movement against apartheid. There was a sense in which Juluka had run out of political road. To have continued after 1985 it would either have had to sustain the turn away from politics that marked the work released in 1984, or find a way to make sense of the fact that many migrant workers, in urban hostels and rural homesteads, had been drawn into the increasingly militarised reactionary politics of Inkatha.

After Juluka split up, Clegg's work took new directions, beginning with the clearly political 1986 solo album *Third World Child*.[64] A live Juluka album, *Juluka Live (The Good Hope Concerts)*, was released the following year, and massive international success came in 1987 with the debut album by Clegg's new band, Savuka, also titled *Third World Child*.[65] The album was primarily a compilation of previously released songs, including '*Asimbonanga*' and a re-recorded, more pop-oriented version of 'Scatterlings' tailored for chart success in the West. It did not address the crisis in the hostels and the wider issue of the increasing violence between Inkatha and the UDF, as well as the violence between Inkatha and the trade unions. It did, though, include the song 'Missing', which deals directly with the urban insurrection and repression under way at the time.

Mchunu returned to recording in 1989 with *Yithi Esavimba* ('We Stopped It'), released under the name Sipho Mchunu Nama Bhubesi ('Sipho Mchunu and the Lions').[66] *Umhlaba Uzobuya*, officially translated on the album cover as 'The World Is Coming Back', in 1990, and then *Iselula* ('Cellular Phone') in 2021 were released as solo projects.[67] The decision to translate *Umhlaba Uzobuya* as 'The World Is Coming Back' is interesting. The word '*umhlaba*' means both 'world' and 'land', but the very explicitly political isiZulu lyrics of the album's title track clearly indicate that here '*umhlaba*' is intended to mean 'land'. The relevant lyrics, which are not recorded on liner notes, are as follows:

>   *Siboshiwe sikhalela inkululeko*
>   *Lomhlaba uzobuya*
>   *Lomhlaba uzobuya izwe lakithi*
>   *Lomhlaba uzobuyo izwe lamaAfrika*
>   *Afrika ngelethu*

>   (We are prisoners we are crying for freedom
>   This land is coming back

> This land is coming back, our country
> This land is coming back the land of Africans
> Africa is ours)[68]

Although artistically credible, none of these three maskanda albums, one of which includes a reworked Mchunu composition from the Juluka catalogue, were able to achieve any commercial success.

As the scale and intensity of the mass struggle against apartheid escalated in the late 1980s, Clegg's work took on more of a pop-world music feel, but it also became, albeit initially in scattered songs, more explicitly political from 1986 to 1993. The most militant song in Clegg's discography is not 'Asimbonanga' but rather the largely overlooked 'One (Hu)'Man One Vote', released on the *Cruel Crazy Beautiful World* album in 1989, during what was still a period of intense repression.[69] It explicitly associates itself with insurrectionary politics, singing sympathetically, and with strong masculinist energy, of armed young men attempting to seize the future: '*Bayeza abafana bancane, wema / Baphethe iqwasha, baphethe ibazooka*' ('The young boys are coming / They carry a homemade pistol, they carry a bazooka').

The Grammy Award-nominated 1993 album *Heat, Dust and Dreams* spoke powerfully to the political drama of the time.[70] The album opens with 'These Days', which sets the scene for the work to come:

> Mass action on the radio
> Like a great river ebbs and flows
> Carrying us to the final close
> When the system has fallen[71]

The next track on the album, 'The Crossing', a song of transcendent power, was written for Dudu Zulu, a murdered band member, but is simultaneously a moving and powerful allegory of a national drama. In 'Foreign Nights (Working Dog in Babylon)', Clegg returned to migrant labour, but this time in an international context:

> I'm a working alien in a land of heat and stone
> A casualty of an economic war

> That took me away from home.
> It's the politics of money and power
>
> ...
>
> I can hear a siren in the workyard
> Another shift and I'll be closer to you[72]

The poetry of *Universal Men* was now well in the past, but migrant labour was not entirely forgotten.

Clegg and Mchunu had shared an extraordinary period of creative brilliance from *Universal Men* in 1979 to the final Juluka album, *Musa Ukungilandela*, in 1984. Both made some solid work after Juluka, with Clegg having sporadic moments of brilliance until 1993, most notably the songs 'Asimbonanga' and 'The Crossing', and the *Heat, Dust and Dreams* album, the only artistically coherent album he released after the Juluka period. The albums he released after 1994, after the end of apartheid, which included the 1997 Juluka reunion album *Ya Vuka Inkunzi* ('The Bull Has Risen' or 'The Bull Awakes') and four solo albums, had no meaningful artistic merit in musical or lyrical terms.[73] Clegg had become a pillar of the new establishment, making forgettable pop music. His live performances were no longer dissident spaces and attracted new audiences. Disturbingly, there were now sometimes white people in the audiences who would take Clegg's explanations of the meaning of isiZulu lyrics or the context of songs as comic when they had no comic element. He did not contest this from the stage.

The sole exception to the post-apartheid drift into forgettable pop is the largely ignored *My Favourite Zulu Street Guitar Songs*, released in 2010.[74] It is a collection of maskanda songs played in the acoustic style of his early work as part of a duo with Mchunu. These were not Clegg's compositions, but for a moment there was a sensitive and successful creative return to the music and life-world of the migrant workers who had embraced him as a teenager and shaped him as a person, an artist and a political protagonist.

In *A Seventh Man* John Berger writes of the migrant worker:

> The naturalness of his inferior status – the naturalness with which he is accorded his inferiority by people, by institutions, by the everyday

etiquette of the metropolis, by ready-made phrases and arguments – would never be so complete and unhesitating if his function, and the inferior status which it entailed was not new.

He has been here from the beginning.[75]

Migrant labour is still here, it's still highly exploitative and, in the dominant symbolic order, migrant workers are seldom recognised as full human beings. The striking miners massacred at Marikana in 2012 were migrant workers. There is no more dangerous job in South Africa than being a motorcycle delivery driver. A newly arrived driver from Malawi must first save R30 000 to cover the cost of repatriating his body to his family before he can start trying to use his income, such as it is, to build a life. He may face intense xenophobia from within society and from the state, including harassment by corrupt and brutish police officers. The media will generally refer to people like him as 'foreign nationals' irrespective of their citizenship status, and often imply a link between this ascribed identity and criminality.

On a Friday night in the Rosebank Mall in Johannesburg, wealthy young people enjoy the promise of life together. The fact that apartheid would have placed them in different racial categories may lead some to see this reverie in terms of diversity and to celebrate it as a realisation of hopes for a future beyond the strictures of race. But the migrant workers coming in and out of the mall on their motorbikes to collect deliveries from the restaurants are not visible as people. They live radically different lives. The cosmopolitanism of their lives is not celebrated. They can be insulted, fired, injured or robbed without consequence. They are disposable. The mall is always 'milling with invisible survivors'.[76]

To reduce Clegg's work to an anticipation of racial diversity among the middle classes while ignoring its deep empathy for migrant workers in the best work of the Juluka period is a failure to understand its enduring power.

NOTES

1. Johnny Clegg & Savuka, *Asimbonanga* (single, Johannesburg: MINC, 12XMC(P) 4054016, 1986); Johnny Clegg & Savuka, *Heat, Dust and Dreams* (album, Sandton: EMI, EMI – CDEMCJ (WF) 5499, 1993).
2. Chris Webb, 'Apartheid, Anthropology and Johnny Clegg', *Africa Is a Country*, 19 July 2019, accessed 31 March 2025, https://africasacountry.com/2019/07/Apartheid-anthropology-and-johnny-clegg.
3. National Union of Metalworkers, 'Condolences on the Passing of Johnny Clegg', 16 July 2019. The statement is not archived online.
4. A growing body of recent scholarship illuminates and examines the complexities of Zulu identities, a project that is beyond the scope of this chapter. See, for instance, Benedict Carton, John Laband and Jabulani Sithole, eds, *Zulu Identities: Being Zulu, Past and Present* (Pietermaritzburg: University of KwaZulu-Natal Press, 2009); Michael Mahoney, *The Other Zulus: The Spread of Zulu Ethnicity in Colonial South Africa* (Durham, NC: Duke University Press, 2012); Carolyn Hamilton and Nessa Leibhamme, eds, *Tribing and Untribing the Archive: Identity and the Material Record in Southern KwaZulu-Natal in the Late Independent and Colonial Periods* (Pietermaritzburg: University of KwaZulu-Natal Press, 2017); Jochen S. Arndt, *Divided by the Word: Colonial Encounters and the Remaking of Zulu and Xhosa Identities* (Johannesburg: Wits University Press, 2002).
5. Johnny Clegg, *Scatterling of Africa: My Early Years* (Johannesburg: Pan Macmillan, 2021), 83.
6. Kristin Ross, *May '68 and Its Afterlives* (Chicago: University of Chicago Press, 2002), 3.
7. Frantz Fanon, *Black Skin, White Masks*, trans. Charles Lam Markmann (New York: Grove Press, 1967), 41.
8. Alice Cherki quoted in Adam Shatz, *The Rebel's Clinic: The Revolutionary Lives of Frantz Fanon* (New York: Farrar, Straus and Giroux, 2024), 354.
9. See Zamalotshwa Sefatsa, *Paulo Freire and Popular Struggle in South Africa* (Johannesburg: Tricontinental Institute for Social Research, 2020), accessed 31 March 2025, https://thetricontinental.org/dossier-34-paulo-freire-and-south-africa/; Richard Pithouse, *The 1972 Durban Strikes: Building Popular Democratic Power in South Africa*, (Johannesburg: Tricontinental Institute for Social Research, 2023), accessed 31 March 2025, https://thetricontinental.org/dossier-1973-durban-strikes/.
10. Frantz Fanon, *The Wretched of the Earth*, trans. Constance Farrington (London: Penguin, 1976), 114; Paulo Freire, *Pedagogy of the Oppressed*, trans. Myra Bergman Ramos (London: Penguin, 1993), 26.
11. Steven Friedman, interview with the author, 25 January 2024.
12. Jonathan and Sipho, *Sengikhumbula Emakhabe Leni/Baba Ungadlali Ngomama* (single, Johannesburg: Jamloti, JM-119, 1976).
13. Jonathan Clegg & Sipho Mchunu, *Uthi Angizule/Silinde* (single, Johannesburg: Jamloti, JM – 100, 1976).
14. Jonathan and Sipho, *Woza Friday/Omam Basemhlabeni* (single, Johannesburg: Jamloti, JM–139, 1977); Jonathan and Sipho, *Ngasala Obala/Bangake Nani?* (single, Johannesburg: Jamloti, JM – 140, 1977).
15. Paul Clingman, *Father to the Child* (album, Johannesburg: Stanyan Africa, 3 EE 7000, 1977).

16 Jonathan Clegg & Sipho Mchunu, 'Ngwaka Nyambe Nkonyane', on Jonathan Clegg & Sipho Mchunu and Ladysmith Black Mambazo, *South Africa: Cologne Zulu Festival* (album, Frankfurt: Network Medien, 54.036, 1992).
17 Hilton Rosenthal, interview with the author, 2000.
18 Juluka, *Universal Men* (album, Johannesburg: Gramophone Records Co./CBS Records, CBS – DNW 2429, 1979); Juluka, *African Litany* (album, Johannesburg: MINC, MINC – (L) 1020, 1981).
19 The recording is available in the Hidden Years Archive, Stellenbosch University, catalogued as 'Hymap-dm-reel-clegg-mchunu-1978-001'.
20 Johnny Clegg & Savuka, *Asimbonanga*.
21 Rosenthal, interview with the author, 2000.
22 Johnny Clegg, interview with the author, 2000. This interview was one of two held with Clegg by the author, the second taking place some years after the first. The exact dates were not recorded.
23 Bruce Springsteen's turn to a focus on migrants in his 1995 album *The Ghost of Tom Joad* resonates with *Universal Men* in some ways (Bruce Springsteen, *The Ghost of Tom Joad* [album, New York: Columbia, C 67484, 1995]). He returned to this theme ten years later on the track 'Matamoros Banks' on the album *Devils and Dust* (Los Angeles: Columbia, CSK 55416, 2005), in which a migrant drowns in the Rio Grande: 'Over rivers of stone and ancient ocean beds / I walk on sandals of twine and tire tread / My pockets full of dust, my mouth filled with cool stone / The pale moon opens the earth to its bones'.
24 The reference is to a line from the poem 'The Watersong Ends': 'reaching the other shore of the sea which has no other shore' (Pablo Neruda, 'The Watersong Ends', in *Selected Poems* [London: Penguin, 1974)], 233–236). Clegg's line is 'Sailing for that shore which has no other shore'. It is important to understand that it only became widely known in 2010 that Neruda had raped a domestic worker in what is now Sri Lanka.
25 All lyrics in this chapter have been transcribed by the author.
26 University of the Witwatersrand, 'Johnny Clegg' [Citation for the Award of an Honorary Doctorate, 2007], accessed 31 March 2025, https://www.wits.ac.za/alumni/distinguished-graduates/honorary-degree-citations/johnny-clegg/.
27 Alain Badiou, *The Age of the Poets and Other Writings on Twentieth-Century Poetry and Prose* (London: Verso, 2014), 6.
28 Clegg, interview with the author, 2000; John Berger and Jean Mohr, *A Seventh Man* (London: Pelican Press, 1975).
29 Juluka, *Universal Men*.
30 Clegg, interview with the author, 2000.
31 Juluka, 'Old Eyes', on *Universal Men*.
32 Clegg, interview with the author, 2000.
33 Various Artists, *Rhythm of Resistance – Music of Black South Africa* (album, London: Virgin, V2113, 1979).
34 Berger and Mohr, *A Seventh Man*, 86.
35 Berger and Mohr, *A Seventh Man*, 145.
36 Juluka, 'Sky People', on *Universal Men*.
37 Juluka, 'African Sky Blue', on *African Litany*. The lyrics appear in the liner notes for the album.
38 Juluka, 'High Country', on *African Litany*.
39 Juluka, *Ubuhle Bemvelo* (album, Johannesburg: MINC, MINC – (E) 1030, 1981).
40 Juluka, 'Woza Friday', on *Ubuhle Bemvelo*.

41 Tracy Chapman, 'Fast Car', on *Tracy Chapman* (album, New York: Elektra, 9 60774-2, 1988); Bruce Springsteen, 'Factory', on *Darkness on the Edge of Town* (album, New York: Columbia, JC 35318, 1978).
42 Juluka, *Scatterlings* (album, Johannesburg: MINC, MINC – (L) 1040, 1982).
43 Johnny Clegg, 'Juluka Iyajuluka: Interview with Johnny Clegg', *MEDU Art Ensemble*, National English Literary Museum, 1983.
44 Juluka. *Impi* (single, London: Safari Records, ZULU 3, 1983).
45 Juluka, 'iJwanasibeki', on *Scatterlings*.
46 Juluka, 'Digging for Some Words', on *Scatterlings*.
47 Richard Harrington, 'Johnny Clegg's Two Cultures: Breaking Barriers with the Zulu Sound of Savuka', *The Washington Post*, 30 August 1988, accessed 31 March 2025, https://www.washingtonpost.com/archive/lifestyle/1988/08/30/johnny-cleggs-two-cultures/be413c35-b118-4322-858e-28f8988d330d/.
48 Juluka, *Work for All* (album, Johannesburg: MINC, MINC – (L) 1070, 1983).
49 Hilton Rosenthal, interview with the author, 19 January 2025.
50 Sipho Mchunu, interview with the author, 20 January 2025.
51 Juluka, 'Baba Nango', on *Work for All*. '*Halala*' is a shout of celebration.
52 Juluka, 'Gunship Ghetto', on *Work for All*.
53 Juluka, 'Mana Lapho', on *Work for All*.
54 Juluka, 'Work for All', on *Work for All*.
55 Juluka, 'Mdantsane', on *Work for All*.
56 Neruda, 'I'm Explaining a Few Things', in *Selected Poems*, 104–105.
57 Juluka, *Stand Your Ground* (album, Burbank: Warner Bros Records – 925 155-1, 1984).
58 Juluka, *The International Tracks* (album, Johannesburg: MINC, MINC(O) – 1098, 1984).
59 Juluka, *Musa Ukungilandela* (album, Johannesburg: MINC, MINC(E) 1100, 1984).
60 Mchunu, interview with the author, 2025.
61 Artists United Against Apartheid, *Sun City* (single, New York: Manhattan Records, V-56013, 1985); Rosenthal, interview with the author, 2025. Rosenthal recalls that Van Zandt met Clegg in New York to discuss the idea of what became Artists United Against Apartheid. They began the evening at a Linton Kwesi Johnson performance at Columbia University before moving on to an Ethiopian Restaurant.
62 Juluka, 'Akanaki Nokunaka', on *Musa Ukungilandela*.
63 Mchunu, interview with the author, 2025.
64 Johnny Clegg, *Third World Child* (album, Johannesburg: MINC, MINC (L) – 1140, 1985).
65 Juluka, *Juluka Live (The Good Hope Concerts)* (album, Johannesburg: MINC, MINC (V) – 4051 1481, 1986); Johnny Clegg & Savuka, *Third World Child* (album, Sandton: EMI, EMCJ (D) – 2407331, 1987).
66 Sipho Mchunu Nama Bhubesi, *Yithi Esavimba* (album, Paris: Totem Records, TOT 760 183, 1989).
67 Sipho Mchunu, *Umhlaba Uzobuya* (album, Durban: 3rd Ear Music, TEAG 3309, 1990); Sipho Mchunu, *Iselula* (album, London: FoundDigitalEntertainment, 859749554462, 2021).
68 Sipho Mchunu, 'Umhlaba Uzobuya' on *Umhlaba Uzobuya*.
69 Johnny Clegg & Savuka, 'One (Hu)'Man One Vote', on *Cruel Crazy Beautiful World* (album, Sandton: EMI, EMCJ (E) – 7934461, 1989).
70 Johnny Clegg & Savuka, *Heat, Dust and Dreams*.

71 Johnny Clegg & Savuka, 'These Days', on *Heat, Dust and Dreams*.
72 Johnny Clegg & Savuka, 'Foreign Nights (Working Dog in Babylon)', on *Heat, Dust and Dreams*.
73 Juluka, *Ya Vuka Inkunzi (The Bull Has Risen)* (album, Sandton: The CCP Record Company, CCCCP (WL) 1127, 1997); Johnny Clegg, *New World Survivor* (album, Pretoria: Value Music, CDVM (WFL) 45, 2002); Johnny Clegg, *One Life* (album, Johannesburg: Sting Music, STIDCD 106, 2006); Johnny Clegg, *Human* (album, Paris: EMI Music France, 5099991791320, 2010); Johnny Clegg, *King of Time* (album, Johannesburg: Universal Music, UMGCD 145, 2017).
74 Johnny Clegg, *My Favourite Zulu Street Guitar Songs* (DVD, Sydney: Scatterlings Pty Ltd and Rhythm Dog Music, 2010).
75 Berger and Mohr, *A Seventh Man*, 113.
76 Berger and Mohr, *A Seventh Man*, 86.

REFERENCES

Arndt, Jochen. *Divided by the Word: Colonial Encounters and the Remaking of Zulu and Xhosa Identities*. Johannesburg: Wits University Press, 2002.

Badiou, Alain. *The Age of the Poets: And Other Writings on Twentieth-Century Poetry and Prose*. London: Verso, 2014.

Berger, John and Jean Mohr. *A Seventh Man*. London: Pelican Press, 1975.

Carton, Benedict, John Laband and Jabulani Sithole, eds. *Zulu Identities: Being Zulu, Past and Present*. Pietermaritzburg: University of KwaZulu-Natal Press, 2009.

Clegg, Johnny. 'Juluka Iyajuluka: Interview with Johnny Clegg'. *MEDU Art Ensemble*, National English Literary Museum, 1983.

Clegg, Johnny. *Scatterling of Africa: My Early Years*. Johannesburg: Pan Macmillan, 2021.

Fanon, Frantz. *Black Skin, White Masks*. Translated by Charles Lam Markmann. New York: Grove Press, 1967.

Fanon, Frantz. *The Wretched of the Earth*. Translated by Constance Farrington. London: Penguin, 1976.

Freire, Paulo. *Pedagogy of the Oppressed*. Translated by Myra Bergman Ramos. London: Penguin, 1993.

Hamilton, Carolyn and Nessa Leibhammer, eds. *Tribing and Untribing the Archive: Identity and the Material Record in Southern KwaZulu-Natal in the Late Independent and Colonial Periods*. Pietermaritzburg: University of KwaZulu-Natal Press, 2017.

Harrington, Richard. 'Johnny Clegg's Two Cultures: Breaking Barriers with the Zulu Sound of Savuka'. *The Washington Post*, 30 August 1988. Accessed 31 March 2025. https://www.washingtonpost.com/archive/lifestyle/1988/08/30/johnny-cleggs-two-cultures/be413c35-b118-4322-858e-28f8988d330d/.

Mahoney, Michael. *The Other Zulus: The Spread of Zulu Ethnicity in Colonial South Africa*. Durham, NC: Duke University Press, 2012.

National Union of Metalworkers, 'Condolences on the Passing of Johnny Clegg', 16 July 2019.

Neruda, Pablo. 'The Watersong Ends'. In *Selected Poems*, 233–236. London: Penguin, 1974.

Pithouse, Richard. *The 1972 Durban Strikes: Building Popular Democratic Power in South Africa*. Johannesburg: Tricontinental Institute for Social Research, 2023. Accessed 31 March 2025. https://thetricontinental.org/dossier-1973-durban-strikes/.

Ross, Kristin. *May '68 and Its Afterlives*. Chicago: University of Chicago Press, 2002.

Sefatsa, Zamalotshwa. *Paulo Freire and Popular Struggle in South Africa*. Johannesburg: Tricontinental Institute for Social Research, 2020. Accessed 31 March 2025. https://thetricontinental.org/dossier-34-paulo-freire-and-south-africa/.
Shatz, Adam. *The Rebel's Clinic: The Revolutionary Lives of Frantz Fanon*. New York: Farrar, Straus and Giroux, 2024.
University of the Witwatersrand. 'Johnny Clegg' [Citation for the Award of an Honorary Doctorate, 2007]. Accessed 31 March 2025. https://www.wits.ac.za/alumni/distinguished-graduates/honorary-degree-citations/johnny-clegg/.
Webb, Chris. 2019. 'Apartheid, Anthropology and Johnny Clegg'. *Africa Is a Country*. Accessed 31 March 2025. https://africasacountry.com/2019/07/Apartheid-anthropology-and-johnny-clegg.

DISCOGRAPHY

Artists United Against Apartheid. *Sun City*. Single. New York: Manhattan Records, V-56013, 1985.
Chapman, Tracy. *Tracy Chapman*. Album. New York: Elektra, 9 60774-2, 1988.
Clegg, Johnny. *Human*. Album. Paris: EMI Music France, 509999179132 0, 2010.
Clegg, Johnny. *King of Time*. Album. Johannesburg: Universal Music, UMGCD 145, 2017.
Clegg, Johnny. *My Favourite Zulu Street Guitar Songs*. DVD. Sydney: Scatterlings Pty Ltd and Rhythm Dog Music, 2010.
Clegg, Johnny. *New World Survivor*. Album. Pretoria: Value Music, CDVM (WFL) 45, 2002.
Clegg, Johnny. *One Life*. Johannesburg: Sting Music, STIDCD 106, 2006.
Clegg, Johnny. *Third World Child*. Album. Johannesburg: MINC, MINC (L) – 1140, 1985.
Clingman, Paul. *Father to the Child*. Album. Johannesburg: Stanyan Africa, 3 EE 7000, 1977.
Johnny Clegg & Savuka. *Asimbonanga*. Single. Johannesburg: MINC, 12XMC(P) 4054016, 1986.
Johnny Clegg & Savuka. *Cruel, Crazy, Beautiful World*. Album. Sandton: EMI, EMCJ (E) – 7934461, 1989.
Johnny Clegg & Savuka. *Heat, Dust and Dreams*. Album. Sandton: EMI, EMI – CDEMCJ (WF) 5499, 1993.
Johnny Clegg & Savuka. *Third World Child*. Album. Sandton: EMI, EMCJ (D) – 2407331, 1987.
Johnny Clegg & Sipho Mchunu and Ladysmith Black Mambazo. *South Africa: Cologne Zulu Festival*. Frankfurt: Network Medien – 54.036, 1992.
Jonathan and Sipho. *Ngasala Obala/Bangake Nani?* Single. Johannesburg: Jamloti, JM – 140, 1976.
Jonathan and Sipho. *Sengikhumbula Emakhabe Leni/Baba Ungadlali Ngomama*. Single. Johannesburg: Jamloti, JM-119, 1976.
Jonathan and Sipho. *Woza Friday/Omama baseMhlabeni*. Single. Johannesburg: Jamloti, JM – 139, 1977.
Jonathan Clegg & Sipho Mchunu. *Uthi Angizule/Silinde*. Single. Johannesburg: Jamloti, JM – 100, 1976.
Juluka. *African Litany*. Album. Johannesburg: MINC, MINC – (L) 1020, 1981.
Juluka. *Impi*. Single. London: Safari Records, ZULU 3, 1983.
Juluka. *The International Tracks*. Album. Johannesburg: MINC, MINC(O) 1098, 1984.
Juluka. *Juluka Live (The Good Hope Concerts)*. Album. Johannesburg: MINC, MINC (V) – 4051 1481, 1986.
Juluka. *Musa Ukungilandela*. Album. Johannesburg: MINC, MINC(E) 1100, 1984.

Juluka. *Scatterlings*. Album. Johannesburg: MINC, MINC – (L) 1040, 1982.
Juluka. *Stand Your Ground*. Album. Burbank: Warner Bros Records, 925 155-1, 1984.
Juluka. *Ubuhle Bemvelo*. Album. Johannesburg: MINC, MINC – (E) 1030, 1982.
Juluka. *Universal Men*. Album. Johannesburg: Gramophone Records Co./CBS Records, CBS – DNW 2429, 1979.
Juluka. *Work For All*. Album. Johannesburg: MINC, MINC – (L) 1070, 1983.
Juluka. *Ya Vuka Inkunzi (The Bull Has Risen)*. Album. Sandton: The CCP Record Company, CDCCP (WL) 1127, 1997.
Mchunu, Sipho. *Iselula*. Album. London: FoundDigitalEntertainment, 859749554462, 2021.
Mchunu, Sipho. *Umhlaba Uzobuya*. Album. Durban: 3rd Ear Music, TEAG 3309, 1990.
Mchunu, Sipho Nama Bhubesi. *Yithi Esavimba*. Album. Paris: Totem Records, TOT 760 183, 1989.
Springsteen, Bruce. *Darkness on the Edge of Town*. Album. New York: Columbia, JC 35318, 1978.
Springsteen, Bruce. *Devils and Dust*. Album Los Angeles: Columbia, CSK 55416, 2005.
Springsteen, Bruce. *The Ghost of Tom Joad*. Album. New York: Columbia, C 67484, 1995.
Various Artists. *Rhythm of Resistance – Music of Black South Africa*. Album. London: Virgin, V2113, 1979.

CHAPTER
6

The Praise Names of Johnny Clegg

Sipho Mchunu and Andrew Grant Innes

Zulu oral traditions are part of the oral traditions of the wider South African Nguni language group (isiXhosa, isiZulu, siSwati and isiNdebele). As Nguni societies did not originally have a literary tradition, oral histories and poems would carry the memories of historical events (*amabali* or *amahubo*) and of people (*izibongo*).[1]

In Zulu culture, praise names relating to people are accorded to clans (*izithakazelo*), royalty (*izibongo zamakhosi*), famous or notable people (*izibongo zabantu abakhulu abagqamile*) and ordinary individuals (*izihasho*).[2] The English translation 'praise names' for the isiZulu '*izibongo*' is somewhat misleading. Praise names in isiZulu can be flattering when used for clans and for royalty. These names are not always flattering when composed for individuals. IsiZulu *izibongo* are short life descriptions that refer to both individual achievements or characteristics and to individual failings or shortcomings. They are often composed by the *izimbongi* (composer/s of the praise name) in a humorous way, using simile and metaphor to allude to or to describe starkly the victories, defeats and peculiarities of an individual.[3] In the oral tradition these names are spoken records of events that stand out in the course of the person's life, giving the listener an understanding of aspects of the person.

Figure 6.1: The authors together with Bafazana Qoma (left) and Charlie Mzila (right) at the launch of Johnny Clegg's book, *Scatterling of Africa: My Early Years*, Johannesburg, 29 September 2021. Photograph © Andrew Innes 2024.

This chapter records the praise names of Johnny Clegg, and provides translations of the names and some insight into events and people referenced in these names that describe Clegg's formative experiences with Zulu culture.

Clegg had two sets of praise names – given to him by people from the areas of Msinga and KwaZulu.[4] He had also originally been given the isiZulu nickname *Madlebe* ('big ears') by Charlie Mzila, his first Zulu guitar teacher and mentor (see figure 6.1), before he received a full set of praise names. The Msinga *izibongo* are based on the original KwaZulu names with a few short additions and small changes. Co-author of this chapter Sipho Mchunu composed Clegg's KwaZulu praise names around the time he was 18 years old, and we will explain them here.

Here are the original KwaZulu praise names:

> *Skeyi jikel'eshobeni, wamudl'umuntu okuphekela, izinduku zehla kabi, zehla ngoRissiki. Kwaze kwadumala umnumzane uMalevu eWemmer hostela. uMalevu waze wabuza ukuthi angikaze ngibone into enje – umlungu odluphuthu nabantu bakhe. Indoda yabaleka nochekazi kanti iphethe odabulanzwane.*

Skeyi⁵ jikel'eshobeni ('The yoke pin spinning on the tail'): The yoke pin harnessing two oxen which broke free and spun on the tails of the oxen.

Wamudla umuntu okuphekela ('You ate a person who cooked for you'): This is an allusion to a romantic liaison Johnny had with a waitron in his younger days.

Izinduku zehla kabi, zehla ngoRissiki ('The *indukus* [Zulu fighting sticks] came down hard, they came down on Rissik Street'): When Johnny was learning Zulu dance styles at Wemmer hostel, he was walking down Rissik Street in Johannesburg with a Zulu dance team. Another (opposing) dance team came down the same street and a physical confrontation happened between the two teams. They fought with Zulu traditional weapons. Johnny was around 17 years old at the time. He describes the area where the incident took place in detail in chapter 12 of his biography.[6]

Kwaze kwadumala umnumzane uMalevu eWemmer hostela ('Mr Malevu was disappointed at Wemmer hostel'): Mr Malevu ran security at the Wemmer hostel, a large property with shared lodgings for migrant labourers in Johannesburg. This reference provides a hint relating to the stories of young Johnny entering the hostel with co-author Mchunu – a more detailed account of these events is described later in this chapter.[7]

uMalevu waze wabuza ukuthi 'angikaze ngibone into enje' – umlungu odluphuthu nabantu bakhe ('Malevu even said [lit. 'asked'] he had never seen something like this – a white person eating *phuthu* [a maize porridge staple food] with his [black] people'): This was unusual as, during the apartheid era, any form of socialising between white and black South Africans was frowned upon and attracted unwanted attention from the authorities.[8]

Indoda yabaleka nochekazi kanti iphethe odabulanzwane ('The man ran away with a Checkers packet containing his dancing sandals'): This line refers again to the clash between the two dance teams, describing young Johnny fleeing the fight. He ran away carrying his pair of *imbadada* dancing sandals in a yellow plastic bag from Checkers, a South African supermarket chain.

Co-author Andrew Grant Innes recalls Clegg's explanation of these praise names during the *South African Story* shows at the Nelson Mandela Theatre in Johannesburg, in 2003: Clegg related that when a Zulu *giya*s (dances at a traditional gathering or dance competition), people will call the dancer's praise names to encourage them in their performance (*ukukhuza*).[9] This performance is similar to the *kata* in karate, where the performer displays their combat prowess and strength to impress the crowd and outdo other performers.[10] No matter how much effort and vigour Clegg put into his performances, at the end of his *giya* people would yell with delight '*wabaleka nochekazi!*' ('he ran away with a Checkers packet!'). As Elizabeth Gunner has noted, the performer is 'helpless to prevent others from [composing praise names] ... commenting upon features which catch their attention and excite their admiration, amusement or distaste'.[11]

Clegg's modified and extended Msinga praise names (with additional content added by Dudu Ndlovu underlined) were as follows:

> *Skeyi jikel'eshobeni, wamudla umuntu <u>owadla umuntu emephekela</u>. Skeyi <u>uNomawisa</u> umuntu wabaleka nochekazi wehla ngoRissiki wabuyela khona eWemmer hostela izinduku <u>zikhala ubufahlafahla</u> eWemmer. <u>Bayakuzonda abelungu, bayakuzonda eflateni, bayakuzonda eKillarney, uyakuzonda ukhetheka. Abafuni</u> umlungu odluphuthu nabantu bakhe <u>eflateni. Thatha!</u> Wabaleka nochekazi!*[12]

Skeyi jikel'eshobeni ('The yoke peg spinning on the tail').

Wamudla umuntu owadla umuntu emephekela ('He ate a person who ate a person who cooked for him').[13]

Skeyi uNomawisa umuntu wabaleka nochekazi wehla ngoRissiki wabuyela khona eWemmer hostela ('Skeyi stumbled about and ran away down Rissik Street with his Checkers packet back to Wemmer hostel').

iZinduku zikhala ubufahlafahla eWemmer ('The fighting sticks made a clacking sound at Wemmer').[14]

> *Bayakuzonda abelungu, bayakuzonda eflateni, bayakuzonda eKillarney, uyakuzonda ukhetheka* ('The white people hate you, they hate you in the apartments, they hate you in Killarney, the caretaker hates you'):[15] The hatred described is a source of pride, as Clegg's unpopularity with his white peers in the suburbs and with figures of authority related to his continued association with black South Africans under apartheid.
>
> *Abafuni umlungu odluphuthu nabantu bakhe eflateni* ('They don't want a white person eating *phuthu* with his people in the apartment'): This line similarly relates to Clegg's adoption of African customs and practices.
>
> *Thatha! Wabaleka nochekazi!* ('Take it away! He ran away with a Checkers packet!')

As mentioned above, the references to Mr Malevu in the KwaZulu praise names relate to Clegg's first experiences at Wemmer hostel after he met Mchunu, as Mr Malevu was in charge of security at Wemmer. Mchunu recalled these events in an interview with Andrew Grant Innes:[16]

> The first time Johnny and I went to Wemmer together, Johnny rode his bicycle. I couldn't ride a bike, so I told Johnny I'd follow behind him on foot. I grew up in the rural areas and never learned to ride a bike. I had learned how to ride a donkey. So we arrived quite late at Wemmer hostel [travelling like this].
>
> When we arrived there, Malevu said 'where are you taking this one?'
>
> I said 'this is my friend, we are going to dance with him'.
>
> Malevu said 'white people can't enter the hostel'. I begged him to let us in, but he said 'no way – the white guy isn't coming in'.
>
> I asked Johnny to just step back and wait a little because Malevu and I wanted to talk. I said to him 'Mr Malevu, I'm asking you to help us. I want to enter with my friend'. I had noticed that Malevu had a half-jack [375 ml bottle] of Viceroy brandy and I glanced at it.

He said, 'I drink this,' and I replied, 'I would like to ask if perhaps I could buy you another one?' There was a bottle store outside the hostel, so Johnny and I went there and bought a bottle of the brandy. We hid it in my jacket and returned to the gate where we quietly handed it to Malevu.

Johnny said to me, 'wow you are very clever, mate!'

After we had given Malevu his brandy he said 'okay ... take your white guy in, but don't take a long time. I will give you just a short time for your white guy to be here'. He opened the gate and Johnny and I entered. Inside the hostel I introduced Johnny to Zwane, the leader of the dance team at Wemmer, explaining that my friend wanted to dance there. We danced for around twenty to thirty minutes then we left. Those people at the hostel were so happy when they saw Johnny dancing with the team.

I had already taught Johnny a little bit of Zulu dancing. Johnny learned to dance *isiBhaca* with Charlie Mzila.[17] I taught him lots of Zulu guitar and some Zulu dances. There are many different Zulu dance styles. There is *Mzansi*, there is *Bhaca*, there is *Shameni*. Johnny learned *Bhaca* first and then later learned *Mzansi* with Dudu Ndlovu. But Dudu didn't specifically teach him. Johnny followed the movements of the style because he was already accustomed to the way Zulu dance works. I had taught him already at my home in Makhabeleni. I took him through all the *Shameni* dances. There he learned *Shameni* and some *Mzansi*. The style that he struggled with was *isiKhomazi*. He eventually didn't learn it. He loved it, but it was beyond his ability to learn the style fluently.

So at the hostel in Wemmer, my friend Malevu had completely changed his tune. He was always asking, 'when are you coming with your white guy?' I'd say, 'oh we'll come don't worry' and he would check that we would bring the brandy along for him. I told Johnny that we would have an easy time of it accessing the Wemmer hostel from then on. We just had to buy Malevu a bottle of Viceroy, which we did regularly. After some time had passed, Malevu said to me one day, 'hey boy – you don't have to buy this any more – I like this white guy and he is amazing me with his progress'.

From then on Clegg had free access to come and go at Wemmer hostel to join the dance teams in the practices and performances. His attendance at hostel dance events continued long after Wemmer hostel closed in 1978; he went to Jeppe and George Goch hostels frequently in later years to dance or spectate.[18] On the 'Final Journey Tour', during the South African legs many of the sons of the dancers from Wemmer hostel came to perform on stage with him, culminating in the final Johannesburg show at the Northgate Dome in November of 2017 when more than 30 Zulu dancers performed together on the night.

These praise names describe the formative period in Clegg's life that forged his Zulu identity and locked his future to Zulu music and culture. His years spent visiting the hostels learning Zulu dance styles, and the revelations they brought to him, are described in his biography as 'pivotal' (figure 6.1).[19] The rhythms of the *Mzansi* and *Shameni* dance drums can be heard in the hit songs that followed – '*Impi*' ('War'), 'African Sky Blue', 'I Call Your Name' and 'Scatterlings of Africa' are good examples of this.[20]

Clegg's praise names (the full set and the shortened 'Skeyi') were used throughout his life by those close to him. At his wedding, at Zulu dance gatherings, at traditional celebrations at the homes of his friends in the Zulu areas, he would be announced with the full set of names. Of course, whenever he participated in dances at the hostels and elsewhere, the final call of '*wabaleka nochekazi!*' would ring in his ears. It is fitting that these words were spoken at his graveside on the day of his funeral, by his old friend.

ACKNOWLEDGEMENTS

The authors thank Zinhle Ndaba for assistance with translations.

NOTES

1. Jeff Opland, *Xhosa Literature: Spoken and Written Words*, Publications of the Opland Collection of Xhosa Literature, vol. 6 (Pietermaritzburg: University of KwaZulu-Natal Press, 2018), 3–5; Ntokozo Madlala, '*Kwasukasukela*: A Practical Exploration of the Impact of Nguni Oral Storytelling Traditions on Contemporary Physical Forms of Storytelling for Theatre' (MA thesis, University of Cape Town, 2001), 3.
2. Noleen Turner, 'A Brief Overview of Zulu Oral Traditions', *Alternation* 1, no. 1 (1994): 59, https://doi.org/10.10520/AJA10231757_140.
3. See for example Turner, 'Zulu Oral Traditions', 61–62.
4. Bafazana Qoma, interview with the authors, 23 November 2023.
5. Literally '*isikeyi*, peg through the yoke [of oxen]', Clement Martyn Doke et al., eds, *English–Zulu, Zulu–English Dictionary*, 1st combined edition (Johannesburg: Witwatersrand University Press, 1990), 372.
6. Johnny Clegg, *Scatterling of Africa: My Early Years* (Johannesburg: Pan MacMillan, 2021), 121.
7. See also Clegg, *Scatterling*, 143–144 for a description of Malevu.
8. See Clegg, *Scatterling*, 127.
9. A recording of this show is available: Johnny Clegg. *A South African Story – Live At The Nelson Mandela Theatre* (album, Johannesburg: EMI, CDEMM (WI), 2003).
10. Clegg learned Shotokan karate as a child.
11. Elizabeth Anne Wynne Gunner, '*Ukubonga Nezibongo*: Zulu Praising and Praises' (PhD thesis, University of London, 1984), 63.
12. Confirmed and transcribed in the interview with Qoma by the authors, 23 November 2023.
13. This also relates to the romantic liaison previously mentioned, but none of the people interviewed are able to satisfactorily explain this addition.
14. '*Ubufahlafahla*' is an onomatopoeic word describing the sound of the sticks connecting.
15. '*Ukhetheka*' is a phonetic adaptation of the English word 'caretaker'.
16. Sipho Mchunu, interview with Andrew Grant Innes, 28 November 2023. Translation by Innes and Zinhle Ndaba.
17. *isiBhaca* is a style of dance from kwaBhaca (formerly Mount Frere).
18. Clegg, *Scatterling*, 121.
19. Clegg, *Scatterling*, 113–114.
20. Juluka, '*Impi*', on *African Litany* (album, Johannesburg: MINC, MINC – (L) 1020, 1981); Juluka, 'African Sky Blue', on *African Litany*; Johnny Clegg & Savuka, 'I Call Your Name', on *Shadow Man* (album, Sandton: EMI, EMCJ (D) – 7904111, 1988); Juluka, 'Scatterlings of Africa', on *Scatterlings* (album, Johannesburg: MINC, MINC – (L) 1040, 1982).

REFERENCES

Clegg, Johnny. *Scatterling of Africa: My Early Years*. Johannesburg: Pan Macmillan, 2021.
Doke, Clement Martyn, D.M. Malcolm, J.M.A. Sikakana and B.W. Vilakazi, eds. *English–Zulu, Zulu–English Dictionary*. 1st combined edition. Johannesburg: Witwatersrand University Press, 1990.
Gunner, Elizabeth Anne Wynne. '*Ukubonga Nezibongo*: Zulu Praising and Praises'. PhD thesis, University of London, 1984.

Madlala, Ntokozo. '*Kwasukasukela*: A Practical Exploration of the Impact of Nguni Oral Storytelling Traditions on Contemporary Physical Forms of Storytelling for Theatre'. MA thesis, University of Cape Town, 2001.

Opland, Jeff. *Xhosa Literature: Spoken and Written Words*. Publications of the Opland Collection of Xhosa Literature, vol. 6. Pietermaritzburg: University of KwaZulu-Natal Press, 2018.

Turner, Noleen. 'A Brief Overview of Zulu Oral Traditions'. *Alternation* 1, no. 1 (1994): 58–67. https://doi.org/10.10520/AJA10231757_140.

DISCOGRAPHY

Clegg, Johnny. *A South African Story – Live At The Nelson Mandela Theatre*. Album. Johannesburg: EMI, CDEMM (WI), 2003.

Johnny Clegg & Savuka. *Shadow Man*. Album. Sandton: EMI, EMCJ (D) – 7904111, 1988.

Juluka. *African Litany*. Album. Johannesburg: MINC, MINC – (L) 1020, 1981.

Juluka. *Scatterlings*. Album. Johannesburg: MINC, MINC – (L) 1040, 1982.

PART 2: GLOBAL RECEPTION

CHAPTER

7

Johnny Clegg and the Cultural Boycott in the United Kingdom

Michael Drewett

Johnny Clegg, as a South African musician born in the United Kingdom (UK), and with dual South African and British citizenship, was integrally caught up in the politics of the cultural boycott. Clegg's band Juluka began to break into the British market in 1983, and in promoting their music through radio and television appearances Clegg confronted the British Musicians' Union (BMU) stance on the cultural boycott. Although Clegg lived and performed in South Africa and merely wanted to tour the UK, the BMU regarded him as breaking the cultural boycott by performing both in South Africa and in the UK. This chapter documents Clegg's attempts to navigate the cultural boycott in the UK, particularly focusing on his confrontations with the BMU on his first trip to the UK with Juluka in 1983, and his confrontation with the British Anti-Apartheid Movement (AAM) leading up to Savuka's exclusion from the Nelson Mandela birthday tribute concert in 1988. Clegg reluctantly accepted the impact of the cultural boycott on his career, but resisted it as far as he could, given his belief in an engaged cultural struggle in which he and his accompanying musicians could freely interact with audiences around the world.

THE CULTURAL BOYCOTT

In October 1954 the seeds of a cultural boycott against apartheid South Africa were sown when British-born Father Trevor Huddleston, an anti-apartheid activist, on returning from a stint in South Africa pleaded for a cultural boycott of the country.[1] He urged 'those who believe racialism to be sinful or wrong ... to refuse to encourage it by accepting any engagement to act, to perform as a musical artist or as a ballet dancer – in short, to engage in any contracts which would provide entertainment for any one section of the community'.[2] In 1957, more than two years before the AAM was established 'and four years ahead of formal opposition to apartheid by the United Nations General Assembly and the International Labour Organization',[3] the BMU passed a resolution expressing 'concern at the apartheid policy of the South African government' and this was followed by an executive committee instruction for members not to perform in South Africa.[4] In April 1960 the British AAM was founded and added its backing to strategies such as the cultural boycott to undermine apartheid.[5] The boycott strategy gained momentum when, in December 1968, the United Nations (UN) General Assembly adopted Resolution 2396, according to which all states and organisations were requested to 'suspend cultural, educational, sporting and other exchanges with the racist regime and with organisations or institutions in South Africa which practice apartheid'.[6] The next significant step came in December 1980 when a 'Register of Artists, Actors and Others who have performed in South Africa' was established (in terms of UN General Assembly Resolution 35/206E).[7] This register was effectively a blacklist of foreign artists who had performed in South Africa. In the UK, being blacklisted by the UN could lead to BMU-imposed penalties, including expulsion, and being barred from television appearances. Furthermore, the British AAM regularly organised pickets at venues where boycott-busters were performing.[8] Although the AAM could not prohibit such performances, it made a concerted effort to shame the musicians and draw attention to their boycott-breaking actions. By 1985 there were more than 500 entertainers' names on the blacklist, and more than 50 whose names had been removed after they apologised and undertook not to perform in apartheid South Africa again.[9] Different organisations instituted aspects of the boycott in various ways. For example, independent record company Rough Trade refused to grant distribution rights in South Africa for any of its recordings.[10]

The effects of the cultural boycott on South African musicians hoping to perform outside of the country varied. During the 1970s several countries, including Japan and the Netherlands, either stopped issuing visas to South African musicians who were based in South Africa or tightened up criteria for performing in their countries. In the UK, the Thatcher government was strongly opposed to sanctions against South Africa, including the cultural boycott.[11] Consequently the Tory government did not prohibit visas being granted to South African musicians wanting to perform in the UK, and the BMU did not control who could perform at venues throughout the UK; but, according to John Williamson, 'for television there was effectively a closed shop – so visiting musicians would have to be a union member either in the UK or with some sort of union brokered exemptions/exchanges with other countries'.[12]

In addition, the AAM placed strict restrictions on both British and overseas musicians who were invited to perform at events that they were sponsoring, including barring blacklisted musicians from performing.[13] While British record companies could technically license South African music and release it in the UK, they were hesitant to do so if the band concerned was all-white. Renee Veldsman of the band Via Afrika related how record companies would tell them: '"This is great, but we can't actually help you because of the policy of your country, you could wait," … but our record company couldn't help us and, well, nobody could help us at that point. So that's actually why Via Afrika dissolved really, because we wanted to push forward, but we did hit walls all the time'.[14] Tom Fox of Afro-rock band Bright Blue said that they didn't even try to release their music overseas and tour there. He explained that he thought 'the record companies at that point would occasionally speak to somebody overseas but they were treated like lepers. So there just really wasn't a chance'.[15] Some black South Africans did release their music in the UK, in other European countries and in the United States of America. Richard Jon Smith and Jonathan

Butler both charted in the UK top 100 singles in the 1980s, and some Shifty Records releases were licensed in the UK or the USA through the record companies Earthworks (UK) and Rounder Records (USA).

The way the cultural boycott was implemented by the BMU and AAM constituted censorship, albeit progressive censorship: they did not allow certain music to be distributed in parts of the world and/or prohibited musicians from performing in certain places. In both cases a core aspect of censorship was present: the monitoring and control of creative work and, crucially, deliberation over whether or not pieces of music would be allowed to be listened to or performed in certain contexts, involving particular people. In other words, the boycott entailed restrictions on expression, movement and association.

JULUKA AND THE UNITED KINGDOM

Clegg's entrance into the music industry was gradual, and by way of his fascination with Zulu culture.[16] As Clegg noted, 'I began in 1970 with Sipho. We played traditional Zulu street guitar music for six years – pure, you know, the authentic street music. And I only added in my western contribution sort of seven or eight years later'.[17] Consequently, it was only after several years of ad hoc performances and musical experimentation that he and Sipho Mchunu first released three singles (in 1976 and 1977) and eventually formed Juluka, so that they could more effectively tour the music they were performing.[18] Their initial focus with the release of their first two albums, *Universal Men* and *African Litany*, was to continue what Clegg referred to as 'a fascinating adventure in trying to construct a meeting point between different forms of musical expression, rhythm, melody, [and] tone'.[19] Not long after the March 1981 release of the *African Litany* album, Juluka (in the original Johnny and Sipho format) conducted a nine-day tour of West Germany (the Federal Republic of Germany), including performing at a concert with Ladysmith Black Mambazo at the Cologne Zulu Festival in Germany on 27 May.[20]

Juluka made minimal initial attempts to release their earlier albums outside of South Africa (*Universal Men* was released in Mozambique in 1979, *African Litany* was released in Israel in 1981, and *Ubuhle Bemvelo* was released in France, Zimbabwe and Zambia in 1982). However, the

Scatterlings album and *Scatterlings of Africa* single marked the beginning of their international career.[21] The album and lead single were released in several countries, including the UK, the Netherlands, the USA, Canada, West Germany, Italy, Japan, Australia and Argentina, in 1982, and in New Zealand and Scandinavia in 1983.

According to Hilton Rosenthal,

> [the] lack of early Juluka international releases was because we simply couldn't attract commercial interest from international companies! We did have a release of Juluka's *Ubuhle Bemvelo* in France before *Scatterlings* (France was the first territory to take notice of African music in general). When we completed the 'Scatterlings of Africa' single I thought it was really special and was more accessible internationally, and started pitching all my international contacts. The first release was by an indie company in Italy – they renamed the single 'African Ideas'! Then John Craig, who owned Safari Records in the UK picked it up and released the single in the UK and once it charted there, the rest of the world took notice.[22]

Safari Records released the *Scatterlings of Africa* single on 14 January 1983,[23] and used some innovative marketing strategies, for example releasing a cut-out Africa-shaped picture disc in addition to a picture-sleeve release. The marketing of the single was effective and it entered the UK charts at number 100 on 30 January 1983. It remained in the top 100 for a further four weeks, peaking at number 44 on 13 February. In addition, it peaked at number 35 on the *UK Radio Stations* playlist chart on 14 February 1983, having entered the chart at number 67 on 24 January.[24] According to *Record Business* magazine, Birmingham's *BRMB* radio station added the song to its playlist in the week of 17 January, while in the same week *Radio Luxembourg* added it to their A-list. On 24 January it was added to the 'Hit Pick' lists on the regional radio stations *Mercia Sounds*, *Severn Sounds* and *Tay*, and made it onto *Victory*'s A-list.[25] On 7 February it was listed as a 'Top Priority' song on *Piccadilly*.[26] On 14 February it made it onto *Metro*'s playlist and again was featured on *Radio Luxembourg*'s A-list, while being added to *Tees*'

A-list.[27] Reviews were generally favourable, with reviewers comparing it to the limited African music they had come across, and usually to British folk music. For example, a *Record Business* review of 31 January 1983 described the lead single as follows:

> **JULUKA – Scatterlings Of Africa (Safari ZULU 1)**
> Juluka are an African band. But the music they make is far removed from the stereotype nurtured by too many hours listening to King Sunny Adé and Pablo. This powerful acoustic song sounds like a cross between Jethro Tull and Chris De Burgh with the odd mass tribal warcry shattering the illusion. They've even got Ian Anderson's flute. Potential off-the-wall smash.[28]

Up to this point Clegg had been working as an academic, and his involvement with Juluka was a serious side-project, but with the breakthrough into the British and other European charts he decided to focus solely on Juluka, with Mchunu in agreement. As he explained: 'Juluka's album *Scatterlings* was released in 1982, and the song for which the album was named took off at home and internationally. Suddenly it was all happening for us. Doors that had been firmly closed now swung open invitingly. Everyone seemed to want a piece of us.'[29]

Clegg took leave from his academic job (to which he never returned) and focused on taking Juluka's music to an international audience. Their first European tour was planned for June and July 1983, and was to include England and West Germany. The tour dates were set and the West German government issued work permits for the group members. However, the BMU advised the Thatcher government not to issue work permits to Juluka. According to the BMU's assistant general secretary, Stan Hibbert, the Department of Employment had consulted the union, which had objected, arguing that 'unless the work under discussion can be taken by our union members or the group concerned can be accommodated under our reciprocal agreement, we say work permits should not be issued'.[30] In addition, the AAM also opposed the tour on the grounds that it went against the cultural boycott.[31]

There were to be gigs in London, Leeds, Manchester and Birmingham. The group also hoped to promote their music through radio and television appearances. In preparation for the tour, in December 1982 Clegg joined the BMU, hoping to pave the way for television appearances, which were tightly controlled by the BMU.[32] However, despite Clegg being a union member, the BMU indicated that it would not permit Juluka to appear on BBC shows. Prior to Juluka's departure from South Africa, negotiations were ongoing between the band's representative and the BMU. Under the headline 'Juluka May Beat the Ban', the *Rand Daily Mail* newspaper reported that 'British television appearances are still possible, as the British Musicians' Union has decided to reconsider their early ban on the South African group's BBC shows'.[33] Nevertheless, *Billboard* magazine reported that on arrival the group 'ran into a performance ban imposed by [the] British Musicians' Union'.[34] In response, Juluka challenged the ban on the grounds that they were a multiracial group. The director of Safari Records, John Craig, explained that

> [they] had to cancel three confirmed television appearances for Juluka because of the MU ban, though the Department of Employment have issued work permits. I understand the reasons why the union has taken this decision, but I think it ought to reconsider, as Juluka is a special case. It is ironic that MU policy, based on repugnance of South African apartheid, should result in the banning of a group which, by its very membership and its actions, breathes life and hope into mere words.[35]

Clegg added that 'we all feel that the union's stand is uncompromising, given the fact that the group stands for a multiracial and integrated society'.[36] In contrast, the general secretary of the BMU, John Morton, explained that

> I've made it clear to the people representing the group that I am not prepared to make an arbitrary decision to vary established union policy. But the executive committee will consider whether there are reasons to relax our rule in this particular case. It's not a new proposition that the exchange of musicians between South Africa and the U.K. will do good because the people concerned are sympathetic to the

same objectives as the Musicians' Union. But when our own members have talked about going to play in South Africa to build bridges and undermine the apartheid policy, the position of the union has been to refuse them this possibility.[37]

When the BMU did convene to deliberate on the issue they reversed their decision and allowed Juluka to go ahead with television shows.[38] However, Clegg told the *Rand Daily Mail* that the BMU go-ahead was on condition that it would withhold Juluka's appearance fee as a face-saving measure.[39] The BMU had wanted to pay the appearance fee to the AAM, which in turn refused to accept the money.[40]

The struggle over television appearances notwithstanding, Juluka's first European tour was a success. It set the path for a flurry of further overseas engagements in the late summer of 1983, including appearances at outdoor music festivals in Reading, Frankfurt and Amsterdam.[41] The band then went on to the USA, where it performed a concert in New York in late October 1983.[42] The impact of the UK tour and television appearances seemed to bear fruit, with the *Scatterlings* album entering the UK album charts at number 94 on 23 July, and '*Impi*' ('War') spending three weeks on the UK Top 100 singles chart, peaking at number 87 on 7 August.[43]

In 1986, soon after launching Savuka, Clegg spoke out against a blanket application of the cultural boycott: 'We would appreciate it if the international music community could find a place for our music and our voices and allow us to participate in events which directly affect music, South Africa, and the dismantling of apartheid.'[44] In the spring of 1987, Savuka began their European tour in France, not entirely sure that their England concerts would go ahead because of resistance from the AAM.[45] Once again Clegg urged a more nuanced view towards the cultural boycott. He argued that

> getting my music heard outside South Africa will not harm that struggle in any way ... I came out knowing I might run into pressure and if I upset people in the anti-apartheid movement outside South Africa and they take measures against me then I can accept that because at least it's coming from the right moral standpoint. I just

feel it's misinformed and cut off from the reality within South Africa. I believe the boycott is now in a transitional stage. I want it redefined to make it more effective because it's become outdated after 20 years … People inside [South Africa] are becoming much more aware of the complexities and subtleties of the situation. They are learning to adapt and manoeuvre accordingly … So I believe it is for the blacks inside South Africa to decide how they want the boycott to help them best.[46]

The AAM and BMU were not persuaded by Clegg's argument for a selective boycott, with the BMU attempting to stop Savuka from performing in the UK on the basis that they opposed performers from South Africa.[47] However, as it had previously done, the Thatcher government went ahead and granted work permits, allowing the UK leg of the tour to go ahead.[48] Pieter De Bruyn Kops reported that Savuka had launched their debut album, *Third World Child*, 'with some electrifying performances in the United Kingdom', including at the Town and Country Club in London on 24 April and again on 20 May.[49] The shows were so successful that Savuka returned for more concerts later that summer.[50] In April 1988 Savuka were performing in the UK again, including a concert at the Top Rank concert venue in Brighton. Later that year Savuka were the support act for Steve Winwood on a tour which began with a 22-concert leg in the USA in July and August. In the UK the tour included concerts at Birmingham's National Exhibition Centre on 25 September and the Royal Albert Hall from 27 September to 6 October. Prior to the tour, *The Hard Report* magazine reporter Lee Carter suggested that the BMU was out of touch, commenting that 'Johnny Clegg and Savuka, the South African multi-racial band are coming to Britain next month to support Steve Winwood (despite an utterly pathetic ban on him by the toothless and obviously ignorant Musicians' Union in Britain)'.[51]

THE NELSON MANDELA 70TH BIRTHDAY CONCERT

Within the AAM's overarching political goal to 'isolate Pretoria on all levels to bring about the collapse of the apartheid regime', the organisation had a history of publicising and campaigning around anti-apartheid political prisoners in South Africa.⁵² The purpose was twofold: first, to highlight the role of liberation movements in South Africa and the violent response of the apartheid regime, and second, to draw attention to human rights issues.⁵³ In 1978 the AAM chose to focus on Nelson Mandela's 60th birthday as a way to highlight these two aspects of its South African political prisoner campaign. The campaign initiated a new focus on Mandela, one which would keep building until his release in 1990. The 1978 campaign centred on raising awareness around Mandela, chiefly through a birthday card campaign, which resulted in more than 3 000 birthday cards being sent to Mandela, including a birthday card signed by most members of the Labour government cabinet.⁵⁴ In June 1983 the AAM turned to musicians to celebrate Mandela's 65th birthday by means of the African Sounds Festival at Alexandra Palace, London. The concert featured performances by South African musicians in exile, including Julian Bahula, Hugh Masekela and John Matshikiza.⁵⁵ In 1988 the AAM planned a much bigger focus on the still incarcerated Mandela, on the occasion of his 70th birthday. The concert featured a host of internationally renowned musicians such as Joan Armatrading, Harry Belafonte, Dire Straits, Peter Gabriel, Whitney Houston, Sting and Stevie Wonder. Exiled South African musicians Miriam Makeba and Hugh Masekela also performed, as did Mahlathini and the Mahotella Queens and Jonathan Butler, who were based in South Africa. The BBC broadcast the event to 67 countries, and it was watched by more than 600 million viewers.⁵⁶

Given his long stand against apartheid, and Savuka's popularity in Europe, Clegg was hoping that Savuka would be invited to perform at the Mandela birthday concert. However, in the months leading up to the concert circumstances conspired against the likelihood of Savuka performing. To begin with, in June 1987 Clegg received a letter from the BMU informing him that unless he stopped performing in South Africa, he would be expelled from the union. The letter arrived at the time when the South African Musicians' Alliance (SAMA) and the broad democratic movement were deliberating over a selective approach to the cultural boycott. While Clegg was waiting for a position to be finalised, a second letter from the BMU was sent to him in January 1988. In the letter the BMU informed him that since he had not replied to the first letter, and had continued to perform in South Africa, he was being charged with 'conduct detrimental to the union'.[57] He was told that a hearing would be convened, and that he would be informed of the venue, date and time. However, the hearing went ahead without any notification, so Clegg was denied the opportunity to present his position to the union, including an update on the SAMA position on the cultural boycott.[58] BMU member and Brighton Branch Secretary Sid Allen had brought a charge against Clegg for contravening BMU policy by performing in South Africa. Clegg had registered his British address as Romney Marsh, Kent, and the charge was accordingly considered at a specially summoned meeting of the Brighton branch committee, held on 22 February 1988. According to a subsequent letter sent to Clegg by Allen, 'by a unanimous decision the Committee found the Charge proven, and also by a unanimous decision decided that you be expelled from the Musicians' Union'.[59] However, the letter to Clegg was sent to his given UK address (where he did not reside), and he consequently did not find out about his expulsion until a South African journalist later informed him of it.[60] Clegg commented: 'When I was told there would be a hearing it was a weight off my shoulders, I thought at last I would be able to present my case and that the hearing would be a blessing in disguise'.[61] Clearly, though, he was denied this opportunity.

In the aftermath of Clegg's expulsion it also became clear that he was not invited by the AAM to participate in the Nelson Mandela 70th birthday concert. John Craig, the director of First Night Records, Savuka's UK label, sent a letter of clarification and appeal to the BMU. He said that he understood that 'the Musicians Union have indicated to the organisers of the Nelson Mandela concert that they would not allow Johnny Clegg and Savuka to appear at the concert because of their South African residence. I am also aware that the Musicians Union is in the process of terminating Johnny Clegg's MU membership due to the fact that he works in South Africa'.[62]

He went on to defend Clegg and Savuka's political credentials, and noted that Clegg was currently in France and was willing to fly over to England to meet with Jack Stoddard, the assistant general secretary of the BMU at the time, to discuss the matter. Craig asked Stoddard to please accept an appointment to meet with Clegg.[63] In a response four days later, Stoddard clarified that Clegg was no longer a member of the union because 'Mr Clegg continues to work in South Africa despite our Union's long-standing embargo on engagements in that country. We have said in the past that Mr Clegg would need to decide whether he wishes to remain a member of the Union or return to South Africa to undertake professional engagements since he cannot do both. Mr Clegg has chosen to work in South Africa'.[64]

Stoddard concluded that 'there would be no point in a meeting between Mr Clegg and myself'.[65] The BMU thus shut the door on any further discussion of Clegg's union membership and removed itself from any role in negotiating Savuka's participation in the Mandela concert. Direct appeals to the AAM were also unsuccessful. In addition to Clegg and his record company appealing the decision, South Africa's central internal organisation opposing apartheid, the United Democratic Front (UDF), and Mandela's wife, Winnie Madikizela-Mandela, sent requests for him to perform. The refusal to allow Clegg to perform became an increasingly controversial incident, with the UDF accusing the BMU of 'deciding for itself what the cultural boycott should be and how it should be applied'.[66] This was despite the SAMA, the UDF and the African National Congress (ANC) all having recently agreed to relax the total boycott and replace it with a selective boycott, 'to allow artists from South Africa who were seen as part of the cultural struggle against apartheid to spread that culture internationally'.[67] Indeed, at the time Clegg noted that 'structures which have been set up in South Africa to help the boycott are being completely ignored … People on the run, cultural activists jeopardise their position every time they go to a meeting. People have put themselves in real danger to discuss my case but this has been totally disregarded by some anti-apartheid forces overseas'.[68]

The Johannesburg Democratic Action Committee (JODAC), a UDF group based in Johannesburg, very aptly expressed the sentiments of those appealing on Clegg's behalf:

> Johnny has shown his commitment to the progressive movement in South Africa by playing for free at protest concerts and by participating in discussions about the role of music and culture in the struggle against apartheid. He gives unflinchingly of his time and energy, and

he consults thoroughly about his actions here and abroad. Johnny has paid heavily both personally and financially for his political stand ... our understanding of the cultural boycott is that it seeks to isolate the Botha regime and related forces of oppression, and NOT isolate those who are active in the struggle against apartheid. We consider Johnny Clegg to be one of the very few musicians who have taken an unequivocal stand against apartheid and who should be given every opportunity both to promote his work, and in doing so, an image of a non-racial, democratic South Africa of the future.[69]

In contrast, and in defending the union's position, union official Stan Martin argued: 'A boycott is a fairly blunt instrument, and there is no way you can start making exceptions for specialist artists. If we had known when Clegg joined the [union] in 1983 who he was, we would have said there is no point in joining because you live and work in South Africa and you obviously can't observe the boycott'.[70] Martin raises a crucial issue here, and one which seems to have confused many people about Clegg not being invited to perform at the Mandela birthday concert. He was expelled from the *British Musicians' Union*, even though he was not, strictly speaking, a British musician. Indeed, when BMU officials realised that Clegg was a member and that he lived in South Africa, they concluded that he had deceived them when he joined. In the aftermath of the Mandela concert debacle, the assistant general secretary of the BMU, Stan Martin, sent a letter to Rupert Perry of EMI Records (UK) in which he reflected on the union's position:

> I nor the union have ever doubted or questioned Johnny Clegg's commitment to the cause of anti-apartheid, and I must assume that he likewise has never questioned our commitment to this cause which dates back to the early 1950's. Our particular problems with Johnny Clegg do not arise because of commitment, honesty or integrity in connection with the cause of anti-apartheid, but arise from his decision to apply and be accepted into membership of the Musician's Union. Johnny Clegg first joined the Union in December 1982 stating that his permanent address was Romney Marsh in Kent, he

was excluded for non-payment of subscriptions in March 1986, he rejoined the Union in April 1986 again giving his permanent address as Romney Marsh in Kent. The question that has never been answered by any of the critics of the Union or the Union's policy is why Johnny Clegg should seek to deliberately mislead when applying for membership of the Union on two occasions. His permanent address since from a young age has been in South Africa.[71]

While the fact of the BMU's expulsion of Clegg featured prominently in the controversy surrounding his absence from the Mandela birthday concert bill, the expulsion was in fact related not to the cultural boycott but to a separate issue altogether.[72] It happened to coincide with the build-up to the concert, but as indicated, the process had begun in 1987. The link between the BMU and AAM in preventing Clegg from performing at the Mandela birthday concert was never formal, if there was a direct link at all. According to Detlef Siegfried, after Clegg had been expelled from the BMU, 'the AAM avoided engaging with the complexity of the issue by refusing to let Clegg perform. This not even unequivocal support of the freedom movement within South Africa was sufficient now to secure an exception to the boycott, as originally planned by the flexible ANC concept'.[73] However, the BMU's Jack Stoddard noted that 'I am not personally aware of anyone from the Union [who] has said that the above named band [Johnny Clegg & Savuka] must not take part in the Nelson Mandela Concert. However, it is possible that an objection has been registered on the grounds that the members of this band are not members of the Union'.[74] Similarly, the BMU assistant secretary, Brian Blair, noted that 'we had nothing whatever to do with the bill for the Mandela concert'.[75] Rather, as noted, it was an AAM event, and it was their policy on the cultural boycott that guided the line-up of musicians. Clegg's management noted that both the AAM and the pressure group Artists Against Apartheid (formed by Jerry Dammers and Dali Tambo), had exerted pressure on Clegg to stop performing in South Africa, based on their interpretation of the cultural boycott.[76]

Although he was disappointed to have been omitted from the line-up for the Mandela 70th birthday concert, Clegg decided to move on. He explained:

'I was denied permission to perform in England at Wembley Stadium. The Anti-Apartheid Movement said they couldn't support my presence there. So, I just said, I'm not going to make an issue of it anymore'.[77]

Clegg later reflected that 'the issue of the boycott was really very messy, basically because culture was never really properly theorised in any way by anybody in the movement'.[78] However, he said, 'the UDF actually became a means whereby we could – by 1986 at least – start to address the boycott and make sense of it, and say "we are the ones who're being boycotted, we are the ones who are being censored, banned, having our shows stopped. We would like to have a say in how the boycott operates"'.[79]

Accordingly, when the SAMA began to develop a position on the cultural boycott their starting point was to acknowledge 'a difference between the culture of the oppressed masses and the culture of the ruling elite'.[80] They argued that it did not make sense to apply the boycott to the culture of the masses, but only to the culture of the ruling elite. Following from this starting point Clegg noted that

> we got three freedoms around which we developed SAMA, and that was freedom of association, freedom of expression and freedom of movement. Those three freedoms were critical for the daily livelihood of musicians because they had to move around, they had to be able to sing about what they want to sing, and they had to be able to associate with people of other races and other ethnic groups to do their work. And so around that we built a political position which we put through the UDF structures.[81]

However, the AAM and BMU did not engage with the UDF's position and were seemingly unconcerned that their approach amounted to censoring progressive South African musicians. Clegg believed that the AAM's rationale 'was around the "problem" of having a white South African in a multiracial band coming out of South Africa. I had letters from JODAC, from the Detainees' Parents Support Committee, I had letters from the UDF, there was an intervention from the UDF to actually say this guy is legit. And it had no effect outside South Africa. So I just left it at that'.[82]

He continued with Savuka, recording and touring, and with his cultural work, especially as vice president of the SAMA. For example, at the first meeting of the Natal branch of the Musicians' Association of Natal held in October 1988, Clegg noted that the power of the anti-apartheid movement to institute blanket cultural boycotts had been reduced. He had attended a UN symposium on culture against apartheid, where a motion was passed in favour of a selective boycott, according to which certain cultural contacts were viewed as beneficial to the fight against apartheid.[83] Clegg reiterated his opposition to a blanket boycott: 'We're living through a very dark corridor in our history and I myself have fought strongly against any cultural policing by radical groups'.[84]

The situation in the UK improved for Clegg over the next year or so, especially after the release of Mandela from prison in February 1990. Thus, when the AAM arranged another Wembley Stadium concert for Mandela to celebrate his release in February of that year, Savuka were invited and performed.[85]

CONCLUSION

Clegg's musical relationship with the UK was a complex one. From the very start he knew that he would have to navigate the controlling influence of the BMU, which insisted that musicians needed to be members of the union or be part of a national reciprocal agreement in order to promote their music on broadcast media. The cultural boycott of South Africa ruled out any reciprocal agreement, and therefore prior to Juluka's first tour of the UK Clegg exploited a potential loophole: he was British and thus would be able to join the union. However, down the line this caused difficulties for him because members of the BMU were not allowed to perform in South Africa. Thus Juluka and Savuka were both affected by Clegg's ongoing tussle with the BMU. Nevertheless, both Juluka and Savuka were able to release their music, appear on broadcast media, and perform on stage in the UK. Later, the AAM's specific application of the cultural boycott meant that Savuka were unable to appear at the Nelson Mandela 70th birthday concert at Wembley in June 1988. But they continued to tour the UK regardless.

Navigating the specific requirements of these different organisations was confusing. Sometimes the confusion was even bizarre. For example, in an interview with Marjolein Rotsteeg in 1990 Clegg related how he had heard that at some point in the 1980s he had been added to the UN blacklist of artists who had performed in South Africa.[86] However, he explained that it had turned out to be a misunderstanding, that the banned musician was British classical pianist John Clegg! If there was indeed a misunderstanding, it might have impacted Juluka and Savuka, especially in relation to television promotion in the UK. Artists blacklisted by the UN were banned by the BMU from doing any television promotion in the UK. But, as with the confusion over the link between the BMU and the AAM, some things might never become absolutely clear. Clegg summed it up very succinctly when he said that 'it's been a very chequered history for me, and my relationship with the hardline left has been obviously one of a yoyo. At moments, I've been really sort of in their bad books, and other times our interests and our beliefs and our values have merged into one, and we've been able to work together and do great things'.[87]

Fortunately, after the release of Mandela in February 1990, Clegg was able to stop fighting the 'hardline left' and simply focus on his work as a musician, with Savuka, with the briefly re-formed Juluka, and also as a solo artist. His final British concert, at the Hammersmith Odeon in August 2017, on his farewell tour, was fortunately a celebration of his life and career, successful despite the effects of the cultural boycott as applied in the UK.

ACKNOWLEDGEMENTS

I would like to express my sincere gratitude for the invaluable support provided by Hilton Rosenthal, John Craig, John Williamson, Dennis Scard and Claude Six. They generously gave of their time to address numerous enquiries I had about Johnny Clegg's music career, particularly his interaction with the British Musicians' Union. I also thank the Rhodes University Research Office for financial support towards writing this chapter and my participation in this book.

NOTES

1. Rob Nixon, *Homelands, Harlem and Hollywood* (London: Routledge, 1994), 157.
2. United Nations Centre Against Apartheid, *Notes and Documents – United Nations Centre Against Apartheid* no. 5/91 (New York: United Nations, 1991), 3, accessed 11 May 2025, https://www.sahistory.org.za/sites/default/files/archive_files/Artists and Entertainers against Apartheid - an update.pdf.
3. Mike Jempson, *Always In Tune with the Times: The Musicians' Union 1893–1993: A Centenary Celebration* (London: Musician's Union, 1983), 51.
4. John Williamson and Martin Cloonan, *Players' Worktime: A History of the British Musicians' Union, 1893–2013* (Manchester: Manchester University Press, 2016), 244.
5. Genevieve Klein, 'The British Anti-Apartheid Movement and Political Prisoner Campaigns, 1973–1980', *Journal of Southern African Studies* 35, no. 2 (2009): 455.
6. United Nations, 'General Assembly Resolution 35/206: Policies of *Apartheid* of the Government of South Africa: Part E Cultural, Academic and Other Boycotts of South Africa', A/RES/35/206A-R, 16 December 1980, accessed 7 April 2025, https://documents-dds-ny.un.org/doc/RESOLUTION/GEN/NR0/392/25/PDF/NR039225.pdf?OpenElement.
7. United Nations, 'General Assembly Resolution 35/206'.
8. The Anti-Apartheid Movement's newsletter, *Anti-Apartheid News*, reported such pickets at concerts by Shirley Bassey in Cardiff in 1982 (*Anti-Apartheid News*, December 1982), Leo Sayer in Newcastle in 1983 (*Anti-Apartheid News*, June 1983), David Essex in Newcastle in 1983 (*Anti-Apartheid News*, October 1983), Cliff Richard in Middlesborough in 1984 (*Anti-Apartheid News*, October 1984), and Paul Simon in London in 1987 (*Anti-Apartheid News*, May 1987).
9. Joseph Hanlon and Roger Omond, *The Sanctions Handbook* (Harmondsworth: Penguin, 1987), 125.
10. *Anti-Apartheid News* January–February 1984.
11. Hanlon and Omond, *Sanctions*, 141.
12. Personal correspondence by the author with John Williamson, co-author of *Players' Worktime: A History of the British Musicians' Union*, 1983–2013 (Manchester: Manchester University Press, 2016). See also Williamson and Cloonan, *Players' Worktime*, 177–178.
13. Andrew Bell, 'Musical Discord', *Time Out*, 29 June–6 July 1988.
14. Renee Veldsman, interview with the author, 16 April 1998.
15. Tom Fox, interview with the author, 20 July 1998.
16. See chapter 2 in this book by Lizabé Lambrechts and Pakama Ncume.
17. Johnny Clegg, interview with the author, April 1998.
18. Johnny and Sipho's first single release (in 1976) was *Uthi Angizule/Silinde* (single, Johannesburg: Jamloti, JM – 100), followed by *Woza Friday/Omam Basemhlabeni* (single, Johannesburg: Jamloti, JM – 139) and *Ngasala Obala/Bangake Nani?* (single, Johannesburg: Jamloti, JM – 140), both released in 1977.
19. Johnny Clegg, interview with the author, April 1998; Juluka, *Universal Men* (album, Johannesburg: Gramophone Records Co./CBS Records, DNW 2429, 1979); Juluka, *African Litany* (album, Johannesburg: MINC, MINC – (L) 1020, 1981).
20. Martin Mahlaba, 'Juluka Stuns Germans with Exciting Shows', *Soweto News*, 19 June 1989. Nine of their isiZulu-language songs were recorded and released on the album Johnny Clegg & Sipho Mchunu and Ladysmith Black Mambazo: *South Africa: Cologne Zulu Festival* (Frankfurt: Network Medien – 54.036, 1992). They are referred to as 'Duo Juluka' on the tracklisting and on the back sleeve.

21 Juluka, *Scatterlings* (album, Johannesburg: MINC, MINC – (L) 1040, 1982); Juluka, *Scatterlings of Africa* (single, Johannesburg: Bullet, MC 92, 1982).
22 Hilton Rosenthal, personal correspondence with the author, 23 September 2023. Rosenthal was Juluka and Savuka's producer and manager; Juluka, *Ubuhle Bemvelo* (album, Johannesburg: MINC, MINC – (E) 1030, 1982).
23 *Record Business*, 10 January 1983.
24 *Record Business*, 24 January 1983; *Record Business*, 14 February 1983.
25 *Record Business*, 24 January 1983.
26 *Record Business*, 7 February 1983.
27 *Record Business*, 14 February 1983.
28 *Record Business*, 31 January 1983.
29 Johnny Clegg, *Scatterling of Africa: My Early Years* (Johannesburg: Pan Macmillan, 2021), 289.
30 'Top SA Pop Group's Hopes in the Balance', *Rand Daily Mail*, 7 June 1983.
31 'Juluka: Plenty to Sing About', *Rand Daily Mail*, 14 July 1983.
32 Letter dated 15 May 1990 from the BMU's assistant general secretary, Stan Martin, to Rupert Perry of EMI Records.
33 John Miller, 'Juluka May Beat the Ban', *Rand Daily Mail*, 9 June 1983.
34 'Juluka Shows Banned in Britain', *Billboard*, 25 June 1983.
35 'Juluka Shows Banned', *Billboard*.
36 'Juluka Shows Banned', *Billboard*
37 'Juluka Shows Banned', *Billboard*.
38 Miller, 'Juluka May Beat the Ban'.
39 'Juluka', *Rand Daily Mail*, 14 July 1983.
40 'Juluka', *Rand Daily Mail*, 14 July 1983.
41 John Miller, 'Juluka Extends Its Horizons', *Rand Daily Mail*, 16 July 1983.
42 The New York concert received a positive review in *The New York Times*. Reviewer Stephen Holden introduced Juluka as 'the most popular interracial South African pop group, [which] blends acoustical English folk music with West African dance rhythms into a style that is consciously pan-African in its cultural sweep ... Led by the singer-guitarist Johnny Clegg and the guitarist Sipho Mchunu, the sextet delivered their bilingual folk tunes with a ritualistic intensity and verve [that] achieved a compelling musical hybrid of two vastly different folkloric cultures' (Stephen Holden, 'Pop: Juluka of South Africa', *The New York Times*, 2 November 1983).
43 Juluka, *Scatterlings*; Juluka, *Impi* (single, London: Safari Records, ZULU 3, 1983); Official Charts, 'Scatterlings by Juluka', accessed 11 May 2025, https://www.officialcharts.com/albums/juluka-scatterlings/; Official Charts, 'Impi by Juluka', accessed 11 May 2025, https://www.officialcharts.com/songs/juluka-impi/.
44 John Miller, 'S.A. Musicians Get Organized', *Billboard*, 5 July 1986.
45 Hugh Fielder, 'Beating the Boycott', *Sounds*, 11 April 1987.
46 Fielder, 'Beating the Boycott'.
47 *New Musical Express* cited in Detlef Siegfried, 'Aporias of the Cultural Boycott: Anti-apartheid Movement, ANC and the Conflict Surrounding Paul Simon's Graceland (1985–1988)', *Studies in Contemporary History* 13 (2016): 23; Robin Denselow, *When the Music's Over: The Story of Political Pop* (London: Faber and Faber, 1989), 201.
48 Denselow, *When the Music's Over*, 201.
49 Pieter De Bruyn Kops, 'Pop with a Zulu Heart', *Music & Media*, 4 July 1987; Johnny Clegg & Savuka, *Third World Child* (album, Johannesburg: EMI, EMCJ(D) – 2407331, 1987).

50 Denselow, *When the Music's Over*, 201.
51 Lee Carter, 'Music News', *The Hard Report* 98 (30 September 1988): 42.
52 Siegfried, 'Aporias', 2.
53 Klein, 'Political Prisoner Campaigns'.
54 Klein, 'Political Prisoner Campaigns'.
55 See the commemorative album Various Artists, *African Sounds! For Mandela* (London: Tsafrika Records, TSA 1003, 1983).
56 Siegfried, 'Aporias', 21.
57 Bell, 'Musical Discord'; letter from Sid Allen, Brighton Branch committee secretary to Johnny Clegg, 2 March 1988, John Craig's personal archive; letter from John Craig, director of First Night Records, to Jack Stoddard, assistant general secretary of the BMU, 20 May 1988, John Craig's personal archive.
58 Bell, 'Musical Discord'; letter from Craig to Stoddard, 20 May 1988; letter from Jack Stoddard to John Craig, 24 May 1988, John Craig's personal archive.
59 BMU letter to Johnny Clegg, 2 March 1988.
60 Bell, 'Musical Discord'.
61 Bell, 'Musical Discord'.
62 Letter from Craig to Stoddard, 20 May 1988.
63 Letter from Craig to Stoddard, 20 May 1988.
64 Letter from Stoddard to Craig, 24 May 1988.
65 Letter from Stoddard to Craig, 24 May 1988.
66 Bell, 'Musical Discord'.
67 Bell, 'Musical Discord'.
68 Bell, 'Musical Discord'.
69 Letter from JODAC to the BMU general secretary, John Morton, quoted in Bell, 'Musical Discord', 12.
70 Nick Robertshaw, 'U.K. Union Ousts Clegg for Performing in South Africa', *Billboard*, 16 July 1988.
71 Letter from Stan Martin to Rupert Perry (EMI Records), 15 May 1990, John Craig's personal archive.
72 For example, Jon Young claimed that Clegg wasn't invited to perform at the Mandela birthday concert 'due to a dispute with the British Musicians' Union, who recently expelled Clegg from its ranks' (Jon Young, 'Faces: Johnny Clegg', *Musician* 120 [October 1988]: 11). More recently, Andrew Donaldson mistakenly claimed that despite support from the ANC and Winnie Madikizela-Mandela, 'the union wouldn't budge. Its hardline stance effectively denied Clegg a massive global audience' (Andrew Donaldson, 'Johnny Clegg and the Stalinists', *Politicsweb*, 19 July 2019, accessed 8 November 2023, https://www.politicsweb.co.za/opinion/johnny-clegg-and-the-stalinists).
73 Siegfried, 'Aporias', 23.
74 Letter from Stoddard to Craig, 24 May 1988.
75 Robertshaw, 'Union Ousts Clegg', 58.
76 Robertshaw, 'Union Ousts Clegg', 58.
77 Immanuel Suttner, 'Johnny Clegg – A Possibility of Wholeness: Interviewed by Immanuel Suttner', in *Cutting Through the Mountain: Interviews with South African Jewish Activists*, ed. Immanuel Suttner, 73–105 (Johannesburg: Penguin, 1997), 102.
78 Clegg, interview with the author, April 1998.
79 Clegg, interview with the author, April 1998.
80 Clegg, interview with the author, April 1998.

81 Clegg, interview with the author, April 1998.
82 Suttner, 'Johnny Clegg'.
83 Anthea Johnston, 'Cultural Boycott Is Waning – Clegg', *Southern Screen & Stage* 1, no. 6 (1988): 1.
84 Johnston, 'Cultural Boycott', 1.
85 Suttner, 'Johnny Clegg', 102.
86 Marjolein Rotsteeg, 'Clegg and His Cruel and Crazy World', *Music & Media*, 17 March 1990.
87 Suttner, 'Johnny Clegg', 102.

REFERENCES

Anti-Apartheid Movement, London. *Anti-Apartheid News*. Various issues, 1982–1987.
Bell, Andrew. 'Musical Discord'. *Time Out*, 29 June–6 July 1988.
Carter, Lee. 'Music News'. *The Hard Report* 98 (30 September 1988): 41–42.
Clegg, Johnny. *Scatterling of Africa: My Early Years*. Johannesburg: Pan Macmillan, 2021.
De Bruyn Kops, Pieter. 'Pop with a Zulu Heart'. *Music & Media*, 4 July 1987.
Denselow, Robin. *When the Music's Over: The Story of Political Pop*. London: Faber and Faber, 1989.
Donaldson, Andrew. 'Johnny Clegg and the Stalinists'. *Politicsweb*, 19 July 2019. Accessed 8 November 2023. https://www.politicsweb.co.za/opinion/johnny-clegg-and-the-stalinists.
Fielder, Hugh. 'Beating the Boycott'. *Sounds*, 11 April 1987.
Hanlon, Joseph and Roger Omond. *The Sanctions Handbook*. Harmondsworth: Penguin, 1987.
Holden, Stephen. 'Pop: Juluka of South Africa'. *The New York Times*, 2 November 1983.
Jempson, Mike. *Always In Tune with the Times: The Musicians' Union 1893–1993: A Centenary Celebration*. London: Musicians' Union, 1983.
Johnson, Anthea. 'Cultural Boycott Is Waning – Clegg'. *Southern Screen & Stage* 1, no. 6 (1988): 1–2.
'Juluka: Plenty to Sing About'. *Rand Daily Mail*, 14 July 1983.
'Juluka Shows Banned in Britain'. *Billboard*, 25 June 1983.
Klein, Genevieve. 'The British Anti-Apartheid Movement and Political Prisoner Campaigns, 1973–1980'. *Journal of Southern African Studies* 35, no. 2 (2009): 455–470.
Mahlaba, Martin. 'Juluka Stuns Germans with Exciting Shows'. *Soweto News*, 19 June 1989.
Miller, John. 'Juluka Extends Its Horizons'. *Rand Daily Mail*, 16 July 1983.
Miller, John. 'Juluka May Beat the Ban'. *Rand Daily Mail*, 9 June 1983.
Miller, John. 'S.A. Musicians Get Organized'. *Billboard*, 5 July 1986.
Nixon, Rob. *Homelands, Harlem and Hollywood*. London: Routledge, 1994.
Official Charts. 'Impi by Juluka'. Accessed 11 May 2025. https://www.officialcharts.com/songs/juluka-impi/.
Official Charts. 'Scatterlings by Juluka'. Accessed 11 May 2025. https://www.officialcharts.com/albums/juluka-scatterlings/.
Record Business Publications Ltd. *Record Business*. Various issues, 1983.
Robertshaw, Nick. 'U.K. Union Ousts Clegg for Performing in South Africa'. *Billboard*, 16 July 1988.
Rotsteeg, Marjolein. 'Clegg and His Cruel and Crazy World'. *Music & Media*, 17 March 1990.
Siegfried, Detlef. 'Aporias of the Cultural Boycott: Anti-apartheid Movement, ANC and the Conflict Surrounding Paul Simon's Graceland (1985–1988)'. *Studies in Contemporary History* 13 (2016): 2–26.

Suttner, Immanuel. 'Johnny Clegg – A Possibility of Wholeness: Interviewed by Immanuel Suttner'. In *Cutting through the Mountain: Interviews with South African Jewish Activists*, edited by Immanuel Suttner, 73–105. Johannesburg: Penguin, 1997.

'Top SA Pop Group's Hopes in the Balance'. *Rand Daily Mail*, 7 June 1983.

United Nations. 'General Assembly Resolution 35/206: Policies of *Apartheid* of the Government of South Africa: Part E Cultural, Academic and Other Boycotts of South Africa', A/RES/35/206A-R, 16 December 1980. Accessed 7 April 2025. https://documents-dds-ny.un.org/doc/RESOLUTION/GEN /NR0/392/25/PDF/NR039225.pdf?OpenElement.

United Nations Centre Against Apartheid. *Notes and Documents – United Nations Centre Against Apartheid* no. 5/91. New York: United Nations, 1991. Accessed 11 May 2025, https://www.sahistory.org.za/sites/default/files/archive_files/Artists and Entertainers against Apartheid - an update.pdf.

Williamson, John and Martin Cloonan. *Players' Worktime: A History of the British Musicians' Union, 1893–2013*. Manchester: Manchester University Press, 2016.

Young, Jon. 'Faces: Johnny Clegg'. *Musician* 120 (October 1988): 10–11.

DISCOGRAPHY

Jonathan Clegg & Sipho Mchunu. *Uthi Angizule/Silinde*. Single. Johannesburg: Jamloti, JM – 100, 1976.

Jonathan and Sipho. *Ngasala Obala/Bangake Nani?* Single. Johannesburg: Jamloti, JM – 140, 1977.

Jonathan and Sipho. *Woza Friday/Omam Basemhlabeni*. Single. Johannesburg: Jamloti, JM – 139, 1977.

Johnny Clegg & Savuka. *Third World Child*. Album. Johannesburg: EMI, EMCJ(D) – 2407331, 1987.

Johnny Clegg & Sipho Mchunu and Ladysmith Black Mambazo. *South Africa: Cologne Zulu Festival*. Album. Frankfurt: Network Medien, 54.036, 1992.

Juluka. *African Litany*. Album. Johannesburg: MINC, MINC – (L) 1020, 1981.

Juluka. *Impi*. Single. London: Safari Records, ZULU 3, 1983.

Juluka. *Scatterlings*. Album. Johannesburg: MINC, MINC – (L) 1040, 1982.

Juluka. *Scatterlings of Africa*. Single. Johannesburg: Bullet, MC 92, 1982.

Juluka. *Ubuhle Bemvelo*. Album. Johannesburg: MINC, MINC – (E) 1030, 1982.

Juluka. *Universal Men*. Album. Johannesburg: Gramophone Records Co. / CBS Records, DNW 2429, 1979.

Various Artists. *African Sounds! For Mandela*. London: Tsafrika Records, TSA 1003, 1983.

CHAPTER

8

Johnny Clegg: *Le Zoulou Blanc* in France

Lucilla Spini

While Johnny Clegg, as part of Juluka, had already gained some international exposure through performances in Canada, the United States of America (US), the United Kingdom (UK), Germany and Scandinavia in 1982–1983, it was only in 1986 that Clegg, with Savuka, reached a vast international audience, worldwide fame and a strong international fan base – thanks to the welcoming and launching stage provided by France, not only for his music but also for his activism. Hence, exploring Clegg's positioning and recognition in France is important to understanding his artistic career, by taking into account the cultural and socio-political contexts in South Africa and France, as well as Clegg's engagement with French culture and socio-political dynamics, from the late 1980s onwards.

THE WHITE ZULU IN ANGOULÊME, FRANCE

In the 1980s, France was already very open to African music and world music generally, leading to the establishment of specialised record companies like Celluloid, which released Juluka's *Ubuhle Bemvelo* (in 1982) and *Musa Ukungilandela* (in 1984) in France.[1] Despite the fact that Juluka did not cover France in their 1982–1983 international tour, Clegg started to become known to the French public in 1985, thanks to an article about him by Christophe Nick in the magazine *Actuel*, which introduced Clegg to a wider public by referring to him as '*Le Zoulou Blanc*' – a term which thereafter was used throughout Clegg's career in a wide variety of countries and languages (such as 'The White Zulu' in English, '*Lo Zulu Bianco*' in Italian and '*El Zulú Blanco*' in Spanish).[2]

Nick's article prompted Christian Mousset, the director of the '*Jazz et Musiques Métisses*' festival in Angoulême (in the western part of France), to invite Johnny Clegg & Savuka to perform at the May 1986 edition of the festival.[3] During the festival, given that Clegg and Savuka did not have a manager on site (since the Savuka project had begun just a few months prior to the festival), they were supported by the festival's general manager, Claude Six, who was already familiar with Clegg's music through his work at Celluloid as tour manager of the Senegalese crossover band Touré Kunda. Six decided to support them, also on the following day, for their opening of the concert by Xalam, a Celluloid-produced Senegalese jazz-fusion band.

Following these two concerts, Six and Mousset were also engaged in the planning and management of the Anti-Apartheid Festival and Forum organised by the *Fédération Mondiale des Villes Jumelées* (also known as the United Towns Organization) in Dakar, Senegal, in June 1986.[4] Mousset and Six were also in charge of the organisation of the show held on the Île de Gorée on 14 June 1986;[5] they added to the list of artists already identified by the federation (for example Miriam Makeba, Diane Dufresne, Pitika Ntuli, Matsemela Manaka and Mongane Wally Serote) other well-known African musicians such as Mory Kanté and Touré Kunda and, then still relatively unknown to the international scene, Johnny Clegg & Savuka. The event was attended by about 300 mayors from all over the world, providing a great launch platform for Clegg to reach out to both an international audience and the French public.

To acknowledge the support provided during the above-mentioned concerts in France and Senegal, Clegg invited Six and Mousset to visit him in South Africa in 1986. Given the ongoing rule of the apartheid regime and the states of emergency in South Africa at the time, the request for visas for them entailed long interviews at the South Africa embassy in Paris and detailed annotations on their passports. However, Six reported that upon arrival in Johannesburg their visit went very smoothly, as Clegg opened many doors to places which otherwise could never have been seen by visitors. While there, Six and Mousset offered to take up Clegg's international management on the basis of their admiration for him. As Six recalled: 'I did not "decide" to become his manager, it just happened. I used to work in the production of the most famous world music festival in Angoulême, I was embedded in such types of music and I was literally "hooked" by Clegg's performances and by the generated atmosphere. There was something "good" in that man'.[6]

Upon acceptance of this offer by Clegg, Six's management began by contacting Renaud Séchan (known most often as Renaud), a very famous French singer/songwriter.[7] Six introduced him to Clegg's work and suggested the possibility of interviewing Clegg in South Africa for a documentary to be included in the very popular programme 'Les Enfants du Rock' ('Rock's Kids') on the French national television station Antenne 2. Renaud reported on this proposal, among other things, in the essay 'Johnny, Je T'adore' ('Johnny, I Adore You') by highlighting that he was a great admirer of Clegg; yet he also underlined his hesitation about travelling to South Africa, given the ongoing violence there.[8] Despite such anxiety, exacerbated by the note on his passport stating that he could not film anything while in South Africa, Renaud accepted the proposal. He then travelled with Six to interview Clegg, first meeting him in a parking lot near a motel in the Cape area (figure 8.1). They started talking through an interpreter, then decided to continue without one, but speaking slowly.[9] The shooting for the documentary started in January 1987.[10]

The ensuing documentary, entitled *Shadow Man*, included images of the conversation between Clegg and Renaud, as well as many contrasting views of South Africa, from the beautiful landscapes and seascapes to urban areas in which hostels were located in Johannesburg.[11] During the conversations with Renaud, Clegg explained the socio-political situation in South Africa (for example, referring to over 20 000 people in detention), some elements of Zulu culture (such as stick fighting), as well as the direction of his music as a personal journey, not as a vehicle for protest.[12] In fact, Clegg underlined the fact that his art was like a photograph of the situation for the public

Figure 8.1: Johnny Clegg and Renaud Séchan in South Africa in 1987. Photograph © Claude Six, 1987.

to interpret and understand: an approach that was a constant throughout Clegg's life and career, also triggered by his application of an ethnographic lens.[13]

The images in the documentary are immersed in several songs by Clegg, including '*Asimbonanga*' ('We Have Not Seen Him') from the 1987 album *Third World Child* (which reached sales of 1.2 million in France alone), as well as 'African Shadow Man' and '*Siyayilanda*' ('We Are Fetching It'), which would be released on the album *Shadow Man* in the following year (1988).[14] The soundtrack also includes 'Miss Maggie', a song by Renaud (1985) about Margaret Thatcher, the prime minister of the UK from 1979 to 1990, who did not support sanctions against South Africa.[15] Some years later, Renaud reported on the documentary as a great and exciting experience: 'We have lived at Clegg's rhythm for some days, and it's difficult to do it ... What an energy! We have seen some horrible things (the townships, the ghettos) in a wonderful country'.[16]

The documentary received support from the French Ministry of Foreign Affairs and was broadcast on national television some months later in 1987: it can be considered a landmark event establishing Clegg's fame in France, and also an opportunity created by Renaud – at that time a very established artist on the French music scene – who encouraged his fans to also become Clegg's fans.[17] Renaud himself became a Clegg fan; in April 1988 he dedicated the song 'Jonathan' to Johnny Clegg on his album *Putain de Camion*, which also allowed the public to further understand Clegg's and Renaud's approach in skilfully intertwining music and activism.[18] The song triggered several joint interviews, including one by Dominique Warluzel during the television programme '*Profil de Renaud*' ('Profile of Renaud') on 27 April 1988, where Renaud explained the song 'Jonathan' and his admiration for Clegg; Clegg suddenly joined him on stage and was asked to comment on the song. Clegg said: 'He [Renaud] has done a very good job with the Zulu chorus, as for the rest I am extremely embarrassed'.[19] Renaud underlined the fact that the song had been a way to record an important part of his life, namely meeting Clegg, who meant the world to him, and that the song was a way to say '*je t'adore*' ('I adore you').[20] In the same interview, Renaud also discussed the great success experienced by Clegg at the festival '*Printemps de Bourges*' where, on 10 April 1988, Clegg's concert had a record-breaking audience of about 18 000 people.[21] Such a success was also exemplified by the fact that in July 1988, 42 000 tickets were sold for Clegg's concert in Lyon scheduled just before Michael Jackson's show (on his '"Bad" World Tour'), which had to be cancelled as a result of Clegg's sold-out concerts in Lyon around the same time.[22]

Renaud and Clegg established a lifelong friendship and mutual admiration, as shown, for instance, by the acknowledgements on Clegg's 1988 album *Shadow Man*: 'Special thanks to Claude Six, Sylvain Mustaki, and to Renaud, famous tall thin paranoid bastard from a small bouncing African Mongrel. Long live the defenders of the special crazy human stew'.[23]

Renaud continued to support Clegg over the years;[24] for example, he invited Clegg to perform in Paris on 8 July 1989 at a concert organised by journalist Gilles Perrault with the support of many individuals (including Renaud), as well as organisations, in order to advocate for writing off the debts of the developing countries in view of the G7 Summit to be held in Paris on 14 July 1989 (figure 8.2).[25] The concert, in Place de la Bastille,

Figure 8.2: Johnny Clegg and Claude Six backstage, July 1989. Photograph courtesy of Claude Six. All rights reserved.

was attended by more than 100 000 people, enabling Clegg and Savuka to become further established on the French music scene.[26]

Hence, by the late 1980s '*Le Zoulou Blanc*' had become a mainstream figure in French popular culture, and a reliable source of information about the current situation in apartheid South Africa, as underlined by François Bensignor.[27] Other key artists on the world music scene also showed admiration for Clegg and his work, including Manu Dibango, who commented that Clegg 'is extraordinary because he is an answer to everything – we do not need philosophy, we can just see it'.[28] Many journalists were also intrigued by the Clegg phenomenon; for instance, in 1988 the journalist Philippe Conrath of the newspaper *Libération* travelled to South Africa to interview Clegg for his book *Johnny Clegg: La Passion Zoulou* ('Johnny Clegg: Zulu Passion').[29]

The success visible through the concerts was also reflected in the music charts and sales of his songs and albums: the album *Scatterlings* remained at number eight in the French Top 50 for 25 weeks in 1987–1988; the song '*Asimbonanga*' remained in the French Top 50 for 30 weeks, reaching number 2 for 7 of those weeks (from May to July 1988); and the song 'I Call Your Name' reached the French Top 10 in 1988.[30] The fans at concerts liked him for his performances, but also for his commitment to the anti-apartheid cause.[31] Such a success was clearly recognised on 3 February 1990 when Michel Rocard, the French prime minister at the time, awarded Clegg the '*Victoire d'Honneur*' ('Honour Victory') at the '*Victoires de la Musique*' ('Victories of Music') event. The ceremony was an opportunity for mutual acknowledgement between Clegg and Rocard. The special and symbolic award honoured Clegg's courage in his fight against apartheid. Clegg had asked to receive the award from the prime minister to recognise his constant and personal support,[32] as exemplified by Rocard's interviewing Clegg for the newspaper *L'Evénement du Jeudi* on 20 August 1987 in order to shed light on the current situation in South Africa.[33]

At this event, another artist received a special award for his career: Serge Gainsbourg, who dedicated one of his last songs to Clegg (he died a year later, on 2 March 1991); the song, '*Zoulou*', was recorded by Vanessa Paradis but has not (yet) been released.[34] The 1990 award at '*Victoires de la*

Musique' testifies to how much Clegg was appreciated by the general public, by French artists and by politicians, as well as to how France paid attention to developments in South Africa.

A few days after the award ceremony, on 11 February 1990, Nelson Mandela was released from prison; Clegg was in Italy with the 'Cruel Crazy Beautiful World' tour and was approached for several interviews to comment on the news.[35] Furthermore, in the following months the interest in witnessing the passage to a democratic, unitary and non-racial South Africa remained high in France, and in Europe generally. In this context, the French government awarded the '*Chevalier de l'Ordre des Arts et des Lettres*' ('Knight of the [French] Order of Arts and Letters') to Clegg, at a ceremony held in 1991 at the Ministry of Culture with the then Minister of Culture Jack Lang, an important advocate of the anti-apartheid struggle who was very supportive of Clegg's work.

Within about five years, Johnny Clegg & Savuka had achieved fame, recognition and a strong fan base in France and Europe at large.[36] This was definitely due to Clegg's energetic and communicative style, and to the key role of individuals – Six, Renaud and Mousset in particular. This was also exemplified by the launch of Johnny Clegg & Savuka's album *Heat, Dust and Dreams* in Paris in 1993 at the Virgin Megastore on the Champs Elysées, which was decorated with posters featuring the album's official photographs taken by the world-renowned French photographer Claude Gassian.[37] The album's success – it was nominated for a 1993 Grammy Award for 'Best World Music Album' – may also be attributable to the fact that it is actually a testimony of a decade of important changes, not just in South Africa but around the world.[38]

The impact of these socio-political and personal dynamics on Clegg can also be inferred from his dialogue with Idir – an Algerian/Kabyle artist living in France – within the programme '*Vis à Vis Idir et Johnny Clegg a capella*', broadcast in 1993 on French national television.[39] This dialogue, conducted between Vauréal-Paris and Johannesburg via satellite, highlighted their lives and interfaces with cultural heritage, enabled them to report on the status quo of the Kabyle people in Algeria and the so-called interregnum in South Africa (as shown by the footage included in the video of the demonstration following Chris Hani's assassination on 10 April 1993), and provided a record of the journeys undertaken by both artists up until the early 1990s, when the world was at a tipping point of imminent and incredible transformations. Such changes may have also triggered the conclusion of the Savuka project in 1994–1995.

THE FRENCH SOCIO-CULTURAL AND POLITICAL CONTEXT SURROUNDING JOHNNY CLEGG & SAVUKA

By the mid-1980s, France had already welcomed and incorporated African music – and more broadly world music – into the national music scene. In fact, while Clegg's music is certainly unique with respect to its crossover style, French audiences had already been exposed to crossover music through other African artists such as the above-mentioned Idir, Manu Dibango, King Sunny Adé and Touré Kunda. France was the fulcrum of world music at the time: in fact, it is certain that there were very few African artists – or artists from Antilles or Réunion – who had not performed at the above-mentioned festival in Angoulême prior to being known elsewhere. Therefore French ears were used to listening to artists mixing and experimenting with different styles.[40] Despite Clegg's amazement at his rapid rise to fame,[41] he was also conscious of the role of France, and Paris in particular, in fostering African music in Europe; this is discussed by Clegg himself in the documentary series *Paris C'est l'Afrique* ('Paris Is Africa'):

> Paris is a meeting point, it is a staging point, I think it is the most important staging point – or platform – that Europe has provided for African music, and I think that it's, more and more, month by month, becoming more and more important ... I think Paris is more important, to a degree, than London, yes, I tell you why: I think that although London and the English music scene has been talking about African music and there has been quite a smaller cult following, there has never been on the pop charts a dramatic breakthrough of African music – there has never been a really top-10 or top-20 African artist singing in his own language, playing his own music. It has never happened. It has

happened in France, many times. And that for me means that not only is there a platform, not only is there a milieu that supports the music, but actually the business side of things, the exposure, and there is a public – a public who has got the ear and who wants to support that. That for me is the crucial difference between the two.[42]

This cultural context was therefore a fertile environment for introducing Clegg's music. While some of the initial fans appeared to come from among Renaud's followers, Clegg seemed to have reached a broader and more diverse fan base. This was probably linked to the fact that concerts were held in many different types of venues, including many summer festivals whose broad participation was also supported by favourable cultural policies; under the leadership of Jack Lang as the French minister of culture (through the 1980s up until 1993), events were either free or accessible through reasonably priced tickets.[43]

Furthermore, at that time in France the anti-apartheid struggle was supported by both government and civil society organisations. This support started early on in the 1960s–1970s, mainly due to the activities of the *Parti Communiste Française* (French Communist Party) and *Mouvement Contre le Racisme l'Antisémitisme et pour la Paix* (Movement Against Racism and Antisemitism and For Peace).[44] Upon the strengthening of the cultural boycott against South Africa in the 1980s, the French *Mouvement Anti-Apartheid* (Anti-Apartheid Movement) shared the position of implementing a selective boycott,[45] as opposed to the indiscriminate boycotts supported by Artists Against Apartheid and by some South African artists in exile in the UK.[46] In fact, Clegg and his management never encountered any pressure or boycotts in relation to their concerts in France, nor were they contacted by the *Parti Communiste Française* or the *Mouvement Contre le Racisme l'Antisémitisme et pour la Paix*.[47]

But there were many other socio-political dimensions of that time that need to be taken into account for an understanding of Clegg's positioning in France. In fact, from the early 1980s, an important, broad movement against racism and for equality developed in France: the national demonstration '*Marche Pour l'Égalité et Contre le Racisme*' ('Demonstration for Equality and Against Racism') – also known as '*Marche des Beurs*'⁴⁸ – held at the end of 1983 is a symbol of that time. As also recalled by Clegg, this was the time of the growth of the extreme right party in France – a fact that triggered young people in France to foster a movement leading to the formation of *SOS Racisme* (an association of anti-racist non-governmental organisations) and the campaign '*Touche Pas à Mon Pote*' ('Hands Off My Friend').⁴⁹ These anti-racist movements and campaigns were focused on eradicating the racism perpetrated against youth and workers from the Maghreb/North Africa or of North African origins. In this context, all the African musicians and bands that performed in France were also integrated into a sort of anti-fascist and anti-racist 'counterculture' aimed at fostering equality, inclusion and socio-cultural integration; upon Clegg's arrival on the French music scene, the situation in South Africa and the *Mouvement Anti-Apartheid* gained further attention and reached a broader sector of society.⁵⁰ This was also furthered by the assassination of the African National Congress representative Dulcie September in Paris on 29 March 1988 – an event also marked in a song, 'September', by the renowned French artist Jean-Michel Jarre.⁵¹

Some parallels can be drawn with other European countries where anti-racist movements triggered by different socio-economic contexts were intertwined with Clegg's performances.⁵² Examples of anti-apartheid events and performances by Clegg related to such movements were the 'World Conference on Sanctions Against Racist South Africa' (Headquarters of the United Nations Educational, Scientific and Cultural Organization, Paris, 16–20 June 1986), the 'Culture in Another South Africa' conference and festival held in Amsterdam (14–19 December 1987) and the (first) 'Symposium on Culture Against Apartheid' hosted by the government of Greece at the Evgenidion Foundation (Athens, 2–4 September 1988), where Clegg participated as a 'dancer, singer, guitarist' from South Africa, along with other artists such as Harry Belafonte, Dennis Brutus, Nadine Gordimer and Wally Serote, and representatives from anti-apartheid movements and associations from many European countries including France, Italy, the Federal Republic of Germany, Ireland and Sweden.⁵³

In other countries, there were socio-cultural dynamics related to reactions to immigration from Africa; for instance, in the early 1990s, Italy was starting to experience important immigration flows from Africa and was confronted with internal racism against African people – an issue that was also discussed with Clegg during the 'Cruel Crazy Beautiful World' tour's concert in Florence.[54] Even in the eastern region of Europe there was engagement in the anti-racism and anti-apartheid movements, as exemplified by the anti-apartheid concert held at the Gdańsk Shipyard in Poland on 13 December 1989.[55] The UK was a very different context; while Clegg had many sold-out shows in London – thanks to, among other things, the local South African community – it was very difficult for him to perform in other towns in the UK, mostly due to the closed approach of Artists Against Apartheid, the artists in exile, and the British Musicians' Union which had 'erased' Clegg from the media sphere,[56] but also due to the different approach of the British music industry to African and world music referred to by Clegg in his interview with Conrath, quoted earlier in this chapter.[57]

JOHNNY CLEGG AND FRANCE: A CONSTANT CONNECTION

From the mid-1990s, Clegg continued to perform in France and elsewhere in Europe; once as Juluka,[58] but mostly with the Johnny Clegg Band. These performances included three more concerts at the festival in Angoulême (in 1995, 2005 and 2007), as well as concerts at the Grand Rex concert venue in Paris (2004 and 2007) and in many other places (such as the cities of Valence, Gardanne, Marseille and Pau). Clegg still attracted crowds and had a strong fan base, which is perfectly exemplified by an amazing project developed (and still managed and updated) by two French fans, Daniel Pontreau and Fabrice Fitoussi, the website *In My African Dream*, established in 2001 'by fans for fans' in order to present 'a collation of the Johnny Clegg discography including Savuka, Juluka and solo work'.[59]

The connection with France was also enabled by Clegg's interest in French culture and knowledge of the language. In fact, during the concerts in France – and in other francophone countries – Clegg spoke a little bit of French to tell the audience about the songs and the situation in South Africa. At the beginning, his manager would write some notes for Clegg to read during the concerts; then he started to memorise them.[60] However, Clegg decided that this was not enough and, as a good anthropologist, decided to learn French by taking intensive individual classes in 1988 and 1989 with a teacher from the Alliance Française in Johannesburg. This allowed him to interact better with the audience and ensured more spontaneous storytelling during the shows. He would start talking in French with the apology *'Je m'excuse si je vais massacrer un peu la langue française'* ('I apologise if I am going to butcher the French language') to attract the attention of the audience, who were very happy to hear him speaking in French.

This connection with France led Clegg to ask Six to write a song for him in French. Six, who had also written songs earlier in his career with the band Imago, took up the challenge of writing lyrics – taking into account Clegg's style and philosophy, as well as adapting to his level of French. The lyrics were developed around the theme of not being caught off guard (in French, *'faut pas baisser les bras'*), inspired by the concept that even in established democracies, it is fundamental to be vigilant and to contribute to maintaining democratic freedom.[61] Clegg liked the theme, and wrote the music to which the final lyrics, also including isiZulu, were adapted. Unfortunately, it was a song that the band found difficult to perform; it was thus mostly included only in the set lists for concerts in France, and therefore was not played enough to become well known. However, Six commented that he was very proud and honoured to have been the only person to have written lyrics for Clegg.[62] This was also the time for Clegg to pay tribute to France as the host of the 2007 Rugby World Cup, as exemplified by the promotional video *'Jongosi* – A Happy Salute to the French & South African Rugby Teams'.[63]

The mixing of the French language with isiZulu, as well as possible collaboration with French artists, was something that continued to intrigue Clegg, as he had an in-depth knowledge of the music scene in France (beyond the world/African music communities based there). In fact, in 2010, when he was asked about which French artists he wanted to collaborate with, he mentioned Bernard Lavilliers – a French artist known for his crossover music that included French song, rock, reggae, salsa and bossa nova.[64] Furthermore, a little hint of the French language is also found on Clegg's last album, *King of Time*, in the song 'Oceanearth', which plays on the similar pronunciations of *'la mer'* (the sea/ocean) and *'la mère'* (the mother) within the sentence '*je suis la mer, ta mère*' ('I am the ocean, your mother').⁶⁵ This was also a demonstration that Clegg had continued to work on his French over the years, in line with his belief in the importance of learning a language to understand other countries. Indeed, in 2018 Clegg returned to the Alliance Française in Johannesburg to improve his French; this time the teacher was Muriel Huet, who interviewed him, in French, about his connection with France.⁶⁶

Upon Clegg's passing, many different tributes were paid to him in the written press and other media.⁶⁷ Furthermore, in 2019 the French/German television station *TV ARTE* released the documentary 'Johnny Clegg, the White Zulu' by Amine Mestari, which provided an account of Clegg's life through his own words and the words of those who had worked with him over the years in different countries.⁶⁸ The development of the documentary, which was finalised in March 2019, provided a great opportunity to record Clegg's account of his life while he was writing his autobiography and saying farewell to his fans.

There was not an official farewell concert in France; in fact, Clegg's last concerts in France date back to the summer of 2016. There was one concert within the 'JAZZ' festival hosted by Gérard Bertrand at the Château l'Hospitalet (Narbonne, 30 July 2016) and another one at the '*Les Escales*' festival (Saint Nazaire, 31 July 2016). The concerts were very successful: the audience sang old and new songs by Clegg in English and isiZulu (with a French accent!) and Clegg (who had not announced his illness yet) was very energetic. Once more – almost exactly 30 years after that first concert in France in May 1986 – his performances were intertwined with the socio-political dynamics of integration and anti-racism, given the extensive immigration flows affecting Europe in 2016. In fact, at the end of the concert in Saint Nazaire, Clegg was asked to be a spokesperson to recall the ongoing immigration crises and to call for support for the work of the non-governmental organisation SOS Méditerrannée. That image of Clegg waving an orange life-jacket and advocating for the importance of rescuing migrants in the Mediterranean Sea can be considered as closing the cycle of the story of the *Zoulou Blanc* in France, as well as underlining that in France Clegg is not just considered an anti-apartheid activist from the past, but also a symbol for social justice across different historical periods.⁶⁹

ACKNOWLEDGEMENTS

Special thanks are due to Claude Six for inputs, discussion and encouragement towards the drafting and completion of this chapter, and for his photographs; many thanks also to Christophe Nick for a prompt and informative reply, to Michael Drewett for useful feedback and to Andrew J. Friedland and Andy Innes for being amazing *Scatterlings*. My gratitude goes also to Johnny Clegg's French management team and crew (all its members over the years), as well to Claude Six's family, for the welcoming atmosphere they created during tours and beyond. A big *Merci* is also due to the many *Scatterlings* from France and from other parts world (such as Belgium, Ireland, the UK and US) whom I met during concerts in France. Et … Johnny, je t'adore!

NOTES

1. Juluka, *Ubhule Bemwelo* (album, Paris: Celluloid, CEL 668071, 1982); Juluka, *Musa Ukungilandela* (album, Paris: Celluloid, CEL 667831, 1984).
2. Christophe Nick, 'Afrique du Sud: Amitié dans la Tempête', *Actuel* 71 (September 1985): 74–81, 145; also reported by Johnny Clegg in an interview with Benjamin Locoge in 2019,'"Je Suis un Zoulou, Donc Je Crois à la Philosophie des Guerriers: Je Dois Endurer pour Survivre": Johnny Clegg – Interview Benjamin Locoge', *Paris Match* 3620, 27 September–3 October 2018.
3. In 1990, the festival changed its name to '*Festival Musiques Métisses*' (see Christian Mousset and André Videau, 'Le Festival d'Angoulême, de "Jazz en France" à "Musiques métisses"', *Hommes et Migrations* 1161 (January 1993): 22–24, https://doi.org/10.3406/homig.1993.1951). The 1986 concert was a success, even though Johnny Clegg & Savuka were at the very beginning of their adventure and their first album, *Third World Child* (Paris: EMI, EMCJ (D) – 2407331, 1987), had not been released yet; it would be released in 1987. Clegg was invited to perform again at the festival several times, in 1988, 1995, 2005 and 2007.
4. At the time, the *Fédération Mondiale des Villes Jumelées* was under the chairmanship of Pierre Mauroy, President François Mitterand's former prime minister and the mayor of Lille.
5. Christiane Chombeau, 'La Conférence des Villes Jumelées Contre L'Apartheid: L'enfant de Gorée et les Écrivains Sud-africains', *Le Monde*, 17 June 1987. See also the television programme '*Gorée Resistances*' broadcast by *Antenne 2* on 3 July 1986, INA Archives, video, 07:34, accessed 3 April 2025, https://www.ina.fr/ina-eclaire-actu/video/cab86017881/goree.
6. Claude Six, email communication with the author, 15 August 2023.
7. Soon after the trip to South Africa, Mousset decided not to pursue the idea of taking on Clegg's management because of other commitments related to the festival in Angoulême.

8   Renaud Séchan, '*Johnny, Je T'adore*', in *Johnny Clegg: La Passion Zoulou*, Philippe Conrath, 189–195 (Paris: Le Club de Stars, Editions Seghers, 1988).
9   Renaud Séchan, '*Visage Pale Recontre Zoulou Blanc*', *Paroles et Musique* no. 27 (March 1990): 38–39.
10 Six, email, 15 August 2023.
11 Jimmy Glasberg, dir. *Shadow Man* (documentary, broadcast on '*Les Enfants du Rock*', Antenne 2, 1987).
12 On the issue of not classifying himself as somebody playing 'protest music' or 'social music', here is the verbatim transcription from *Shadow Man* of Clegg's statement: 'The direction of my music is a personal journey to explore my identity as an African. But I am in between, I was born in England, I came here as an immigrant. So, my music is a mixture of different cultures; and it's crossover. My music is not social music or protest music, I am not protesting anything. I see myself as just describing, and making a record, like a photograph of this thing. And you the consumer, or the listener, must decide. I do not preach. I do not say this is good or that is bad. I think it is very important for an artist to be like that.' (Johnny Clegg quoted in Glasberg, *Shadow Man*.)
13 Lucilla Spini and Andrew Grant Innes, 'Johnny Clegg: A Polycultural Anthropologist on Stage for Social Justice', *International Journal of Anthropology* 37 no. 1–2 (2022): 75–94, https://doi.org/10.14673/IJA2022121089.
14 Guillaume Vieira, 'France Best Selling Albums Ever: Third World Child by Johnny Clegg & Savuka (1987)', *Chartmasters*, 15 March 2016, accessed 3 April 2025, https://chartmasters.org/2016/03/france-best-selling-albums-ever-third-world-child-by-johnny-clegg-savuka-1987/; Johnny Clegg & Savuka, *Third World Child*; Johnny Clegg & Savuka, *Shadow Man* (album, London: EMI, EMCJ (D) – 7904111, 1988).
15 Renaud Séchan, 'Miss Maggie', on *Mistral Gagnant* (album, Paris: Virgin France, 70425, 1985).
16 Renaud Séchan, '*Visage Pale*'; translation by the author.
17 The documentary had a similar impact in other countries, for example through WOMAD in Italy (personal observation). WOMAD (World of Music, Arts and Dance) is an international festival (established by Peter Gabriel and others). Its main venue is in the UK, but the festivals also travels to locations in other countries.
18 Renaud Séchan, 'Jonathan', on *Putain de Camion* (album, Paris: Virgin France, 70600, 1988).
19 The original title of the 1988 television programme broadcast by RTS was '*Profil de Renaud*', The interview is available at RTS Archives, '*Renaud et Johnny Clegg (1988)*', YouTube video, 04:13, accessed 3 April 2025, https://www.youtube.com/watch?v=UYFv57Yicxo.
20 RTS Archives, '*Renaud et Johnny Clegg*'.
21 Six, email, 15 August 2023.
22 See for instance the documentary by Amine Mestari, 'Johnny Clegg, the White Zulu' (documentary/DVD, Paris: Screenshot Group, Arte France, 2019).
23 Johnny Clegg & Savuka, *Shadow Man*.
24 Clegg's album *One Life* (album, Angoulême: Marabi Productions, 46817.2, 2006) was produced by Renaud, who is acknowledged by Clegg as follows: 'Special thanks to Renaud for his constant support'. See also Renaud Séchan, '*Reposez en Paix, Monsieur Clegg*', *Parlez-moi de Renaud Website*, July 2019, accessed 3 April 2025, https://parlezmoiderenaud.com/tag/les-enfants-du-rock/.

25 The slogan of the concert was '*Ça suffa comme ci!*', a humorous way to say '*Ça suffit comme ça! (y en a assez!)*', which means 'that's enough'.
26 '*La Manifestation et le Concert de la Bastille à Paris*', *Le Monde*, 11 July 1989.
27 François Bensignor, '*Un Diable d'Anglais Se Fait Zoulou*', *Paroles et Musique* 27 (March 1990): 32–33.
28 Brief interview with Manu Dibango within the context of the '*Printemps de Bourges*' festival in 1988; translation by the author. See the full interview and others at France 3 Centre – Val de Loire, '*Printemps de Bourges 1988: Johnny Clegg*', television programme 1988, YouTube video, 02:03, accessed 3 April 2025, https://www.youtube.com/watch?v=lF6orU-826c.
29 Philippe Conrath, *Johnny Clegg: La Passion Zoulou* (Paris: Le Club de Stars, Editions Seghers, 1988).
30 Juluka, *Scatterlings* (album, Johannesburg: MINC, MINC – (L) 1040, 1982); Johnny Clegg & Savuka, '*Asimbonanga*', on *Third World Child*; Johnny Clegg & Savuka, 'I Call your Name', on *Shadow Man*.
31 See France 3 Centre – Val de Loire, '*Printemps de Bourges 1988*'.
32 Fred Hidalgo, '*Editorial: Où Vas-tu Johnny Clegg?*', *Paroles et Musique* 27 (March 1990): 4.
33 See Frédèric Ploquin, '*Michel Rocard et les Zoulous*', interview compiled by Frédèric Ploquin, *L'Evénement du Jeudi*, 20 August 1987, accessed 3 April 2025, https://www.vie-publique.fr/discours/254228-interview-de-m-johnny-clegg-chanteur-sud-africain-par-m-michel-rocar.
34 Six, email, 15 August 2023.
35 See for instance Raffaella Carrà, 'Interview of Johnny Clegg by Raffaella Carrà', *Raffaella Venerdì, Sabato e Domenica* (television programme, Rome: *RAI 2*, 1990).
36 While France has been the main fulcrum for Clegg's fame and fan base in Europe, it is important to note that other countries such as Belgium, Germany, Italy and Switzerland have also recognised him; but this is beyond the scope of this chapter.
37 Johnny Clegg & Savuka. *Heat, Dust and Dreams* (album, UK/Europe: EMI, 7 98795 2, EMI – 0777 7 98795 2 6, EMI – CDEMC 3650, 1993).
38 As exemplified by the album's song 'Inevitable Consequences of Progress'.
39 Jean-Jacques Birgé, dir., '*Vis-à-vis: "Idir et Johnny Clegg a capella"*', documentary, France 3 & Point du Jour co-production with Internews, 1993, available at YouTube, 54:42, accessed 3 April 2025, https://www.youtube.com/watch?v=npNsceGRn98.
40 Six, email, 15 August 2023.
41 For example, he referred to this in his television interview for the *Printemps de Bourges* festival in 1988 (France 3 Centre – Val de Loire, '*Printemps de Bourges 1988: Johnny Clegg*').
42 Transcription by the author of an interview with Johnny Clegg by Philippe Conrath in the first episode '*Les Précurseurs*' ('The Pioneers') of the documentary series '*Paris C'est l'Afrique*'. (Philippe Conrath, dir., '*Paris C'est l'Afrique*', Paris: Organisation internationale de la francophonie, 1989.)
43 The establishment of the '*Fête de la Musique*' by Jack Lang – an annual one-day open music event held in France on 21 June, since 1982 – is an example of such policies.
44 Six, personal communication with the author.
45 Six, email, 15 August 2023.
46 See chapter 7 in this book by Michael Drewett. Artists Against Apartheid was established in London in February 1986 by Jerry Dammers, Dali Tambo and Chandra Sekar.

At its official launch on 22 April 1986, many artists, such as Bob Geldof and Midge Ure of Band Aid, were in attendance. On 28 June 1986, the Festival for Freedom in Namibia and South Africa was successfully held at Clapham Common, also in London. See also reference to Artists Against Apartheid in chapter 7 by Drewett.

47 Six, email, 15 August 2023.
48 '*Beur*' is a French term that defines the Arabs born in the French territory, but whose parents are immigrants from an Arab country.
49 See Muriel Huet, '*Entretien avec Johnny Clegg, Élève à l'Alliance Française de Johannesburg, Afrique du Sud, depuis Septembre 2018*', *Fondation des Alliances Françaises Website*, 30 October 2018, accessed 3 April 2025, https://www.fondation-alliancefr.org/?p=37853.
50 Six, email, 15 August 2023.
51 Jean-Michel Jarre, 'September', on *Revolutions* (album, Paris: Disques Dreyfus, 837 421-4, Dreyfous Disques, 1988).
52 Six, email, 15 August 2023.
53 See the UN Digital Library reference at https://digitallibrary.un.org/record/147367, accessed 3 April 2025; Amadou-Mahtar M'Bow, 'Address by Amadou-Mahtar M'Bow, Director-General of Unesco, on the Occasion of the Opening of the United Nations World Conference on Sanctions against Racist South Africa' (Paris: Unesco House, 16 June 1986), accessed 3 April 2025, https://unesdoc.unesco.org/ark:/48223/pf0000069086_spa.locale=en; Willem Campschreur and Joost Divendal, eds., *Culture in Another South Africa* (London: Zed Books, 1989). At the 'Second Symposium on Culture Against Apartheid' held in Los Angeles, Clegg participated as a representative of the South African Musicians' Alliance Executive (see chapter 10 by Lucilla Spini and Andrew J. Friedland in this book).
54 Personal observation, Florence, March 1990.
55 For further information see Positive Music Promotion/BBC, 'BBC Report: *Solidarność* Anti-Apartheid Concert at the Gdańsk Shipyard, 13-12-1989', 14 December 1989, YouTube video, 03:41, accessed 3 April 2025, https://www.youtube.com/watch?v=NArQyinvYzY
56 See chapter 7 by Michael Drewett in this book.
57 Conrath, '*Paris C'est l'Afrique*'.
58 For example, at the '*Festival de Confolens*' in 2000 (Michael Drewett, personal communication with the author).
59 Daniel Pontreau and Fabrice Fitoussi, *In My African Dream Website*, http://inmyafricandream.free.fr/. The website is available in both French and English.
60 Six, email, 15 August 2023.
61 Reference is made to the text in the booklet within Clegg's 2006 album *One Life*.
62 Six, email, 15 August 2023.
63 Johnny Clegg, '*Jongosi* – A Happy Salute To The French & South African Rugby Teams' (promotional edition CD and video, 03:11, Angoulême: Marabi Productions, 46817.S3, 2007). The cover can be seen at https://www.discogs.com/release/13101720-Johnny-Clegg-Jongosi-A-Happy-Salute-To-The-French-South-African-Rugby-Teams, accessed 3 April 2025. Clegg's official video for the song, released in 2007 within the promotional edition, is available at https://www.dailymotion.com/video/x2ynst, accessed 3 April 2025.
64 NRJ - Hit Music Only, 'Johnny Clegg – Spirit is the Journey – Interview – *Le 6/9 NRJ*' YouTube video, 09:34, accessed 3 April 2025, https://www.youtube.com/watch?v=6ff6WTZ7rHg&t=559s.

65 Johnny Clegg, 'Oceanearth', on *King of Time* (album, Paris: BMG, 384 279-5, 2017).
66 Huet, *'Entretien avec Johnny Clegg'*.
67 See for instance the tribute by Bertrand Lavaine, *'Johnny Clegg, la Dernière Danse du Zoulou Blanc'*, Radio France Internationale (RFI) Musique, 17 July 2019, accessed 3 April 2025, https://musique.rfi.fr/musique-africaine/20190717-johnny-clegg-mort-zoulou-blanc.
68 Mestari, 'Johnny Clegg'. The interviews in the documentary were conducted in Johannesburg in September 2018.
69 SOS Méditerrannée France, '[*On Nous Soutient*] *Johnny Clegg Soutient SOS Méditerrannée aux Escales de St Nazaire 2016*', 2016, YouTube video, 01:18, accessed 3 April 2025, https://www.youtube.com/watch?v=DLZ7fu6AnO0.

REFERENCES

Antenne 2. 'Gorée Resistances'. 1986. Video, 07:34, INA Archives. Accessed 3 April 2025. https://www.ina.fr/ina-eclaire-actu/video/cab86017881/goree.

Bensignor, François. '*Un Diable d'Anglais Se Fait Zoulou*'. *Paroles et Musique* no. 27 (March 1990): 32–33.

Birgè, Jean-Jacques, dir. *Vis-à-Vis: 'Idir et Johnny Clegg a capella'*. Documentary film. Paris: France 3 and Point du Jour co-production with Internews, 1993.

Campschreur, Willem and Joost Divendal, eds. *Culture in Another South Africa*. London: Zed Books, 1989.

Carrà, Raffaella. 'Interview of Johnny Clegg by Raffaella Carrà', *Raffaella Venerdì, Sabato e Domenica*. Television programme. *RAI 2*, 1990.

Chombeau, Christiane. '*La Conférence des Villes Jumelées Contre L'Apartheid: L'enfant de Gorée et les Écrivains Sud-africains*'. *Le Monde*, 17 June 1987.

Clegg, Johnny. 'Jongosi – A Happy Salute to the French & South African Rugby Teams'. Promotional edition CD and video, 03:11. Angoulême: Marabi Productions, 46817.S3, 2007. Accessed 3 April 2025. https://www.dailymotion.com/video/x2ynst.

Conrath, Philippe. *Johnny Clegg: La Passion Zoulou*. Paris: Le Club de Stars, Editions Seghers, 1988.

Conrath, Philippe, dir. '*Paris C'est l'Afrique*'. Paris: Organisation internationale de la francophonie, 1989.

France 3 Centre – Val de Loire. '*Printemps de Bourges 1988: Johnny Clegg*' 1988. YouTube video, 02:03. Accessed 3 April 2025. https://www.youtube.com/watch?v=lF6orU-826c.

Glasberg, Jimmy, dir. *Shadow Man*. Documentary. Broadcast on '*Les Enfants du Rock*', Antenne 2, 1987.

Hidalgo, Fred. '*Editorial: Où Vas-tu Johnny Clegg ?*' *Paroles et Musique* no. 27 (March 1990): 4.

Huet, Muriel. '*Entretien avec Johnny Clegg, Élève à l'Alliance Française de Johannesburg, Afrique du Sud, depuis Septembre 2018*'. Fondation des Alliances Françaises Website, 30 October 2018. Accessed 3 April 2025. https://www.fondation-alliancefr.org/?p=37853.

'*La Manifestation et le Concert de la Bastille à Paris*'. *Le Monde*, 11 July 1989.

Lavaine, Bertrand. '*Johnny Clegg, la Dernière Danse du Zoulou Blanc*'. Radio France Internationale (RFI) Musique, 17 July 2019. Accessed 3 April 2025. https://musique.rfi.fr/musique-africaine/20190717-johnny-clegg-mort-zoulou-blanc.

Locoge, Benjamin. '"*Je Suis un Zoulou, Donc Je Crois à la Philosophie des Guerriers: Je Dois Endurer pour Survivre*": Johnny Clegg – Interview Benjamin Locoge'. *Paris Match* 3620, 27 September–3 October 2018.

M'Bow, Amadou-Mahtar. 'Address by Amadou-Mahtar M'Bow, Director-General of Unesco, on the Occasion of the Opening of the United Nations World Conference on Sanctions against Racist South Africa'. Paris: Unesco House, 1986. Accessed 3 April 2025. https://unesdoc.unesco.org/ark:/48223/pf0000069086_spa.locale=en.

Mestari, Amine. 'Johnny Clegg, the White Zulu'. Documentary. DVD. Paris: Screenshot Group, Arte France, 2019.

Mousset, Christian and André Videau. '*Le Festival d'Angoulême, de "Jazz en France" à "Musiques Métisses"*'. *Hommes et Migrations* 1161 (January 1993): 22–24. https://doi.org/10.3406/homig.1993.1951.

Nick, Christophe. '*Afrique du Sud: Amitié dans la Tempête*'. *Actuel* 71 (September 1985): 74–81, 145.

NRJ - Hit Music Only. 'Johnny Clegg – Spirit is the Journey – Interview – *Le 6/9 NRJ*'. YouTube video, 09:34, Accessed 3 April 2025. https://www.youtube.com/watch?v=6ff6WTZ7rHg&t=559s.

Pontreau, Daniel and Fabrice Fitoussi. *In My African Dream Website*. Accessed 3 April 2025. http://inmyafricandream.free.fr/.

Ploquin, Frédèric. '*Michel Rocard et les Zoulous*'. Interview compiled by Frédèric Ploquin. *L'Evénement du Jeudi*, 20 August 1987.

Positive Music Promotion/BBC. 'BBC Report: *Solidarność* Anti-Apartheid Concert at the Gdańsk Shipyard, 13-12-1989', 12 December 1989. YouTube video, 03:41. Accessed 3 April 2025. https://www.youtube.com/watch?v=NArQyinvYzY.

RTS Archives. '*Renaud et Johnny Clegg* (1988)'. YouTube video, 04:13. Accessed 3 April 2025. https://www.youtube.com/watch?v=UYFv57Yicxo.

Séchan, Renaud. '*Johnny, Je T'adore*'. In *Johnny Clegg: La Passion Zoulou*, Philippe Conrath, 189–195. Paris: Le Club de Stars, Editions Seghers, 1988.

Séchan, Renaud. '*Reposez en Paix, Monsieur Clegg*'. *Parlez-moi de Renaud Website*, July 2019. Accessed 3 April 2025. https://parlezmoiderenaud.com/tag/les-enfants-du-rock/.

Séchan, Renaud. '*Visage Pale Recontre Zoulou Blanc*'. *Paroles et Musique* no. 27 (March 1990): 38–39.

SOS Méditerranée France. '[On Nous Soutient] Johnny Clegg Soutient SOS Méditerranée aux Escales de St Nazaire 2016'. YouTube video, 01:18. Accessed 3 April 2025. https://www.youtube.com/watch?v=DLZ7fu6AnO0.

Spini, Lucilla and Andrew Grant Innes. 'Johnny Clegg: A Polycultural Anthropologist on Stage for Social Justice'. *International Journal of Anthropology* 37 no. 1–2 (2022): 75–94. https://doi.org/10.14673/IJA2022121089.

Vieira, Guillaume. 'France Best Selling Albums Ever: Third World Child by Johnny Clegg & Savuka (1987)'. *Chartmasters*, 15 March 2016. Accessed 3 April 2025. https://chartmasters.org/2016/03/france-best-selling-albums-ever-third-world-child-by-johnny-clegg-savuka-1987/.

DISCOGRAPHY

Clegg, Johnny. *King of Time*. Album. Paris: BMG, 384 279-5, 2017.

Clegg, Johnny. *One Life*. Album. Angoulême: Marabi Productions, 46817.2, 2006.

Jarre, Jean-Michel. *Revolutions*. Album. Paris: Disques Dreyfus, 837 421-4, 1988.

Johnny Clegg & Savuka. *Heat, Dust and Dreams*. Album. UK/Europe: EMI, 7 98795 2, EMI – 0777 7 98795 2 6, EMI – CDEMC 3650, 1993.

Johnny Clegg & Savuka. *Shadow Man*. Album. London: EMI, EMCJ (D) – 7904111, 1988.

Johnny Clegg & Savuka. *Third World Child*. Album. Paris: EMI, EMCJ (D) – 2407331, 1987.
Juluka. *Musa Ukungilandela*. Album. Paris: Celluloid, CEL 667831, 1984.
Juluka. *Scatterlings*. Album. Johannesburg: MINC, MINC – (L) 1040, 1982.
Juluka. *Ubhule Bemwelo*. Album. Paris: Celluloid, CEL 668071, 1982.
Séchan, Renaud. *Mistral Gagnant*. Album. Paris : Virgin France, 70425, 1985.
Séchan, Renaud. *Putain de Camion*. Album. Paris: Virgin France, 70600, 1988.

CHAPTER

9

Lost or Misconstrued: Johnny Clegg in Hollywood

Chris Letcher

At the height of his fame in the late 1980s and early 1990s, Johnny Clegg's Savuka-era music appeared on the soundtracks of a number of Hollywood films with American settings. A remixed version of the song 'Scatterlings of Africa' occupies over two minutes of soundtrack time near the beginning of *Rain Man* (1988), and 'Cruel, Crazy, Beautiful World' dominates sections of the otherwise unrelated films *Opportunity Knocks* (1990) and *Career Opportunities* (1991).[1] There were other appearances of Clegg's music in films during this period – 'Great Heart' in South African adventure film *Jock of the Bushveld* (1986), 'Life Is A Magic Thing' in the Australian-American animated film *Fern Gully: The Last Rainforest* (1992), and specially written songs for *The Power of One* (1992), which was set in South Africa in the 1940s – but it is the presence of Clegg's music in the US films with US settings that is in many ways the most remarkable.[2] On the one hand, the songs' presence in these films feels fitting – the hard-surfaced, glossy sound Clegg and his long-time producer and collaborator, Hilton Rosenthal, adopted for the Savuka albums was a more commercial proposition than Juluka's music, and the songs sat comfortably alongside the other contemporary pop music in the films. On the other hand,

I remember thinking as a teenage audio-viewer of the films in the late 1980s, something felt oddly, interestingly misplaced in hearing Clegg's intrinsically South African music while seeing US landscapes, shopping malls and living rooms.

In this chapter I take a close listen to two of these 'sync placements': 'Scatterlings of Africa' in Barry Levinson's *Rain Man* and 'Cruel, Crazy, Beautiful World' in the John Hughes-written romantic comedy *Career Opportunities*.[3] I have selected them as a way of exploring what the songs might mean in these cinematic contexts. As with all music on screen they are involved in what Miguel Mera and Anna Morcom describe as complex processes of de- and recontextualisation: music is taken out of one cultural context (for example, as stand-alone music in the real world) and placed in new cinematic (in this case fictional) contexts.[4] In relation to Clegg's music in these films, transnational and cross-cultural issues make the process additionally layered, and my analysis considers how the music seems to both converge with and diverge from other storytelling elements in the scenes. In terms of the sound of the music in the context of the soundtracks, I am interested in how the films seem to want to invoke the songs' South Africanness while also seeking to obscure or disconnect the music from its origins.

I am also interested in thinking through what the placement of the songs in these films might tell us about how Clegg's Savuka-era music was received globally. Can a reading of the music in the films tell us something about what might be lost in taking music from the periphery into the global mainstream? Through email correspondence with Rosenthal, I have also learned more about the production of the songs for the films and how the licensing agreements came about. Sync deals, particularly ones as prized as these with top-tier Hollywood names, can be enormously lucrative and useful in helping artists find audiences; this was perhaps even more the case in the pre-internet 1980s and 1990s, and particularly key for bands whose music fell outside of the stylistic norms of radio playlists – but might a song's meaning be diminished in the process?[5] Johnny Clegg & Savuka's music itself might be heard as a strategic set of compromises – generic commercialisation in certain respects (the use of contemporary, often sequenced synthesisers, hard-compressed and quantised drums, squared-out time signatures, radio-tooled hooks) balanced with something far more unique and African.[6] I explore how the US films seem to want us to hear Clegg's South African music in a particular way, and how the music might ultimately resist such readings.

SYNC DISPLACEMENTS: 'SCATTERLINGS OF AFRICA' IN *RAIN MAN*

Clegg's appearance on the soundtrack of *Rain Man*, the highest-grossing film of 1988 and the only film to have won both the Berlin Film Festival's highest award and the Academy Award for Best Picture, marked his arrival as a truly international star.[7] While the song is somewhat buried in the mix in the film, as I discuss below, Rosenthal said the association with the film and the inclusion of the song on the soundtrack album 'certainly contributed to the awareness of the group, particularly in the USA'.[8]

Rain Man is a road movie in which an abrasive young car dealer, Charlie Babbitt (played by Tom Cruise), discovers his estranged father has died leaving most of his US$3 million estate to his other son, Raymond (Dustin Hoffman), an autistic savant, of whose existence Charlie was unaware. While Hoffman's portrayal of Raymond won the year's Best Actor Oscar and was much discussed, the film is not primarily interested in Raymond's experience of the world. The dominant dramatic trajectory is the shift that occurs in Charlie's character – in connecting with Raymond, Charlie moves away from selfishness and self-interest to caring about other people and appreciating family.

The film incorporates more non-Western musical elements than one might expect. This is, in some ways, less surprising when one considers that the film was made at a time when 'world music' had become a marketing phenomenon, and less than two years after the release of Paul Simon's *Graceland* (1986).[9] The influence of African music, and specifically South African music, is notable across *Rain Man*'s soundtrack, in both the compiled music (the pre-existing pop music licensed for use in the film) and Hans Zimmer's specially composed score. Zimmer's score is revealing of the film's overall musical approach and is worth considering briefly here.

Rain Man's director, Barry Levinson, said he had asked Zimmer to score the film after hearing his score for the anti-apartheid film *A World Apart* (released early in 1988), which was influenced by South African music.[10] Zimmer himself is explicit about the world music influence on his *Rain Man* music, telling an *Entertainment Weekly* journalist in 2008 that 'the Raymond character doesn't actually know where he is. The world is so different to him. He might as well be on Mars. So, why don't we just invent our own world music for a world that doesn't really exist?'[11] Zimmer's Fairlight-heavy score does indeed conjure an odd, generically exotic musical world by jumbling up musical instruments and signifiers: marimbas, didgeridoos, pan-pipes and steel pans are all thrown together.[12]

A similar concept seems to have informed the selection of pre-existing pop music for the soundtrack. The film opens with a contemporary reworking of the New Orleans song 'Iko Iko' by the Belle Stars, which draws explicitly on West African music.[13] We hear it as we see one of Charlie's futuristic cars hoisted by crane, framed so that it resembles a spacecraft in a Martian landscape. It creates a sense of disconnection: an incongruous combination of music, place and image, casting 1980s America as alien and unfamiliar.

Johnny Clegg & Savuka's 'Scatterlings of Africa', a song initially recorded with Juluka but reworked six years later as a Savuka song on the album *Third World Child*, is the second piece of music we hear in the film and it does something similar.[14] The song appears as diegetic car radio music as Charlie and his girlfriend head out from Los Angeles for a weekend in Palm Springs. On the way, Charlie receives news, on his new-fangled car phone, of his father's death, to which he appears indifferent. We hear the song primarily at the beginning and end of the sequence – in the middle the music is mixed so far below the sound of the car and dialogue that only the faintest hints are audible. At the end of the scene, over the iconic long shot of southern Californian wind turbines, the music is allowed to swell briefly for the song's isiZulu vocable outro.[15]

Zimmer's argument about music in the film needing to create an exotic world because Raymond 'doesn't actually know where he is' does not work here – Raymond isn't in the scene, and at this point Charlie isn't even aware of his existence. The physical and emotional disconnection between Charlie and the world, however, seems to be the point of the scene and the song helps to emphasise that disconnection.

The song is clearly also incongruous on numerous levels. Clegg wrote the song as an implicit critique of apartheid ideology; 'rather than subscribing to the dogma of an essential difference between races', Caleb Mutch writes in his analysis of the Juluka version, the song 'emphasise[s] all of humanity's common origin in Africa and our shared journey'.[16] 'They are the scatterlings of Africa', Clegg sings in the chorus we hear at the beginning of the scene, 'each uprooted one'. The African/apartheid context of the song is obviously hard to square with the film's narrative, but the deeper meaning in the song about an essential commonality between disconnected and dislocated humans resonates with Charlie's shift from an inability to connect to an appreciation of human connection and a sense of familial belonging. There are other ways in which the music is congruous with the film: the song is also a kind of road trip – we can just about make out Clegg singing 'we're on the road to Phelamanga, where the world began' at the end of the chorus.[17]

The music thus criss-crosses from convergence to divergence in relation to the film's narrative, something pre-existing music in cinema often does.[18] The apparent incongruities act as prompts, encouraging audiences to attempt actively to extract meaning from the interaction of music, image and story.

Adding a consideration for context to film sound theorist Michel Chion's conception of cinema as a system in which sound/music and visuals synergistically situate and resituate each other, Mera and Morcom argue that 'as soundtrack and visuals are matched, each re-contextualises the (de-contextualised) other'.[19] While all music is in a constant state of syncretic evolution, they argue, 'these characteristics have many and, in some cases, potentially infinite new layers on top of a "traditional" history, making screened music fundamentally different from non-screened performances and performance traditions'.[20] Mera and Morcom outline 'the myriad ways' in which music and visuals situate and resituate each other: 'With the multiple shots and multiple scenes and location in the visual dimension, and

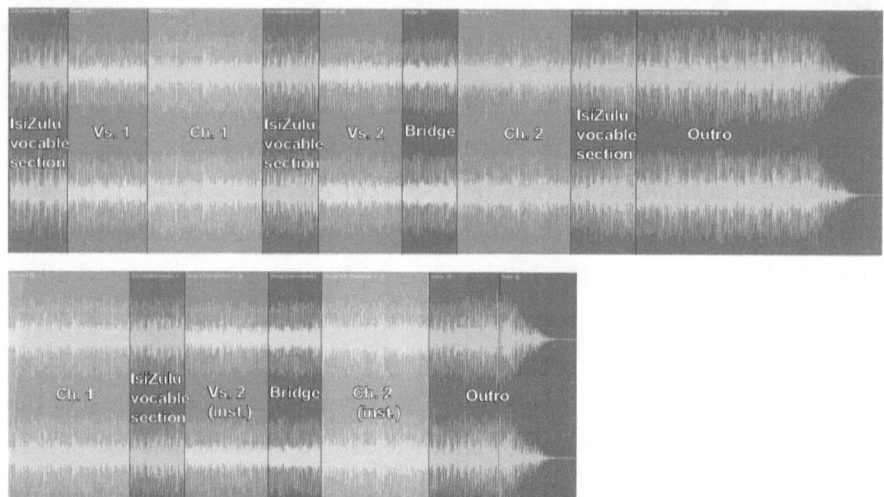

Figure 9.1: The wave form (top) shows the structure of the album version of 'Scatterlings of Africa' compared with the edited remix used in the film (bottom). Transcription by author.

equivalent use of sound in the aural dimension that film and sound design enable, contextualisations with and within other contextualisations tend to exist at many levels. Even the crudest filmed snippets of music making involve de- and re-contextualisations as a new text is created'.[21]

De- and recontextualisation as a concept feels particularly apt with regard to the distinctly South African or, more specifically, Zulu-connoting aspects of 'Scatterlings of Africa' in *Rain Man*. A close comparison of the edit of the song in the film with the album version (figure 9.1) shows how the filmmakers sought to emphasise the performed Zulu-ness in the music – the song fades up with the first chorus (presumably to include the 'on the road' reference as well as repeated mentions of Africa), before cutting straight to the isiZulu vocable section that references neo-Zulu vocal styles; Clegg's verses in English are removed entirely. In correspondence for this chapter, Rosenthal recalled music supervisor Allan Mason telling him that he had 'played [director] Barry [Levinson] the Savuka version of the song, and Barry liked the arrangement but preferred the "sound" of the Juluka version'. Rosenthal said he then suggested that they go into the studio and do a remix with that in mind.[22] The 'sound' and production of the version of the song in the film are, however, the same as the version that appears on *Third World Child*, while the arrangement differs. Rosenthal told me he gave the filmmakers a mix of the song without the lead vocal, which they could keep in or leave out as much as they needed.[23] An instrumental version of the second verse is just audible under the film's dialogue, and at the end of the scene, when the music swells, there is a cut to the end of the song. Here though, in the film mix, Clegg's English vocal ad lib overdubs have been removed ('we are the scatterlings of Africa' repeated six times on the album version) leaving just the isiZulu vocables (*'Jimm o hmm ... Hawu beke mama ye!'*) and the flute solo as it appears on the album version.

This feels significant: the African or, more specifically, Zulu elements are emphasised, used to defamiliarise the American setting so as to set up the metaphor for the lead character's disconnection. For the film, the actual Zulu-ness matters less than the alien nature of the song (we 'might as well be on Mars', to quote Zimmer again), and the explicit anti-apartheid narrative in the music is obviously not of any use to the film either; specific associations are therefore suppressed through careful selection of the bits of the music that are used and those that are given relative prominence in the mix. Mera and Morcom's discussion of the ways in which all music is de- and recontextualised in film is useful here. We might also see this as a more mainstream kind of 'schizophonic transmogrification' – a process Michael Bakan describes as 'involving the rematerialisation and thorough reinvention of people and places whose voices and sounds, as inscribed on sound recordings, have been separated from their original sources of identity and meaning and resituated in entirely alien contexts ... for purposes that serve especially to evoke the strange, and often the grotesque and sinister as well'.[24] There is not the same evidence of the grotesque and sinister here as in the *kecak* examples Bakan explores, but the evocation 'of the strange' feels entirely apposite.

The music works in the scene for many reasons, and its incongruity in terms of signifying place is paradoxically fitting in terms of the metaphorical work it does in the film. The erasure of the South African specificities in the song in its recontextualisation in the film is nevertheless discomforting, perhaps especially for a South African audio-viewer. The year 1988 was a particularly brutal period in the dying days of apartheid, and Clegg's empathetic song for the lives crushed and disrupted by apartheid was an important intervention. One feels delight at the fact that Clegg's iconic South African song appears in this iconic US film, but also irritation at the way the film asks us to hear the music: as strange and foreign-sounding, relegated to metaphor.

SCHIZOPHONIC PLACEMENT: 'CRUEL, CRAZY, BEAUTIFUL WORLD' IN *CAREER OPPORTUNITIES*

There are related schizophonic processes at work in the use of Clegg's song 'Cruel, Crazy, Beautiful World' in the romantic comedy *Career Opportunities*, which I will look at more briefly.[25] The film is far less significant than *Rain Man*; although it was written and co-produced by John Hughes. Hughes was disappointed with how it turned out and tried unsuccessfully to take his name off it.[26] Like *Rain Man* it is a film about a persuasive but irresponsible young man – Jim Dodge (played by Frank Whaley) in this case – who lands a job as an overnight janitor at a local Target store. On his first shift in his new job, Jim is locked alone in the store by his boss, who leaves him there until his shift ends at 7 a.m. The edit of Clegg's song accompanies a slapstick montage of Jim cleaning the store. One could either read the music as diegetic, perhaps emanating from the in-store sound system – and there are moments of clear synchronisation between strong beats in the music and actions on screen[27] – or else, more straightforwardly, as a music video-like montage sequence, a kind of *entr'acte* in which narrative progression is suspended for the duration of the song. Either way, Clegg's song dominates the soundtrack – we can hear every word and audiences are likely to seek connections between the song's narrative and that of the film. On the surface, the song is about taking the rough with the smooth: accepting and dealing with the bad or unpleasant things that happen in life in addition to the good or pleasant things. On that level the song chimes with the film's exploration of life's ups and downs (having no money but finding love). The sunny cheerfulness of the music also makes a good match for the lead character's boundless positivity, and there are other more specific points

Figure 9.2: Transcription by the author of the first verse of 'Cruel, Crazy, Beautiful World', used in the film *Career Opportunities* at 00:24:30.

of connection – the line about having to live with 'the crooked politician' (figure 9.2) fits well with the abusive state officials in the plot.

The song also makes a comfortable fit with the soundtrack because it has sonic similarities to other contemporary international pop hits. In a discussion of the recording of the song, Rosenthal said he 'loved the production of "She Drives Me Crazy" by Fine Young Cannibals, which was a hit at the time. When Johnny first played me "Cruel, Crazy", I suggested that we take a similar approach'.[28] Rosenthal said that programmed synthesiser/ MIDI elements were sequenced using an Atari 1040ST, a personal computer released in 1986 that had a MIDI port, which was used by numerous contemporary hit-makers including Depeche Mode and the Pet Shop Boys.

If the film attempts to impose a straightforwardly optimistic reading of the song ('Every time you wake up I hope it's under a blue sky'), for listeners aware of the song's wider context, the scene might feel more dissonant and the music incongruent again. 'Cruel, Crazy, Beautiful World' was written in the wake of anthropologist and anti-apartheid activist David Webster's assassination by apartheid security forces outside his home on 1 May 1989.

Clegg was one of Webster's students and later his colleague at the University of the Witwatersrand, where Clegg studied and worked before his music career took off. He was working on the album, later also titled *Cruel, Crazy, Beautiful World*, when Webster was murdered.[29] Speaking about the murder to *Rolling Stone* journalist Samuel Freedman in 1990 he said: 'I felt like I'd been axed, like a cleaver had come into my brain ... I was seized once again by this fucking paralysis, an impotence, a real fright. In a death like this, you realise the contingency of history, the reality of existing in chaos. We have a superficial web of order we place over things. This smashed my web.'[30]

Clegg frames 'Cruel, Crazy, Beautiful World' as a farewell letter to his son. Jesse Clegg was born in 1988 and is depicted on Clegg's shoulders on the album cover. Knowing the context of Webster's murder, it is hard not to hear the song as an expression of his own fear of assassination in a cruel and violent world. The lines '*Ayeye* Jesse, *mfana*' ('watch out or beware, Jesse, my boy') are repeated numerous times in the song and are heard in the edit used in the film, as Jim finds ways to amuse himself as he cleans the store. There is, however, no way to make sense of the lines in terms of the film's narrative. As in *Rain Man*, there are aspects of the song – lyrics and music – that converge with the other storytelling elements in the film, while others diverge disquietingly.

As in the 'Scatterlings of Africa' recontextualisation, the film seems to want to partially disassociate the music from its original South African context in order for it to work in the scene where it occurs. Such decontextualisations, however, are not always accomplished successfully. Musical meaning is hard to regulate, and there is something in the plaintive, heartbroken tone of Clegg's high tenor voice in the verse, and the rise and fall of the melody on the words 'say goodbye', that, in combination with the perky bass pattern and maskanda guitar licks, conveys something far more complex than the scene might need or the filmmakers want.

CONCLUSION

If mainstream cinema at this time invited a wider range of non-Western musics onto its soundtracks, the invitations were, perhaps unsurprisingly, partial, and often made on the basis that some connection to the music's original context be severed. As other writers have observed, that is generally true of all uses of pop music in on-screen narratives: the music fits and doesn't fit in complex ways.[31] The Zulu-music references and specific political contexts of Johnny Clegg & Savuka's music make its mediation in US-set Hollywood films additionally layered and complex. If the songs' use in these films comes at a cost to how they are heard and understood, there is also something pleasingly ungovernable about their presence on these soundtracks – a complex South African vitality that refuses to be entirely incorporated.

NOTES

1   'Scatterlings of Africa' (soundtrack), in *Rain Man*, directed by Barry Levinson (Hollywood: United Artists, 1988); 'Cruel, Crazy, Beautiful World' (soundtrack), in *Opportunity Knocks*, directed by Donald Petrie (Los Angeles: Universal Pictures, 1990); 'Cruel, Crazy, Beautiful World' (soundtrack), in *Career Opportunities*, directed by Bryan Gordon (Los Angeles: Universal Pictures, 1991).
2   'Great Heart' (soundtrack), in *Jock of the Bushveld*, directed by Gray Hofmeyr (Sandton: Toron International, 1986); 'Life Is A Magic Thing' (soundtrack), in *Fern Gully: The Last Rainforest*, directed by Bill Kroyer (Los Angeles: 20th Century Fox, 1992); *The Power of One*, directed by John Avildsen (Burbank: Warner Bros Pictures, 1992). The music for both films was issued as separate recordings: Johnny Clegg & Savuka, *Great Heart* (single, Los Angeles: Capitol Records, B-73029, 1987); Johnny Clegg, *Life Is A Magic Thing* (single, Los Angeles: Capitol Records, DPRO 79287, 1992).
3   Producers who want to use a pre-existing song in a film need to secure a 'synchronisation licence' for its use from the song's copyright holders. The licence allows the film's producers to use music – called 'sync placements' – timed to or synchronised with the film's visual images.
4   Miguel Mera and Anna Morcom, 'Introduction: Screened Music, Trans-contextualisation and Ethnomusicological Approaches', *Ethnomusicology Forum* 18 no. 1 (2009): 5.
5   In the late 1990s, about 60 per cent of performance royalties were derived from the use of music in television, radio and films, according to Harold Vogel, *Entertainment Industry Economics: A Guide for Financial Analysis* (Cambridge: Cambridge University Press, 1998), with the US being the biggest exporter of cultural products (films, television and recorded music).
6   Caleb Mutch describes the sound of Savuka's synths as 'a distinctly 1980s sound', in chapter 11 in this book. In the same chapter he describes how the rhythmic changes made to the re-recording 'serve to make Savuka's version more familiar to Western audiences'.
7   'Top 1988 Movies at the International Box Office', *The Numbers*, 1988, accessed 10 September 2023, https://www.the-numbers.com/box-office-records/international/all-movies/cumulative/released-in-1988.
8   Hilton Rosenthal, email correspondence with the author, 7 April 2024.
9   Paul Simon, *Graceland* (album, Burbank: Warner Bros Records, 925 447-1, 1986).

10. *A World Apart*, directed by Chris Menges (Anchorage: Atlantic Entertainment Group, 1988); D.R. Stewart, 'Zimmer and Howard Discuss Remote Collaboration', *Variety*, accessed 10 September 2023, https://web.archive.org/web/20090205021906/http://www.variety.com/article/VR1117990043.html?categoryId=3179&cs=1. Rosenthal, in response to my emailed questions, elaborated on the connection with Zimmer: in his first meeting with music supervisor Allan Mason about licensing 'Scatterlings' for *Rain Man*, Rosenthal said Mason 'played me some music composed by Hans Zimmer from the movie *A World Apart*, telling me that he was considering using Hans as the composer for *Rain Man*. I was blown away, even more, after watching the movie premiere. Soon after, when I was music supervisor for *The Power of One* it was obvious to me that Hans should do our soundtrack!' (Rosenthal, email, 7 Apr 2024).
11. John Young, 'Hans Zimmer Reflects on 15 of His Memorable Film Scores', *Entertainment Weekly*, 5 August 2008, accessed 10 September 2023, https://web.archive.org/web/20090309180419/http://www.ew.com/ew/gallery/0,,20216261,00.html.
12. Introduced in 1979, the Fairlight was the first commercially available digital synthesizer with an inbuilt sampler, enabling users to reproduce acoustic instruments as playable 'samples'. Along with Zimmer, Kate Bush and Peter Gabriel helped popularise its distinctive sound.
13. The Belle Stars, *Iko Iko* (single, Los Angeles: Capitol Records, 7PRO-79543, 1982). In 'Hearing *Thelma & Louise*', Claudia Gorbman notes how many of the New Hollywood directors of the time (Martin Scorsese, Quentin Tarantino, Jonathan Demme) took exceptional care with music in their films, not least with the choice of pop music to help define characters and their worlds. Gorbman writes: 'By means of their titles, lyrics, style, and/or performers, the songs invite a more active reading than orchestral underscoring: they define action, setting, and character, they engage references, parallelism, and metaphors, and sometimes they elaborate complex structures of point of view' (Claudia Gorbman, 'Hearing *Thelma & Louise*': Active Reading of the Hybrid Pop Score', in *Thelma & Louise Live! The Cultural Afterlife of an American Film*, edited by Bernie Cook [Texas: University of Texas Press, 2007], 65). This is equally true of Levinson's use of pop music in *Rain Man*.
14. Juluka, 'Scatterlings of Africa', on *Scatterlings* (album, Johannesburg: MINC, MINC – (L) 1040, 1982; Johnny Clegg & Savuka, 'Scatterlings of Africa', on *Third World Child* (album, Sandton: EMI, EMCJ (D) – 2407331, 1987). For an excellent analysis of the Juluka version of the song see Caleb Mutch, '"Something Else Is Possible": Transcultural Collaboration as Anti-apartheid Activism in the Music of Juluka', *Popular Music* 40, no. 3–4 (2021): 450–469. Mutch's close analysis and comparison of the Juluka and Savuka versions in chapter 11 in this book is also pertinent.
15. An album from the film that included the pre-existing pop music used in the film as well as two of Hans Zimmer's cues was released on CD by Capitol Records in 1989 in the US and Europe (Various Artists, *Rain Man Original Motion Picture Soundtrack* [album, Hollywood: Capitol Records, CDP 7 91866 2, 1989]; see https://www.discogs.com/release/1111513-Various-Rain-Man-Original-Motion-Picture-Soundtrack, accessed 5 April 2025). As in the film, 'Scatterlings of Africa' is the second piece of music on the album.
16. Mutch, 'Something Else Is Possible', 463.
17. The song had another life on the soundtrack album for the film and was widely played on MTV and radio, so if it is hard to hear the lyrics in the scene, some listeners to the album may have been able to make the connections.

18 See Phil Powrie and Robynn Stilwell, *Changing Tunes: The Use of Pre-existing Music in Film* (Aldershot: Ashgate, 2006).
19 Michel Chion, *Audio-Vision: Sound on Screen*, trans. Claudia Gorbman (New York: Columbia University Press, 1994); Mera and Morcom, 'Introduction', 6.
20 Mera and Morcom, 'Introduction', 6.
21 Mera and Morcom, 'Introduction', 6–7.
22 Rosenthal, email, 7 April 2024.
23 Rosenthal, email, 7 April 2024.
24 Michael B. Bakan, 'The Abduction of the Signifying Monkey Chant: Schizophonic Transmogrifications of Balinese *Kecak* in Fellini's *Satyricon* and the Coen Brothers' *Blood Simple*', *Ethnomusicology Forum* 18, no. 1 (2009): 84–85.
25 Rosenthal (email, 7 April 2024) told me how it was music supervisor Tim Sexton, 'a big fan of Johnny's', who made the decision to license 'Cruel, Crazy, Beautiful World' in *Career Opportunities*, as well as in the previous film he had worked on, *Opportunity Knocks*. Sexton isn't credited as a music supervisor on *Career Opportunities*, but he is on *Opportunity Knocks* and on another film featuring Clegg's music, *Fern Gully: The Last Rainforest*.
26 Bill Carter, 'Him Alone', *The New York Times*, 4 August 1991, accessed 10 September 2023, https://www.nytimes.com/1991/08/04/magazine/him-alone.html.
27 In the first chorus, the first syllable of the line 'Every day you wake up' on the first beat of the bar coincides with the percussive hit of Whaley pushing open the 'Employees Only' swing doors; a bit later the polishing machine crashes into a display of flower pots synchronised with a downbeat; the song ends abruptly on a downbeat synchronised precisely with Whaley bashing through the swing doors again.
28 Rosenthal, email, 7 April 2024.
29 Johnny Clegg & Savuka, *Cruel, Crazy, Beautiful World* (album, London: EMI, EMCJ (E) – 7934461, 1989).
30 Samuel G. Freedman, 'Johnny Clegg's War on Apartheid', *Rolling Stone*, 22 March 1990, accessed 10 September 2023, https://www.rollingstone.com/music/music-features/johnny-clegg-south-africa-apartheid-samuel-freedman-860888/.
31 See Miguel Mera, 'Reap Just What You Sow: *Trainspotting*'s Perfect Day', in *Pop Fiction: The Song in Cinema*, ed. Matthew Caley and Steve Lannin, 86–97 (Bristol: Intellect Books, 2005), 90, and Jeff Smith, *The Sounds of Commerce: Marketing Popular Film Music* (New York: Columbia, 1998), 221.

REFERENCES

Bakan, Michael B. 'The Abduction of the Signifying Monkey Chant: Schizophonic Transmogrifications of Balinese *Kecak* in Fellini's *Satyricon* and the Coen Brothers' *Blood Simple*'. *Ethnomusicology Forum* 18, no. 1 (2009): 84–85.

Carter, Bill. 'Him Alone'. *The New York Times*, 4 August 1991. Accessed 10 September 2023. https://www.nytimes.com/1991/08/04/magazine/him-alone.html.

Chion, Michel. *Audio-Vision: Sound on Screen*. Translated by Claudia Gorbman. New York: Columbia University Press, 1994.

Freedman, Samuel G. 'Johnny Clegg's War on Apartheid'. *Rolling Stone*, 22 March 1990. Accessed 10 September 2023. https://www.rollingstone.com/music/music-features/johnny-clegg-south-africa-apartheid-samuel-freedman-860888/.

Gorbman, Claudia. 'Hearing *Thelma & Louise*: Active Reading of the Hybrid Pop Score'. In *Thelma & Louise Live! The Cultural Afterlife of an American Film*, edited by Bernie Cook, 65–90. Texas: University of Texas Press, 2007.

Mera, Miguel. 'Reap Just What You Sow: *Trainspotting*'s Perfect Day'. In *Pop Fiction – the Song in Cinema*, edited by Matthew Caley and Steve Lannin, 86–97. Bristol: Intellect Books, 2005.

Mera, Miguel and Anna Morcom. 'Introduction: Screened Music, Trans-contextualisation and Ethnomusicological Approaches'. *Ethnomusicology Forum* 18, no. 1 (2009): 3–19.

Mutch, Caleb. '"Something Else Is Possible": Transcultural Collaboration as Anti-apartheid Activism in the Music of Juluka'. *Popular Music* 40, no. 3–4 (2021): 450–469.

Powrie, Phil and Robynn Stilwell. *Changing Tunes: The Use of Pre-existing Music in Film*. Aldershot: Ashgate, 2006.

Smith, Jeff. *The Sounds of Commerce: Marketing Popular Film Music*. New York: Columbia University Press, 1998.

Stewart, D.R. 'Zimmer and Howard Discuss Remote Collaboration'. *Variety*, 4 August 2008. Accessed 10 September 2023. https://web.archive.org/web/20090205021906/http://www.variety.com/article/VR1117990043.html?categoryId=3179&cs=1.

'Top 1988 Movies at the International Box Office'. *The Numbers*, 1988. Accessed 10 September 2023. https://www.the-numbers.com/box-office-records/international/all-movies/cumulative/released-in-1988.

Vogel, Harold. *Entertainment Industry Economics: A Guide for Financial Analysis*. Cambridge: Cambridge University Press, 1998.

Young, John. 'Hans Zimmer Reflects on 15 of His Memorable Film Scores'. *Entertainment Weekly*, 5 August 2008. Accessed 10 September 2023. https://web.archive.org/web/20090309180419/http://www.ew.com/ew/gallery/0,,20216261,00.html.

DISCOGRAPHY

The Belle Stars. *Iko Iko*. Single. Los Angeles: Capitol Records, 7PRO-79543, 1982.
Clegg, Johnny. *Life Is A Magic Thing*. Single. Los Angeles: Capitol Records, DPRO 79287, 1992.
Johnny Clegg & Savuka. *Cruel, Crazy, Beautiful World*. Album. London: EMI, EMCJ (E) – 7934461, 1989.
Johnny Clegg & Savuka. *Great Heart*. Single. Los Angeles: Capitol Records, B-73029, 1987.
Johnny Clegg & Savuka. *Third World Child*. Album. Sandton: EMI, EMCJ (D) – 2407331, 1987.
Juluka. *Scatterlings*. Album. Johannesburg: MINC, MINC – (L) 1040, 1982.
Simon, Paul. *Graceland*. Album. Burbank: Warner Bros Records, 925 447-1, 1986.
Various Artists. *Rain Man Original Motion Picture Soundtrack*. Album. Hollywood, CA: Capitol Records, CDP 7 91866 2, 1989.

FILMOGRAPHY

Avildsen, John, dir. *The Power of One*. Burbank: Warner Bros Pictures, 1992.
Gordon, Bryan, dir. *Career Opportunities*. Los Angeles: Universal Pictures, 1991.
Hofmeyr, Gray, dir. *Jock of the Bushveld*. Sandton: Toron International, 1986.
Kroyer, Bill, dir. *Fern Gully: The Last Rainforest*. Los Angeles: 20th Century Fox, 1992.
Levinson, Barry, dir. *Rain Man*. Hollywood: United Artists, 1988.
Menges, Chris, dir. *A World Apart*. Anchorage: Atlantic Entertainment Group, 1988.
Petrie, Donald, dir. *Opportunity Knocks*. Los Angeles: Universal Pictures, 1990.

CHAPTER

10

Digging for Some Words: Johnny Clegg's Academic Experiences in North America

Lucilla Spini and Andrew J. Friedland

Jonathan (Johnny) Clegg officially left academia and lecturing duties in the early 1980s after requesting sabbatical leave from which he never returned. What followed was a highly successful full-time artistic career at home and internationally. However, while becoming an accomplished and world-renowned full-time artist, Clegg did establish links with two universities in the United States of America (US): the City University of New York (CUNY) and Dartmouth University in Hanover, New Hampshire.[1]

Clegg was an anthropologist by training and this fact was noticeable throughout his artistic career. His direct engagement with academic institutions was publicised mostly through coverage of his receipt of honorary degrees in the 2000s and 2010s, and less because of his academic contributions made through visits to university classes. In this chapter we examine these engagements with academic institutions by providing the historical background to this part of Clegg's life, highlighting the interconnections among his art, activism and academic contributions, and by providing a record of his engagement with universities in the US.

LEAVING ACADEMIA: CLEGG'S EARLY EXPERIENCES IN NORTH AMERICA

During his university years – as a student at the University of the Witwatersrand (Wits) from his first year in 1971 until he received his BA Honours in 1977, then as a junior lecturer from 1980 to 1983 at Wits, and as a replacement for a senior lecturer in anthropology at the University of Natal, Durban, in 1979 – Clegg did not have many opportunities to meet foreign academics, as would have been possible today.[2] This was in part due to the restrictions of the cultural and academic boycotts of South Africa, as expressed, for example, in United Nations General Assembly Resolution 35/206: 'To cease any cultural and academic collaboration with South Africa, including the exchange of scientists, students and academic personalities, as well as cooperation in research programmes'.[3] The boycotts also had an impact on academic exchange programmes (such as the US Fulbright Program).[4] Yet, we know that Clegg established dialogues with scholars from the US, including David Coplan, who was in 1975 a graduate student in ethnomusicology at Indiana University on his first research visit to South Africa, and Helen Q. Kivnick, a lecturer at the University of Minnesota (and a singer/songwriter) on her visit to South Africa in 1984, as recalled in her 1990 book: 'During the trip I had spent an evening talking with Johnny Clegg. In a few hours Johnny had given me a private lecture-demonstration of traditional Zulu music, and he had named several performers whose music I would have to hear to get a feel for contemporary black popular singing'.[5]

Furthermore, in those years, Clegg did not have the opportunity to visit academic institutions abroad, not even in a personal capacity (although, when he was 21 years old, he did travel to the United Kingdom to meet his biological father).[6] The prospect of further travel abroad was triggered, in 1982, by Juluka's fame established through the song 'Scatterlings of Africa'.[7] This led Clegg to request a one-year sabbatical leave from Wits through the head of the Department of Anthropology, Professor David Hammond-Tooke, in order to explore the opportunity to tour as a professional artist overseas.[8] Clegg has reported numerous times that Hammond-Tooke granted the one-year leave, but also famously said: 'Jonathan the moment you walk out that door we'll never see you again'. Clegg responded that he enjoyed teaching and that the leave was only for one year.[9] Later on, Clegg acknowledged that Hammond-Tooke had been right: he never resumed an academic career.[10] However, he did remain faithful to his academic discipline (anthropology), through his songwriting and performances in addition to invited lectures as well as documentaries.[11]

The above-mentioned cultural boycott also related to artists' performances. However, as highlighted by Clegg himself, 'boycotts are usually messy and uneven affairs'.[12] In fact, each country applied the boycott in a different way: there were many European and North American countries that were applying boycott measures on a case-by-case basis.[13] Among them was the US, where the anti-apartheid movement allowed for South African artists committed to the anti-apartheid struggle to perform and to have their message heard.[14] Such a context enabled Juluka to be supported by the anti-apartheid movement in the US and to be featured in well-known venues in 1983 and 1984 (such as The Ritz in New York and Toad's Place in New Haven), and to receive important press coverage in publications such as *The New York Times*, *Newsweek* and *USA Today*, but also to have Clegg invited to give a guest lecture in New York in 1983.[15]

Clegg was invited by Dr Larry Shore – a South African-born immigrant to the US in 1973, Wits alumnus, and someone active in the anti-apartheid movement in the US in the 1980s – to talk to CUNY Hunter College's students in a class on the music industry in late 1983.[16] Unfortunately, there are no written or audiovisual records of the class, but Shore reported that Clegg covered the following topics: music in South Africa, the role of music in the anti-apartheid struggle, how he viewed the role of culture, and his band Juluka and the challenges it faced.[17] At that time, Clegg had just departed from academia and it must have been quite a comfortable experience for him to step back into the classroom.

As far as we know, Shore was the first person to invite Clegg to lecture in a US university, and we do not have other evidence of Clegg's engagement with academic institutions in the US or Canada in the 1980s and 1990s (neither through guest lectures nor through participation in any anti-apartheid demonstrations or other events organised by US or Canadian students).

In fact, Clegg's tours in North America in the 1980s can be considered mostly related to his work as a professional artist, as also confirmed by the fact that Clegg and Juluka attracted the interest of major American artists. Among these artists was Paul Simon, whose interest in South African music led him to contact Hilton Rosenthal – then the producer of Juluka. Rosenthal arranged to introduce Simon to Clegg in South Africa in February 1985, at a time when Simon was developing what then became the *Graceland* album,[18] and Clegg and Juluka were at the height of their recognition and fame, as exemplified by the successful 'Concert in the Park' in Johannesburg on 12 January 1985.[19]

Despite the dissolution of Juluka, also in 1985, and after a short spell as a solo artist, in 1986, Clegg initiated the Savuka project, Johnny Clegg & Savuka, which brought his international exposure as an artist and as an anthropologist to greater prominence.

THE SAVUKA PROJECT: CLEGG RETURNS TO NORTH AMERICA

During the 1986–1994 period, Johnny Clegg & Savuka's music and performances reached international fame. The song '*Asimbonanga*', written by Clegg, became an international hit; it was also recorded by a major American artist, Joan Baez, who released it in 1987 on her album *Recently*.[20] The *Third World Child* album on which the song appeared also included a new version of 'Scatterlings of Africa' which further increased this song's fame worldwide, as shown by its selection for the soundtrack of the 1988 movie *Rain Man*.[21]

With Savuka, Clegg continued his innovative work of mixing different styles of music and he addressed geopolitical and environmental challenges, in line with the events occurring in South Africa and around the world (for example, the fall of the Soviet Union). The late 1980s and 1990s were still years of transition and political tension in South Africa, including civil unrest and violence, despite the fact that Nelson Mandela was released on 11 February 1990.[22] During those years, several of Clegg's friends were killed, including his academic mentor, Dr David Webster, who was assassinated on 1 May 1989 because of his anti-apartheid activism.

In addition, in this tense geopolitical context, Clegg's producer and friend Hilton Rosenthal left South Africa to move to Los Angeles, where he established his own recording studio (Plus 4 Studio). Clegg and Savuka recorded three of their albums there: this enabled Clegg to spend time in Los Angeles and to have the opportunity to perform additional concerts in the US and Canada as well as to participate in promotional events and receive high-level recognition.[23] For example, Thomas (Tom) Bradley – Los Angeles' first black mayor – declared 25 July 1988 'Johnny Clegg & Savuka Day'.[24] Such an event created visibility for Clegg and Savuka, as well as underlining the anti-apartheid stance taken by Mayor Bradley, which also resulted in the hosting of the 'Second International Symposium on Cultural and Academic Links with South Africa, organised by the Special Committee against Apartheid' in Los Angeles on 12 May 1991).[25] Clegg was one of the symposium participants: he participated as a representative of the executive of the South African Musicians' Alliance (SAMA), accompanied by Jabu Ngwenya (the SAMA coordinating secretary) and Rashid Lanie (a SAMA executive member), who publicly expressed positive feedback on the symposium's outcome in the 'Los Angeles Statement'.[26]

From the available documents relating to the symposium we do not see any evidence of direct engagement by Clegg with universities, but we imagine that this symposium probably provided him with the opportunity to engage with world-renowned intellectuals and academics (such as Nigerian Wole Soyinka, then professor of comparative literature at the Obafemi Awolowo University/University of Ife in Nigeria, and recipient of the 1986 Nobel Prize for Literature; South African Dennis Brutus, at the time professor of African literature at the University of Pittsburgh but also an activist, educator, journalist and poet; and Nadine Gordimer, the South African writer and activist and 1991 recipient of the Nobel Prize for Literature) and to further develop, and be acknowledged, as a public intellectual.[27]

CLEGG'S RE-ENGAGEMENT WITH ACADEMIA IN THE US

In the early 2000s, Clegg's work focused on contemporary challenges affecting the new democratic South Africa and the world, as exemplified by the lyrical content of the 2002 album *New World Survivor*.[28] In 2004, he toured in both Europe and North America with the Johnny Clegg Band, and performed in front of audiences that included more recent expatriates from South Africa but also concertgoers who had previously attended Juluka and/or Savuka shows. During this time, Clegg's unique South African story and his role as a public intellectual addressing global socio-political and environmental matters were reinvigorated, which led to the reinstatement of the academic side of his life in the US.

The invitation to give a lecture at Dartmouth University in 2004 conveyed to Clegg by co-author Andrew Friedland, a professor of environmental studies at Dartmouth, can be seen as the trigger for a more direct engagement with academia in the US. The invitation was developed within the framework of a programme at Dartmouth that brought students to Africa (to countries such as Kenya and South Africa) for a ten-week off-campus term to study the interlinkages between people, wildlife and the environment. The invitation to Clegg was motivated by the fact that his songs conveyed the strong connection between people and the natural environment, through an interdisciplinary approach that was of interest to students and faculty from a wide variety of scholarly fields (for example environmental sciences, anthropology, political science and music) at Dartmouth.

When first invited in early 2004 to offer an academic lecture, Clegg politely declined, explaining that he was not delivering academic lectures any more. This was probably in part a result of his training in a university system which did not include practitioners as lecturers; and, in part because it would have been difficult for him to engage in an academic visit of any length while touring with a band, manager and sound technicians. However, he suggested that if he and his band were invited to Dartmouth for a concert, he would make himself available to a class earlier on the same day. On 7 July 2004, Clegg arrived at Dartmouth just one hour before the class starting time (having just travelled from Washington DC by overnight tour bus). He discussed with Friedland what would be covered in the talk, and then he addressed 'a combined meeting of classes from Environmental Studies, History, African and African American Studies, Anthropology and Government' (about 150 students) in 105 Dartmouth Hall.[29]

Clegg gave the talk entirely without notes, and demonstrated acuity and fluency with academic concepts and lecture style. It became apparent within seconds of the start of the talk that even though he had not been lecturing formally since he left his academic position in South Africa, he was still adept at academic discourse, probably because of the above-mentioned 'mini-lectures' he gave during performances and his overall communication skills, as also underlined more recently by Coplan.[30] In that engaging, articulate and energetic 60-minute talk, Clegg compared Western and Zulu culture, described various types of traditional African dance, and demonstrated some of the dances as well as humming and chanting. He also sang three songs accompanied by his own acoustic guitar-playing. The music continued in the ensuing concert that evening in the sold-out Spaulding Auditorium, where 900 people from the campus and local communities enjoyed not only the songs, but also the 'mini-lectures' – as highlighted by one of the students who said after attending the concert: 'His anecdotes and explanations in between songs were almost as fascinating as the songs themselves'.[31]

While we cannot suggest a causal relationship between the Dartmouth occasion and subsequent events, we note that in the years following his Dartmouth visit, Clegg also re-engaged with academia in South Africa, as shown for instance by the fact that in 2007 his *alma mater*, Wits University, awarded him an honorary doctorate in music with the motivation that his 'life and productions give meaning to the multiculturalism and social integration South Africans yearn for'.[32] However, it is certain that this first lecture at Dartmouth led to further engagements with Dartmouth (in 2011, 2014 and 2016) and it may also have attracted the attention of other North American universities.

In 2011, within the context of the 'Human Tour'– an extensive and successful tour in Europe, the US and Canada – Clegg and the Johnny Clegg Band also performed in or near university campuses, including Brock University in St Catherines, Ontario.[33] That event occurred at the invitation of Debbie Slade, the then director of the Brock University Center for the Arts. It does not appear that there was any sort of outreach or student event on the margins of the concert, nor in any other Canadian universities.

Yet, just before the concert at Brock University, Clegg was on tour in the US and stopped at two universities: CUNY School of Law and Dartmouth.

On 5 April 2011, Clegg was awarded an honorary doctor of laws degree from CUNY School of Law. He was nominated for the honorary degree by Professor Penelope Andrews, then academic dean at the School of Law. Professor Andrews, who was South African-born, trained at the University of Natal at the time when Clegg was lecturing there in anthropology in 1979. Having been familiar with Clegg's music since the time of Juluka, in 2010 she had the chance to talk to Clegg in person following a concert in New York. As a result of that interaction and others, she nominated him for an honorary degree.[34] The nomination was based on three main points, namely shared history between the US and South Africa with respect to racial justice (that is, the US civil rights and South African anti-apartheid struggles); long-standing CUNY engagement with South Africa (for example, through a reading group on South Africa, and internship programmes and faculty engagement with South Africa, both established in 1993–1994); and the role of music in the anti-apartheid struggle. Not only was the nomination approved, but special permission was given to hold the *honoris causa* ceremony in an event prior to the regular commencement ceremony in order to accommodate Clegg's touring schedule in the US.[35] It was also an opportunity for the CUNY community to mark the 15-year anniversary since the school's second dean, Haywood Burns, and faculty member Shanara Gilbert had died in a car accident while in South Africa working on post-apartheid judicial reform.[36]

The ceremony was attended by many high-level CUNY representatives, including CUNY Board Vice Chairperson Philip Alfonso Berry – a student leader activist in the 1970s – who during the ceremony 'praised Clegg and his melding of music, activism and philanthropy as the essence of *ubuntu*, the African humanist concept of the individual's interconnectedness to the community and the world'.[37] Other attendees included Executive Vice Chancellor for Academic Affairs and Provost Alexandra Logue, who highlighted that in 'combining Western and Zulu rhythms and stimulating audiences to think more deeply about racial identity and justice, Clegg embodied values similar to bedrock CUNY principles, such as the celebration of diversity and the equality of opportunity'.[38] Clegg gave a speech during the ceremony in which he stated that 'it was appropriate that his honorary degree was a Doctor of Laws, for he [had] spent a lifetime questioning "why the fence exists"', alluding to the plethora of laws and institutions (a 'legal Lego set') that legislated the separation of races and social spaces in South Africa. He further added that 'he found it fitting that his journey to 'find a way around the fence' (that is, obstacles imposed by apartheid) had brought him to CUNY'.[39]

Just prior to the CUNY event, on 6 April 2011, Clegg returned to Dartmouth to speak for a second time with a group of students in a crowded Environmental Studies Library in the Fairchild Science Center.[40] In his talk, he spoke about his adopted homeland, South Africa, the struggle to end apartheid, and his musical influences. He also addressed South African cultural development, including the music industry. The cyclical approach in music is an important topic that Clegg brought up there and in many 'minilectures' and other talks. He also introduced this topic while describing the structure of walking songs. Clegg concluded the class by providing advice for future artists and activists, drawing on his past and current experiences and arguing that activism should engage in 'conscription' of the audience (that is, recruiting them to the cause) rather than triggering guilt for their faults and wrongdoings.[41] Later on the same day, Clegg delivered the George Link Jr Environmental Awareness Lecture to about 175 students, faculty and community members in the Filene Auditorium. He focused on the metaphors and symbols in relationships among people, domesticated animals and the natural world in South Africa. He then connected these cultural symbols to concepts of masculinity, stick fighting and sorcery that figure prominently in traditional societies. He also incorporated a multimedia aspect into his talk with a few video clips, including an interview with Sipho Mchunu. The symbol of the bull was prominent in the talk, not simply as a powerful, masculine animal but as an animal that guarantees the life and prosperity of the family. Clegg played one Zulu melody on acoustic guitar, demonstrating his ability to switch from academic discourse to musical expression. The audience of local residents, faculty and undergraduate and graduate students appeared to enjoy the diverse presentation. Without a formal performance scheduled, it was a non-workday for the band, and most of them were in attendance, which we think might have been the first time the band heard Clegg give an academic talk. After answering a few questions, he described the song 'Digging for Some Words' and its connection to the theme of environmental change, including global climate change today.[42] Then, in a spontaneous and unrehearsed event, he and fellow band members Mandisa Dlanga and Andy Innes, who had been in the audience listening to the lecture, performed the song, with Dlanga on vocals and Innes on acoustic guitar.[43] The next day, 'the Johnny Clegg Band was in its element during a Thursday, April 7th, 2011 concert in front of an almost sold-out audience at the Lebanon Opera House'.[44]

In the following years, Clegg was awarded two other honorary doctorates: one in South Africa (an honorary doctorate in social sciences from the University of KwaZulu-Natal [formerly the University of Natal, where Clegg had taught in 1979]) in April 2013, and the other one at Dartmouth in the US on 10 June 2012.[45] The Dartmouth degree was preceded by a nomination in August 2011 from co-author Friedland, who highlighted previous engagements by Clegg with Dartmouth but also stressed Clegg's role at the time 'as a private citizen in building and strengthening a democratic South Africa'. Friedland also identified Clegg's involvement in 'environmental business ventures as an advocate for local empowerment creating jobs for black South Africans and his becoming an "elder statesman" in the country'.[46] Clegg received an honorary doctorate of humane letters from the president of Dartmouth, Jim Yong Kim, an anthropologist and medical doctor (figure 10.1), who shortly thereafter became the president of the World Bank (a position he held from July 2012 to February 2019).[47]

With this honorary doctorate, the linkages between Clegg and Dartmouth became more consolidated; he was invited back to Dartmouth in 2014 through the prestigious Montgomery Fellowships – a fellowship that has been bestowed on eminent people such as J. William Fulbright, Chinua Achebe, Merce Cunningham, Wangari Maathai, Toni Morrison, Desmond Tutu and Yo-Yo Ma.[48] In the same year, along with Clegg, the Montgomery Fellowship was also awarded to archaeologist Daniel Potts. On the occasion

Figure 10.1: Johnny Clegg receives an honorary doctorate of humane letters from the president of Dartmouth University, Jim Yong Kim, on 10 June 2012. Photograph © Jeff Woodward, 2012.

of the announcement, the Montgomery Endowment reported that 'Potts and Clegg promise to enrich our campus in very different but complementary ways', and said that Clegg 'as an artist and activist in Apartheid South Africa, reminds us that individual action can make a significant difference to history'.[49]

As a Montgomery Fellow, Clegg visited the campus on 13–14 April 2014. He was a guest lecturer in a class taught by naturalist and writer

Figure 10.2: The Dartmouth undergraduate class with, front row from left, Terry Tempest Williams, Johnny Clegg, Andrew Friedland, 13 April 2014. Photograph © Lars Backmore, 2014.

Terry Tempest Williams (figure 10.2), and he gave the public Montgomery Lecture under the title 'A Conversation with Johnny Clegg' about arts and activism in the Filene Auditorium on 14 April, (discussed below), and met with students from the Environmental Studies Program's Southern Africa Foreign Study Program.[50]

In the same year, 2014, Clegg was also interviewed for the programme 'Higher Education Today' which is produced by the University of the District of Columbia. The interview, hosted by the educational consultant and author Steven Roy Goodman, provides great insight into Clegg's view of academia, his experience as a lecturer, as well as his passion for teaching and learning.[51]

In 2016, Clegg returned to Dartmouth as a guest of the Geisel School of Medicine and performed with the Johnny Clegg Band at Lebanon Opera House. In the context of the Geisel School of Medicine, he participated in a panel discussion with Patrick L. Osewe (the lead health specialist for the Southern Africa region of the World Bank) and Vama Jele (the executive secretary of the Swaziland Migrant Mineworkers Association and an advocate for mine workers' health). Clegg's participation on this panel was linked to his engagement with the campaign 'TB [tuberculosis] positive' in South Africa, among other things.

In 2017, Clegg returned to North America with the 'Final Journey' tour. During the tour he added a stop on 15 October 2017 at the Berklee College of Music for World Music/CRASHarts, for 'A Conversation with Johnny Clegg' moderated by a local radio station.[52] This 'outreach activity' in which Clegg talked about his life, his music and his views on different issues, was organised by Maure Aronson, the Boston music promoter, who is also a South African and a big fan of Clegg.[53]

CLEGG'S APPROACH TO ACADEMIC CONVERSATIONS

Concerning his time teaching in South Africa in the late 1970s and early 1980s, Clegg reported that he had started by teaching first-year students, in a six-week first-year course on 'Race and Racism', and in 'mainly white classes of above 90% white students'.[54] These incoming first-year students could have made a fairly homogeneous and, in a way, easy audience for Clegg to define lectures for, but he highlighted that it was a very challenging process to enable students to identify their racial biases and stereotypes prior to introducing them to anthropology.[55] In contrast, Clegg's audiences in North American universities were more diverse with respect to disciplinary backgrounds, especially in high-level, university-wide lectures. Such a different context did not pose an obstacle to Clegg, as his communication and rhetorical styles, as well as the content he chose to focus on, were easily adaptable to a diverse audience, probably benefiting from the extensive practice he had had when 'storytelling' to diverse audience during concerts.

Unfortunately, there are not many video recordings of his lectures; the above-mentioned lecture he gave for the Montgomery Fellowship at Dartmouth is one of the few audiovisual recordings of an entire Clegg lecture (longer than one hour) available with open access on YouTube.[56] Hence, this lecture provides an opportunity to analyse the content, structure and style of a lecture, which was entitled 'A Conversation with Johnny Clegg' and not a 'lecture', at Clegg's own request. The lecture was delivered without a written paper, slides or videos and without notes – as was also the case for other lectures and talks he delivered at Dartmouth.[57] Furthermore, Clegg used his knowledge of stage-space to ensure that he held the attention of the entire auditorium (right, left and centre, as during a concert) with extensive use of gestures; this was definitely not a formal lecture delivered through reading of a written paper while standing behind a lectern (unlike the lecture he delivered at the University of KwaZulu-Natal during the commencement ceremony there, in a much more formal and staid setting).

This high-level, university-wide lecture was intended for a multidisciplinary academic audience; and in fact, Clegg addressed many different – yet intertwined – themes. He mentioned the themes explicitly at the beginning of the lecture in order to guide the audience:

> Activism: 'it's the story of how somebody becomes an activist, what is activism?'
> Identity: 'it's a story of the search for an identity in a country where the politics of identity were supreme …'
> Music: 'it's also about a journey to create a new music, a music that tried to offer alternatives to what was going on in the country'.[58]

However, the audience was also warned that the themes were strongly intertwined, as highlighted by Clegg himself, who stated at the very beginning of the talk: 'It's not a linear presentation. I'm going to tell a number of different narratives at the same time, and would ask you to bear with me.'[59] In fact, the lecture seems to be built on the above-mentioned cyclical concept of traditional music (versus the linear approach of Western music) – a cyclical mode that appeared to provide a safer space for a conversation.

In this context, we suggest that the lecture followed the style of a 'creative nonfiction' essay or talk and not that of the classical academic lecture. Such a style, which employs techniques and methodologies of literature, will provide factual details but not necessarily in a chronological order. Rather, this style uses techniques found in literature, such as presenting the reader with the details from the middle stages of a story or event before presenting the beginning. This style was probably chosen by Clegg for many different reasons. It allowed him to provide interlinkages among the many different themes addressed in the lecture, and to better explain causal relationships and even paradoxes; and it enabled him to establish empathy with the audience, given the personal anecdotes he was conveying. It also allowed him to utilise a very strong evidence-based approach to describe a totalitarian – and isolated – state like South African during the apartheid period. Furthermore, it allowed him to convey his 'life experience' as an inspiration to others so as to 'comply' with the expectations of him – to allow young people to be inspired by 'a kind, generous person who is a great musician and a person who has acted heroically'.[60]

In fact, many of the shifts or interfaces between the different themes dealt with in the lecture were introduced by personal-life anecdotes, including what Clegg referred to as 'epiphany' moments, starting with his unexpected encounter with Charlie Mzila when he was 14 years old and asked Mzila to teach him Zulu guitar technique.[61] Using such an example allowed Clegg to engage in the discourse on how he was exposed to new music styles and genres as well as to describe the life of migrant workers in Johannesburg under the apartheid regime. Other personal episodes, such as the instance when he was first caught 'breaking the Group Areas Act', introduced his narrative about activism and how activism had been slowly 'intruding' into his life and his search for identity.[62] The lecture included some terms he had used in other instances (such as in interviews and documentaries), for example the expression 'politics found me' (mentioned twice in the lecture) and used in several interviews, and the metaphor of 'the fence' of apartheid.[63]

In addition, indicating the importance he attributed to selecting the right words for the audience, Clegg also used academic jargon by referring to specific theories (such as 'social engineering' and 'labour theory of value') to further attract the attention of his academic audience.[64] The fact that he mentioned different theories and approaches and schools of thought was not just a mechanism to get the audience engaged; it was also intended to show that there were several approaches to the topic under discussion, and to emphasise that he was not adhering completely to any particular approach. This is very similar to the techniques he used in his music: he did not choose a single musical genre as much as he created new ones. Such theoretical references were not just 'add-ons', but were based on Clegg's knowledge acquired through university training and extensive reading.

Through the above-mentioned 'creative non-fiction' style, these main themes of the lecture were then summarised at the end in a non-traditional way that had the potential to leave his audience with something of a puzzle: namely, that his music was a testimony to many of the events that had happened in South Africa since he started recording in the 1970s. This 'puzzle' can best be demonstrated in the concluding paragraph of the lecture:

> So just closing now. I was going to try and cleverly weave a narrative of music in, but I'm sorry, I failed to do that. And I'd like to just close up now and say thank you for coming. I hope you got some sense of this story. And that my music is embedded in the entire trajectory of South Africa, from the time I started recording. A lot of my music is, in fact, a record of those events. Devilishly and cleverly concealed.[65]

This closing statement was very much in line with Clegg's approach of making the audience think about and reflect on what they had just heard – whether a song or a lecture – and also leaving them with a desire to find out more through his music. In fact, while the record of events in South Africa is 'devilishly and cleverly concealed' in the music,[66] so are the references to Clegg's songs (such as '*Utshani Obulele*' and '*Mdantsane* (Mud Coloured Dusty Blood)', hinted at in the lecture – recognisable to those who had already listened to the music.[67] Hence, this closing enabled more reflections on the music and introduced the actual conversation with the audience.

In the question-and-answer section – maybe better defined as the 'encore' to the lecture – Clegg intertwined playing, talking and singing to give examples of traditional Zulu music and its linkages with Western music, and to provide further insight into his life (for example, describing his praise names).[68] Some of the songs and music were also played by Clegg during his commencement lecture at the University of Kwazulu-Natal in 2013, but of course with a different perspective on them, as the isiZulu lyrics were probably not understood by very many in the audience at Dartmouth.[69]

THE CYCLE BRINGING CLEGG BACK TO ACADEMIA

From this review of the portion of Clegg's life journey that focused on re-engagement with academia, we suggest that concerts were in some ways an academic setting for Clegg; and that his willingness to step into the classroom – and notably that he did so in a very respectful way, namely through 'conversations' and not lectures – could symbolise a cyclical approach to some of the endeavours in his life. In fact, after a young Clegg experienced his identity-seeking journey among the Zulu migrant community in Johannesburg, he went to university to further understand his experience through the lenses of anthropology and the socio-political context of the time. He then repackaged and applied this academic knowledge to his successful artistic and performing career.

Hence, by willingly engaging in academic events, Clegg may have felt that he would further make sense of his experiences as a full-time professional artist. Furthermore, his autobiography – which he started writing in the early 2010s – was also part of that framework of 'studying' his amazing journey and unique South African story.[70]

These opportunities were a response to Clegg's passion for teaching and learning, as he highlighted in interviews, and for creating dialogues with his fellow human beings within the spirit of *ubuntu*.[71] In fact, his lectures and mini-lectures very much revealed aspects of his personal life. He was not shy about discussing personal events (such as his work on a chicken farm and his engagement in investing, and leading, an electronic waste business, 'New Earth Waste Solutions') in public, to ensure that the human beings he was addressing could recognise the difficulties and challenges (as well as successes and aspirations and dreams) faced by another human being.[72] Furthermore, adopting such an approach made the topic of the lecture or talk timeless – as Clegg had done with his songs, which were developed in a particular historical period but could actually continue to be sung 'across the centuries', as the world revolved around cycles of 'the same human story'.[73]

When Clegg left university for a 'sabbatical', the university environment – in both South Africa and North America – was probably not ready for his transdisciplinary approach to applied anthropology, and Professor

Hammond-Tooke probably knew that when he talked to Clegg in the early 1980s. Later on, Clegg was recognised by and reintroduced into the academic space as a high-level lecturer, a recipient of honorary doctorates and a case study in textbooks.[74] Yet, we are left grappling with the question of whether Clegg would have formally returned to a university or other research-related institutions as a long-term fellow or professor of practice. Considering his statement that he had been feeling 'a certain kind of a loss not being able to have completed my career, as you know, going to do my PhD ... and watch[ing] other students, you know, carry on either as anthropologists or to go off and do something', we like to think that he would have formally returned from the 'sabbatical'.[75] What we know for sure is that he has inspired and motivated generations of students, in lecture halls and concert venues alike.

ACKNOWLEDGEMENTS

We thank Ethan Friedland for his lecture transcription and text analysis, and Hilton Rosenthal, Larry Shore, Penny Andrews, Andrew G. Innes, AnneMarie Martins, Terry Finley, Bobby Summerfield and Michael Drewett for assistance with various aspects of this chapter.

NOTES

1. See https://www.cuny.edu/; https://home.dartmouth.edu/. Dartmouth is officially called a 'college' in the US but functions as a university with PhD-level graduate programmes and professional graduate degrees.
2. Johnny Clegg, *Scatterling of Africa: My Early Years* (Johannesburg: Pan Macmillan, 2021).
3. United Nations, 'General Assembly Resolution 35/206: Policies of *Apartheid* of the Government of South Africa: Part E Cultural, Academic and other Boycotts of South Africa', A/RES/35/206A-R, 16 December 1980, accessed 7 April 2025, https://documents-dds-ny.un.org/doc/RESOLUTION/GEN/NR0/392/25/PDF/NR039225.pdf?OpenElement. See also chapter 7 in this book by Michael Drewett.
4. Adelaide M. Cromwell, 'The Fulbright Program in Africa, 1946 to 1986', *Annals of the American Academy of Political and Social Science* 491 (1987): 92–103.
5. David Coplan, 'Johnny Clegg: South Africa's Universal Man of Uncommon Passion', *The Conversation*, 24 July 2019 (updated 25 July 2019), accessed 14 January 2024, https://theconversation.com/johnny-clegg-south-africas-universal-man-of-uncommon-passion-120794; Helen Q. Kivnick, *Where is the Way: Song and Struggle in South Africa* (New York: Penguin, 1990), 126.

6   Clegg, *Scatterling*, 95.
7   Juluka, 'Scatterlings of Africa', on *Scatterlings* (album, Johannesburg: MINC, MINC – (L) 1040, 1982).
8   See Steven Roy Goodman, 'Higher Education Today: Johnny Clegg, Musician and Anthropologist', interview by Steven Roy Goodman, *Higher Education Today*, University of the District of Columbia, 8 April, 2014, YouTube video, 29:52, accessed 10 December 2023, https://www.youtube.com/watch?v=zh4ox9DPV4Q.
9   Goodman, 'Higher Education Today'.
10 Goodman, 'Higher Education Today'.
11 See David Coplan, *In Township Tonight! South Africa's Black City Music and Theatre* (Cape Town: Jacana, 2007); Lucilla Spini, 'Johnny Clegg: Anthropologist, Artist and Global Citizen', *International Journal of Anthropology* 35, no. 3–4 (2020): 145–160, https://doi.org/10.14673/IJA2020341060; Clegg, *Scatterling*. Among the documentaries, we recall the television series presented by Clegg, *A Country Imagined*, directed by Ella Terri, Liza Key, Feizel Mamdoo, Vincent Moloi, Guy Spiller and John Trengove (season 1, Johannesburg: South African Broadcasting Corporation/Curious Pictures, 2010), but also an earlier documentary on Juluka, *Juluka*, directed by Ashley Lazarus, produced for the South African Broadcasting Corporation by Cinevision Motion Pictures Producers (Johannesburg: South African Broadcasting Corporation, 1984), YouTube video, 27:33, accessed 10 December 2023, https://www.youtube.com/watch?v=JOc87cm9XKs.
12 Clegg, *Scatterling*, 257.
13 Claude Six, email to co-author Lucilla Spini, 1 September 2023.
14 Larry Shore, personal communication with the authors, 7 August 2023.
15 Hilton Rosenthal, personal communication with the authors, 9 August 2023.
16 Shore, personal communication, 7 August 2023. See Shore's biography on the *CUNY Website*, accessed 9 December 2023, https://fm.hunter.cuny.edu/facultystaff/full-time-faculty/larry-shore/.
17 Shore, personal communication, 7 August 2023.
18 Paul Simon, *Graceland* (album, Burbank: Warner Bros Records, 925 447-1, 1986). The first edition of the *Graceland* album cover highlighted the pivotal role of Rosenthal and Juluka in the development of the concept of the album.
19 Rosenthal, personal communication, 9 August 2023. See also Emily Boulter, 'The Unforgettable Concert that History Somehow Forgot,' *Forward*, 18 May 2021, accessed 10 December 2023, https://forward.com/culture/469773/the-unforgettable-concert-that-history-somehow-forgot/.
20 Johnny Clegg & Savuka, 'Asimbonanga', on *Third World Child* (album, Hollywood: Capitol Records, CLT-46778, 1987); Joan Baez, *Recently* (album, Hollywood: Gold Castle Records, 171 004-1, 1987). See also chapter 4 in this book by Martina Viljoen.
21 Johnny Clegg & Savuka, 'Scatterlings of Africa', on *Third World Child*. *Rain Man*, directed by Barry Levinson (film, Hollywood: United Artists, 1988) had its premiere at the 39th Berlin International Film Festival in February 1988. See also chapter 9 by Chris Letcher and chapter 11 by Caleb Mutch in this book.
22 Gilles Teuliè, *Histoire de l'Afrique du Sud* (Paris: Tallandier, 2019).
23 The albums recorded at Plus 4 Studio were *Shadow Man* (Hollywood: Capitol Records – C1 90411, EMI – C1 90411, 1988), the 1989 album *Cruel, Crazy Beautiful World* (Hollywood: Capitol Records, C4-93446) and the 1993 album *Heat, Dust and Dreams* (Hollywood: Capitol Records/EMI, CDP 0777 7 98795 2 6/CDP 0777 7 98795 2 6), whose album cover and booklet photographs were shot by French photographer

Claude Gassian at Death Valley in California. In 1990 Rosenthal established the music label Rhythm Safari (see https://www.rhythmsafari.com.au/, accessed 14 January 2024).

24 Rosenthal, personal communication, 9 August 2023. A photograph of the event can be seen in the magazine *Black Radio Exclusive*, 26 August 1988.
25 Frank Clifford, 'Bradley Proposes Wider City Policy Against Apartheid', *Los Angeles Times*, 19 March 1986.
26 United Nations, 'Report of the Symposium on Cultural and Academic Links with South Africa, held at Los Angeles, United States of America, on 11 and 12 May 1991', A/AC.115/L.677, 18 July 1991, accessed 7 April 2025, https://digitallibrary.un.org/record/126789. The 'Los Angeles Statement' was presented as an annex to another document, United Nations, 'Letter from the Acting Chairman of the Special Committee against Apartheid to the Secretary-General', A/46/177, 16 May 1991, accessed 7 April 2025, https://digitallibrary.un.org/record/114425?v=pdf. See also Arthur Goldstuck, 'U.N. Group Lift S. Africa Boycott for Certain Acts', *Billboard* (Archive: 1963–2000), 15 June 1991.
27 See the list of participants in Annex III of the 1991 'Report of the Symposium' (A/AC.115/L.677) cited above.
28 Johnny Clegg, *New World Survivor* (album, Pretoria: Value Music, CDVM (WFL) 45, 2002).
29 A brief description of that talk and some photographs can be found at Andrew J. Friedland, 'Johnny Clegg at Dartmouth 2004', *Dartmouth University Website*, accessed 10 December 2023, https://sites.dartmouth.edu/ajf/johnny-clegg-at-dartmouth-2004/. 105 Dartmouth Hall is the same room where Martin Luther King, Jr spoke in May 1962 – a coincidence that interested Clegg (Friedland, personal observation).
30 Coplan, *In Township Tonight!*; Coplan, 'Universal Man'.
31 Friedland, 'Clegg at Dartmouth'.
32 University of the Witwatersrand, 'Johnny Clegg', *Alumni Relations* (n.d.), accessed 9 December 2023, https://www.wits.ac.za/alumni/distinguished-graduates/honorary-degree-citations/johnny-clegg/.
33 See 'Johnny Clegg', *Concert Archives*, accessed 10 December 2023, https://www.concertarchives.org/concerts/johnny-clegg-951e4c10-e4d3-4fcb-9c44-e90ee658b769.
34 Penny Andrews, personal communication with the authors, 29 August 2023.
35 Andrews, personal communication, 29 August 2023.
36 CUNY Matters, 'Law School Awards Doctorate to South African Activist Musician', *CUNY Website*, 15 April 2023, accessed 10 December 2023, https://www1.cuny.edu/sites/matters/2011/04/15/law-school-awards-honorary-doctorate-to-south-african-activist-musician/.
37 CUNY Matters, 'Law School Awards Doctorate'.
38 CUNY Matters, 'Law School Awards Doctorate'.
39 CUNY Matters, 'Law School Awards Doctorate'.
40 Andrew J. Friedland, 'Johnny Clegg at Dartmouth 2011 (and 2014) (and 2016)', *Dartmouth University Website*, accessed 10 December 2023, https://sites.dartmouth.edu/ajf/johnny-clegg-at-dartmouth-2011/.
41 Friedland, 'Clegg at Dartmouth 2011'.
42 Juluka, 'Digging for Some Words', on *Scatterlings*.
43 There is a low-quality video of this unplanned performance available online: Johnny Clegg, Mandisa Dlanga and Andy Innes, 'Digging for Some Words', YouTube video, 03:10, accessed 10 December 2023, https://youtu.be/izhQwlxavf8?feature=shared.

44 Friedland, 'Clegg at Dartmouth 2011'.
45 Johnny Clegg, 'Commencement Lecture', University of KwaZulu-Natal, 16 April 2013. See excerpts from the lecture at University of KwaZulu-Natal on the recording 'Johnny Clegg Sings Warsongs at UKZN Graduation', YouTube video, 03:28, 17 April 2013, accessed 10 December 2023, https://www.youtube.com/watch?v=k33MuE-qMTM.
46 Andrew J. Friedland, 'Nomination for Johnny Clegg as Honorary Degree Recipient at Commencement in 2012', Dartmouth College, 26 August 2011.
47 Friedland, 'Clegg at Dartmouth 2011'.
48 Dartmouth University, 'The Montgomery Fellows Program: Johnny Clegg'. *Dartmouth University Website*, accessed 10 December 2023, https://montgomery.dartmouth.edu/johnny-clegg; Dartmouth University, 'The Montgomery Fellows Program: Meet the Fellows', *Dartmouth University Website*, accessed 10 December 2023, https://montgomery.dartmouth.edu/fellows/meet-fellows?page=0.
49 Dartmouth University, 'The Montgomery Fellows Program: Musician, Archaeologist Are the Next Montgomery Fellows', *Dartmouth University Website*, 7 March 2014, accessed 10 December 2023, https://montgomery.dartmouth.edu/news/2014/03/musician-archaeologist-are-next-montgomery-fellows.
50 Friedland, 'Clegg at Dartmouth 2011'; Johnny Clegg, 'A Conversation with Johnny Clegg', Montgomery Lecture, Dartmouth University, 14 April 2014 (the lecture is available from the Dartmouth YouTube channel at YouTube video, 01:26:21, accessed 10 December 2023, (https://www.youtube.com/watch?v=sDMawnPw2SQ); Dartmouth University, 'Environmental Studies: Foreign Study', *Dartmouth University Website*, accessed 10 December 2023, https://envs.dartmouth.edu/foreign-study/foreign-study.
51 Goodman, 'Higher Education Today', 2014.
52 Johnny Clegg, 'A Conversation with Johnny Clegg', Berklee College of Music, Berklee Performance Center, Boston, 15 October 2017. AnneMarie Martins, email to the authors, 3 August 2023.
53 Martins, email to the authors.
54 Goodman, 'Higher Education Today', 2014.
55 Goodman, 'Higher Education Today', 2014.
56 Clegg, 'A Conversation', Montgomery Lecture.
57 For both the Montgomery Lecture at Dartmouth and the lecture at the Berklee College of Music, Clegg asked explicitly to define and title the event as 'A Conversation with Johnny Clegg'.
58 Clegg, 'A Conversation', Montgomery Lecture.
59 Clegg, 'A Conversation', Montgomery Lecture.
60 Andrew J. Friedland, 'Montgomery Fellowship Nomination Letter for Johnny Clegg', Dartmouth College, 30 July 2004.
61 Clegg, *Scatterling*, 67.
62 The Group Areas Act (No. 41 of 1950) was legislation introduced by the apartheid government to require people with different racial classifications to live in separate areas within a city, town or region.
63 See for example the documentary by Amine Mestari, *Johnny Clegg, the White Zulu* (DVD, Paris: Screenshot Group, Arte France, 2019).
64 Johnny Clegg, personal communication with co-author Lucilla Spini, 7 October 2017; Clegg, 'A Conversation', Montgomery Lecture.
65 Clegg, 'A Conversation', Montgomery Lecture.
66 Clegg, 'A Conversation', Montgomery Lecture.

67. In the lecture, Clegg says: 'And they'd say, "*Utshani obulele buvuswa wumlilo*". The old, dry grass that's crispy it's so dry, is renewed when you set it on fire'. This is a concealed reference to a song from his 2006 album *One Life* (Johnny Clegg, '*Utshani Obulele*', on *One Life* [album, Angoulême: Marabi Productions, 46817.2]). He also says: 'I don't want to write about a strike. I don't want to write about the fact that four people were shot dead in Mdantsane', even if he has done so in the song recorded by Juluka, 'Mdantsane (Mud Coloured Dusty Blood)', on the album *Work for All* (Johannesburg: MINC, MINC – (L) 1070, 1983).
68. On Clegg's praise names, see chapter 6 in this book by Sipho Mchunu and Andrew Grant Innes.
69. Clegg, 'Commencement Lecture', University of Kwa-Zulu Natal.
70. Clegg, *Scatterling*.
71. Goodman, 'Higher Education Today', 2014.
72. For further information on Johnny Clegg and electronic waste (e-waste), see UNEP, 'Johnny Clegg', *Our Planet Magazine*, February 2007; Andrew J. Friedland and Rick Relyea, *Environmental Science for the AP Course*, 4th edition (New York: Macmillian, 2023).
73. Johnny Clegg, 'Dance Across the Centuries' (lyrics), accessed 10 December 2023, https://www.rhythmsafari.com.au/dance-across-the-centuries-lyrics; Johnny Clegg, 'Human Rainbow' (lyrics), accessed 10 December 2023, https://www.rhythmsafari.com.au/dance-across-the-centuries-lyrics. Both songs are included on the album *Shadow Man* by Johnny Clegg & Savuka.
74. See for example Friedland and Relyea, *Environmental Science*.
75. Goodman, 'Higher Education Today'.

REFERENCES

Boulter, Emily. 'The Unforgettable Concert that History Somehow Forgot'. *Forward*, 18 May 2021. Accessed 10 December 2023. https://forward.com/culture/469773/the-unforgettable-concert-that-history-somehow-forgot/.

Clegg, Johnny. 'Commencement Lecture'. Public lecture. University of KwaZulu-Natal, Durban, 16 April 2013.

Clegg, Johnny. 'A Conversation with Johnny Clegg'. Public lecture. Berklee College of Music, Berklee Performance Center, Boston, 15 October 2017.

Clegg, Johnny. 'A Conversation with Johnny Clegg'. Public lecture. Montgomery Lecture, Dartmouth University, Filene Auditorium, Hanover, 14 April 2014.

Clegg, Johnny. 'Johnny Clegg Sings Warsongs at UKZN Graduation'. Excerpts from commencement lecture at the University of KwaZulu-Natal, 16 April 2013. YouTube video, 03:28. Accessed 10 December 2023. https://www.youtube.com/watch?v=k33MuE-qMTM.

Clegg, Johnny. *Scatterling of Africa: My Early Years*. Johannesburg: Pan Macmillan, 2021.

Clegg, Johnny, Mandisa Dlanga and Andy Innes. 'Digging for Some Words'. YouTube video, 03:10. Accessed 10 December 2023. https://youtu.be/izhQwlxavf8?feature=shared.

Clifford, Frank. 'Bradley Proposes Wider City Policy Against Apartheid'. *Los Angeles Times*, 19 March 1986.

Coplan, David. *In Township Tonight! South Africa's Black City Music and Theatre*. Cape Town: Jacana, 2007.

Coplan, David. 'Johnny Clegg: South Africa's Universal Man of Uncommon Passion'. *The Conversation*, 24 July 2019 (updated 25 July 2019). Accessed 14 January 2024. https://

theconversation.com/johnny-clegg-south-africas-universal-man-of-uncommon-passion-120794.

Cromwell, Adelaide M. 'The Fulbright Program in Africa, 1946 to 1986'. *Annals of the American Academy of Political and Social Science* 491 (1987): 92–103.

CUNY Matters. 'Law School Awards Doctorate to South African Activist Musician'. *CUNY Website*, 15 April 2023. Accessed 10 December 2023. https://www1.cuny.edu/sites/matters/2011/04/15/law-school-awards-honorary-doctorate-to-south-african-activist-musician/.

Dartmouth University. 'Environmental Studies: Foreign Study'. *Dartmouth University Website*. Accessed 10 December 2023. https://envs.dartmouth.edu/foreign-study/foreign-study.

Dartmouth University. 'The Montgomery Fellows Program: Johnny Clegg'. *Dartmouth University Website*. Accessed 10 December 2023. https://montgomery.dartmouth.edu/johnny-clegg.

Dartmouth University. 'The Montgomery Fellows Program: Meet the Fellows'. *Dartmouth University Website*. Accessed 10 December 2023. https://montgomery.dartmouth.edu/fellows/meet-fellows?page=0.

Dartmouth University. 'The Montgomery Fellows Program: Musician, Archaeologist Are the Next Montgomery Fellows'. *Dartmouth University Website*, 7 March 2014. Accessed 10 December 2023. https://montgomery.dartmouth.edu/news/2014/03/musician-archaeologist-are-next-montgomery-fellows.

Friedland, Andrew J. 'Johnny Clegg at Dartmouth 2004'. *Dartmouth University Website*. Accessed 10 December 2023. https://sites.dartmouth.edu/ajf/johnny-clegg-at-dartmouth-2004/.

Friedland, Andrew J. 'Johnny Clegg at Dartmouth 2011 (and 2014) (and 2016)'. *Dartmouth University Website*. Accessed 10 December 2023. https://sites.dartmouth.edu/ajf/johnny-clegg-at-dartmouth-2011/.

Friedland, Andrew, J. 'Montgomery Fellowship Nomination Letter for Johnny Clegg'. Dartmouth College, 30 July 2004.

Friedland, Andrew J. 'Nomination for Johnny Clegg as Honorary Degree Recipient at Commencement in 2012'. Dartmouth College, 26 August 2011.

Friedland, Andrew J. and Rick Relyea. *Environmental Science for the AP Course*, 4th edition. New York: Macmillan, 2023.

Goldstuck, Arthur. 'U.N. Group Lift S. Africa Boycott for Certain Acts'. *Billboard* (Archive: 1963–2000), 15 June 1991.

Goodman, Steven Roy. 'Higher Education Today: Johnny Clegg, Musician and Anthropologist'. Interview by Steven Roy Goodman. *Higher Education Today*, University of the District of Columbia. YouTube video, 29:52. Accessed 10 December 2023. https://www.youtube.com/watch?v=zh4ox9DPV4Q.

'Johnny Clegg'. *Concert Archives*. Accessed 10 December 2023. https://www.concertarchives.org/concerts/johnny-clegg-951e4c10-e4d3-4fcb-9c44-e90ee658b769.

'Johnny Clegg & Savuka Day', *Black Radio Exclusive*, 26 August 1988. Photograph.

Kivnick, Helen Q. *Where is the Way: Song and Struggle in South Africa*. New York: Penguin, 1990.

Lazarus, Ashley dir. *Juluka*. Television programme. Produced by Cinevision Motion Pictures for the South African Broadcasting Corporation. Johannesburg: South African Broadcasting Corporation, 1984. YouTube video, 27:33. Accessed 10 December 2023. https://www.youtube.com/watch?v=JOc87cm9XKs.

Levinson, Barry, dir. *Rain Man*. Hollywood: United Artists, 1988.

Mestari, Amine. *Johnny Clegg, the White Zulu*. DVD. Paris: Screenshot Group, Arte France, 2019.

Parliament of South Africa. *Group Areas Act (No. 41 of 1950)*. Cape Town: Parliament of South Africa, 1950.

Spini, Lucilla. 'Johnny Clegg: Anthropologist, Artist and Global Citizen'. *International Journal of Anthropology* 35, no. 3–4 (2020): 145–160. https://doi.org/10.14673/IJA2020341060.

Terri, Ella, Liza Key, Feizel Mamdoo, Vincent Moloi, Guy Spiller and John Trengove, dirs. *A Country Imagined*. Television series. Season 1, presented by Johnny Clegg. Johannesburg: South African Broadcasting Corporation/Curious Pictures, 2010.

Teuliè, Gilles. *Histoire de l'Afrique du Sud*. Paris: Tallandier, 2019.

UNEP (United Nations Environment Programme). 'Johnny Clegg'. *Our Planet Magazine*. February 2007.

United Nations. 'General Assembly Resolution 35/206: Policies of *Apartheid* of the Government of South Africa: Part E Cultural, Academic and other Boycotts of South Africa', A/RES/35/206A-R, 16 December 1980. Accessed 7 April 2025. https://documents-dds-ny.un.org/doc/RESOLUTION/GEN/NR0/392/25/PDF/NR039225.pdf?OpenElement.

United Nations. 'Letter from the Acting Chairman of the Special Committee against Apartheid to the Secretary-General', A/46/177, 16 May 1991. Accessed 7 April 2025. https://digitallibrary.un.org/record/114425?v=pdf.

United Nations. 'Report of the Symposium on Cultural and Academic Links with South Africa, held at Los Angeles, United States of America, on 11 and 12 May 1991', A/AC.115/L.677, 18 July 1991. Accessed 7 April 2025. https://digitallibrary.un.org/record/126789.

University of the Witwatersrand. 'Johnny Clegg'. *Alumni Relations*, n.d. Accessed 9 December 2023. https://www.wits.ac.za/alumni/distinguished-graduates/honorary-degree-citations/johnny-clegg/.

DISCOGRAPHY

Baez, Joan. *Recently*. Album. Hollywood: Gold Castle Records, 171 004-1, 1987.

Clegg, Johnny. *New World Survivor*. Album. Pretoria: Value Music, CDVM (WFL) 45, 2002.

Clegg, Johnny. *One Life*. Album. Angoulême: Marabi Productions, 46817.2, 2006.

Clegg, Johnny. *A South African Story (Live at the Nelson Mandela Theatre)*. Album. Johannesburg: EMI, CDEMM (WI) 067, 2003.

Johnny Clegg & Savuka. *Cruel, Crazy Beautiful World*. Album. Hollywood: Capitol Records, C4-93446, 1989.

Johnny Clegg & Savuka. *Heat, Dust and Dreams* Album. Hollywood: Capitol Records/EMI, CDP 0777 7 98795 2 6/CDP 0777 7 98795 2 6, 1993.

Johnny Clegg & Savuka. *Shadow Man*. Album. Hollywood: Capitol Records, C1 90411, EMI – C1 90411, 1988.

Johnny Clegg & Savuka. *Third World Child*. Album. Hollywood: Capitol Records, CLT-46778, 1987.

Juluka. *Scatterlings*. Album. Johannesburg: MINC, MINC – (L) 1040, 1982.

Juluka. *Work for All*. Album. Johannesburg: MINC, MINC – (L) 1070, 1983.

Simon, Paul. *Graceland*. Album. Burbank: Warner Bros Records, 925 447-1, 1986.

PART 3: TRANSITIONS IN JOHNNY CLEGG'S MUSIC AND LIFE

CHAPTER

11

From Juluka to Savuka: Johnny Clegg's Changing Compositional Practices

Caleb Mutch

Johnny Clegg's formation of the band Savuka in 1986 was an artistic turning point in his career. Juluka (1976–1985), founded and led by Clegg and Sipho Mchunu, had largely focused on blending Zulu and Western folk styles; Savuka, by contrast, has been characterised nearly from its inception as drawing from a broader cultural palette. Clegg himself stated that when forming Savuka, 'I changed the sound slightly [from Juluka's]: I brought in a few more synthesizers, I kept the Zulu street guitar music intact. But I looked further north for a greater African musical input, looking at the Malawian, the Zimbabwean, Zairean and West African guitar techniques and styles and harmonics. And this has basically made our music a lot more pan-African than particularly South African in certain regards'.[1]

Yet the artistic differences between Clegg's Savuka-era recordings and his earlier music cut far more deeply than has previously been appreciated, as I demonstrate in this chapter by analysing his songs. First, I argue that the music released by Johnny Clegg & Savuka (hereafter 'Savuka') is much more indebted to Western pop-rock music than was Juluka's. By comparing the two songs recorded by both bands, namely, '*Siyayilanda*' and 'Scatterlings of Africa', I show that Savuka's reworking of these songs to sound more like 1980s pop-rock affected a wide range of parameters: they added new sections, altered instrumentation and even changed the metre. I closely analyse these revisions, first to draw conclusions about how the two bands presented themselves to listeners and then to find meaning in the divergent compositional and performance decisions of the bands. Second, I demonstrate that Clegg and Savuka did not merely broaden their cultural palette beyond Juluka's: they also extended and deepened Juluka's practice of engaging with South African musical idioms, as I show by analysing 'I Call Your Name', one of Clegg's early compositions for Savuka. Together, these analyses reveal that Clegg's musical path from Juluka to Savuka ranged more widely than has been previously appreciated, and also continued his lifelong artistic exploration of South African culture.

'SIYAYILANDA'

'*Siyayilanda*' ('We Are Fetching It') serves a bookend function in Clegg's catalogue: it opens Juluka's 1982 album *Scatterlings*, and it closes Savuka's *Shadow Man* (1988).[2] Fittingly, the song's beginning and ending themselves merit particular attention: the former because it intriguingly plays with metre and the latter owing to the dramatic difference between the endings on the two recordings. In Juluka's version the song's opening texture is spare: the first notes are sung by Clegg, unaccompanied, and in the song's first 16 seconds he is joined by only male backing vocals and drums.[3] Listeners trying to locate the music's downbeat are given two quite different sets of metrical cues by these three parts. On the one hand, the drums hammer out what sounds like a stereotypical two-step pattern: floor tom attacks (plus a fast pickup to those attacks) on what could be the strong beats, and on the alternating beats hand claps, substituting for the conventional snare drum hits. The backing vocals can reinforce that interpretation, as they enter at the same time as the floor tom's main beat. And those backing vocals align with Clegg's singing of the song's title, '*Siyayilanda*', suggesting that his unaccompanied first word is a pickup to that strong beat (see 'Interpretation 1' in figure 11.1).[4] On the other hand, the lead vocals suggest that the song could start on the downbeat, in which case

Figure 11.1: Two metrical interpretations of the opening of Juluka's and Savuka's versions of '*Siyayilanda*'. Transcription by the author.

the drum hits occur on weak beats (see 'Interpretation 2' in figure 11.1).[5] (The parenthesised '*Siya*' only occurs in Savuka's version of the song.)

The remainder of the song's opening 16 seconds proceeds in much the same way: this initial material is repeated, with a minor tweak to make the ending stronger the second time, creating a period.[6] This period is then repeated again (0:17–0:33), but with the addition of electric bass, guitar hits and more percussion. These added parts, however, do not resolve the metric ambiguity. The bass largely doubles the backing vocals' part, with added pickups, the kick drum plays a steady pulse of four beats per measure, and auxiliary percussion takes over the fast repeated rhythm that had been played on closed hi-hat (not included in the transcription). The guitar hits are even more ambiguous, as they come on weak off-beats (aligned with the '-ba' of 'bamba' and '-da' of '*siyayilanda*').

It is only with the entrance of the verse's material, more than 30 seconds into the song, that Interpretation 1 ceases to be viable. The electric bass

Figure 11.2: Two interpretations of the drums in Savuka's *'Siyayilanda'*. Transcription by the author.

emphasises Interpretation 2's beats one and three, and first the flute and then Clegg's singing of the verse aligns with that downbeat. The drum part, which in the opening had conflicted with Interpretation 2, also now lines up with the downbeat: the two-step pattern's alternation of low drum (earlier the floor tom, now the kick drum) and snare drum doubles in speed and is shifted back a beat, so that the kick drum lands on beats one and three (as well as the pickup to beat three). At the arrival of the chorus section, which copies the second, fuller-instrumentation period from the opening material (0:17–0:33), the drums revert to the half-speed alternation of floor tom and snare on the weak beats, thereby establishing the play between different metric possibilities as one of the song's compositional ideas.

Savuka's version introduces yet another metrical stream to the song's opening. The kick drum enters at the song's first strong beat, whereas in Juluka's version it only enters at the second statement of the opening period (0:16).[7] The alternating timbres of the floor tom and snare drum that support the two-step hearing of Interpretation 1 are still present, but Savuka's recording introduces a new, conflicting two-step pattern (see figure 11.2). This two-step pattern alternates between the kick drum on strong beats and other drums on the weak beats and it starts a quaver earlier, so it supports the other interpretation of where the downbeat is.

Crucially, this drum pattern that Savuka introduces behaves just like the two-step pattern usually does in pop-rock music: it persists steadily through the entire song (unlike the other two-step pattern, which breaks off when the verse enters) and demarcates the song's main pulse (whereas the other pattern progresses at half that rate). In fact, Savuka's pairing of the characteristic rock two-step pattern with the newly introduced prominent synthesizers shifts the song's instrumentation firmly into the sound-world of 1980s pop-rock, which Clegg had embraced in his 1985 solo album *Third World Child*.[8] These changes do not entirely resolve the metric ambiguity that still persists throughout the song's opening, but they do provide extra support to those listeners who favour Interpretation 2.

Since the chorus section in '*Siyayilanda*' copies the introduction's fuller-instrumentation second period, listeners have already heard that melodic material six times by the time the song concludes the second verse and launches into the chorus yet again. As a result, both bands take that opportunity to play with the material's metric ambiguity once more. In Juluka's version the second verse is followed by the expected melodic material, but now with an unexpected accompaniment. Instead of the full instrumental backing the chorus has thus far received, the melody is paired with the metrically underdetermined drums-and-vocals setting of the song's introduction. And in a further twist, the established alternation of weaker and stronger line endings in the introduction/chorus material is upset, as the material from the second, strong-ending half of the introduction's first period is placed first (2:14–2:22). Only after that does a usual weak-strong periodic version of the chorus follow, with the expected fuller instrumentation, adding up to a chorus section that is 50 per cent longer than the first chorus.

Savuka's version of the second chorus makes two notable changes. On the one hand, this version normalises it: by removing the second half of the opening period found at the beginning of Juluka's second chorus, Savuka reduces the chorus to the length of one period. On the other hand, Savuka's version heightens the opening material's metric indeterminacy. The entirety of Savuka's second chorus features the spare vocals-and-drums instrumentation found in the song's opening, but this time Clegg abandons his lead vocal part, instead joining in with the backing chorus. As a result, the only sounds supporting the downbeat of Interpretation 2 (which is the downbeat unmistakably established by the preceding verse) are a kick-drum hit and a quiet guitar part, which plays three semiquaver-length Es beginning at each downbeat.

But it is in the ending of '*Siyayilanda*' that the two bands' recordings diverge most dramatically. In Juluka's version the song progresses in a fairly standard verse-chorus form: the expanded second chorus is followed by a saxophone solo above the verse's backing material, and then the first half of the first verse and twice-repeated chorus ensue. Thereafter the song quickly fades out with a few seconds of saxophone solo. Savuka's version likewise has an instrumental section (now a composed synthesizer passage instead of an improvised flute solo) following the second chorus, but the commonalities end there. Instead of the final half-verse and repeated chorus of the earlier version, Savuka ends the song with a very different 'outro'. This begins with a new bridge-like section (2:48–3:08) featuring a guitar 'melodic-rhythmic pattern' similar in style to those heard at the beginnings of maskanda songs.[9] After this pattern is established, Clegg enters with the new lyrics, 'I can feel it in the air', set to a new melody and with synthesizers accompanying the guitar pattern. After this lyric is repeated twice more the song's lengthy final section begins, which combines old and new. The most prominent instrument at the beginning is a synthesizer, introducing a new, sinuous melody. The bass part and chord structure reproduce the song's verse section, but the backing singers borrow from the introduction/chorus, singing the same '*siyayilanda*' lyric with the same rhythm, though a shifted melody. Furthermore, Clegg returns to the 'I can feel it in the air' melody from the bridge-like section, to which he also adds new lyrics about his 'day coming nearer'. After about 45 seconds of repeating this music, a slow fade-out concludes the song.

What do these compositional changes reveal about the discrepancies between the two bands' music and self-presentation? The rhythmic differences largely serve to make Savuka's version more familiar to Western audiences. Many of the rhythmic characteristics of Savuka's recording result from implications of the new two-step drum pattern it introduces atop the off-set drum pattern found in Juluka's recording. In Juluka's version Interpretation 1 is suggested more strongly, although that hearing requires shifting the downbeat back a beat when the verse enters. Savuka's added two-step pattern, by contrast, weakens the salience of Interpretation 1 and makes it easier to hear Interpretation 2, which can easily be sustained through the entirety of the song, as Western listeners usually expect of their pop songs.

The different endings of the two versions also show Savuka's recording practice shifting away from tight pop-music formal conventions towards a looser, rock-based structure. In Juluka's recording the song's formal organisation hews closely to a conventional verse-chorus structure, though with the slight twist of the chorus being based on the introduction. The radically changed last third of Savuka's recording rejects this relatively standard formal organisation that Juluka used in the studio in favour of a rock-sounding anthemic culmination. In addition, the new ending also reflects how both bands performed the song live. Videos of performances from the late 1980s show that Savuka used the new ending as vamping material to accompany their dancing, and the audio recording of Juluka's live performance released as *Juluka Live (The Good Hope Concerts)* documents the same practice.[10] It appears that as Juluka and then Savuka repeatedly played this song live, the vamp ending ceased to seem like an extraneous addition to the song's verse-chorus structure and instead became an integral part of 'Siyayilanda', giving rise to a richer, more idiosyncratic composition.

'SCATTERLINGS OF AFRICA'

After Savuka's formation Clegg's producer, Hilton Rosenthal, had a suggestion. Why not re-record Juluka's biggest international hit, 'Scatterlings of Africa', with changes to make it more radio-friendly? Clegg was resistant, saying it was like asking Picasso to paint one of his pictures again. Why would people want to hear Johnny Clegg covering a song by Johnny Clegg?[11] In the end, though, Clegg relented and the resulting re-recording went on to introduce Savuka to the world, just as Juluka's version had done for that band.[12] And as Savuka had done with 'Siyayilanda', they changed Juluka's version in ways that brought their re-recording closer to the sound-world of 1980s pop-rock music, particularly when it came to the song's metric and rhythmic particularities.

The verse section of 'Scatterlings of Africa' introduces listeners to the rhythmic complexity that characterises much of the song. In both Juluka's and Savuka's versions it sets out a complex interweaving of guitar and bass parts that divides an eight-beat cycle into groupings of three, three and two beats, above which Clegg sings a highly syncopated melody.[13] Once Juluka reaches the lead-in to the chorus the complexity is heightened even more as the eight-beat cycle is shortened to seven beats (see the top half of figure 11.3a).

Above a steady kick-drum pulse, the bass and Clegg's melody articulate a repeated rhythm of two dotted crotchets at the start of each seven-beat cycle, leading to a division of the cycle into a pattern of three, two and two beats.

It is in the context of this seven-beat-cycle chorus section that Savuka makes its most major intervention by adding an extra beat to each cycle. This creates a standard eight-beat grouping in which the newly added two-step drum pattern fits in its conventional place (see the lower halves of figures 11.3a and 11.3b, where the boxes indicate approximately when the extra beats occur). These extra beats are inserted highly artfully, in a variety of ways. In one method the added beat occurs towards the end of the cycle, after Clegg has finished his lyric, but before the thundering quaver-crotchet rhythm in the tom drums that ends each cycle (see the first and fourth cycles of the chorus, setting 'scatterlings of Africa' and 'where the world began'). In the second method the extra beat seems to come at the end of the cycle, as a crotchet rest is added after the singing concludes (see the second and third cycles, 'each uprooted one' and 'on the road to Phelamanga'). Yet this means that the tom drum's quaver-crotchet rhythm is now shifted too, so that it no longer coincides with the vocal part (as it does in Juluka's version), but occurs mostly or entirely after it. The lead-in to the chorus ('refuge in the night') adds the extra beat in yet another way, stretching out the melodic line early in the cycle.

Figure 11.3a: The lead-in and start of the chorus of 'Scatterlings of Africa', Juluka and Savuka versions. Transcription by the author.

Figure 11.3b: The continuation of the chorus of 'Scatterlings of Africa', Juluka and Savuka versions. Transcription by the author.

As in '*Siyayilanda*', Savuka's clarification or normalisation of Juluka's unusual metres shifts the song further towards the soundscape of 1980s pop-rock music.[14] Indeed, Clegg recounted that changing the metre of 'Scatterlings of Africa' to 4/4 was one of Rosenthal's suggestions for making it more radio friendly.[15] Changes in instrumentation also reinforce the impression of a more rock-oriented sound: besides Savuka's addition of the two-step drum pattern, the fairly prominent sustained organ tones found in Juluka's version of the chorus are buried in the mix in Savuka's version; new synthesizer interjections are also added, which have a distinctly 1980s sound. Furthermore, Clegg also changes his singing for the Savuka recording. In the Juluka recording he frequently glides into and away from notes; in the Savuka version, by contrast, he lands on pitches more squarely, conforming more closely to Western singing mores. He shifts his vocal timbre, too: in the Juluka recording he produces a smooth phonation with some nasal twang, resonance in his chest and strong breath support. In the Savuka version, by contrast, his phonation is grainier, has less nasal twang, vocal resonance in his head and softer breath support.[16] Finally, he even shifts his pronunciation to sound more US-American in places, starting 'Africa' with an open front unrounded sound (International Phonetic Alphabet: a, 'short a') in the Savuka recording, whereas he gives it an open central unrounded sound (International Phonetic Alphabet: ä, 'short o') in the Juluka one.[17]

Although these changes served to make 'Scatterlings of Africa' fit more easily into Savuka's context of 1980s global pop music, Clegg did not treat them as Savuka-specific. When Juluka re-formed in the 1990s and toured in support of a new album, they performed 'Scatterlings of Africa' as Savuka had done, with eight-beat cycles, two-step drums, added interjections (now played by flute instead of synthesizer) and the like.[18] Nor were the extra beats dependent on the two-step drum pattern. Recordings of late-career performances by Clegg on solo guitar or with small backing ensembles still keep the eight-beat cycles, even when the lack of drum kit means they could have easily returned to the original seven-beat cycle.

This raises a question: given that Juluka, Savuka and Clegg's solo act performed substantially different versions of this song over the decades, what parts of 'Scatterlings of Africa' might have been integral to Clegg's conception of the song? The melody and harmonies certainly seem to qualify as integral, as they occur largely unchanged in each recording I have heard.[19] The lyrics, too, are mostly invariant, though Juluka's initial studio recording contains lyrics later eliminated to fashion the tighter version found in their music video and recorded concerts, and in Savuka's performances and recordings as well.[20] The arrangement of larger formal sections is even less fixed, as the transition out of the first chorus shows. Juluka's *Scatterlings* and *Juluka Live* (*The Good Hope Concerts*) recordings cut straight to the instrumental lead-in to verse 2, while their music video and Savuka's version interpose forms of the intro/outro material.[21] (This added material is retained in many of Clegg's recorded performances, but not all.) Changing a song's metre is a very unusual move, and it is tempting to view Savuka's shift to eight-beat cycles as entirely replacing or rewriting Juluka's seven-beat form of the song, since it appears that Clegg practically always performed it that way thereafter. The sole exception I have found proves the rule: in one undated live solo performance, Clegg drops a beat from the mid-point of the first chorus.[22] Juluka's seven-beat pattern was still in his muscle memory, evidently, ready to re-emerge during an unguarded moment, but this happened exceedingly rarely. In sum, by comparing recordings of 'Scatterlings of Africa' from different points in Clegg's career it appears that the song's defining elements were most of its lyrics, its melody and the way that melody was harmonised. Other significant aspects of the song, including its instrumentation, formal structure and even metre, were less fixed and could be revised to serve different purposes.

'I CALL YOUR NAME'

Since at least 1987 a narrative has spread that Savuka had a broader range of cultural influences than Juluka; as we saw in the introduction, Clegg called attention to Savuka's cultivation of a pan-African sound. In subsequent years several writers surveying the scope of Clegg's career have sought to place that characteristic within the larger perspective of 1980s 'world music', though without acknowledging Clegg's explicit words on the matter. Samuel Freedman, for instance, writes: 'Clegg's music metamorphosed from Juluka's folkloric stylings to a more accessible interweaving of Celtic and African influences – one thinks at turns of Sting, Peter Gabriel and Richard Thompson'.[23] Louise Meintjes similarly notes that

> in Savuka, he imagined his composition as a blend of several African styles and rock, especially that of rock musicians engaged in their own fusions, such as Jethro Tull's Celtic interests, the Police incorporating reggae and Peter Gabriel's world music intersections and collaboration with Senegalese musician Youssou N'Dour ... He also extended his harmonic palate [properly: palette] beyond 'three cord [sic] music in a cyclical format' ('A Marginal Man' 1987), sang more English lyrics and moved further away from Juluka's early folksy image and sound.[24]

While the overall thrust of these claims is largely accurate, they do merit two qualifications. First, inasmuch as Clegg shifted away from a 'folksy' and specifically South African style to a more generically pop-based pan-African or 'world music' sound, this metamorphosis was already well under way with Juluka's album *The International Tracks* (1984).[25] And second, as I will now demonstrate, Savuka continued to engage in sophisticated, creative ways with Zulu-connoting musical idioms. Indeed, 'I Call Your Name', from

Savuka's 1988 album *Shadow Man*, explores the compositional potential of South African music in a way never found in Juluka's output.

The neo-traditional Zulu song genre known variously as maskanda, umaskande and umaskandi was a frequent source for Juluka's 'crossover' music, which blended Western and South African musical styles.[26] They drew on maskanda for aspects of its formal organisation, harmonic patterns, typical instrumentation and more, as I have shown in previous research.[27] Juluka's use of the Zulu-associated genre of mbaqanga has received less investigation, though they wrote many songs in that style, such as 'Umbaqanga Music' (a resetting with English lyrics of their earlier song '*Umfazi Omdala*') and numerous tracks from their isiZulu albums *Ubuhle Bemvelo* (1982) and *Musa Ukungilandela* (1984).[28] These songs all express the characteristics of mbaqanga listed by Norbert Nowotny: 'Most mbaqanga pieces begin with a lead guitar (or electric organ, violin or accordion [properly: concertina]) introduction before a heavy bass line and a rock beat entry [properly: enter] playing a short I IV V I cycle over a bouncing 8/8 rhythm … There is often a lead singer and a group of backing vocalists who sing about three or four different melodies. The vocal texts are usually in African languages'.[29] Nowotny's stipulation of a 'I IV V I cycle' is overly simplistic, as mbaqanga songs often substitute other chords in place of the IV or even reorder the cycle to 'I V IV I', but the remainder of the description is on firm ground.[30]

As 'I Call Your Name' begins, it initially appears to fit the same pattern. Solo accordion starts the song introducing an eight-beat melodic-harmonic pattern. Halfway through the second statement of that pattern the drums enter, and the bass joins in at the start of the third statement.[31] The bass outlines an unmistakable 'I IV V' root-progression cycle that lines up well with the pattern Nowotny identified in mbaqanga songs, and the entirety of the rest of the song is composed of these three chords, in typical mbaqanga fashion. But in 'I Call Your Name' Clegg does more than what is expected with these simple and limited harmonic resources: he explores their compositional potential by making each chord the tonal focus of a different section.

The song's introduction (which also provides the material for its chorus section) clearly focuses on the I chord, B-flat major (see figure 11.4).

That chord enters at the beginning of each eight-beat cycle, lasts twice as long as any other chord in the section, and the notes that comprise it are emphasised by the accordion in the introduction and Clegg's lead vocals in the chorus. At 0:17, however, the song suddenly changes. New synthesizer parts bury the accordion: busy figuration in a lower range and trumpet-imitating interjections in a higher one. The eight-beat cycle is now occupied by different chords, too. The V chord (F major) takes up the first half of each cycle and the IV chord (E-flat major) serves as a neighbouring chord in the second half. After two statements of this cycle Clegg enters with the first verse, accompanied by the backing vocalists.

At 0:50 the song changes yet again, as the verse gives way to the pre-chorus. The bass drops its propulsive rhythm in favour of a simple pulse that alternates with synthesizer hits. A new, sustained synthesizer line enters above Clegg's melody as well, while the accordion is no longer audible. The harmonies comprising the eight-beat cycle reverse, as the IV chord (E-flat major) is now the new tonal focus. It lands at the start of each cycle and Clegg's melody, consisting largely of a repeated G, fits with that chord. When Clegg keeps repeating that G in the second half of the cycle, though, the underlying chord switches to the V chord (F major), which gives a greater sense of instability and forward momentum to the cycle's ending.

Figure 11.4: Bass and lead vocals of 'I Call Your Name', beginning of each type of section. Transcription by the author.

As the cycle repeats it builds up energy, as is the characteristic function of pre-chorus sections, and finally it yields, with a strong sense of harmonic resolution, to the arrival of the chorus section at 1:06.[32]

The chorus section returns to the introduction's mbaqanga sound, 'I IV V' root-progression cycle and all, now with the addition of Clegg's melody. As Meintjes notes, in his work with Savuka Clegg 'extended his harmonic [palette] beyond "three [chord] music in a cyclical format"'.[33] In 'I Call Your Name' Clegg uses only three chords, arranged cyclically. Yet by the time listeners come to the chorus section, developments in instrumentation, texture and tonal focus have taken them on a journey through the surprisingly rich compositional possibilities offered by these three simple chords. Clegg has paid tribute to the conventions of mbaqanga music while at the same time demonstrating just how much room for exploration its economy of harmonic means can provide.

CONCLUSION

In his autobiography Clegg draws attention to Juluka's artistic contribution to the South African debates of the late 1970s and early 1980s: 'More than anything, Juluka was a concept. It was saying, there's a black and a white experience and we're going to have a conversation between these different styles of music and find a way to make a hybrid music. So that there's a musical conversation going on in a country that has laws of cultural segregation and seeks to prevent conversation'.[34] Savuka, by contrast, sought to participate in the musical conversation of popular music across the Western world.

With both '*Siyayilanda*' and 'Scatterlings of Africa' Savuka alters the soundscapes of Juluka's songs, making them resemble standard pop-rock music more closely and ironing out some of the songs' idiosyncrasies. In Juluka's version of '*Siyayilanda*' the song's introduction and related chorus are metrically ambiguous to an extent very rare for pop music, both in South Africa and more broadly. On the one hand, Savuka's introduction of the rock-connoting two-step drum pattern reduces that metric ambiguity, while also providing a foundation for the vocals in the second chorus to be even further metrically underdetermined. On the other, Savuka replaces the rather conventional verse-chorus form of Juluka's recording with a looser organisation that reflects the particularities of their live performances, while also evoking a rock-like anthemic 'outro'. In 'Scatterlings of Africa' Savuka likewise introduces a two-step drum pattern, making the song sound closer to rock norms, but in this case that pattern necessitates normalising Juluka's highly unusual seven-beat cycles. Other changes in instrumentation, vocal timbre and the like also shift the song's sonic profile closer to 1980s pop-rock norms. With both songs Savuka's alterations largely serve to make Juluka's songs more legible to the musical conversation happening beyond the bounds of South Africa.

Yet attenuating South Africa-specific musical elements was not Savuka's only move. As 'I Call Your Name' shows, Clegg continued to draw upon specific Zulu musical idioms, such as mbaqanga, to fashion new songs. Even here, though, his practice had changed from that of his Juluka days: whereas many Juluka songs were composed entirely within the norms of mbaqanga, Savuka's 'I Call Your Name' builds its verse and pre-chorus sections out of the abstracted harmonic materials of the mbaqanga-based chorus. Attending closely to these three songs has revealed a circuitous trajectory in the development of Clegg's compositional practice from Juluka to Savuka, one that engages more closely with the conversation of global popular music while also continuing to draw on and develop the musical languages of South Africa.

NOTES

1   Johnny Clegg, '1987 VHS: Johnny Clegg Interview and Music Compilation 60 FPS', unattributed interview, 1987, YouTube video, 23:45, accessed 17 October 2023, https://youtu.be/c5NOZsoHqhw.
2   Juluka, '*Siyayilanda*', on *Scatterlings* (album, Johannesburg: MINC, MINC – (L) 1040, 1982); Johnny Clegg & Savuka, '*Siyayilanda*', on *Shadow Man* (album, Sandton: EMI, EMCJ (D) – 7904111, 1988).
3   As I have explained elsewhere, even when songs by Juluka are credited solely to Clegg I attribute compositional decisions to Juluka as a group (Caleb Mutch, '"Something Else Is Possible": Transcultural Collaboration as Anti-Apartheid Activism in the Music of Juluka', *Popular Music* 40, no. 3–4 [2021]: 453–454). I do this both to reflect Clegg's collaborative approach to learning Zulu culture and to avoid minimising the significance of the other band members. For consistency's sake I will apply the same approach to recordings by Savuka.

4 The transcriptions, which are mine, are intended to emphasise the songs' most pertinent features, not to record exhaustively every performed detail.
5 My intention in describing these two interpretations is not to adjudicate which is right and wrong, but to attend to how the song's rhythmic complexity and interest make two conflicting hearings possible simultaneously.
6 My use of the term 'period' draws on that of William E. Caplin, referring to a pair of similar-length phrases each starting with the same melodic material, where the second phrase ends more conclusively than the first. See William E. Caplin, *Classical Form: A Theory of Formal Functions for the Instrumental Music of Haydn, Mozart and Beethoven* (Oxford: Oxford University Press, 1998), 49–55.
7 Savuka's version also adds an extra syllable, '*Siya*-', as a pickup at the song's onset, so that the music now starts on a weak quaver. This lends yet more emphasis to the song's first strong beat than it has in Juluka's version.
8 Johnny Clegg, *Third World Child* (album, Johannesburg: MINC, MINC (L) – 1140, 1985). This album is not to be confused with Johnny Clegg & Savuka's 1987 album of the same name, which has only two tracks in common with Clegg's solo album: the title track and 'Don't Walk Away' (Johnny Clegg & Savuka, *Third World Child* [Sandton: EMI, EMCJ (D) – 2407331, 1987]). Savuka's album reuses the 1985 recording of 'Third World Child'; I have not been able to assess whether 'Don't Walk Away' is likewise copied.
9 Tom Collins, 'Constructing Maskanda', *SAMUS: South African Music Studies* 26–27 (2006–2007): 4.
10 Juluka, *Juluka Live (The Good Hope Concerts)* (album, Johannesburg: MINC, MINC (V) – 4051 1481, 1986). See video footage of Savuka's 1988 Paris concert, 'Siyayilanda – Johnny Clegg & Savuka – Live at Zenith (Paris)', YouTube video, 04:23, accessed 9 September 2023, https://youtu.be/cZHoJIhkhOM; a 1989 concert in Italy, 'Johnny Clegg & Savuka – Siyayilanda (Live in Italy – Shadow Man Tour, 1989) Videomusic', YouTube video, 04:13, accessed 9 September 2023, https://youtu.be/oVIl3-7ks4U; and a 1990 concert in Germany, 'Johnny Clegg & Savuka Rock Life, Germany, 1990', YouTube video, 01:07, accessed 9 September 2023, https://youtu.be/1lNiapt8F7U.
11 Clegg recounted this story many times, including during his final tour (for example at Montecasino Teatro, Johannesburg, 7 August 2017). My thanks to Andrew Grant Innes for providing audio of that concert and for fleshing out the anecdote as Clegg told it at other performances (Andrew Grant Innes, e-mail to the author, 15 November 2023).
12 Juluka's recording reached 44 on the Official Singles Chart in the United Kingdom in February 1983 ('Official Singles Chart: 13 February 1983–19 February 1983', accessed 14 October 2023, https://www.officialcharts.com/charts/singles-chart/19830213/7501/). Savuka's recording reached 75 ('Official Singles Chart: 10 May 1987–16 May 1987', accessed 14 October 2023, https://www.officialcharts.com/charts/singles-chart/19870510/7501/). The lower peak of the Savuka recording may have been due to competition from other tracks on *Shadow Man*, most notably '*Asimbonanga*' (my thanks to Lucilla Spini for this observation).
13 For a more detailed analysis of the verse's rhythmic implications see Mutch, '"Something Else Is Possible"', 463–465.
14 The driving sound of the two-step drum pattern is strengthened by the song's faster speed: Juluka's recording of 'Scatterlings of Africa' is played at 122 beats per minute, whereas Savuka's recording has 127.
15 Innes, e-mail, 15 November 2023.

16 My description of Clegg's vocal timbre draws on the system proposed by Kate Heidemann in 'A System for Describing Vocal Timber in Popular Song', *Music Theory Online* 22, no. 1, (2016), accessed 11 September 2023, https://mtosmt.org/issues/mto.16.22.1/mto.16.22.1.heidemann.html.
17 My thanks to Lucilla Spini for the observation that when Clegg addressed North American audiences he likewise shifted his speaking accent to sound more like the locals.
18 As captured on an audio recording of their 1997 tour, 'Johnny Clegg & Juluka "Juluka Tour 1997"', YouTube video, 1:09:25, accessed 11 September 2023, https://youtu.be/eRoUr4ouvv8. The album was Juluka, *Crocodile Love* (International: HR BV Music/ One World Music/ CNR Music, 3032202, 1997).
19 See chapter 4 in this book by Martina Viljoen for a sensitive reading of the song's lyrics.
20 The initial studio recording is on Juluka, *Scatterlings*. The condensed version omits chorus 2, and it also combines the first half of the long version's verse 3 and the second half of verse 2 to create a single verse 2, omitting the other halves. Most later versions also reduce the lines Clegg speaks in the fade-out section to a mere 'We are the scatterlings of Africa'.
21 Juluka, Scatterlings, 1982; Juluka, *Juluka Live (The Good Hope Concerts)*; Juluka, 'Scatterlings Of Africa – Johnny Clegg & Juluka', YouTube video, 03:08, accessed 1 May 2025, https://youtu.be/2X-o7Kfqbuw; Johnny Clegg & Savuka, 'Johnny Clegg and Savuka – Scatterlings of Africa (1987)', YouTube video, 03:48, accessed 1 May 2025, https://youtu.be/qnYtcH4YS44.
22 At 01:20–01:24 of the recording labelled 'Johnny Clegg Unplugged: Scatterlings', YouTube video, 03:52, accessed 9 September 2023, https://youtu.be/4dOgIyKJ72Y. Other solo recordings are consistently in eight-beat cycles, suggesting that the anomalous seven-beat cycle was an accident (compare 'Johnny Clegg Performs "Scatterlings" Unplugged from the Expresso Studio', YouTube video, 04:20, accessed 9 September 2023, https://youtu.be/GorJ_xXgs7Q).
23 Samuel G. Freedman, 'Johnny Clegg's War on Apartheid', *Rolling Stone*, 22 March 1990, accessed 14 September 2023, https://www.rollingstone.com/music/music-features/johnny-clegg-south-africa-apartheid-samuel-freedman-860888/.
24 Louise Meintjes, *Dust of the Zulu: Ngoma Aesthetics after Apartheid* (Durham, NC: Duke University Press, 2017), 160. 'A Marginal Man' is an anonymous article from the newspaper *New Nation*, which I have been unable to access.
25 Juluka, *The International Tracks* (album, Johannesburg: MINC, MINC(O) – 1098, 1984). My thanks to Michael Drewett for this observation. See also chapter 3 by Andrew Grant Innes in this book. Most of the material from *The International Tracks* was released for American and European markets on the Juluka album *Stand Your Ground* (Burbank: Warner Bros Records, 925 155-1, 1984). ('Umbaqanga Music' and the dance mixes of 'Fever' and 'Kilimanjaro' were not included.) Clegg's 1985 *Third World Child* solo album exhibits an emphatic shift to 1980s-style pop and pop-rock, like much of Savuka's music, but without the clear 'world music' allusions, which differentiates it from Savuka's musical agenda.
26 Concerning the name of this genre, see Thomas Mathew Pooley, '*Umaskandi Izibongo*: Semantic, Prosodic and Musical Dimensions of Voice in Zulu Popular Praises', *African Music: Journal of the International Library of African Music* 10, no. 2 (2016): 7. Kathryn Olsen provides an invaluable overview of the genre's signification of Zulu tradition and its post-apartheid transformation in *Music and Social Change in South Africa: Maskanda Past and Present* (Philadelphia: Temple University Press, 2014).

27 Mutch, "'Something Else Is Possible'", 450–469.
28 Juluka, *Ubuhle Bemvelo* (album, Johannesburg: MINC, MINC – (E) 1030, 1982) and Juluka, *Musa Ukungilandela* (album, Johannesburg: MINC, MINC(E) 1100, 1984). From *Ubuhle Bemvelo*: '*Umfazi Omdala*' and '*Biza*'; from *Musa Ukungilandela*: 'Zodwa', 'Thoko' and 'Trouble *Musa Ukungilandela*'. 'Thandazani' from *Crocodile Love* (1997) is another example.
29 Norbert Nowotny, 'Mbaqanga and Mahlathini', in *Papers Presented at the Eleventh Symposium on Ethnomusicology*, ed. Carol Muller (Grahamstown: Rhodes University [International Library of African Music], 1995): 106.
30 This correction of Nowotny's harmonic generalisation draws upon my research on analysing mbaqanga, which is in preparation for publication elsewhere.
31 The song's first three statements of the melodic-harmonic pattern in the accordion take an ABA form. The A version of the statement is favoured for the song's first three minutes, but then the altered B form of the pattern returns for a while, before giving way to the original form for the rest of the song's closing groove and fade-out.
32 For more on the function of the pre-chorus in pop songs, see Jay Summach, 'The Structure, Function and Genesis of the Prechorus', *Music Theory Online* 17, no. 3 (2011), accessed 8 April 2025, https://mtosmt.org/issues/mto.11.17.3/mto.11.17.3.summach.html.
33 Meintjes, *Dust of the Zulu*.
34 Johnny Clegg, *Scatterling of Africa: My Early Years* (Johannesburg: Pan Macmillan, 2021), 269.

REFERENCES

Caplin, William E. *Classical Form: A Theory of Formal Functions for the Instrumental Music of Haydn, Mozart and Beethoven*. Oxford: Oxford University Press, 1998.

Clegg, Johnny. '1987 VHS: Johnny Clegg Interview and Music Compilation 60 FPS'. Unattributed interview, 1987. YouTube video, 23:45. Accessed 17 October 2023. https://youtu.be/c5NOZsoHqhw.

Clegg, Johnny. 'Johnny Clegg Performs "Scatterlings" Unplugged from the Expresso Studio'. YouTube video, 04:20. Accessed 9 September 2023. https://youtu.be/GorJ_xXgs7Q.

Clegg, Johnny. 'Johnny Clegg Unplugged: Scatterlings'. YouTube video, 03:52. Accessed 9 September 2023. https://youtu.be/4dOgIyKJ72Y.

Clegg, Johnny. *Scatterling of Africa: My Early Years*. Johannesburg: Pan Macmillan, 2021.

Collins, Tom. 'Constructing Maskanda'. *SAMUS: South African Music Studies* 26–27 (2006–2007): 1–26.

Freedman, Samuel G. 'Johnny Clegg's War on Apartheid'. *Rolling Stone*, 22 March 1990. Accessed 8 April 2025. https://www.rollingstone.com/music/music-features/johnny-clegg-south-africa-apartheid-samuel-freedman-860888/.

Heidemann, Kate. 'A System for Describing Vocal Timber in Popular Song'. *Music Theory Online* 22, no. 1 (2016). Accessed 8 April 2025. https://mtosmt.org/issues/mto.16.22.1/mto.16.22.1.heidemann.html.

Johnny Clegg & Savuka. 'Johnny Clegg & Savuka Rock life, Germany, 1990'. YouTube video, 01:07. Accessed 9 September 2023. https://youtu.be/1lNiapt8F7U.

Johnny Clegg & Savuka. 'Johnny Clegg and Savuka – Scatterlings of Africa (1987)'. YouTube video, 03:48. Accessed 1 May 2025. https://youtu.be/qnYtcH4YS44.

Johnny Clegg & Savuka. 'Johnny Clegg & Savuka – Siyayilanda (Live in Italy – Shadow Man Tour, 1989) Videomusic'. YouTube video, 04:13. Accessed 9 September 2023. https://youtu.be/oVIl3-7ks4U.

Johnny Clegg & Savuka. 'Siyayilanda – Johnny Clegg & Savuka – Live at Zenith (Paris)'. YouTube video, 04:23. Accessed 9 September 2023. https://youtu.be/cZHoJIhkhOM.

Juluka. 'Johnny Clegg & Juluka "Juluka Tour 1997"'. YouTube video, 1:09:25. Accessed 11 September 2023. https://youtu.be/eRoUr4ouvv8.

Juluka. 'Scatterlings Of Africa – Johnny Clegg & Juluka'. YouTube video, 03:08. Accessed 1 May 2025. https://youtu.be/2X-o7Kfqbuw.

'A Marginal Man'. *New Nation*, 26 January–1 February 1987.

Meintjes, Louise. *Dust of the Zulu: Ngoma Aesthetics after Apartheid*. Durham, NC: Duke University Press, 2017.

Mutch, Caleb. '"Something Else Is Possible": Transcultural Collaboration as Anti-Apartheid Activism in the Music of Juluka'. *Popular Music* 40, no. 3–4 (2021): 450–469.

Nowotny, Norbert. 'Mbaqanga and Mahlathini'. In *Papers Presented at the Eleventh Symposium on Ethnomusicology*, edited by Carol Muller, 105–115. Grahamstown: Rhodes University (International Library of African Music), 1995.

'Official Singles Chart: 13 February 1983–19 February 1983'. Accessed 14 October 2023. https://www.officialcharts.com/charts/singles-chart/19830213/7501.

'Official Singles Chart: 10 May 1987–16 May 1987'. Accessed 14 October 2023. https://www.officialcharts.com/charts/singles-chart/19870510/7501/.

Olsen, Kathryn. *Music and Social Change in South Africa: Maskanda Past and Present*. Philadelphia: Temple University Press, 2014.

Pooley, Thomas Mathew. '*Umaskandi Izibongo*: Semantic, Prosodic and Musical Dimensions of Voice in Zulu Popular Praises'. *African Music: Journal of the International Library of African Music* 10, no. 2 (2016): 7–34.

Summach, Jay. 'The Structure, Function and Genesis of the Prechorus'. *Music Theory Online* 17, no. 3 (2011). Accessed 8 April 2025. https://mtosmt.org/issues/mto.11.17.3/mto.11.17.3.summach.html.

DISCOGRAPHY

Clegg, Johnny. *Third World Child*. Album. Johannesburg: MINC, MINC (L) – 1140, 1985.

Johnny Clegg & Savuka. *Shadow Man*. Album. Sandton: EMI, EMCJ (D) – 7904111, 1988.

Johnny Clegg & Savuka. *Third World Child*. Album. Sandton: EMI, EMCJ (D) – 2407331, 1987.

Juluka. *Crocodile Love*. Album. International: HR BV Music/One World Music/CNR Music, 3032202, 1997.

Juluka. *The International Tracks*. Album. Johannesburg: MINC, MINC(O) – 1098, 1984.

Juluka. *Juluka Live (The Good Hope Concerts)*. Album. Johannesburg: MINC, MINC (V) – 4051 1481, 1986.

Juluka. *Musa Ukungilandela*. Album. Johannesburg: MINC, MINC(E) 1100, 1984.

Juluka. *Scatterlings*. Album. Johannesburg: MINC, MINC – (L) 1040, 1982.

Juluka. *Stand Your Ground*. Album. Burbank: Warner Bros Records, 925 155-1, 1984.

Juluka. *Ubuhle Bemvelo*. Album. Johannesburg: MINC, MINC – (E) 1030, 1982.

CHAPTER

12

What We Don't See: The Afterlives of 'Asimbonanga'

Nicol Hammond

'*Asimbonanga*' ('We Have Not Seen Him') is a powerful opening number for a Savuka concert.[1] It begins with Johnny Clegg's sinuous tenor, issuing a call: '*Asimbonanga*'. His voice is exposed and isolated. In live performance he is introduced with an instrumental riff, but this is not an accompaniment.[2] Clegg, soon joined by the rest of Savuka's male vocalists, is performing in the *a cappella* call and response (antiphonal) choral style characteristic of so much Southern African choral music.[3] The relationship between a solo call and the choral support provided by the harmonised response in this style demonstrates why it has worked so well in political and protest song. The structure of the music represents the philosophy of sociality and individual support for collective power known in the wider southern Bantu-language communities of Africa as *ubuntu*.[4] '*Asimbonanga*', Johnny Clegg calls, and before the responding ensemble has even completed the first word he joins them, affirming his role as both soloist and part of the ensemble: '*Asim* ...' '... *bonang' uMandela thina*' ('We have not seen Mandela').

'*Asimbonanga*' is structured like a Western or Euro-American commercial pop song, with a verse-chorus form. It incorporates a meditative middle section that both rehearses material from the chorus and introduces a new call, which builds in energy to a final chorus with full accompaniment and an added wordless descant sung by the band's only female member, Mandisa Dlanga. The familiarity of this structure to a popular music audience lends the song a predictable symmetry that, like much of Savuka's repertoire, scaffolds the less familiar isiZulu-language and South African choral music features. The structure is also, however, flexible in a manner characteristic of protest music, which must often be repeatable to accommodate the unpredictable circumstances of protest actions.

On 10 September 1999 in Frankfurt, Germany, Mandisa Dlanga interrupted and redirected the song by introducing her descant early. As she arrived on stage, a cheer went up from the audience. Clegg turned around to see Nelson Mandela, hand in hand with Dlanga, dancing his characteristic 'Mandela shuffle' onto the stage. Clegg danced over to Mandela and he and Dlanga escorted the statesman, only recently retired from the presidency of the new South Africa, to the front of the stage. Mandela smiled and waved his hand, signalling to the audience to join in. Savuka finished the song, a slight quiver colouring Clegg's voice, and the audience roared. Clegg invited Mandela to speak. 'It is music and dancing that makes me at peace with the world, and with myself,' Mandela said, before goading the audience to join, and asking the band to play the song again. They reprised the final chorus, singing the main call and response three times, before Clegg and Mandela slowly exited the stage, hand-in-hand.

This performance in many ways functions like a new version of this iconic Savuka song, rearranged not so much in the usual musical ways (despite Dlanga's in-the-moment redirection of the band to skip the middle section), but by a context that changed the song, and subsequently significantly changed its meaning. In this chapter I consider the shifting meanings of one of Clegg's most frequently covered songs by examining both musical and extra-musical features of meaning-making in two versions of the song by Savuka, a performance by the Soweto Gospel Choir, and a recontextualisation of the song in the context of a medley by Karen Zoid and Snotkop.

'ASIMBONANGA': BACKGROUND AND HISTORY

'*Asimbonanga*' was written and first performed in the 1970s by Johnny Clegg and Sipho Mchunu as a protest song against Chief Kaiser Matanzima of Transkei.[5] The song was originally sung entirely in isiZulu, and comprised only the isiZulu-language sections of the more familiar version (without the meditative recitation of names that Clegg and Savuka typically include in the middle section), in an infinitely repeatable A/B structure. The lyrics of the first section of the original song are almost identical to the lyrics of the chorus of the more familiar version, except for the use of Matanzima's name, later replaced by the name Mandela. Clegg and Mchunu performed their original version significantly faster than the later version, with an accompaniment in Juluka's characteristic fast-picking maskanda guitar style. This version is also structured around the interwoven vocal call and response of the more familiar version. The infinite repeatability of the A/B structure, and lack of more wordy verses (the verses are in English in the later Savuka version) highlights the song's function as a protest song. While this early version was never released commercially, a recording of a live Juluka performance at the Market Café on 7 May 1978 has been digitised by archivists at the Hidden Years Music Archive.[6] The more familiar version of '*Asimbonanga*' was one of the first songs Clegg released with Savuka (whose name means 'Arise' or 'Awake'), the multiracial and multicultural Afro-pop group Clegg formed in 1986 after Juluka disbanded. The song was released as a single and on a South African EP and cassette in 1986, and then as the second track on the internationally released album *Third World Child* in 1987.[7] It was also covered frequently, including by Joan Baez in 1987, and is included on several struggle song compilations, which contributed considerably to Clegg's international reputation.[8]

'*Asimbonanga*' is a characteristic example of the crossover style for which Clegg and Savuka are well known.[9] The more narrative verses of the song are in English and consequently easily comprehensible to a broad international audience, while the frequently repeated chorus is in isiZulu. Mandela's name, which is easily recognisable to an international audience, is a key word in the chorus. The chorus is also easily singable by minimally skilled singers, with a clear melodic hook and easily harmonisable pentatonic tonality. Its frequent repetition increases the chorus's memorability for a non-Zulu audience, and audience participation is encouraged by the choral call and response structure.

Pop songs frequently employ unison or choral-style harmonies, or even sometimes overdubbing, reverb or delay effects in sections of the song designed to encourage audience participation in live settings. This approach is effective because audiences are more likely to join in when their voices feel supported by other voices, and when a song seems to create space for group participation instead of encouraging more focused listening. Examples of this effect include the outro of the Beatles' 'Hey Jude' on the single *Hey Jude/Revolution*, the chorus of Queen's 'We Will Rock You' on the album *Queen Live Killers* and the chorus of Bok van Blerk's 'De La Rey' on the album *De La Rey*.[10] This choral audience participation mechanism has been used particularly effectively in activist pop songs, including Peter Gabriel's 'Biko' on the album *Biko* and Jerry Dammers and The Special A.K.A.'s 'Nelson Mandela' on *Nelson Mandela/Break Down the Door*.[11] Call and response structures further amplify this effect by both creating space for audience participation and cuing that participation so that audiences know exactly when and what to sing. In many cases, the singalong mechanism of these songs turns them into anthems of a sort, by creating both a shared experience for the immediate audience and an imagined community.[12] As a crossover song, '*Asimbonanga*' deploys this familiar participatory mechanism to interpellate its audience into the song as more than just bystanders or observers. The chorus lyrics reference an inclusive 'we', and by encouraging participation, that 'we' becomes simultaneously performer and audience. Moreover, by coaching the audience into singing in isiZulu, Clegg and Savuka demonstrate one of the particular absurdities of South Africa's apartheid-era segregation. In addition to censoring songs on the basis of their lyrical content, radio stations were language-segregated, which meant that songs that mixed languages could be denied airplay on the basis that they did not fit clearly into the language framework of one station or another.[13] By encouraging a large international audience to sing in isiZulu, then, '*Asimbonanga*' disrupts the apparently neat segregation of the apartheid system.[14]

The first rendition of the chorus in *'Asimbonanga'* is *a cappella*, with minimal percussion. Subsequent choruses and all verses of the song feature the standard rock instrumentation of drum kit augmented by hand-held percussion, keyboard, bass guitar, and lead and rhythm guitars. In most recordings and performances there is a mostly *a cappella* middle section after the second (and final) verse and third chorus, in which Clegg invokes the names of anti-apartheid activists killed by apartheid operatives: 'Stephen Biko', 'Victoria Mxenge', 'Neil Aggett (and all the others)'.[15] After the recitation of each name, the call and response chorus is repeated with minor lyrical variations, mostly unaccompanied except for sparse percussion and sometimes a didgeridoo-like drone.[16] The effect of this section is chant-like and meditative, suggesting a commemorative ritual or prayer rather than music for popular entertainment, and resisting the pop ballad character of the more poetic verses.

After this recitation of names, Clegg addresses the listener more directly with a new *a cappella* call and its corresponding choral response: '*Hawu ngithi, hey wena (Hey wena), hey wena, hey wena nawe, s'zofika nini la siyakhona?*' ('Oh! I say: hey you, hey you, hey you and you, when will we get there?'). Once again this call and response begins with Clegg singing alone, followed by the chorus' response, but by the second response Clegg joins the chorus, and the line ends with him singing as part of the ensemble rather than with his voice isolated. This structure, while common in South African choral music, is atypical in global pop songs, which tend to maintain a clearer division between lead singer and back-up voices, or between call and response. In South African call and response, however, the relationship between soloist and ensemble, and therefore of the individual with the community, is re-emphasised through a song structure that lets one person initiate a call, but then sweeps them along with the collective. In protest or congregational situations this means that a single singer can quickly instigate collective singing, and the cyclical nature of these songs means that they can be repeated as often as the community is moved to repeat them. New singers can also redirect a singing group with a new call, and community agreement can be expressed by individual voices offering new harmonies or decorative vocalisations.[17] The shift from a collective to a transitive pronoun (from 'we' to 'you') in this section of '*Asimbonanga*' is accompanied by a more driving, insistent tone in the music created by shorter, more frequently repeated phrases that begin on the downbeat, and follow a clearly descending melody rather than the more complex lyricism of the chorus melody. Consequently, this section propels the song forward and builds energy in a manner that sets up the final chorus as a clear climax rather than simple recapitulation.

Part of what amplifies the energy of this final chorus is Dlanga's wordless descant, which suggests both ululation (typically an expression of joy or praise) and keening or weeping. The descant is reminiscent of typical South African choral call and response songs, which frequently feature vocal improvisations expressing participants' and audiences' appreciation or engagement, and which also frequently include a soprano descant added once all other vocal layers are established. It also, however, is characteristic of global pop songs of the era, which frequently include high-energy vocal or instrumental improvisations, typically by the lead performer, though sometimes by an ensemble member. In '*Asimbonanga*' this feature therefore helps to signal the approaching end of the song, despite the potential for additional repetition.

'*Asimbonanga*' is a ballad-like song, with a swaying rather than danceable rhythm, despite Mandela's exhortation to the audience in Frankfurt to stand up and dance. Combined with the unaccompanied opening and chant-like middle section, this rhythm recalls a style of South African protest song that is derived from Christian hymn traditions, and often uses a prayer-like petition or question to bring attention to injustice. In the context of its original release and early performances, this is exactly what '*Asimbonanga*' did. After the release of Mandela from prison in 1990, however, the signification of the song shifted from petition to celebration, and its meaning revolved more around the name of Mandela than around the statement 'we have not seen him'. In fact, in the context of Mandela's appearance on stage in 1999, the statement seems rhetorical, or perhaps even playful. This was not the intention of the musicians, as Clegg's introduction to the song suggested. Before he began singing it, he discussed the political circumstances in which it was originally released, and described the song as a tribute to 'one of the greatest

South Africans in history'.[18] Nonetheless the structural reconfiguration of the song that happened when the middle section was skipped reinforced the more celebratory character of the Mandela-era version.

THE SOWETO GOSPEL CHOIR COVERS 'ASIMBONANGA'

On 7 December 2013, the Soweto Gospel Choir surprised shoppers at a mall in Pretoria with a flash mob performance of '*Asimbonanga*'.[19] The choristers dressed as shop employees and customers, and mingled unobtrusively with shoppers until one member of the group began singing. The rest of the choir distributed around the store joined in, quickly silencing the shoppers, who gathered to watch and film the performance on cell phones. At the end of the performance the singers rapidly dispersed, regrouping soon after in their regular choir costumes to perform a short concert for the assembled shoppers. The event was organised by national retailer Woolworths as part of a fundraising effort for a local charity that organises cleft lip and cleft palate repair surgeries for South African children. Originally the choir had planned to perform an upbeat American pop song, but the death of Mandela two days before the event led them to change their plans, and '*Asimbonanga*' was chosen as a tribute to the former president.

The Soweto Gospel Choir performed only the isiZulu sections of the song. They sang the chorus three times, augmenting the responsive harmony on each repetition, followed by the isiZulu lyrics of the middle section of the song (excluding the lament) repeated twice, and then repeating the chorus twice with the added descant. Finally, they added a wordless outro, borrowed from the multivoiced outro to Peter Gabriel's 'Biko', which they sang twice, ending the performance with fists raised in salute. This arrangement of the song facilitated their *a cappella* performance, as the English parts of the song are structured around a solo voice with instrumental accompaniment, while the isiZulu sections are choral call and response, and work well unaccompanied. The arrangement also kept the song focused on Mandela by eliminating overt reference to other anti-apartheid activists. While the wordless outro from 'Biko' indexes the song and the person of Biko to an audience familiar with the song, not all audiences will recognise the reference.

Finally, the elimination of the verses updated the song to the present by removing references to Mandela's imprisonment on Robben Island. Suddenly the refrain 'We have not seen him' has shifted from referencing a temporary political situation to describing a permanent reality. Moreover, the middle section, which before suggested a call to action, in this context becomes a reminder of the mortality of the audience.

The Soweto Gospel Choir are certainly not the first, or only, performers to eliminate references to other anti-apartheid activists when performing '*Asimbonanga*' in the post-apartheid era. One might argue that Mandela himself first prompted this arrangement when he interrupted Savuka in 1999. Moreover, the original Juluka version was in isiZulu only. I would argue, however, that this arrangement has a somewhat paradoxical impact on the possible interpretation of the song as an expression of *ubuntu*, or communal interconnectedness. The parts of the song that the choir eliminate are the more soloistic elements, which might suggest that their arrangement refocuses the song on a more collective performance. Nonetheless, by eliminating the references to other anti-apartheid activists, this new performance leans in to an interpretation of the song as a celebration of Mandela's individual achievements, rather than his function as one leader among a collective representing the anti-apartheid struggle. Moreover, while the elimination of the sections of the song that are more like pop music and less clearly South African could be interpreted as a decolonising gesture, it also removes the productive tension that was such an important part of the activism of Savuka. The band were remarkable in part because they were multicultural. It is precisely the interaction of the different sections of the song that generates the complex web of significations that characterises South Africa's political struggle.

It is perhaps not insignificant that this version of '*Asimbonanga*' was a corporate marketing event. Samer Al-Khateeb and Nitin Agarwal note that flash mobs began as intentionally pointless performances with potentially playful or humorous outcomes but no clear goals. They define a flash mob as 'analog[ous] to a "flash flood" where all participants arrive at once, then disperse within minutes just like water from a sudden storm'.[20] The earliest events these authors identify as flash mobs disrupted business and consumer culture by mobilising large numbers of people to interact with store employees. They note, however, that flash mobs have been adapted to organise protests, for marketing purposes, and for the purposes of social or political disruption. It is not uncommon for business interests to use flash mobs for indirect marketing, by generating positive feelings among employees and customers. The performance of 'Asimbonanga' was part of an event originally intended as a fundraising campaign by a company collecting donations from customers for a third party. Charity fundraisers like this function as marketing strategies by generating positive feelings and beliefs about the community involvement of the company, while simultaneously permitting the customers who donate to feel as if they are involved, with minimal direct engagement with the cause in question. Moreover, charitable giving shields corporations and governments from more directly addressing wide-ranging social needs by presenting these needs as beyond the scope of policy change, and reliant instead on individual generosity or social responsibility. In this context, then, a performance that highlights one heroic figure, positioning Mandela as both a singular sufferer and a singular saviour, aligns more effectively with the goals of the project than would a performance that highlights more systemic inequality and shared activism.

This Soweto Gospel Choir arrangement of 'Asimbonanga' is based on a version of the song performed in a medley with Peter Gabriel's 'Biko' that the Soweto Gospel Choir regularly perform live, and which they first recorded for their 2005 album *Blessed*.[21] This arrangement begins with a steady and simple djembe introduction which accompanies the chorus sections of the song. No other instrumental accompaniment is used, and the djembe drops out entirely as the choir sing the bridge section, '*ngithi, hey wena (Hey wena)*'. Only the isiZulu sections of the song are performed, with two renditions of the chorus, sung through twice each time, and separated by the isiZulu part of the middle section, also performed twice. The descant is added to the chorus after the middle section. The choir then launch straight into the wordless melody that Gabriel repeats many times to end 'Biko'. This melody is sung on an open 'oh' sound, and consists of four notes moving stepwise downwards from the tonic to the dominant of the scale, and functionally resolving in a IV-I plagal cadence. The first two notes are detached, sounding like sobs, while the third note is held for two full bars, and slides down to the final held note, like a cry, or keening. The plagal resolution is so typical of Western church music that it is often known as the 'amen cadence', and consequently it underlines the feel of the song as grief-filled or prayer-like. In live performances Gabriel typically goads the audience into singing along during this section of the song, often with fists raised in an *amandla* (power) salute. In their medley version of the song, the Soweto Gospel Choir use this melody to connect the two songs, and move from this to the third verse of 'Biko'. They follow this single verse with only half of a chorus before returning to the wordless cry, repeated at a progressively lower volume to the end of the song. By skipping the scene-setting first verse and the personal narrative of the second verse, and leaping straight to a verse with a metaphor about a movement igniting like a fire, the Soweto Gospel Choir seem to draw attention to the continuity between the activism of two individuals (Mandela and Biko) and the larger political movement that encompassed the musical activism from which both songs emerged.

This medley epitomises the larger musical ecosystem that both '*Asimbonanga*' and 'Biko' characterise. Clegg and Gabriel performed together – both on the same programmes at the 1990 concert at Wembley Stadium for Nelson Mandela and at the 2003 46664 Aids benefit concert in Cape Town, where in addition to performing separately, Gabriel joined Clegg to perform '*Asimbonanga*'.[22] Moreover, both '*Asimbonanga*' and 'Biko' were covered by folk singer Joan Baez on her 1987 album *Recently*, with minimal variation from the original recordings.

SNOTKOP AND KAREN ZOID RECONTEXTUALISE '*ASIMBONANGA*'

In 2016, Karen Zoid launched the third season of her Afrikaans television talk show '*Republiek van Zoid Afrika*' ('Republic of Zoid Africa') by releasing a duet recorded during the first episode with Afrikaans singer and rapper Snotkop.[23] The song was a cover of a rearrangement of an Afrikaans popular song first released in 1987 by Carike Keuzenkamp, a singer particularly known for her recordings of Afrikaans children's songs. '*Dis 'n Land*' ('It's a Country', also sometimes known as '*Daar's 'n Land*' ['There's a Country']).[24]

The 1987 song was included on an album, *Ek Sing* ('I Sing') originally released as the End Conscription Campaign, coupled with a brain drain precipitated by the departure of young white men seeking to avoid compulsory conscription, was creating a crisis for an apartheid government dependent on its military to suppress anti-apartheid activism. It followed in the wake of an extremely expensive propaganda song called 'Together We'll Build a Brighter Future', which Keyan Tomaselli and Bob Boster have suggested may have been influenced by the pop charity songs 'We Are the World' and 'Do They Know it's Christmas?'[25] Schalk van der Merwe notes that while 'the idea of Schlager music as a tool of population control during times of national duress might be an extreme accusation … when one considers Carike Keuzenkamp's translated Schlager hit, "*Dis 'n Land*" ("It's a Country"), along with the timing of its release (during the third year of the South African State of Emergency in 1987), as well as the music video accompanying the release, such an accusation seems appropriate and legitimate'.[26] The 1980s was the final decade of apartheid, and the possibility of civil war or social catastrophe loomed large for many white South Africans. '*Dis 'n Land*' and its accompanying music video, which depicted racial segregation as successful and included imagery of military airplanes and parachuting soldiers, was clearly created as propaganda. The song employed musical material from a German popular song, with new Afrikaans lyrics praising the diversity of South Africa and asserting that the nation includes a place for the singer, who stands in for all white South Africans.[27] While the verses are sung by Keuzenkamp alone, the chorus is multitracked, with back-up singers adding a chorus effect to the catchy melody, and creating, as described above, an anthem-like encouragement to the audience to sing along.

In 2013, Snotkop rearranged the song with new rapped verses and a chorus that sampled Keuzenkamp's original in its entirety.[28] While his voice is isolated, with sparse accompaniment, and a somewhat strained delivery that creates an impression of anxiety in the verses, Snotkop sings along with Keuzenkamp in the chorus, and his voice is far enough back in the mix that it seems to join with hers and the other backing singers. Consequently, he sounds supported and included in the chorus, and the effect, especially in comparison to the verses, is celebratory. The new verses along with the music video of the song celebrate post-apartheid South African diversity and culture, but also describe the singer's nostalgic remembrance of his childhood experiences, and express somewhat anxious hopefulness that there is still a place for him in South Africa.[29]

Karen Zoid and Snotkop's performance covers Snotkop's version of 'Dis 'n Land', but incorporates a chorus and the choral part of the middle section of 'Asimbonanga'. They maintain the circular piano melody that Snotkop uses to introduce his song, but augment it with rock guitar, bass and percussion to fill out the sound space and make the introduction of the song feel more supported and less isolating. The two singers' voices enter in unison, and while Zoid drops out in the second line, letting Snotkop continue alone, she joins him at the end of several subsequent phrases. In the second verse, Zoid inserts a wordless melody sung in the rich lower register of her voice, supporting Snotkop's rapping with what sounds like a soothing croon. They sing together in full voice in the chorus, and while the live setting of the recording reduces the potential for multitracking, the effect is still of an anthemic sing-along chorus.

Zoid inserts the chorus of 'Asimbonanga' after the second verse of 'Dis 'n Land', where the second chorus would usually go. The insertion is seamless, and Snotkop and Zoid's cover band join her for the choral responses. The song then returns to 'Dis 'n Land' for a third verse and second chorus, and immediately after the chorus Zoid returns to 'Asimbonanga', calling 'I say hey *wena*' ('I say hey you'). The accompaniment drops out and Zoid, Snotkop and the cover band complete the song with a full-throated *a cappella* rendering of the response.

Zoid and Snotkop's incorporation of these fragments of 'Asimbonanga' in Snotkop's rearranged 'Dis 'n Land' gestures towards the fragmentation of the South Africa of the 1980s. 'Asimbonanga' and 'Dis 'n Land' were originally released at almost the same time, but the two songs represented radically different experiences and visions of South Africa. For the primary audience of 'Dis 'n Land', the segregation of cultures was presented as natural and desirable, while state violence was visualised as though it represented technological development and white progress. For audiences of 'Asimbonanga', however, it was cultural, musical and language mixing that occurred naturally, while state violence was implicitly condemned through references to imprisoned and murdered activists. The combination of the two songs in Zoid and Snotkop's performance generates an ambiguous musical message. On the one hand, the medley seems to suggest that Mandela's legacy is a democratic South Africa. On the other hand, the singers' choice to end on the question 'when will we get there?' implies an incomplete transition or a failure of the struggle for freedom.

CONCLUSION

It is a testament to Johnny Clegg's songwriting, and the artistic visions of Juluka and Savuka, that *'Asimbonanga'* is able to shift signification so effectively across such a wide range of contexts. The song endures not only because of its importance as a historical text, but because its musical richness permits such diverse reinterpretations. Moreover, the song's meaning-making is not limited to what can be gained from either musical or textual analysis. Rather, the song invites interpretation of the manner in which these elements interact with changing social and performance contexts.

NOTES

1   Apologies to Saidiya Hartman, whose concept of the afterlife of slavery informs my thinking in this chapter. See Saidiya Hartman, *Lose Your Mother: A Journey Along the Atlantic Slave Trade Route Terror* (New York: Farrar, Straus and Giroux, 2007).
2   Johnny Clegg & Savuka with Nelson Mandela, '"Asimbonanga" Live in Frankfurt', 1999, available as a bonus track on the DVD *Live and More ... Johnny Clegg with Savuka and Juluka* (Sydney: Rhythm Safari, RSDV5001, 2003); see also 'Johnny Clegg (With Nelson Mandela) – Asimbonanga – 1999 Fran', YouTube video, 06:12, accessed 1 September 2023, https://youtu.be/BGS7SpI7obY?si=UTJT6U_ZKZPLhCHU.
3   See Omotayo Jolaosho, 'Singing Politics: Freedom Songs and Collective Protest in Post-Apartheid South Africa', *African Studies Review* 62, no. 2 (2019): 6–29 for a discussion of the ways that call and response or antiphonal music works as protest music in South Africa, and see Lee Hirsch, dir. *Amandla: A Revolution in Four-Part Harmony* (DVD, Santa Monica: Artisan, 2002) for a history of choral protest music in the anti-apartheid struggle.
4   While *ubuntu* has deeper roots and more contested meanings, the definition most closely connected with South Africa's transitional years is the one I evoke here. In that context, *ubuntu* is understood to have been derived from the Nguni-language proverb *'umuntu ngumuntu ngabantu'* ('a person is a person because of [other] people'). Consequently *ubuntu* may be understood for the purposes of this chapter

as a philosophy that locates an individual's identity in the context of that person's relationships. See, for example, Desmond Tutu, *No Future Without Forgiveness* (London: Rider/Doubleday, 1999); Christian Gabe, 'What Is Ubuntu? Different Interpretations among South Africans of African Descent', *South African Journal of Philosophy* 31, no. 3 (2012): 484–503; C.W. Maris, 'Philosophical Racism and Ubuntu: In Dialogue with Mogobe Ramose', *South African Journal of Philosophy* 39, no. 3 (2020): 308–326.

5   Matanzima (also spelled Mathanzima) was raised in a position of relative power, alongside Nelson Mandela, within traditional Thembu society. During the apartheid years, however, he significantly increased his power by collaborating with the apartheid government in support of the homeland (Bantustan) system, while Mandela, as an African National Congress leader, opposed this stance. Matanzima was appointed 'paramount chief' and later state president of Transkei by the apartheid government. See Timothy Gibbs, *Mandela's Kinsmen: Nationalist Elites and Apartheid's First Bantustan* (Martlesham, Suffolk: Boydell & Brewer, 2014); Nelson Mandela, *Long Walk to Freedom: The Autobiography of Nelson Mandela* (Boston: Little, Brown and Company, 1994); Lungisile Ntsebeza, *Democracy Compromised: Chiefs and the Politics of the Land in South Africa* (Leiden: Brill, 2005).

6   The Hidden Years Archive is housed at Stellenbosch University, and this recording is catalogued as 'Hymap-dm-reel-clegg-mchunu-1978-001'. I am immensely grateful to Pakama Ncume and Lizabé Lambrechts for sharing this recording with me, and to Michael Drewett for making the connection and sharing this information.

7   Johnny Clegg & Savuka, *Asimbonanga* (single, Johannesburg: MINC, 12XMC(P) 4054016, 1986); Johnny Clegg & Savuka, *Third World Child* (album, Sandton: EMI, EMCJ (D) – 2407331, 1987).

8   Joan Baez, 'Asimbonanga', on *Recently* (album, Hollywood: Gold Castle Records, 171 004-1, 1987); Joan Baez, *Brothers in Arms* (compilation album, Los Angeles: Gold Castle Records, D2-71363, 1991); Various Artists, *United Voices of Africa* (compilation album, Paris: Atoll Music, 523 820-2, 2000); Various Artists, *The Winds of Change* (compilation album, Johannesburg: African Cream, ACM-CD023/3, 2004).

9   Lara Allen describes 'crossover' music as 'differentiated [from other popular music] first by the self-consciousness with which such fusion [between elements of different musical styles] took place, and secondly by the political significance intended by stylistic fusion' (Lara Allen, 'Kwaito versus Crossed-Over: Music and Identity during South Africa's Rainbow Years, 1994–99', *Social Dynamics* 30, no. 2 [2004]: 91–92).

10 The Beatles, *Hey Jude/Revolution* (single, London: Apple Records, R 5722, 1968); Queen, *Queen Live Killers* (album, New York: Elektra, BB-702, 1979); Bok van Blerk, *De La Rey* (album, Tshwane: Mozi Records MZCD 01, 2006).

11 Peter Gabriel, *Biko* (album, London: Charisma, CBDJ 370, 1980); The Special A.K.A., *Nelson Mandela/Break Down the Door* (single, New York: Chrysalis Records, 601 247, 1984).

12 Benedict Anderson notes that the ability of citizens to imagine others participating in the same rituals as them, even when they can't literally see one another doing so, creates a sense of national identity, or what he calls an 'imagined community' (Benedict Anderson, *Imagined Communities: Reflections on the Origin and Spread of Nationalism* [London: Verso, 1987]). Shana Redmond argues that 'anthems require subscription to a system of beliefs', suggesting that participation in the singing of an anthem creates the conditions for shared ideology that, in the case of the Black anthems Redmond is analysing, 'inspires its listeners to believe that the circumstances

or world around them can change for the better' (Shana Redmond, *Anthem: Social Movements and the Sound of Solidarity in the African Diaspora* [New York: NYU Press, 2014], 2). Lucilla Spini argues that Johnny Clegg's music, and *'Asimbonanga'* in particular, function as 'new traditional songs' or even as a national anthem (Lucilla Spini, 'Johnny Clegg: Anthropologist, Artist and Global Citizen', *International Journal of Anthropology* 35, no. 3–4 (2020): 156–157).

13 Clegg and Drewett explain that the *Juluka* song 'Woza Friday' ('Come Friday') was described by the censors as 'an insult to the Zulu people' due to its mixing of languages (Johnny Clegg and Michael Drewett, 'Why Don't You Sing About the Leaves and the Dreams? Reflecting on Music Censorship in Apartheid South Africa', in *Popular Music Censorship in Africa*, ed. Martin Cloonan and Michael Drewett [London: Ashgate, 2006]). See also Drewett's examination of 'aesopian strategies' for disguising protest content in South African popular music: Michael Drewett, 'Aesopian Strategies of Textual Resistance in the Struggle to Overcome the Censorship of Popular Music in Apartheid South Africa', *Critical Studies* 22, no. 1 (2004): 189–207.

14 Muff Andersson presents numerous examples of the disruption of apartheid's segregationist ideals through music, in particular in her discussion of crossover music, where she describes not only Clegg and Mchunu's partnership, but also the impact of Black American music on South Africa's urban, (mostly) black audiences, set ironically against white South African's clamouring for Margaret Singana's recordings of songs from the musical *Ipi Tombi* (Muff Andersson, *Music in the Mix: The Story of South African Popular Music* [Johannesburg: Ravan Press, 1981]). *Ipi Tombi* was a 1974 South African musical starring Margaret Singana, written and produced by white artists for primarily white audiences, but purporting to represent black life in apartheid South Africa. While the show achieved some initial success, it was heavily criticised and protested against for misrepresenting African culture and creating an inaccurate impression of the reality of black lives under apartheid. See Bertha Egnos (composer) and Gail Lakier (lyricist), *Ipi Tombi: Original Cast Recording* (album, Johannesburg: Satbel, BELD 23009, 1975), performed by the musical group Ipi 'n Tombia with lead singer Margaret Singana.

15 Clegg did not say 'and all the others' in the first releases of this song in 1986 and 1987; however, he frequently added the phrase in subsequent live performances and later recordings.

16 Instead of *'uMandela thina'* ('our Mandela') Savuka sing *'mfowetu thina'* ('our brother') after Biko's and Aggett's names, and *'udadewethu thina'* ('our sister') after Mxenge's name. Drones similar to those used in *'Asimbonanga'* are a regular feature in 'world' music of this era, frequently evoking 'exotic' or 'spiritual' imagery. While the instruments are different, the effect is similar to what Drewett describes as '[Peter] Gabriel's experimentation with layering sounds of different origins on top of one another' to enhance 'the global aesthetic of the song, forging a space which is everywhere yet in a sense nowhere in particular' (Michael Drewett, 'The Eyes of the World Are Watching Now: The Political Effectiveness of "Biko" by Peter Gabriel', *Popular Music and Society* 30, no. 1 [2007]: 41). Gabriel used a synthesized bagpipe sound in 'Biko'. Similarly, Timothy Taylor (2000) notes that a 'drone on an octave with a perfect fifth up from the bottom [is] a sound that for at least a couple of centuries has signified "rustic" or "primitive" to western listeners' (Timothy Taylor, 'World Music in Television Ads', *American Music* 18, no. 2 (2000): 172).

17 Jolaosho ('Singing Politics') explains that the level of communal engagement or agreement can be gauged by the uptake of a song or a variation by the collective.

18 Johnny Clegg, with Nelson Mandela, *Asimbonanga*.
19 Soweto Gospel Choir, 'Woolies and Soweto Gospel Choir Madiba Tribute', YouTube video, 03:09, accessed 1 September 2023, https://youtu.be/8GD55vY6Qiw?si=9YlUhHY1yfU8S2oi.
20 Samer Al-Khateeb and Nitin Agarwal, 'Flash Mob: A Multidisciplinary Review', *Social Network Analysis and Mining* 11, no. 97 (2021): 1.
21 Soweto Gospel Choir, *Blessed* (album, Johannesburg: Universal Music, CDRBL 331, 2005).
22 The concert in 1990 was the second of the Wembley Stadium concerts for Mandela, and was called 'Nelson Mandela: An International Tribute for a Free South Africa'. While Gabriel performed at the first Wembley concert for Mandela in 1988, Clegg was excluded from that concert due to the ongoing cultural boycott against South Africa (see chapter 7 by Michael Drewett in this book). Johnny Clegg & Savuka's performance at the 1990 'Tribute to Nelson Mandela' concert at Wembley Stadium can be viewed at 'Johnny Clegg & Savuka (feat Jackson Browne) Tribute to Nelson Mandela 1990', YouTube video, 08:59, accessed 10 May 2025, https://www.youtube.com/watch?v=sMMNacs5N74. Peter Gabriel and Geoffrey Oryema's performance at the 1990 'Tribute to Nelson Mandela' concert at Wembley Stadium can be viewed at 'PETER GABRIEL & GEOFFREY ORYEMA: "BIKO" [LIVE:1990]', YouTube video, 13:11, accessed 10 May 2025, https://www.youtube.com/watch?v=B0wIrkXcE8Y. Johnny Clegg & Savuka with various artists singing '*Asimbonanga*' can be seen on the DVD release of the 46664 concert that was originally performed in Cape Town in 2003: Various Artists, *46664: The Event* (DVD, Disc 1, Cape Town: Warner Music Vision, 2564-61475-2, 2004). A video of this performance can also be viewed at 'Johnny Clegg & Savuka with Peter Gabriel Asimbonanga Mandela Live at The 46664 Aids Concert South Africa 2003', YouTube video, 04:53, accessed 10 May 2025, https://www.youtube.com/watch?v=pYjfOmBEXVs.
23 Snotkop and Karen Zoid, '*Dis 'n Land*', on *Republiek van Zoid Africa,* vol. 3 (album, Cape Town: Karen Zoid Music, X3M-DHN-UEH-1, 2016).
24 Carike Keuzenkamp, *Ek Sing* (album, Johannesburg: Decibel Musiekmaatskappy Beperk, DCB (E) 187, 1987). The music video of the song, 'Daar's 'n Land [sic] – Carike Kuezenkamp', is available as a YouTube video, 04:06, accessed 1 September 2023, https://youtu.be/8r2uLdSlyg0.
25 Keyan G. Tomaselli and Bob Boster, 'Mandela, MTV, Television and Apartheid', *Popular Music and Society* 17, no. 2 (1993): 5; USA for Africa, 'We Are the World', on *We Are the World* (album, New York: Columbia, US2-05179, 1985); Band Aid, 'Do They Know It's Christmas', on *Do They Know It's Christmas* (album, London: Phonogram, FEED 112, 1984). 'Together We'll Build a Brighter Future' (Various artists, Bureau for Information, South African Government, 1986) was never commercially released and there are no known recordings of it.
26 Schalk van der Merwe, *On Record: Music and Society in Recorded Popular Afrikaans Music Records, 1900–2015* (Stellenbosch: African Sun Media, 2017): 12. Van der Merwe explains that *Schlager* are northern European pop songs that were regularly re-recorded with Afrikaans lyrics for a South African market during the latter half of the twentieth century. Both in Europe and in South Africa, *Schlager* are frequently criticised as easily consumable sentimental songs with low artistic value, which have been used by oppressive regimes like the apartheid regime to pacify the populace.

27 The music is from Nicole, *'Laß Mich Nicht Allein'* ('Don't Leave Me Alone'), Ralph Siegel (composer), Bernd Meinunger (lyricist) (single, Munich: Jupiter Records, 885 022-7, 1986). See Van der Merwe, *On Record*, 14.
28 Snotkop, *'Dis 'n Land'*, on *Ek Laaik van Jol* (album, Johannesburg: Select Musiek, SELBCD 931, 2011).
29 Snotkop, 'Snotkop – Dis 'n Land', YouTube video, 03:39, accessed 1 September 2023, https://youtu.be/xAx3I-y1FHU?si=jr87r6asUzxT15D.

REFERENCES

Al-Khateeb, Samer and Nitin Agarwal. 'Flash Mob: A Multidisciplinary Review'. *Social Network Analysis and Mining* 11, no. 97 (2021): 1–18.
Allen, Lara. 'Kwaito versus Crossed-Over: Music and Identity During South Africa's Rainbow Years, 1994–99'. *Social Dynamics* 30, no. 2 (2004): 82–111.
Anderson, Benedict. *Imagined Communities: Reflections on the Origin and Spread of Nationalism*. London: Verso, 1987.
Andersson, Muff. *Music in the Mix: The Story of South African Popular Music*. Johannesburg: Ravan Press, 1981.
Clegg, Johnny and Michael Drewett. 'Why Don't You Sing About the Leaves and the Dreams? Reflecting on Music Censorship in Apartheid South Africa'. In *Popular Music Censorship in Africa*, edited by Martin Cloonan and Michael Drewett, 127–135. London: Ashgate, 2006.
Clegg, Johnny, with Nelson Mandela. 'Johnny Clegg (With Nelson Mandela) – *Asimbonanga* – 1999 Fran'. YouTube video, 06:12. Accessed 1 September 2023. https://youtu.be/BGS7SpI7obY?si=UTJT6U_ZKZPLhCHU.
Drewett, Michael. 'Aesopian Strategies of Textual Resistance in the Struggle to Overcome the Censorship of Popular Music in Apartheid South Africa'. *Critical Studies* 22, no. 1 (2004): 189–207.
Drewett, Michael. 'The Eyes of the World Are Watching Now: The Political Effectiveness of "Biko" by Peter Gabriel'. *Popular Music and Society* 30, no. 1 (2007): 39–51.
Gabe, Christian. 'What Is Ubuntu? Different Interpretations Among South Africans of African Descent'. *South African Journal of Philosophy* 31, no. 3 (2012): 484–503.
Gabriel, Peter and Geoffrey Oryema. 'PETER GABRIEL & GEOFFREY ORYEMA: "BIKO" [LIVE:1990]'. YouTube video, 13:11. Accessed 10 May 2025. https://www.youtube.com/watch?v=B0wIrkXcE8Y.
Gibbs, Timothy. *Mandela's Kinsmen: Nationalist Elites and Apartheid's First Bantustan*. Martlesham, Suffolk: Boydell & Brewer, 2014.
Hartman, Saidiya. *Lose Your Mother: A Journey Along the Atlantic Slave Trade Route Terror*. New York: Farrar, Straus and Giroux, 2007.
Hirsch, Lee, dir. *Amandla: A Revolution in Four-Part Harmony*. DVD. Santa Monica: Artisan, 2002.
Jolaosho, Omotayo. 'Singing Politics: Freedom Songs and Collective Protest in Post-Apartheid South Africa'. *African Studies Review* 62, no. 2 (2019): 6–29.
Johnny Clegg & Savuka. 'Johnny Clegg & Savuka (feat Jackson Browne) Tribute to Nelson Mandela 1990', YouTube video, 08:59. Accessed 10 May 2025. https://www.youtube.com/watch?v=sMMNacs5N74.

Johnny Clegg & Savuka with Peter Gabriel. 'Johnny Clegg & Savuka with Peter Gabriel Asimbonanga Mandela Live at The 46664 Aids Concert South Africa 2003'. YouTube video, 04:53. Accessed 10 May 2025. https://www.youtube.com/watch?v=pYjfOmBEXVs.

Keuzenkamp, Carike. 'Daar's 'n Land [sic] – Carike Kuezenkamp'. YouTube video, 04:06. Accessed 1 September 2023. https://youtu.be/8r2uLdSlyg0.

Mandela, Nelson. *Long Walk to Freedom: The Autobiography of Nelson Mandela*. Boston: Little, Brown and Company, 1994.

Maris, C.W. 'Philosophical Racism and Ubuntu: In Dialogue with Mogobe Ramose'. *South African Journal of Philosophy* 39, no. 3 (2020): 308–326.

Ntsebeza, Lungisile. *Democracy Compromised: Chiefs and the Politics of the Land in South Africa*. Leiden: Brill, 2005.

Redmond, Shana. *Anthem: Social Movements and the Sound of Solidarity in the African Diaspora*. New York: New York University Press, 2014.

Snotkop. 'Snotkop – Dis 'n Land'. YouTube video, 03:39. Accessed 1 September 2023. https://youtu.be/xAx3I-y1FHU?si=jr87r6asUzxT15D.

Soweto Gospel Choir. 'Woolies and Soweto Gospel Choir Madiba Tribute'. YouTube video, 03:09. Accessed 1 September 2023. https://youtu.be/8GD55vY6Qiw?si=9YlUhHY1yfU8S2oi.

Spini, Lucilla. 'Johnny Clegg: Anthropologist, Artist and Global Citizen'. *International Journal of Anthropology* 35, no. 3–4 (2020): 145–160.

Taylor, Timothy. 'World Music in Television Ads'. *American Music* 18, no. 2 (2000): 162–192.

Tomaselli, Keyan G. and Bob Boster. 'Mandela, MTV, Television and Apartheid'. *Popular Music and Society* 17, no. 2 (1993): 1–19.

Tutu, Desmond. *No Future Without Forgiveness*. London: Rider/Doubleday, 1999.

Van der Merwe, Schalk. *On Record: Music and Society in Recorded Popular Afrikaans Music Records, 1900–2015*. Stellenbosch: African Sun Media, 2017.

Various Artists. *46664: The Event*. DVD, Disc 1. Cape Town: Warner Music Vision, 2564-61475-2, 2004.

DISCOGRAPHY

Baez, Joan. *Brothers in Arms*. Compilation album. Los Angeles: Gold Castle Records, D2-71363, 1991.

Baez, Joan. *Recently*. Album. Hollywood: Gold Castle Records, 171 004-1, 1987.

Band Aid. *Do They Know It's Christmas*. Album. London: Phonogram, FEED 112, 1984.

The Beatles. *Hey Jude/Revolution*. Single. London: Apple Records, R 5722, 1968.

Egnos, Bertha (composer) and Gail Lakier (lyricist). *Ipi Tombi: Original Cast Recording*. Performed by the musical group Ipi 'n Tombia with lead singer Margaret Singana. Album. Johannesburg: Satbel, BELD 23009, 1975.

Gabriel, Peter. *Biko*. Album. London: Charisma, CBDJ 370,1980.

Johnny Clegg & Savuka. *Asimbonanga*. Single. Johannesburg: MINC, 12XMC(P) 4054016, 1986.

Johnny Clegg & Savuka. *Third World Child*. Album. Sandton: EMI, EMCJ (D) – 2407331, 1987.

Johnny Clegg with Savuka and Juluka. *Live and More … Johnny Clegg with Savuka and Juluka*. DVD. Sydney: Rhythm Safari, RSDV5001, 2003.

Keuzenkamp, Carike. *Ek Sing*. Album. Johannesburg: Decibel Musiekmaatskappy Beperk, DCB (E) 187, 1987.
Nicole. *Laß Mich Nicht Allein*. Ralph Siegel (composer), Bernd Meinunger (lyricist). Single. Munich: Jupiter Records, 885 022-7, 1986.
Queen, *Queen Live Killers*. Album. New York: Elektra, BB-702, 1979.
Snotkop. *Ek Laaik van Jol*. Album. Johannesburg: Select Musiek, SELBCD 931, 2011.
Snotkop and Karen Zoid. *Republiek van Zoid Africa*, vol. 3. Album. Cape Town: Karen Zoid Music, X3M-DHN-UEH-1, 2016.
Soweto Gospel Choir. *Blessed*. Album. Johannesburg: Universal Music, CDRBL 331, 2005.
The Special A.K.A. *Nelson Mandela/Break Down the Door*. Single. New York: Chrysalis Records, 601 247, 1984.
USA for Africa. *We Are the World*. Album. New York: Columbia, US2-05179, 1985.
Van Blerk, Bok. *De La Rey*. Album. Tshwane: Mozi Records, MZCD 01, 2006.
Various Artists. *46664: The Event*. DVD, Disc 1. Cape Town: Warner Music Vision, 2564-61475-2, 2004.
Various Artists. 'Together We'll Build a Brighter Future'. No album released. Pretoria: Bureau for Information, South African Government, 1986.
Various Artists. *United Voices of Africa*. Compilation album. Paris: Atoll Music 523 820-2, 2000.
Various Artists. *The Winds of Change*. Compilation album. Johannesburg: African Cream, ACM-CD023/3, 2004.

CHAPTER

13

Clegg is Cancelled? Johnny Clegg and Questions of Zulu Cultural Appropriation

Brett Houston-Lock

> 'These things come to us by way of much pain
> Don't let us slip back into the dark'
>
> — 'One (Hu)'Man One Vote', Johnny Clegg & Savuka,
> *Cruel, Crazy, Beautiful World*, 1989.

In August 2017, like many South Africans living abroad, I was determined to see Johnny Clegg perform one last time when his farewell tour came to London. Of course, I had seen him countless times over the years, starting in the mid-1980s when I was still in high school. For my generation of liberal white South Africans coming of age in the 1980s, Clegg's great friendship and musical partnership with Sipho Mchunu in the band Juluka represented a clear way ahead for South Africa and a non-racial democratic future.

In 2017, he knew he didn't have long left and embarked on a final world tour, 'The Final Journey'. This show took time to review some of the standout moments of his long career, soon to be cut short by the cancer that would kill him. One of those key moments, of course, is shown in the famous clip of Nelson Mandela surprising Clegg on stage at a concert in Frankfurt in 1999, and, standing arm-in-arm with him, cajoling the audience to dance.[1] Could any South African artist have been paid a greater tribute?

I was therefore stunned and surprised when the American liberal newspaper of record, *The Washington Post*, chose to memorialise Johnny Clegg after his death with an article that questioned whether it was okay to love Clegg's music in spite of alleged problematic aspects of his career, central to which was the issue of so-called 'cultural appropriation'.[2] The author of the piece, Zoé Samudzi, is an American academic of Zimbabwean heritage. Among her expressed grievances is a notion that Clegg's white fans 'laughed' at his Zulu persona and thus 'indigenous language could still be treated like some kind of novelty or spectacle' (something which I do not believe to be in the slightest bit true). While acknowledging Clegg's enthusiasm for promoting Zulu culture to a global audience, she asks rhetorically 'but was it "his place" to do so?' Samudzi has form on this theme. Previously she had written for *Media Diversified*, taking Annie Lennox to task for allegedly culturally appropriating the song 'Strange Fruit' from Billie Holiday, seemingly unaware that the song had been written, not by Holiday, but by a white Jewish songwriter, Lewis Allan (born Abel Meeropol).[3] It would seem that untying the Gordian Knot of culture isn't as straightforward as activists imagine it is. Attacking it with bluster and hubris isn't going to cut it.

There is little evidence that these questions were being asked in South Africa by many South Africans of any colour or culture, and this raises a question that may point to the real problem: are the assumptions of the progressive left in the United States of America (US) about race – based on their own experience, and because of American cultural, media and academic dominance – toxic to race relations in other parts of the world? There is a growing feeling that they may be, as evidenced by books such as the one by black British social commentator Tomiwa Owolade, *This Is Not America*, in which he argues that 'too much of the debate around racism in Britain is viewed through the prism of American ideas'.[4] It is this sort of thoughtless appropriation of more dominant foreign cultural narratives that does real damage to countries struggling with their own histories and racial dynamics.

Perhaps because of the preponderance of social media – largely managed and facilitated by US-based companies – American social trends tend to take on greater significance than they otherwise might, and the corollary in this globalised world is that Americans see other cultures through their own eyes. The irony of this frequently escapes those in American institutions complaining about 'cultural appropriation'. In a real sense, the social discourse of the entire world has been appropriated to serve American narratives about society, race and gender.

An example is the globalisation of the Black Lives Matter movement following the death in custody of George Floyd in Minnesota in 2020. The presence and activities of BLM should more appropriately have been limited to a few American cities, but instead spread even to the United Kingdom, a country where police are not routinely armed and police killings are so rare as to barely make double figures in a decade, and are largely found to be justified by an independent board of inquiry.[5] There was not, however, a global protest movement spawned after the killing of protesting mine workers by the South African police at Marikana in 2012, for the simple reason that South African domestic issues are not globalised in the way American issues are. A South African active on social media might be expected to have an opinion on President Donald Trump or President Joe Biden, but few Americans are likely to even know who President Jacob Zuma and President Cyril Ramaphosa are.[6]

Unfortunately, the concerns of North American 'wokeness' emanating from the campuses and corporations of the US have nevertheless travelled to South Africa, and now infect local discourse around the music and legacy of Clegg and his contemporaries in similar 'crossover' bands like Hotline and Mango Groove. Younger critics who were not yet born at the height of these bands' cultural relevance and importance now critique them without awareness of the social and political context in which they existed. For example, in a podcast called *Deep Cut* on the Spotify platform, two young South African pundits, Zwide Ndwandwe and Nomonde Tshomi, reflect on how Clegg's cultural appropriation was 'in your face', remarking that, 'as an anthropologist' (Clegg was an academic before becoming a full-time professional musician) Clegg's music, to Tshomi, sounds like 'travel writing in musical form'.[7] The implication is that Clegg was a tourist rather than someone who immersed himself in any authentic way in Zulu culture. The podcast represents a fair summary of the various accusations thrown at Clegg by those who claim he was a cultural thief.

These verdicts are delivered with a troubling moral certainty that is completely at odds with the testimony of Clegg's many Zulu friends and collaborators. If the question is 'who has the right to speak?', is it a younger generation that knows little of the era and environment Clegg operated in, US-based journalists suffering the same knowledge deficiency, or the black people Clegg lived and worked with during the apartheid years, when the cultural impact of black and white musicians working together was a powerful and subversive statement against a regime intent on maintaining the divide between them? Former African National Congress (ANC) policy-maker and academic Nomboniso Gasa sums it up best, in a 2019 tweet: 'Johny [sic] Clegg was an activist who worked closely with David Webster, (assassinated in 1989). Clegg was an anthropologist by training. He didn't study "Zulu culture", he lived with the people. A bridge whose music brought people together'.[8]

In the 1970s, Juluka's music was blocked from airplay because it fell foul of the apartheid government's broadcast policy of not allowing the mixing of languages in radio programmes.[9] Bands with multiracial personnel were harassed, faced arrest and were severely limited in their chances of commercial success. In one instance, three police officers in camouflage uniforms and carrying shotguns invaded the stage while Juluka were performing to stop the show.[10] Had Clegg wished to simply 'appropriate' Zulu music, he could just as easily have done so by replicating a toned-down version of the music and performing it with an all-white band. Had he wanted merely to make an entertaining 'spectacle' of Zulu culture, he could have simply hired dancers fresh from a theatre run of *Ipi Tombi The Musical* to dance at his shows.[11] Instead, he chose to partner with authentic collaborators, not costumed actors hired for spectacle; he partnered as an equal with Mchunu and formed a band whose success would be an uphill and dangerous struggle against banning, censorship and other forms of harassment.

Nevertheless, the young *Deep Cut* podcaster snorts derisively: 'Is that a Zulu? Oh no … it's Johnny Clegg!' Her co-host chimes in with 'Yeah, my God, it's not the best example of South African music, is it?' Well, what is?

That this might be a contentious and complicated question to answer – if indeed it could be answered at all – does not occur to them. The questions that 'problematise' culture, particularly where there is an element of 'whiteness' involved, seem performative rather than sincere.

'It sounds like Toto in Africa', the podcaster goes on to sneer, while Juluka's *'Impi'* ('War') plays in the background.[12] It is not authentically 'African', in other words. Funnily enough, this echoes the complaints of some overseas 'World Music' aficionados who have listened to Juluka's music and found the blend of maskanda – Zulu folk music – and Western rock unpalatable. A reviewer for the UK music paper of record, *Melody Maker*, called Clegg 'a cultural transvestite', for example.[13] In another example, a review for the *Trouser Press Record Guide* spoke of Juluka as 'a failed experiment in combining rock with Zulu chants and the mbaqanga sound of the South African township'.[14] Similarly, *Rolling Stone*'s review of *Shadow Man* – Johnny Clegg & Savuka's second album – was scathing about its efforts to 'make itself more attractive to European and American Ears'.[15] Perhaps the reviewer, Jimmy Gutterman, didn't appreciate that mbaqanga music itself was a product of African and American fusion in the first place, and hardly 'authentic' – whatever that actually is.[16]

One rather suspects that the 'authenticity' Western European collectors demand of so-called 'World Music' doesn't apply to their own Western European music, which is expected to be constantly innovating and progressing – whereas African music, for their listening pleasure, should apparently remain hermetically sealed in and unchanging. If anything, this is – to adopt another fashionable progressive term – the real 'othering' of Africa and African people.

Take for example this review of Johnny Clegg & Savuka's *Heat, Dust and Dreams* album from the influential online *AllMusic* guide. Describing Clegg's vocals as a mixture of American singers Bob Dylan and Bruce Springsteen, it reads:

> A nice album of pieces ... The guitar work seems slightly influenced by reggae, which wouldn't be too surprising given the half-South African membership of the group. Overall rather pop-like, but a decently higher quality of pop than the majority that's generally pushed on the

American market. For those curious as to what's happening in cross-cultural pop music, it would be a great addition. For those who are looking for strictly South African music, Ladysmith Black Mambazo or the Mahotella Queens might be a better choice.[17]

It betrays the international reviewer's prejudices about national identities in Africa, in that he does not regard the white members of Savuka as truly 'South African', nor the music they have created together as authentically African. Instead he points to music less adulterated by modernity as 'traditional' South African music. Would any reviewer say The Beatles, for example, were not a truly British band and instead point to Spiers and Boden, or some other practitioners of music to Morris dance to?

At the core of this attitude is an assumption that 'culture' – when it isn't Western – is sacrosanct, an idea that Clegg explicitly rejected. 'Culture isn't "liberal" or "conservative",' he said, 'it is what you *do* with it.'[18]

Writing in the journal *Reality* in 1981, essayist Nhlanhla Ngcobo notes: 'Juluka's socio-cultural modality is forceful in dissolving racial stereotypes and prejudice; it attacks the problem of racial stereotype and prejudice at its rock-bottom foundation. The common error of equating "traditional" with "primitive" and "Western" with "civilised" is challenged and replaced by attitudes of compatibility and equality. Jonathan's profound understanding of and appreciation of black culture and language brings white and black cultures together in South Africa.'[19] This contemporary account of (white) Clegg's role by a (black) writer addresses both the importance of cultural integration in breaking down the racial barriers put in place by apartheid ideology, as well as the hidden prejudice at the core of a desire to keep non-Western culture 'pure', and its implications, entirely overlooked or unappreciated by present-day critics.

There are well-known African musicians who agree with this argument. Senegalese musician Youssou N'Dour reminds us that cultural exchange is a two-way street: 'In Dakar we hear many different recordings. We are open to these sounds. When people say my music is too Western, they must remember that we, too, hear this music over here. We hear the African music with the modern.'[20] Beninese singer Angélique Kidjo argues: 'There is a kind of cultural racism going on where people think that African musicians have to make a certain kind of music. No one asks Paul Simon, "Why did you use black African musicians? Why don't you use Americans? Why don't you make your music?" What is the music that Paul Simon is supposed to do? Answer: Any music he wants.'[21] Of course, Paul Simon has had his detractors, but the point is nonetheless well made. We will return to Paul Simon in due course.

At least the *Deep Cut* team admit in their podcast to having been introduced to the concept of 'cultural appropriation' through the social media platform X (formerly *Twitter*), even as they remark that any white people wearing Zulu attire are guilty of 'cosplay'. One wonders what style of clothing they were wearing in the studio. It would be disgustingly racist to accuse them of 'cosplay' because they were probably dressed in Western fashion, but that the reverse might also be true does not occur to them. If a person were to convert to Judaism or Islam, for example, and adopt traditional religious dress, would anyone regard this as 'cosplay'? Is there any reason to believe that Clegg's immersion in Zulu culture was any less sincere?

Still, citing Clegg's background in anthropology, the *Deep Cut* hosts conclude that his 'going native' (their words) is 'fifty layers of messed up'. They profess to admire artists like Johannes Kerkorrel and Koos Kombuis who opposed apartheid in their own language (that is, Afrikaans), 'without gimmick', unlike Clegg. There would have been little disagreement with this view during the apartheid era by any National Party-appointed director general of the South African Broadcasting Corporation (SABC), the state-run broadcaster. Keep in mind that '*Woza* Friday' ('Come Friday') is another example of a song banned from airplay for 'mixing languages'.[22]

Back at *The Washington Post*, Samudzi – also strangely obsessed with Clegg's background in anthropology – concludes that on balance Clegg's contribution, regardless of its 'questionable' aspects, was positive and that he was widely loved. She writes: 'His story and his life's work lovingly demand we consider and reconsider the nature of and our capacity for a confrontational and self-sacrificial interracial solidarity (and, for whites, not simply political actions that are personally convenient), the historical and contemporary power of music and culture in anti-oppression struggles, and what it means to ethically and responsibly participate in the cultural forms of a people that is not yours.'[23]

Really? What in the life and work of Johnny Clegg 'demands' these 'questions', and why, particularly, is it necessary or fitting to ask them in place of a decent obituary? What was so questionable about his life that it begged to be questioned? Whatever the pressing question, it never seemed to occur to even Mandela to ask it, though he had the opportunity. Nor did it occur to Sipho Mchunu to do so. Instead, Mchunu spoke of his friend thus at his funeral: 'I have lost more than a friend, more than a brother; he was everything to me'.[24]

Mchunu and Clegg met when they were both teenagers in 1969 and became friends and musical collaborators for the best part of two decades until Mchunu retired in the late 1980s, resurrecting their collaboration periodically until Clegg's death in 2019. No one (so far) has accused Mchunu of appropriating Western rock music in order to become more successful as a maskandi artist; the focus is entirely on the proposition that Clegg appropriated maskanda to be more successful in rock music. But this makes little sense, because apartheid policies pertaining to arts and culture in the 1970s and 1980s meant neither one furthered his career by participating in this unwelcome fusion. One can therefore conclude only that the partnership was heartfelt and artistically satisfying to both.

Furthermore, since the only logical motive for cultural appropriation is fame and the attendant commercial rewards, Clegg's accusers must face up to the absurdity of ascribing these motives to a child who could not have hypothesised the success that would be decades away. To imagine the friendship between two teenagers, Clegg and Mchunu, to be anything more than it appeared to be presupposes a prescience that is hard to support. By Clegg's own account, he was captivated by the sound of maskanda music and wanted to learn everything about it, and to this end befriended the people who would introduce him to the culture and traditions from where it came. This behaviour is typically described as assimilation rather than appropriation, especially given that it was entirely free of malign intentions. Indeed, Clegg believed that for there to be hope for the future, it was important that white South Africans 'search for an African identity'.[25] He would later say, in an interview ahead of his final South African concerts: 'People say, "Gee you guys were clever," but to be honest we were just buddies; I loved guitar music ... I didn't think that I was going to do this and in 20 years' time be celebrated as some sort of cultural missionary'.[26]

The reason no one ever suggests that Sipho Mchunu 'appropriated' the stylings of Western rock music for commercial advantage and with malign intentions is that the accusations of appropriation only ever flow in one direction. But the reality is that such appropriation simply would not have made economic sense to either Clegg or Mchunu – even if this had been on their minds at the time – given the commercial realities of the music business in apartheid South Africa. Certainly, as they moved forward with their careers in music years later, it may have occurred to them – and most likely did – that they had created something unique together and that it had established their brand, spawning many imitators. But the key word here is 'together'. What they had done by assimilating a part of each other's cultures is create a new, uniquely South African musical form that was neither quite white, nor entirely black, but which shone a light on the dream of a non-racial South Africa of the future.

It is this quality of 'not being entirely black and not being entirely white', but retaining and blending the most exciting elements of both traditions, that, ironically, frustrates the aforementioned 'World Music' purists and leads them to dislike Juluka's (and later Savuka's) music. Clegg's response to this attitude is recorded in a 1987 edition of *Sounds* magazine. Speaking to Hugh Fielder, he remarked: 'That puritanical attitude makes the African culture sacrosanct from the normal pressures that affect all cultures. We need to get rid of this form of paternalism'.[27] For some, this is precisely the problem. As musicologist Christopher Ballantine observes, there is 'an emergent discourse of African essentialism'. This means that 'blackness is understood in terms of Africanness, and black or African identity is simply associated with authenticity, resistance and subversion, while whiteness is associated with Europe, in-authenticity, domination and collusion. This discourse denies creolisation and hybridity as constitutive of African experiences'.[28]

But the focus on Clegg touches on another tenet of the peddlars of 'cultural appropriation' critiques, the 'magic black person', through which they, again, unintentionally 'other' black people as having some mystical power in music which a white person needs to steal (or 'appropriate') in order to succeed in the field. This denies any possibility of genuine artistic cooperation and collaboration between black and white musicians. Again, this is a cultural nihilism that places modern progressives in a chilling concordance with the racists and reactionaries who designed apartheid, while at the same time essentialising black people as custodians of 'singing and dancing', another unfortunate racist trope.

The obsession in 'woke' ideology with power differentials, and the article of faith that white people are always 'privileged' and thus more powerful, implies that no genuine collaboration between musicians of different races – who are simply 'turned on' by each other's styles and talents (as the young Clegg and Mchunu were) – can take place. This is a bleak terrain, and a world view generally antipathetic to artists and creators. Significantly, Mchunu's estimation of his relationship with Clegg differs entirely from this. He puts it down to fate that they happened to meet in the street, changing the future for both of them, but he says, 'what made us get very tight together was respect. We respected each other in a very strong way'.[29] He stresses friendship, partnership, respect and a brotherhood, recalling memories stretching back to their teenage years. The notion that his friend was a cultural thief and he the victim does not square in the slightest with his testimony: '"We didn't care about politics because we didn't know about politics. I was just happy with a friend," Mchunu said of their boyhood friendship'.[30] If there is disrespect present, it is in the reluctance to acknowledge that Mchunu can express his own truth, and in the patronising and insulting implication that he is the unwitting facilitator of the cultural theft by Clegg, or the illegitimate conduit through which the alleged appropriation occurred.

For a so-called 'progressive' movement in America that stresses that authentic voices should be heard, it seems odd that many involved in it are not prepared to listen to those who actually lived through the turbulent times in South Africa that Clegg, Mchunu and other musicians operated in. Most are still alive. The concerns imported in recent times from the American political maelstrom were not their concerns then – and are not now; these concerns should not be transplanted into the South African context and overlaid on the musicians' *actual lived experience* (another popular modern expression). The current blanket obsession with imagined 'cultural appropriation' risks smothering the real history of South African music and musicians. Their voices should not be drowned out by those who like to hear only their own voices.

Another of the delusions of the *Deep Cut* team is that 'Johnny Clegg shot to international stardom' on the back of his 'dabbling' in 'black art' (meaning the art of black people, not seeking the help of the devil, as Robert Johnson is famously thought to have done).[31] In the first place, Clegg never 'shot' to stardom at all. His rise to success, together with Mchunu, was a hard uphill slog in South Africa taking more than a decade before they achieved any international attention. Even when he did achieve some visibility – chiefly with Savuka – Clegg's efforts to achieve success in the UK were frustrated following lobbying by the British Anti-Apartheid Movement seeking to enforce the cultural boycott against South Africa, and he was expelled as a member of the British Musicians' Union for refusing to stop performing in South Africa.[32] It was hardly Savukamania! Clegg was even barred from playing at the 1988 Nelson Mandela Tribute Concert at Wembley Stadium, despite appeals by the ANC itself for an exception to be made.[33] This was the esteem in which he was held by the leaders of South Africa's liberation movement. But of course, young millennial critics who were not even alive at the time profess to know better.

The reality of overseas success is very different. By far the most successful South Africans in terms of international success during the apartheid era were black artists in the exile community, like Miriam Makeba and Hugh Masekela, both household names in every country where pop music and jazz were consumed. Artists like Abdullah Ibrahim and Dudu Pukwana also did very well in jazz circles. Commercially, white artists like Manfred Mann, Trevor Rabin, Duncan Faure, and – later on – Dave Matthews did better sticking to straightforward rock music. White crossover bands like Hotline, eVoid, Via Afrika and Bright Blue who followed in the wake of Juluka tried to reach audiences beyond South Africa but never really found international success with a hybrid rock/African sound.

The artist who did finally make a huge commercial and artistic splash through the blending of black South African music with Western rock and a singer-songwriter ethos was Paul Simon, with his 1986 *Graceland* album.[34]

Simon was inevitably himself accused of cultural appropriation, but never by the South African musicians he worked with, many of whom went on to very successful international careers of their own via the doors that opened following their collaborations with him. Many continued playing with Simon for decades after *Graceland*. Musicians are generally curious people, and want to find new sounds and collaborate with interesting people. Often what they make together is transcendent and beautiful. It is, sadly, politicians and academics who seek to make this approach divisive and ugly. It would be tragic if progressive politics succeeded where apartheid ideologues like prime ministers Hendrik Verwoerd and John Vorster failed in keeping musicians from different cultural backgrounds from finding each other.

Yet the issue persists. Reviewing Clegg's autobiography in *Daily Maverick*, Lucas Ledwaba starts by noting: 'Clegg's immersion into Zulu culture and traditional music that catapulted him into superstardom has always raised uncomfortable questions about the appropriation of African culture and gaining commercial success from it'.[35] In *Business Day* a few days after Clegg's death, Chris Thurman began his tribute – acknowledging the general heartfelt mourning of the nation – with these words: 'Questions of cultural appropriation aside ...'.[36] Is any of this a fitting way to memorialise a man who has made such a contribution to South African music that Mandela himself was a fan? One wonders if this will now be a standard preface that blights every future article about Clegg's legacy.

One cannot help noticing that Harry Belafonte, who made the album *Paradise in Gazankulu* (1988), after the success of Simon's *Graceland*, is not typically accused of appropriation, despite being a rich and successful American artist, and despite the fact that the album was less collaborative than Simon's; for example, there are tracks on it which are essentially the original recordings with the original vocals erased and replaced with new English lyrics written by American songwriter Jake Holmes.[37] That is not to say the original artists were not given full credit – they were – but it was not the sort of 'boots on the ground' collaborative situation that created *Graceland*. Belafonte's boots did not touch South African soil for the project. It is likely that he escapes accusations of appropriation because he was black. It seems a particularly racist view to regard all black people, regardless of their own cultural backgrounds, nationality, economic power and social status, as of the same 'culture' and therefore unable to 'appropriate' from one another. A similar view is taken with regard to white artists who arguably appropriate from one another. Paul McCartney has not been accused of 'appropriating' French *chanson* with his song 'Michelle'.[38]

Similarly, in South Africa, David Kramer – English-speaking, Jewish – is not accused of appropriating Afrikaans Christian culture for his stage persona. While he was condemned by the apartheid censors early in his career for 'mixing languages' and probably raised some concerned eyebrows in the corridors of power due to his liberal, anti-apartheid stance, his wit, humour and keen sense of social satire ensured that he became an Afrikaans cultural icon, too. He has, lately, faced accusations of both 'cultural appropriation' and even a sort of cultural 'blackface' through a few objections to the coloured characters in his songs and the persona he adopts to tell their stories.[39] But significantly, once again, these accusations have never been made by the coloured musicians he has worked with, who are numerous, including the late Taliep Pietersen with whom he wrote many successful stage shows. It is evidence, once again, of South Africans with a non-racial outlook getting along and working together as equals. Kramer acknowledges that there has been a history of exploitation in the entertainment world which 'goes right down to the Saartjie Baartman days'. (Baartman was a Khoekhoe woman who was exhibited for the amusement of European eyes in a travelling 'Freak Show' in the early 1800s.) 'But,' he says, 'I think we're in a different time now and it is about working together; it's about creating together.'[40] You would expect this artistic collaboration to be unpalatable to the remaining Afrikaner nationalists, but it appears that it is just as unpalatable to a growing number of the black millennial 'born-free' generation in South Africa (those born after the advent of democracy in 1994) and to supposedly progressive sociologists abroad who have abandoned the non-racialism of the old guard of liberals and liberationists in favour of a black nationalism that may prove as ugly and destructive as the nationalism of their white counterparts was in a previous era.

Of course, there have always been the separatist analogues of the apartheid old guard on the other side of the racial divide. Infamously, Mabi Thobejane of the band Sakhile once criticised Clegg in the *Weekly Mail*, saying: 'We can do this music thing on our own with a pure black African race'.[41] It is understandable that some of Thobejane's generation might have such antipathy to whites that they would take this stance, and of course the similarly stanced Pan Africanist Congress has always been a political force, if only a minority one. The majority of South Africans called for 'a democratic, non-racial South Africa based on one person, one vote'.[42] It is disappointing to see the achievement of this democratic South Africa through blood, sweat, tears and sacrifice being undone through the efforts of modern-day progressive sociologists and academics in the field of cultural studies, and self-styled 'social justice warriors' who have latched on to a fashionable catchphrase.[43] The notion of the 'dangers' of cultural appropriation is echoed in the media by public intellectuals talking of the 'harmful' effects of the 'unauthorised use of another culture's dance, dress, music, language, folklore'.[44]

Traditionally the far Left's criticism of Clegg was quite different. As he remarked to Tymon Smith of the *Sunday Times*, 'I was called a crypto-tribalist by the Left. I was promoting tribal values in a time that we should be promoting universal, counterculture values'.[45] All this is not to say that there isn't a case for accusations of 'cultural appropriation', even if Johnny Clegg isn't the right target to choose. You might make that argument in relation to Malcolm McLaren, who practically plundered black South African music for the album *Duck Rock* released in 1983.[46] But even in this case I'd dispute the claim, because McLaren stole from a named composer – Petrus Manile of The Boyoyo Boys, whose hit song 'Puleng' McLaren had copied for his own track 'Double Dutch' on the album – not from 'a culture'.[47] It was an issue of plagiarism, and copyright violation, which have legal remedies, and these were pursued successfully.[48] The music belonged to a composer, not to 'a culture'.

'Cultural appropriation' – except in rare instances where an insincere attempt has been made to profit off a culture without collaboration or attribution – is an absurd notion. The nature of culture is reliant on assimilation and synthesis as people come together, and this is only accelerating in the modern 'connected' world. Jazz music would not exist without the blending of African vocal and percussive music with Irish folk music,

Jewish klezmer music, Spanish guitar-based flamenco, classical music, popular song and other styles coming together in the immigrant melting pot of early twentieth-century America. Maskanda itself would not have existed without the introduction by European settlers to Africa of guitars, violins, concertinas and penny whistles. But instead of obsessing about who brought what in the distant past, we should celebrate what was made with it and from it, and celebrate those – like Johnny Clegg – who defied the forces attempting to stop that mixing together.

If Hendrik Verwoerd, the architect of apartheid, could hear young (supposedly) progressive writers today obsessing over cultural purity, he'd be smiling. And that should make us all weep.

NOTES

1. Toni Jaye Singer, 'When Nelson Mandela Couldn't Speak, Johnny Clegg Spoke for Him', *Sunday Times*, 17 July 2019, accessed 10 April 2025, https://www.timeslive.co.za/sunday-times/lifestyle/2019-07-17-when-nelson-mandela-couldnt-speak-johnny-clegg-spoke-for-him/; Johnny Clegg & Savuka, 'Johnny Clegg (With Nelson Mandela) – Asimbonanga – 1999 Fran', YouTube video, 06:12, accessed 10 May 2025, https://youtu.be/BGS7SpI7obY?si=UTJT6U_ZKZPLhCHU; Johnny Clegg with Savuka and Juluka, *Live and More … Johnny Clegg with Savuka and Juluka* (DVD, Sydney: Rhythm Safari, RSDV5001, 2003).
2. Zoé Samudzi, 'Johnny Clegg's Music Was Full of Contradictions. But I Loved It', *The Washington Post*, 17 July 2019, accessed 10 April 2025, https://www.washingtonpost.com/outlook/2019/07/17/johnny-cleggs-music-was-full-contradictions-i-loved-it/.
3. Billie Holiday and Her Orchestra, *Strange Fruit* (single, New York: Commodore, 526, 1939); Zoé Samudzi, 'The Unbearable White Ignorance of Annie Lennox', *Media Diversified*, 18 December 2014, accessed 10 April 2025, https://mediadiversified.org/2014/12/18/the-unbearable-white-ignorance-of-annie-lennox/.
4. Tomiwa Owolade, *This Is Not America* (Leicester: W. F. Howes Ltd, 2022), cover text.
5. Wikipedia, 'List of Killings by Law Enforcement Officers in the United Kingdom', accessed 10 April 2025, https://en.wikipedia.org/wiki/List_of_killings_by_law_enforcement_officers_in_the_United_Kingdom.
6. Laura Silver et al., 'What Do Americans Know About International Affairs?'(Pew Research Center, 25 May 2022), accessed 10 April 2025, https://www.pewresearch.org/global/2022/05/25/what-do-americans-know-about-international-affairs/.
7. Zwide Ndwandwe and Nomonde Tshomi, 'Music of the Rainbow', *Deep Cut*, 30 March 2020, podcast, accessed 10 April 2025, https://podcasts.apple.com/gb/podcast/music-of-the-rainbow/id1483941186?i=1000470002449.
'Cultural appropriation' is defined by *The Concise Oxford Companion to English Literature* as 'a term used to describe the taking over of creative or artistic forms, themes, or practices by one cultural group from another. It is in general used to describe Western appropriations of non-Western or non-white forms, and carries

connotations of exploitation and dominance' (Oxford Reference, *The Concise Oxford Companion to English Literature*, accessed 10 April 2025, https://www.oxfordreference.com/display/10.1093/oi/authority.20110803095652789).

8 Nomboniso Gasa (nombonisogasa), Twitter, 16 July 2019, accessed 10 April 2025, https://twitter.com/nombonisogasa/status/1151210129104297986.

9 Johnny Clegg and Michael Drewett, 'Why Don't You Sing About the Leaves and the Dreams? Reflecting on Music Censorship in Apartheid South Africa', in *Popular Music Censorship in Africa*, ed. Martin Cloonan and Michael Drewett, (London: Routledge, 2016), 128.

10 Clegg and Drewett, 'Why Don't You Sing', 130.

11 Bertha Egnos (composer) and Gail Lakier (lyricist), *Ipi Tombi: Original Cast Recording* (album, Johannesburg: Satbel, BELD 23009, 1975), performed by the musical group Ipi 'n Tombia with lead singer Margaret Singana.

12 Juluka, '*Impi*', on *African Litany* (album, Johannesburg: MINC, MINC (L) 1020, 1981).

13 Timothy D. Taylor, *Global Pop: World Music, World Markets* (London: Routledge, 1997), 138.

14 Ira A. Robbins, ed., 'Johnny Clegg & Savuka, Juluka', in *Trouser Press Record Guide*, ed. Ira A. Robbins (London: Collier Books, 1991), 137.

15 Johnny Clegg & Savuka, *Shadow Man* (album, Sandton: EMI, EMCJ (D) 7904111, 1988); Jimmy Gutterman, 'Shadow Man', *Rolling Stone* 536, 6 October 1988.

16 'Mbaqanga', *AllMusic*, n.d., accessed 10 April 2025, https://www.allmusic.com/style/mbaqanga-ma0000002677/albums.

17 Johnny Clegg & Savuka, *Heat, Dust and Dreams* (album, Sandton: EMI, CDEMCJ (WF) 5499, 1993); Adam Greenberg, 'Heat, Dust and Dreams Review', *Allmusic*, n.d., accessed 10 April 2025, https://www.allmusic.com/album/heat-dust-and-dreams-mw0000097820.

18 Taylor, *Global Pop*, 177.

19 Nhlanhla Ngcobo, 'Glimpses into South Africa: A Perspective through Juluka Music', *Reality* 14, no. 1 (1982): 6.

20 Youssou N'Dour quoted in Taylor, *Global Pop*, 135.

21 Angélique Kidjo quoted in Taylor, *Global Pop*, 201.

22 Jonathan and Sipho, *Woza Friday* (single, Johannesburg: EMI Brigadiers/Jamloti, JM 139, 1977); Clegg and Drewett, 'Why Don't You Sing', 128.

23 Samudzi, 'Johnny Clegg's Music'.

24 Sipho Mchunu speaking at Johnny Clegg's televised funeral (SABC [South African Broadcasting Corporation], 'South Africa Pays Tribute to Johnny Clegg', *SABC News*, 17 July 2019, accessed 10 April 2025, https://www.sabcnews.com/sabcnews/south-africa-pays-tribute-to-johnny-clegg/).

25 Samuel G. Freedman, 'Johnny Clegg's War on Apartheid', *Rolling Stone* 574, 22 March 1990.

26 Johnny Clegg quoted in Tymon Smith, 'I Didn't Think I'd Be Celebrated as a Cultural Missionary: Johnny Clegg', *Sunday Times*, accessed 10 April 2025, https://www.timeslive.co.za/sunday-times/lifestyle/2017-07-29-i-didnt-think-id-be-celebrated-as-a-cultural-missionary-johnny-clegg/.

27 Hugh Fielder, "Beating the Boycott', *Sounds*, 11 April 1987.

28 Christopher Ballantine, 'Re-thinking "Whiteness"? Identity, Change and "White" Popular Music in Post-apartheid South Africa', *Popular Music* 23, no. 2 (2004): 123.

29 Sipho Mchunu speaking to *SABC News* after Clegg's death; see SABC, 'Johnny Clegg's Long-Time Musical Partner Sipho Mchunu Pays Tribute', *SABC News*, 17 July 2019, YouTube video, 07:44, accessed 10 April 2025, https://www.youtube.com/watch?v=Z7R-xL7aC5o).
30 Freedman, 'Johnny Clegg's War on Apartheid'.
31 Ndwandwe and Tshomi, 'Music of the Rainbow'.
32 Garth Cartwright, 'Johnny Clegg: South African Singer Whose Cross-cultural Music Was a Direct Challenge to Apartheid', *Independent*, 24 July 2019, accessed 10 April 2025, https://www.independent.co.uk/news/obituaries/johnny-clegg-death-singer-south-africa-apartheid-nelson-mandela-obituary-a9008716.html; Gutterman, 'Shadow Man'. See also chapter 7 in this book by Michael Drewett.
33 Rob Tannenbaum, 'British Organization Boots South African', *Rolling Stone* 539, 6 October 1988.
34 Paul Simon, *Graceland* (album, Burbank: Warner Bros Records, 925 447-1, 1986).
35 Lucas Ledwaba, 'It's Not Black and White: The Grey World that Shaped Johnny Clegg', *Daily Maverick*, 4 November 2021, accessed 10 April 2025, https://www.dailymaverick.co.za/article/2021-11-04-its-not-black-and-white-the-grey-world-that-shaped-johnny-clegg/.
36 Chris Thurman, 'Johnny Clegg Deserves More than Political Grandstanding', *Business Day*, 19 July 2019, accessed 10 April 2025, https://www.businesslive.co.za/bd/opinion/columnists/2019-07-19-chris-thurman-johnny-clegg-deserves-more-than-political-grandstanding/.
37 Harry Belafonte, *Paradise in Gazankulu* (album, Los Angeles: EMI-Manhattan Records, TOL (Y) 7469711, 1988). The title track, 'Paradise in Gazankulu', for example, is just the song 'Kazete No. 2' by Obed Ngobeni on his album *My Wife Bought a Taxi*, but based on the performance by Mahlathini and the Mahotella Queens on their album *Paris–Soweto*, with new English lyrics. Belafonte didn't go to South Africa, and instead dispatched his arranger and (English) lyricist to the country to capture performances by the Soul Brothers and the Makgona Tsohle Band and turn them into songs for an American audience. See Robert Christgau's disapproving review, 'Consumer Guide Album: Harry Belafonte: *Paradise in Gazankulu*', accessed 10 May 2025, https://www.robertchristgau.com/get_album.php?id=6183.
38 Paul McCartney, 'Michelle', on The Beatles, *Rubber Soul* (album, London: Parlophone, PCSJ 3075, 1965).
39 Marianne Thamm, 'David Kramer's New Musical – Making Right with Music', *Daily Maverick*, 9 May 2023, accessed 10 April 2025, https://www.dailymaverick.co.za/article/2023-05-09-david-kramers-new-musical-making-right-with-music/.
40 David Kramer quoted in Roger Young, 'Never Forget District Six', *City Press*, 8 February 2016, accessed 10 May 2025, https://www.news24.com/citypress/trending/never-forget-district-six-20160208.
41 Mabi Thobejane quoted in Andrew Donaldson, 'Johnny Clegg and the Stalinists', *PoliticsWeb*, 19 July 2019, accessed 10 April 2025, https://www.politicsweb.co.za/opinion/johnny-clegg-and-the-stalinists.
42 The call for a democratic non-racial South Africa based on one person one vote is the foundation of the 'Freedom Charter', which was adopted, broadly speaking, by almost all anti-apartheid organisations. See 'South Africa', *Documents on Democracy* 1, no. 4 (1990): 128–134, accessed 10 May 2025, https://www.journalofdemocracy.org/articles/documents-on-democracy-88/.

43 Kennan Malik, 'Away With The Gatekeepers', *Pandaemonium*, accessed 10 April 2025, https://kenanmalik.com/2016/04/14/away-with-the-gatekeepers/. Some universities and non-governmental organisations now offer courses on how to avoid 'the dangers' of cultural appropriation, as if it were a settled issue; see Bangor University, 'Avoiding Cultural Appropriation', accessed 10 April 2025, https://www.bangor.ac.uk/courses/other-courses/avoiding-cultural-appropriation; Language and Equity: Education Solutions, 'Cultural Appropriation vs Cultural Appreciation', https://socialjusticeandeducation.org/2021/02/16/cultural-appropriation-vs-cultural-appreciation/.
44 Nadra Kareem Nittle, 'A Guide to Understanding and Avoiding Cultural Appropriation', *ThoughtCo.*, accessed 10 April 2025, https://www.thoughtco.com/cultural-appropriation-and-why-iits-wrong-2834561.
45 Clegg quoted in Smith, 'Cultural Missionary'.
46 Malcolm McLaren, *Duck Rock* (album, London: Charisma, STAR 5311, 1983).
47 The Boyoyo Boys, *Puleng/Mapule*, (single, Johannesburg: Jumbo Jet, JJB 275, 1975).
48 Carsten Rasch, 'Criminal Record: How Malcolm McClaren Ripped Off SA Musicians', *Sunday Times*, 28 March 2021, accessed 10 April 2025, https://www.timeslive.co.za/sunday-times/lifestyle/2021-03-28-criminal-record-how-malcolm-mcclaren-ripped-off-sa-musicians/.

REFERENCES

Ballantine, Christopher. 'Re-thinking "Whiteness"? Identity, Change and "White" Popular Music in Post-apartheid South Africa'. *Popular Music* 23, no. 2 (2004): 105–131.

Bangor University. 'Avoiding Cultural Appropriation'. Accessed 10 April 2025. https://www.bangor.ac.uk/courses/other-courses/avoiding-cultural-appropriation.

Cartwright, Garth. 'Johnny Clegg: South African Singer Whose Cross-cultural Music Was a Direct Challenge to Apartheid'. *Independent*, 24 July 2019. Accessed 10 April 2025. https://www.independent.co.uk/news/obituaries/johnny-clegg-death-singer-south-africa-apartheid-nelson-mandela-obituary-a9008716.html.

Clegg, Johnny and Michael Drewett. 'Why Don't You Sing About the Leaves and the Dreams? Reflecting on Music Censorship in Apartheid South Africa'. In *Popular Music Censorship in Africa*, edited by Martin Cloonan and Michael Drewett, 127–135. London: Routledge, 2016.

Christgau, Robert. 'Consumer Guide Album: Harry Belafonte: *Paradise in Gazankulu*'. Accessed 10 May 2025. https://www.robertchristgau.com/get_album.php?id=6183.

Donaldson, Andrew. 'Johnny Clegg and the Stalinists'. *PoliticsWeb*, 19 July 2019. Accessed 10 April 2025. https://www.politicsweb.co.za/opinion/johnny-clegg-and-the-stalinists.

Fielder, Hugh. 'Beating the Boycott'. *Sounds*, 11 April 1987.

Freedman, Samuel G. 'Johnny Clegg's War On Apartheid'. *Rolling Stone* 574, 22 March 1990.

Greenberg, Adam. 'Heat, Dust and Dreams Review'. *Allmusic*. Accessed 10 April 2025. https://www.allmusic.com/album/heat-dust-and-dreams-mw0000097820.

Gutterman, Jimmy. 'Shadow Man'. *Rolling Stone* 536, 6 October 1988.

Johnny Clegg & Savuka, 'Johnny Clegg (With Nelson Mandela) - Asimbonanga - 1999 Fran'. YouTube video, 06:12. Accessed 10 May 2025. https://youtu.be/BGS7SpI7obY?si=UTJT6U_ZKZPLhCHU.

Language and Equity: Education Solutions. 'Cultural Appropriation vs Cultural Appreciation'. Accessed 10 April 2025. https://socialjusticeandeducation.org/2021/02/16/cultural-appropriation-vs-cultural-appreciation/.

Ledwaba, Lucas. 'It's Not Black and White: The Grey World that Shaped Johnny Clegg'. *Daily Maverick*, 4 November 2021. Accessed 10 April 2025. https://www.dailymaverick.co.za/article/2021-11-04-its-not-black-and-white-the-grey-world-that-shaped-johnny-clegg/.

Malik, Kennan. 2016. 'Away with the Gatekeepers'. *Pandaemonium*. Accessed 10 April 2025. https://kenanmalik.com/2016/04/14/away-with-the-gatekeepers/.

'Mbaqanga'. *AllMusic*. Accessed 10 April 2025. https://www.allmusic.com/style/mbaqanga-ma0000002677/albums.

Ndwandwe, Zwide and Nomonde Tshomi. 'Music of the Rainbow'. *Deep Cut*, 30 March 2020. Podcast. Accessed 10 April 2025. https://podcasts.apple.com/gb/podcast/music-of-the-rainbow/id1483941186?i=1000470002449.

Ngcobo, Nhlanhla. 'Glimpses into South Africa: A Perspective through Juluka Music'. *Reality* 14, no. 1 (1982): 4–6.

Nittle, Nadra Kareem. 2021. 'A Guide to Understanding and Avoiding Cultural Appropriation'. *ThoughtCo*. Accessed 10 April 2025. https://www.thoughtco.com/cultural-appropriation-and-why-iits-wrong-2834561.

Owolade, Tomiwa. *This Is Not America*. Leicester: W.F. Howes Ltd, 2022.

Oxford Reference. *The Concise Oxford Companion to English Literature*. Accessed 10 April 2025. https://www.oxfordreference.com/display/10.1093/oi/authority.20110803095652789.

Rasch, Carsten. 2021. 'Criminal Record: How Malcolm McClaren Ripped Off SA Musicians'. *Sunday Times*, 28 March 2021. Accessed 10 April 2025. https://www.timeslive.co.za/sunday-times/lifestyle/2021-03-28-criminal-record-how-malcolm-mcclaren-ripped-off-sa-musicians/.

Robbins, Ira, A., ed. 'Johnny Clegg & Savuka, Juluka'. In *Trouser Press Record Guide*, edited by Ira A. Robbins, 137. London: Collier Books, 1991.

SABC (South African Broadcsting Corporation). 'Johnny Clegg's Long-Time Musical Partner Sipho Mchunu Pays Tribute'. *SABC News*, 17 July 2019. YouTube video, 07:44. Accessed 10 April 2025, https://www.youtube.com/watch?v=Z7R-xL7aC5o.

SABC (South African Broadcasting Corporation). 'South Africa Pays Tribute to Johnny Clegg'. *SABC News*, 17 July 2019. Accessed 10 April 2025. https://www.sabcnews.com/sabcnews/south-africa-pays-tribute-to-johnny-clegg/.

Samudzi, Zoé. 'Johnny Clegg's Music Was Full of Contradictions. But I Loved It'. *The Washington Post*, 17 July 2019. Accessed 10 April 2025. https://www.washingtonpost.com/outlook/2019/07/17/johnny-cleggs-music-was-full-contradictions-i-loved-it/.

Samudzi, Zoé. 'The Unbearable White Ignorance of Annie Lennox'. *Media Diversified*, 18 December 2014. Accessed 10 April 2025. https://mediadiversified.org/2014/12/18/the-unbearable-white-ignorance-of-annie-lennox/.

Silver, Laura, Christine Huang, Laura Clancy, Aidan Connaughton and Sneha Gubbala. 'What Do Americans Know About International Affairs?' *Pew Research Center*, 25 May 2022. Accessed 10 April 2025. https://www.pewresearch.org/global/2022/05/25/what-do-americans-know-about-international-affairs/.

Singer, Toni Jaye. 'When Nelson Mandela Couldn't Speak, Johnny Clegg Spoke for Him'. *Sunday Times*, 17 July 2019. Accessed 10 April 2025. https://www.timeslive.co.za/sunday-times/lifestyle/2019-07-17-when-nelson-mandela-couldnt-speak-johnny-clegg-spoke-for-him/.

Smith, Tymon. 'I Didn't Think I'd Be Celebrated as a Cultural Missionary: Johnny Clegg'. *Sunday Times*, 30 July 2017. Accessed 10 April 2025. https://www.timeslive.co.za/sunday-times/lifestyle/2017-07-29-i-didnt-think-id-be-celebrated-as-a-cultural-missionary-johnny-clegg/.

'South Africa'. *Documents on Democracy* 1, no. 4 (1990): 128–134. Accessed 10 May 2025. https://www.journalofdemocracy.org/articles/documents-on-democracy-88/.
Tannenbaum, Rob. 'British Organization Boots South African'. *Rolling Stone* 539, 6 October 1988.
Taylor, Timothy D. *Global Pop: World Music, World Markets*. London: Routledge, 1997.
Thamm, Marianne. 'David Kramer's New Musical – Making Right With Music'. *Daily Maverick*, 9 May 2023. Accessed 10 April 2025. https://www.dailymaverick.co.za/article/2023-05-09-david-kramers-new-musical-making-right-with-music/.
Thurman, Chris. 'Johnny Clegg Deserves More than Political Grandstanding'. *Business Day*, 19 July 2019. Accessed 10 April 2025. https://www.businesslive.co.za/bd/opinion/columnists/2019-07-19-chris-thurman-johnny-clegg-deserves-more-than-political-grandstanding/.
Wikipedia. 'List of Killings by Law Enforcement Officers in the United Kingdom'. Accessed 10 April 2025. https://en.wikipedia.org/wiki/List_of_killings_by_law_enforcement_officers_in_the_United_Kingdom.
Young, Roger. 'Never Forget District Six'. *City Press*, 8 February 2016. Accessed 10 May 2025. https://www.news24.com/citypress/trending/never-forget-district-six-20160208.

DISCOGRAPHY

The Beatles. *Rubber Soul*. Album. London: Parlophone, PCSJ 3075, 1965.
Belafonte, Harry. *Paradise in Gazankulu*. Album. Los Angeles: EMI-Manhattan Records, TOL (Y) 7469711, 1988.
The Boyoyo Boys. *Puleng/Mapule*. Single. Johannesburg: Jumbo Jet, JJB 275, 1975.
Holiday, Billie and Her Orchestra. *Strange Fruit*. Single. New York: Commodore, 526, 1939.
Egnos, Bertha (composer) and Gail Lakier (lyricist). *Ipi Tombi: Original Cast Recording*. Performed by the musical group Ipi 'n Tombia with lead singer Margaret Singana. Album. Johannesburg: Satbel, BELD 23009, 1975.
Johnny Clegg & Savuka. *Cruel, Crazy, Beautiful World*. Album. Sandton: EMI, EMCJ (D) 7934461, 1989.
Johnny Clegg & Savuka. *Heat, Dust and Dreams*. Album. Sandton: EMI, CDEMCJ (WF) 5499, 1993.
Johnny Clegg & Savuka. *Shadow Man*. Album. Sandton: EMI, EMCJ (D) 7904111, 1988.
Johnny Clegg with Savuka and Juluka. *Live and More ... Johnny Clegg with Savuka and Juluka*. DVD. Sydney: Rhythm Safari, RSDV5001, 2003.
Jonathan & Sipho. *Woza Friday*. Single. Johannesburg: EMI Brigadiers/Jamloti, JM 139, 1977.
Juluka. *African Litany*. Album. Johannesburg: MINC, MINC (L) 1020, 1981.
McLaren, Malcolm. *Duck Rock*. Album. London: Charisma, STAR 5311, 1983.
Simon, Paul. *Graceland*. Album. Burbank: Warner Bros Records, 925 447-1, 1986.

CHAPTER
14

King of Time: A Lament for Johnny Clegg

Marguerite de Villiers Coetzee

'There is a place for lamenting …
But to live in the shadow of lamenting
is disempowering and futile'

— Johnny Clegg, *Scatterling of Africa: My Early Years*, xix.

FOUNDATION

> We have all been sentenced to this life, everyone is a defendant
> We are all prisoners of time, we are destined to spend it
> But we must be free to choose the way we serve the sentence[1]

Time is not linear, but intertwined: a braiding of what has been, what is and what is yet to be. It is a crossing over of multiple, simultaneous temporalities. Anthropologists have contemplated how time erupts, swells, converges, gnaws, inflects and intersects. Time cannot be divided into distant and distinct states: everything exists in time, all the time. The non-contemporaneity of art – its timeless quality – makes it capable of mediating between real and imagined worlds. The magical quality of myth means that there is no end to the mystery, only new layers of meaning. That is why creative forms like music endure.

Figure 14.1: Johnny Clegg at The Teatro, Montecasino, Johannesburg, 15 July 2016. Photograph © Marguerite de Villiers Coetzee, 2016.

In relation to the notion of time (as in finality and mortality), anthropologists have long studied the material and embodied phenomenon of death, and the diverse and dynamic structures of awareness and actions surrounding the expectation and anticipation of death. Questions are often raised around intention, preventability, randomness, displacement and impact. Essentially, it is a paradox: death is a fundamental part of life. It is certain that all living things must die, but it is uncertain what that actually entails. Recurrent themes in the study of death are those of time and space. Death might be an abrupt, catastrophic end, or a lingering decline into a tragic demise. It could be the haunting presence of a glaring absence, or a reconfiguration of relationships across physical and etheric realms. Whatever the circumstances, the mysteries and silences surrounding death beget stories, evoke reactions and raise questions in an attempt to render meaningful the incomplete.

Central to this chapter is the chronotope: how configurations of time are projected onto space. Time materialises in space and space moves through time. Assessing anthropological elements of time and space could offer a foundation from which to construct a lament for the death, grief and memory of an anthropologist and artist: Johnny Clegg. Soundscape, for example, creates a rhythm and realm in which we can be immersed and interact with such notions. 'I know that time's a distance and distance is a space', as the song goes.[2] Through first-hand extended experiences with isiZulu-speaking communities, Clegg gathered raw material that was then organised into songs, stories and shows.

The topics of time and space were a recurring theme throughout each 'incarnation' of his music.[3] One way of identifying Clegg's symbolic imagination and conventions of place-making is to search for clues to the spatio-temporal basis of his music. The intention is to recognise and understand the passage and preservation of time, as well as the dynamic between physical absence and ethereal presence as it relates to the Zulu philosophies and 'cultural sensibilities' that shaped Clegg's world view, value system, musical expression and sense of self.[4]

Juluka's representation of space-time largely takes the form of duration, repetition and change in relation to nature. 'Mama Shabalala', who 'had lost everything that she ever had to lose', returns home to Weenen County in the springtime, 'the long gone summer has passed' in 'December African Rain' and a new summer brings with it 'a new hope in the dawn' with a future 'written in the sky' for the 'Sky People', 'Deliwe' walks in a foreign land and is haunted by a melody 'like falling autumn leaves', and 'Universal Men' 'share with the swallows all their winters and their hopes' as they 'undo that distance just once more'.[5] There is a long view of time ('timeless,'[6] 'always,'[7] 'centuries,'[8] and 'lifetimes'[9]) contrasted with the emptying of time ('left behind,'[10] 'fly away,'[11] 'remain with nothing,'[12] 'where did the time go?'[13]). It is clear that the repetition involved in migration and the slow-paced change of village life, as well as the stark contrast between constructed and natural environments, influenced Juluka's notions of time and place.

The songs performed by Johnny Clegg & Savuka continue to express the notion of the occasional and temporary ('sometimes')[14] present in Juluka's lyrics, and add to it 'last time,'[15] 'one more time,'[16] 'no time,'[17] 'any time'[18] and 'every time'.[19] These are 'dark and troubled times,'[20] but the times are changing and there's an encouragement to 'change with the times'.[21] There is 'a sign of the times'[22] and a 'time [that] will come'.[23] Some 'dance across the sea of time'[24] and hunt their tomorrow 'on the edge of time',[25] while others are 'lost in time'[26] or 'killing time'.[27] The future – hope, destiny, dream and promise – is fetched, grabbed, changed, given shape, left forever far below and kept on hold.[28] The lyrics communicate a finality: an ending of an era ('a hard day is coming to an end',[29] 'at the end of all bloody human storms',[30] 'it's all over now',[31] 'we will reach our final destination',[32] 'picture the end of a cycle'[33]). The tide was turning in South African politics as it shifted from the urgency of violence to the promise of peace.

In his solo work, Clegg juxtaposes the past with the future: trapped between yesterday's hopes and dreams of tomorrow.[34] It is almost as if the future imagined in the past was not realised: there is loss in change and a haunting of the past in the future ('the future lost its way',[35] 'I see the future on hold',[36] 'rushing for tomorrow where the future used to be',[37] 'the hopes of yesterday drowning in shifting sands',[38] 'there's another life that I know could have been',[39] 'yesterday's gone and tomorrow is just a dream',[40] 'we're trapped in the past; the future won't flow'[41]). Overall, time and space in Clegg's music take on contradictory, incompatible and conflicting properties of continuity and change, fixity and flux.

This is a fitting basis on which to disentangle threads of endings, beginnings and transitions in relation to prolonged grief, death trajectories, legacies of loss and journeys of healing. My aim is not to explain away the magic of the music or to demystify the mystery surrounding the man, but to be faithful and tactful in describing what I consider to be right and realistic in my interpretations. Clegg's songs and stories are rich with semantic density, complexity and gravity. What follows are my thoughts on only a fraction of a meaningful life lived and wealth of music made. The chapter is divided into three parts: the first unpacks how Clegg confronted his own death, the second considers how he dealt with the death of others, and the third reviews how others have processed his death.

ENDINGS: THE LATER YEARS

A little more than a decade before Clegg's passing, his elder son, Jesse, debuted as an artist in his own right (see figures 14.2 and 14.3). Also at this time, a

Figure 14.2: Jesse Clegg's debut concert at The Venue, Melrose Arch, Johannesburg, 2 May 2009. Photograph © Marguerite de Villiers Coetzee, 2009.

Figure 14.3: Guest appearance by Arno Carstens at Jesse Clegg's debut concert at The Venue, Melrose Arch, Johannesburg, 2 May 2009. Photograph © Marguerite de Villiers Coetzee, 2009.

Figure 14.4: Jesse Clegg at the 'Joburg Day' festival held on Riversands Farm, Fourways, 17 October 2009. Photograph © Marguerite de Villiers Coetzee, 2009.

compilation of cover songs by artists around the world was released called *Power of One: the Songs of Johnny Clegg*.[42] Soon after, father and son both performed at a festival in Johannesburg, 'Joburg Day', held on 17 October 2009, but as separate acts (see figures 14.4 and 14.5). Johnny Clegg celebrated his 30th year in the music industry, which had started in 1979 with Sipho Mchunu, performing a series of anniversary concerts in 2010 and 2011 in Johannesburg and Cape Town, with Juluka reuniting briefly on stage, taking audiences on a historical journey through an expansive musical career. In hindsight, this was a pivotal time: a recollection of musical moments in time that had shaped a shared history, a coming together of artists honouring their collective musical ancestor, and a handing over of the torch from one artist to another. When one door closes, another opens. As Clegg had said in the song written for his son two decades earlier: 'beyond the door, strange cruel beautiful years lie waiting for you'.[43]

During this time, Clegg recorded a series of his favourite Zulu street guitar songs set in Kwa Mai Mai Market, where his journey into maskanda music originally began.[44] In an interview he said that 'it's a record of my

Figure 14.5: Johnny Clegg at the 'Joburg Day' festival held on Riversands Farm, Fourways, 17 October 2009. Photograph © Marguerite de Villiers Coetzee, 2009.

experience of maskand[a] music ... and shows the door which opened a career in music to me.'[45] He also contributed a song (called 'Golden Country') to the soundtrack of the animated film *Jock the Hero Dog*, released an album, *Human* (appropriately named for an anthropologically trained artist), and hosted a documentary series called *A Country Imagined* (travelling the length and breadth of South Africa to gather stories from artists of all kinds).[46] In the years that followed, he received several awards and acknowledgements (such as various honorary doctorates from international universities). In 2013, the world learned of Nelson Mandela's passing and South Africans mourned the dimming of their beacon of peace, with Clegg reciting (on the 11th day of the memorial) a praise poem he had written.[47] In 2014, *Carte Blanche*, a South African investigative journalism television series, investigated the killing of the musician and member of Clegg's band Bongani Masuku; Clegg appeared in the episode dealing with Masuku's murder, and participated in a benefit concert held in support of his family.

In 2015 Clegg was presented with an Order of the British Empire (OBE) by Queen Elizabeth II for his contribution to music and the fight against

Figure 14.6: Johnny Clegg and Sipho Mchunu backstage at Kirstenbosch National Botanical Garden, Cape Town, 29 March 2015. Photograph © Marguerite de Villiers Coetzee, 2015.

apartheid. According to the British High Commission in South Africa, the award was a 'recognition of Johnny's unique services to the Arts, vulnerable people and children and to democracy in South Africa'.[48] Clegg had returned home to Johannesburg from a couple of concerts in Cape Town, and was diagnosed with cancer (see figure 14.6 before his diagnosis and figure 14.7 afterwards). He had been confronted suddenly by the surreal reality of his own imminent mortality. In a subsequent interview he was asked what had changed in his psyche, his thought process, when he was faced with such a diagnosis, to which he responded that it is the sudden closing down of an open-endedness of the world that brings closer the intimations of mortality, but also an appreciation for the simpler things.[49]

As a *ngoma* dancer, Clegg understood the importance of ending on the off-beat (see figures 14.8 and 14.9).[50] In a paper presented at an anthropology symposium at Rhodes University in 2004, he stated: 'Deeper social values have found their way into the dance and contributed to this constant drive for a "better ending".[51] Stepping into the dance, the *ngoma* dancer encounters peripheral meanings: the ambiguous experience of being a

Figure 14.7: Johnny Clegg at the Walter Sisulu National Botanical Garden, Johannesburg, 30 August 2015. Photograph © Marguerite de Villiers Coetzee, 2015.

Figure 14.8: Johnny Clegg shakes hands with an audience member and fan who recognised him at a dance event outside Jeppe Hostel in central Johannesburg, 7 December 2014. Photograph © Marguerite de Villiers Coetzee, 2014.

Figure 14.9: Prior to posing for a photograph together, a leader at Denver Men's Hostel in Johannesburg playfully comments on how Johnny Clegg's face has changed over the years, 13 November 2016. Photograph © Marguerite de Villiers Coetzee, 2016.

distinct individual and of blending into a united and uniform whole. A good leader is balanced and unbiased in how they handle what unfolds, whether prepared for or spontaneous. The off-beat is the killing blow: unexpected and hidden, a switching of identities, and a demonstration of surprises or a mastery of tricks. Clegg's medical diagnosis was an off-beat moment: a war declared, concealed and later revealed. In true warrior fashion, he formulated a plan of attack. 'Between debilitating chemo sessions', he wrote and recorded a final album (*King of Time*), performed a final world tour ('The Final Journey Tour'), and worked on his autobiography (published posthumously as *Scatterling of Africa: My Early Years*).[52] He still had a few tricks up his sleeve (see figures 14.10 and 14.11). What follows is a triangulation of these last three works – the album, the tour, the memoir – in an attempt to determine how Clegg dealt with the prospect of his own death, roughly related to the psychological stages of grief.

When first confronted with the potential for loss, an initial reaction might be one characterised by a disbelief in a presented truth, or a belief

Figure 14.10: Jesse Clegg joins Johnny Clegg on stage at the first of the 'Final Journey Tour' concerts at Cape Town's Grand West Casino, 30 June 2017. Photograph © Marguerite de Villiers Coetzee, 2017.

Figure 14.11: Sipho Mchunu and Johnny Clegg perform together at the second 'Final Journey Tour' concert at Cape Town's Grand West Casino, 1 July 2017. Photograph © Marguerite de Villiers Coetzee, 2017.

in a distorted truth: 'I feel like I can keep on going forever, but I know that it is an illusion', said Clegg.[53] This can result in denial, avoidance and a refusal to accept or recognise a particular reality of or relationship with loss, especially if it occurs outside of the realm of human agency. This is often followed by feelings of anger, wrath and rage when reality sets in. Existential questions are raised: why me? 'Life is hard, you don't get what you deserve', Clegg acknowledged, 'you have to understand that these things will afflict everybody at some time. It's not about why me. It's about how can I get around this, how can I find a way through this?'[54] It would seem that Clegg's approach to a challenge was to face it head on.

Invoking a similar image of a barrier to be crossed, in the introduction to his book Clegg uses the analogy of a road to explain his motivation for entering the world of the Zulu migrant worker. Apartheid's laws of segregation were potholes in the road and the system was a fence put arbitrarily across it. Walking down the metaphorical road and facing these obstacles, he was confronted by a challenge: he needed to get to the other side, and so he would find a hole in the fence to get through. Problem solved. 'I learned to operate with what I had … I never let the fence stop me. I always found a hole.' Again now he faced a fence. In his book his illness is not named, but personified as a living thing that 'will get on with its own course dictated by its own laws and design'. He and it are neighbours: apathetic strangers divided and united by a fence in need of mending. 'What unfolds will be dealt with when it arrives.'[55]

In an attempt to impose today's will on tomorrow, someone faced with potential loss might engage with change in creative ways. Instead of 'why me?', the responses become 'what if?' and 'if only'. Bargaining and making promises become a form of false hope: thinking that making a major change will negotiate a different future outcome that does not yet exist, or that an exchange could result in reverting to a past that no longer exists. Take for example the title track of Clegg's last album, 'King of Time'.[56] The title refers to endurance: Clegg had been around for a long time, withstood change, overcome challenges and emerged still standing. He was the king of time and his songs were immortal. 'To endure. To keep going. I kept going.'[57] The album is a collection of songs on the theme of choices and their consequences, and the shifting sense of time as infinite to indispensable. It reflects Clegg's change of perspective from thinking that there is all the time in the world to realising that time is running out. The value of time increased in its scarcity.

The title track opens with a metacognitive statement: 'I've been thinking about the way I think about my thinking'. The chorus contains an expression in isiZulu: '*Wolibamba ilanga lingashoni*' ('grab the sun so that it does not set').[58] Freeze time if you can, because it passes so quickly. It is about holding on to a beautiful moment and not letting it become just another memory. However, it also references the idea that when the sun goes down, the potential for trouble arises. The surface-level narrative of the song is about someone wishing to reverse time and return to the moment when a mistake was made, and make things right, but knowing that it is not possible to do so. 'Nobody is the king of time,' said Clegg wistfully.[59]

It is also known that the passing of Clegg's half-sister, Diane, is memorialised in the song 'Touch the Sun' on the album *One Life*.[60] While this song has obvious parallels with 'King of Time' in incorporating symbolism of the sun, there appears to be a parallel also in the siblings' experience of the gradual loss of their own lives: 'Time is not her own, and she feels it in her bones / There's a strange hand tugging at her soul'. The lyrics also carry traces of the courage invoked in Juluka's song '*Impi*' ('War'), about being engaged in battle: '*Impi! Wo nans' impi iyeza / Obani bengathinta amabhubesi?*' ('War! Here comes war / Who will be brave enough to touch the lions?') compared with '*Ubani bengathinta thina / Sibamba ilanga nangezandla?*' ('Who can touch us / For we can hold the sun even with our bare hands?').[61]

The song 'King of Time' is a counterfactual. Counterfactual thinking is a conjuring up of alternative outcomes to an event that has already occurred and cannot be undone, usually with questions that start with 'what if' or 'if only'. This is evident in the lines: 'If I could only go back to that day / Maybe we'll find our way'. The reality of what happened is contrasted with an imagining of an improbable alternative trajectory. Then reality sets in. Reflection in this state involves an inward orientation, an appreciation for ephemerality, and changes in consciousness and attitude in order to adapt to and cope with the anticipated experience of loss. 'There's a deep sense of melancholy and sadness that I have to do this … It's a bittersweet moment', said Clegg.[62]

Towards the end of his autobiography, Clegg reflects on '[a] feeling of being left behind [that] drifts through the heart' when the swallows instinctively migrate in search of a summer elsewhere.[63] There is a sense of sadness but also acceptance of the natural order of things. Such is the way of the world. Acceptance is a process of evolving into a new reality. It allows for novelty to emerge, while feeling a sense of comfort in certainty. 'The misfortunes of life have hidden lessons, and those hidden lessons are valuable and even in what I'm going through now, I'm discovering things. Meanings and things that were important to me before have slowly dissipated,' Clegg disclosed.[64] Just as the dry, dead grass is made new again by fire, 'you were fast asleep, this woke you up, now you are aware of your surroundings'.[65] Like the swallows, he has to be a bird in winter and learn how to fly away. Acceptance, in this sense, is moving towards change, rather than fighting against it.

The 'Final Journey Tour' was one such movement: a type of disengagement from the world and a farewell to those who had supported Clegg through the various stages of his life.[66] It was a way of consoling the liminal experience of lingering between 'no longer' and 'not yet'. The first of these final shows ended with the song 'December African Rain': 'I hear the owls calling my name' – a premonition of death? 'Where did the time go?' In a metaphorical rite of passage, the tour marked a phase of separation. Perhaps Clegg's memoir marks a phase of transformation. The prologue to *Scatterling* contains a quote from the poem 'Self-Pity' by the English writer D.H. Lawrence, about how '[a] small bird will drop frozen dead from a bough without ever having felt sorry for itself'. A wild thing is spared the complexities of existential reflection.[67]

> Much of what is written in an autobiography or memoir is a kind of existential archaeology, fraught with hindsight and the reconstruction of scattered shards, dead convictions and unclear choices … Digging around old geographies and awkward sites of personal struggle, sifting through passing moments that carried hints of tomorrow and its promises, and then failed.[68]

As the existential archaeologist unearths these buried and forgotten artefacts, questions and perspectives change. The anthropologist is the apparatus through which anthropology occurs, and in this instance, Clegg is reflecting, thinking and observing (through the lens of six decades), knowing that his observation will influence what is observed.[69] He looks at the beginning with the end in mind. '[He] knows if you look back in anger you will never be free.'[70]

> The shape of my story is not strictly chronological or linear. It winds through canyons of neural pathways with mental sinews hardened by the repetition of days. This flickering landscape is where I collect and make sense of all the incidents and the meanings that are attached to this gnarled mind's eye like some ancient cataract.[71]

TRANSITIONS: THE IN-BETWEEN YEARS

In the foreword to Clegg's book by Roddy Quin, two occurrences are mentioned that are said to have shaken him visibly: the death of David Webster and the death of Dudu Mntowaziwayo Ndlovu.[72] In dealing with the sudden, secretive and suspicious deaths of these two pivotal figures in his life, Clegg wrote two songs. These songs give us some insight into the manner in which he dealt with the death of others.

Webster was an anthropology lecturer at the University of the Witwatersrand (Wits), with a particular interest in the correlation between tuberculosis and the migrant labour system.[73] He was also interested in the informal economy, and so put together a group of people to conduct research on the topic in Soweto. While studying at Wits, Clegg was one of Webster's students and a member of his research group. They became friends and, later, colleagues. Webster was an early fan of Juluka. He founded an organisation, the South African Musicians' Alliance (SAMA), that united musicians across the country who opposed apartheid and sought freedom of speech, movement and association.[74]

Webster was shot outside his home on Workers' Day (1 May) in 1989. He and his partner, Maggie Friedman, had been working on research concerning the 'death squads' that assassinated people who opposed the government and its laws.[75] 'Assassinations have the effect of controlling government opposition when all other methods – such as detention or intimidation – have failed', Webster wrote.[76] A couple of months prior to his assassination, there had been plans to organise a show called 'Human Rainbow', but it was banned when the SAMA refused to provide song lyrics intended to be performed at the show to the authorities in advance.[77] 'Same old human story, the saddest winds do blow, while we are trapped in the language of dark history, underneath a human rainbow.'[78] Clegg was in the US recording an album – *Revolution with a Smile* – when he received a phone call telling him: 'they shot David. David Webster'.[79] The album's title was changed to *Cruel, Crazy, Beautiful World*, and the first track on it, 'One (Hu)'Man, One Vote', with lyrics by Johnny Clegg and music by Johnny Clegg and Bobby Summerfield, was dedicated to Webster.

Clegg recalled:

> I felt like I'd been axed, like a cleaver had come into my brain. I was seized once again by this fucking paralysis, an impotence, a real fright. In a death like this, you realize the contingency of history, the reality of existing in chaos. We have a superficial web of order we place over things. This smashed my web ... I felt lost in the world ... I didn't trust the universe anymore ... Every time I come offstage, I feel 'another nail in the coffin'.[80]

The title track had been written for Clegg's son Jesse as little life lessons, but also in anticipation of Johnny's own potential assassination for being a cultural activist.[81] Towards the end of 1992 an inquest was held to determine the motivation and identity of those involved in Webster's death.[82] Earlier that same year, in February, it was announced that apartheid would be coming to an end. In March of 1992, a South African film, *The Power of One*, was released based on a book of the same title.[83] Clegg had worked on some of the songs that featured on the movie's soundtrack. The title track was an adaptation of his 1985 song 'All Is Not Lost' on the album *Third World Child*, and he was responsible for the musical arrangement of two songs: 'Southland Concerto' and '*Senzeni Na*?' ('What Have We Done?').[84] The former was referred to as a requiem (a song of remembrance) and the latter was a well-known political-turned-mourning song that featured in the film's funeral scene. The song is known to be sung when someone is killed who was not ready to die.[85]

In May of 1992, Dudu Ndlovu was killed. He was known for his dance performances on stage with Clegg as part of Johnny Clegg & Savuka. Reports say that Ndlovu was shot on a dusty road near Greytown in what was then the province of Natal (later renamed KwaZulu-Natal).[86] He had died before his time, 'too early for the sky'. He was not ready to go. Clegg wrote 'The Crossing (*Osiyeza*)'[87] to send him on his way. On one level it was a song about crossing over from the physical world to the spiritual realm, on another it was a metaphor for the country transitioning from oppression to democracy. Clegg explained this five years later:

> The Zulu believe that if you're not ready to die, then your spirit doesn't really believe it's dead. There are all sorts of rituals that have to be performed to convince the spirit that it's dead ... It has to make a crossing from this world to the next world to become an ancestor ... In order to go forward and change yourself, we know you have to let a part of yourself die, so that a new part of yourself can be born. He was one of the very unfortunate casualties of that birth.[88]

Thanatological themes were less obvious or prominent in the Juluka years, perhaps alluded to in references to endings and emptiness. In a recording from 1977, Clegg introduced the song 'Sky People' as a sad song about an old man who has a premonition about dying.[89] When Juluka reunited briefly in 1997, their album *Crocodile Love* featured a song called '*Ubaba Akalele*' ('The Father Is Not at Peace').[90] It tells the story of a son who dreamt of his late father telling him that he wanted to be sent on his last journey by means of a white ox. Despite his wishes, the family had buried him in a coffin. The son was concerned that this would bring misfortune. His father's spirit was not at peace, it felt trapped, and it was wandering around the cattle enclosure.

Perhaps owing to the rise in violence and unrest in South Africa during the late 1980s, Johnny Clegg & Savuka's songs dealt more directly with the topic of death and its metaphorical associations ('underneath all some things never die',[91] 'it's a world of do or die',[92] 'one day when you wake up I will have to say goodbye',[93] 'would you leave me here to die on your shore stranded?',[94] 'I would die a thousand times to get you out of here',[95] 'I'm slowly dying, I have to make a stand'[96]). In an interview, Clegg mentioned the narrowing of time as one gets older;[97] and perhaps this is the introspective perspective from which he dealt with loss in his solo work ('I'm not gonna curl up and die here',[98] 'only someone who gives up will grow old',[99] 'it's hard to fight on your own against the fading of the light',[100] 'where does that day live where part of you did drown?'[101]).

In later years, reflecting on 'The Crossing', Clegg said singing it brought Ndlovu closer to him, and brought that reality of loss closer to himself, which enabled him to deal with it: to confront it and face it.[102] Mere months before his passing, a number of artists came together and surprised Clegg with a recording of them performing 'The Crossing' in his honour.[103] 'It's funny how those once so close and now gone, still so affect our lives.'[104]

BEGINNINGS: THE AFTER YEARS

Clegg died on 16 July 2019, two days before Mandela Day.[105] A winter's day in South Africa. The end of a cycle. Socio-political cartoonist Zapiro produced an image of Clegg doing his signature kick, while Mandela dances at heaven's gates and sings the Johnny Clegg & Savuka song '*Asimbonanga*' ('We Have Not Seen Him').[106] The Ndlovu Youth Choir sang this song in tribute.[107] Many the world over have echoed the sentiment of Harry Belafonte's message at the start of Clegg's autobiography: that he was a uniting voice against injustice, that he will be remembered for his generosity of spirit and gift of heart, that we were blessed that he moved among us, and that he is an inspiration to us all.[108] He is loved and missed. I received a voice note on WhatsApp from Bafazana Qoma, Clegg's life-long friend: '*lihambile iqhawe. Asinamuntu lapha, futhi sisele obala.*' ("The hero is gone. We have nobody here, and we are exposed.").[109] The appropriate response is: '*Akwehlanga olungehli. Nilale ngenxeba.*' ('What has happened to you is not something that has never happened to anyone. You must lay on your wound.').[110]

King of Time: A Lament for Johnny Clegg

Figure 14.12: Various artists on stage take a bow at the end of Johnny Clegg's public memorial service held in Sandton, Johannesburg, 26 July 2019. Photograph © Marguerite de Villiers Coetzee, 2019.

A formal memorial was held soon after at the Sandton Convention Centre in Johannesburg and broadcast live (see figures 14.12 and 14.13).[111] 'We contend with the loss of a torchbearer of our struggle for freedom', Nathi Mthethwa, South Africa's minister of culture, said. Clegg remained 'the personification of what's possible when we genuinely embrace non-racialism'. People gathered and shared their thoughts, 'acknowledging that Johnny sought to understand where we come from in order to understand where we are going, that he was a "towering African giant" that strove for the "oneness of humanity" by creating social cohesion through music, that he was "as colourful as his country", that he encouraged his sons to be curious about the world, and that he was a teacher who "made ideas sing and dance"'.[112]

At the memorial there was a mixed atmosphere of wanting to both celebrate and preserve Clegg's life and mourn the loss of a forefather of a new South Africa. Clegg had grown up without his father, and his stepfather had left the family early on. He had mentioned in an interview that he had read

Figure 14.13: Sipho Mchunu speaks at the public memorial service held for Johnny Clegg in Sandton, Johannesburg, 26 July 2019. Photograph © Marguerite de Villiers Coetzee, 2019.

the book *Black Dogs*, in which the protagonist proclaims that in fathering his children, he had fathered himself.[113] Clegg fulfilled a similar role for himself, his sons and people around the world who shared his vision and values. When his elder son Jesse wrote the song 'I've Been Looking' for him, and his younger son Jaron created a phantasmagorical music video for the album's title track as well as for the remix of 'Take My Heart Away', Clegg said it was like coming full circle from when he had written 'Cruel, Crazy, Beautiful World' when he became a father (see Fig 14.14).[114] A couple of years after Clegg's passing, in 2021, Jesse became a father himself to daughter Mylah Thandolwethu Clegg – Johnny Clegg's first grandchild. Some believe that when a baby is born, an ancestor returns.[115]

Soon after the memorial, on the first day of spring, a tribute Zulu dance event was organised (see figures 14.15, 14.16 and 14.17).[116] Riots had broken out nearby in Jeppestown (driven by xenophobia, according to some people present on the day) and there were concerns that the event would be prevented from taking place. Many were deterred from attending, but

Figure 14.14: Johnny Clegg is joined on stage by his sons Jesse and Jaron and Sipho Mchunu at the end of the 'Final Journey Tour' performance in Cape Town, 30 June 2017. Photograph © Marguerite de Villiers Coetzee, 2017.

Figure 14.15: Johnny Clegg's sons, Jesse and Jaron, speak at a tribute held by Johnny Clegg's former dance teammates at Jules Park in central Johannesburg, near Jeppe Hostel, 1 September 2019. Photograph © Marguerite de Villiers Coetzee, 2019.

Figure 14.16: Dancers perform a tribute for Johnny Clegg at Jules Park in central Johannesburg, near Jeppe Hostel, 1 September 2019. Photograph © Marguerite de Villiers Coetzee, 2019.

Figure 14.17: Bafazana Qoma, Johnny Clegg's long-time friend, who organised and participated in the tribute to Clegg held at Jules Park in central Johannesburg, near Jeppe Hostel, 1 September 2019. Photograph © Marguerite de Villiers Coetzee, 2019.

there were many others who came to pay their respects and be part of an effervescent moment. Dancers kicked up dust in a spirited spectacle. It was mentioned by someone close to him that one of the last things Clegg had said, in isiZulu, was: burn the *impepho*, I'm dying.[117]

As the world shut down in 2020 amidst a global pandemic, tributes, memories and condolences continued to pour in as the loss of Clegg lingered. It is believed by some that when a person dies, linear time stops and 'everything happens in the same moment, if you can imagine that'.[118] It is also believed that their spirit remains connected to those left behind. What came next was an *ukubuyisa* (a traditional crossing ceremony) at Mchunu's home in Makhabaleni.[119] Some say that human beings are composed of *umzimba* (body), *indlozi* (spirit), *inhliziyo* (heart), *ingqondo* (mind) and *isithunzi* (shadow). It is believed that *isithunzi* becomes an ancestral spirit after an *ukubuyisa* ceremony is performed in order to bring it back home, to *umsamo* (a sacred place) where the living can converse with their ancestors.[120] Clegg was given his own *ukubuyisa* ceremony. It is the final phase of a rite of passage: returning and being reincorporated.

Clegg was once asked what kind of ancestor he hoped to be.[121] He responded:

> All ancestors should be a source of auspiciousness and good fortune, all ancestors should guard their offspring and guard the ones they left behind, they should take care and be connected, which is hard for them because they're in another place so they have to be reminded. The living must remember the dead, and they do that through real rituals, and say 'we are still here and you must look after us and you must bide with us, don't go wandering off somewhere and forget about us'.

He went on to say that he wanted to be the kind of ancestor that held people together: someone with that magic ability to have people gather around and to keep things going. 'That's the kind of ancestor I'd like to be.' Clegg will be remembered by many for having *inkani*, *isibindi* and *isigqi* (stubborn determination, unwavering courage, and rhythmic power). 'It is the braves who

Figure 14.18: Johnny Clegg's sons, Jesse and Jaron, speak at the Tribute Show at Emmarentia Botanical Gardens, Johannesburg, 17 July 2022. Photograph © Marguerite de Villiers Coetzee, 2022.

would rather perish than surrender,' said Nathi Mthethwa at the memorial, referring to a poem by Samuel Edward Krune (S.E.K.) Mqhayi, 'that have died and given birth to a new awakening.'[122]

In the years that have passed since his death, Clegg's autobiography was published posthumously,[123] and Wits University hosted a 'Free People's Concert' in 2022 to celebrate its centenary and its alumnus Johnny Clegg. Jesse Clegg recorded a song about the fear of change inherent in loss (whose music video features home movie clips from his childhood), and together with the solo artist Msaki, with whom he sometimes collaborates, released a reimagining of a cluster of Johnny Clegg's songs.[124] A tribute concert was held at Emmarentia Dam in 2022 (see figures 14.18 and 14.19), where Mchunu sang a song about losing someone who meant the world to him. It is the same song that Clegg and Mchunu had sung at a 'Free People's Concert' in 1974.[125] In the recording of their original performance of this song, Clegg had introduced it as a lament about being exposed after the death of a loved one, and asking to be guarded from harm.[126]

Figure 14.19: Former band members Andy Innes (of Savuka) and Sipho Mchunu (of Juluka) perform together at Johnny Clegg's Tribute Show at Emmarentia Botanical Gardens, Johannesburg, 17 July 2022. Photograph © Marguerite de Villiers Coetzee, 2022.

CLOSURE

> I know you are thinking that
> for something to be born
> something has to die.[127]

Clegg was buried in a plain pine coffin, as per his request. Here lay the remains of a meaningful life lived 'devoid of airs and graces'.[128] His gravestone is engraved with a collection of song lines. The words 'You enchanted us...' are etched between the lyrics. 'As I expected, Johnny Clegg was laid to rest in accordance with the practices of his mother's people – within 3 days of passing, in a Jewish cemetery', wrote Canada-based cultural anthropologist Shelley TSivia Rabinovitch.[129] She went on to explain that, for her, Clegg embodied the Jewish teaching of *tikkun olam*: the act of repairing and improving upon the world through ritual performance. Clegg had constructed a kaleidoscopic image of himself out of fragments, and found

Figure 14.20: Jesse Clegg performs 'Cruel, Crazy, Beautiful World' while home videos of him and his father are displayed on a screen behind him at The Teatro, Montecasino, Johannesburg, 25 November 2023. Photograph © Marguerite de Villiers Coetzee, 2023.

strength in those broken parts.[130] 'I am inherently a meaning-maker as a musician and an anthropologist. I look for webs of significance in my life and what unfolds around me.'[131]

The last time Clegg had entered a recording studio was with US band Walk The Moon and his son Jesse (see figures 14.20 and 14.21). The song they recorded – 'Fire in Your House' – was released in 2021.[132] Lead singer Nicholas Petricca spoke of the collaboration with Clegg occurring at a time in which he was trying to make sense of an experience in his life, and Clegg had framed a narrative thereof.[133] The overarching theme of the song seems to be one of finding solace in the depths of love; however, it is obscured by a shadowy presence: dwelling in the sorrow of regret and what 'could have been'. Hope persists ('[a] place to start again'), juxtaposed against a lingering weariness ('I cannot hide it / Is it nearly over? / Are we near the end?') and a fear of not knowing what will remain and what will return. As if coming full circle, the song tugs at threads entangled with Clegg's greater body of work. Consider, for example, the lines 'After all of the words have been spoken'

King of Time: A Lament for Johnny Clegg

Figure 14.21: Nicholas Petricca of Walk the Moon performs with Jesse Clegg at his 'Songs and Memories' gig at Montecasino in Johannesburg, 25 November 2023. Photograph © Marguerite de Villiers Coetzee, 2023.

and 'How much longer must I twist in the wind?' 'The Crossing' expresses a sad realisation: 'All the words in truth that were spoken, that the wind has blown away'.[134]

The isiZulu verse '*Lomshika shika / Wendaba / Wawushisa umuzi wami*' translates as 'this thing you did – what you were busy with – look, it has burned down my house'.[135] The image of the house appears in several of Clegg's songs ('The homes of my fathers are burning').[136] 'What burns in the fire we'll find again in the ashes' Clegg sings as the song comes to a close. We are reminded of an earlier lesson: the dry, dead grass is made new and fresh again by fire.[137] We are awakened by hardship: we learn to live again in difficult moments. 'Sometimes we step into the dark so we can see the light / We only see the stars at night'.[138]

The final thematic chapter of Clegg's autobiography, 'The River', invokes an image of 'the mighty Tugela, carving its slow, magnificent way to the sea'. As the river passes by, finding its way around and over obstacles to

Figure 14.22: The first photograph the author took of Johnny Clegg, at the 'Joburg Day' festival in September 2006. Photograph © Marguerite de Villiers Coetzee, 2006.

Figure 14.23: The last photograph the author took of Johnny Clegg, at the 'Final Journey Tour' performance in Cape Town's Grand West Casino, 1 July 2017. Photograph © Marguerite de Villiers Coetzee, 2017.

reach the final destination it has dreamed of, so too has Clegg's life been guided by 'something secret, invisible and magical … unfolding'.[139] We, too, were hypnotised and comforted by watching him do what was in his nature. I bring this chapter to a close in celebration of the magical, paradoxical and untranslatable enigma that is Johnny Clegg. This is my lament for him. Now we can step out of the shadow of lamenting: empowered by what has come to light, illuminated by the stories, silences and spirit surrounding Skeyi's life and legacy.[140]

ACKNOWLEDGEMENTS

This chapter would not have come to pass were it not for Thandeka Tembe, who made poetic worlds accessible in her translation of language and sentiment, and Bafazana Qoma, whose gracious storytelling and generous spirit embody his philosophy: 'My heart is a church'.

NOTES

1   Johnny Clegg, 'Tell Him Again', on *Third World Child* (album, Johannesburg: MINC, MINC (L) – 1140, 1985).
2   Johnny Clegg & Savuka, 'I Call Your Name', on *Shadow Man* (album, Sandton: EMI, EMCJ (D) – 7904111, 1988).
3   John Perlman, '#UnderTheSkin: Johnny Clegg: Final Journey Part 1,' *eNCA*, 28 February 2018, YouTube video, 14:09, accessed 11 April 2025, https://www.youtube.com/watch?v=yOLRnIYlQtI.
4   Johnny Clegg, *Scatterling of Africa: My Early Years* (Johannesburg: Pan Macmillan, 2021), 5.
5   Juluka, 'Mama Shabalala', on *African Litany* (album, Johannesburg: MINC, MINC – (L) 1020, 1981); Juluka, 'December African Rain', on *Work For All* (album, Johannesburg: MINC, MINC – (L) 1070, 1983); Juluka, 'Sky People', on *Universal Men* (album, Johannesburg: Gramophone Records Co./CBS Records, CBS – DNW 2429, 1979); Juluka, 'Deliwe', on *Universal Men*; Juluka, 'Universal Men' on *Universal Men*.
6   For example, 'Memory upon memory binds you into a timeless web' (Juluka, 'African Litany', on *African Litany*).
7   For example, 'But you will always be a child of Africa, always a wilderness' (Juluka, 'Deliwe', on *Universal Men*).
8   For example, 'And for centuries they've travelled on a pale phantom ship' (Juluka, 'Universal Men', on *Universal Men*).
9   For example, 'Where a million lifetimes flow' (Juluka, '*iJwanasibeki*', on *Scatterlings* [album, Johannesburg: MINC, MINC – (L) 1040, 1982]).

10   For example, 'The old ones gone before / Weep for those they left behind' (Juluka, 'Sky People', on *Universal Men*); 'And one day the skies will clear and eagles fly above those you left behind' (Juluka, 'Deliwe', on *Universal Men*).

11   For example, 'Will you join the swallows and fly away' (Juluka, 'Deliwe', on *Universal Men*).

12   For example, 'I remain totally empty, I remain with nothing' (Juluka, 'Crocodile Love', on *Crocodile Love* [album, International: HR BV Music/One World Music/CNR Music, 3032202, 1997]).

13   Juluka, 'December African Rain', on *Work For All*.

14   For example, 'Sometimes hard to keep up the fight' (Juluka, 'Kilimanjaro', on *Stand Your Ground* [album, Burbank: Warner Bros Records, 925 155-1, 1984]); 'Sometimes I feel that you really know me / Sometimes there's much you can show me' (Johnny Clegg & Savuka, 'Great Heart', on *Third World Child*); 'Sometimes you will smile while you're crying inside' (Johnny Clegg & Savuka, 'Cruel, Crazy, Beautiful World', on *Cruel, Crazy, Beautiful World* [album, Sandton: EMI, EMCJ (E) – 7934461, 1989]).

15   For example, 'This could have been the last time I ever saw you smile' (Johnny Clegg & Savuka, 'Too Early for the Sky', on *Shadow Man*).

16   For example, 'Let the wheel turn one more time' (Clegg, 'Don't Walk Away', on *Third World Child*).

17   For example, 'No time to hide or fight' (Johnny Clegg & Savuka, 'Warsaw 1943', on *Cruel, Crazy, Beautiful World*).

18   For example, 'He believes in a magic wave that rolls on the sea of time / At any time it can appear' (Johnny Clegg & Savuka, 'Bombs Away', on *Cruel, Crazy, Beautiful World*).

19   For example, 'Every time you wake up I hope it's under a blue sky' (Johnny Clegg & Savuka, 'Cruel, Crazy, Beautiful World', on *Cruel, Crazy, Beautiful World*).

20   Johnny Clegg & Savuka, 'Woman Be My Country', on *Cruel, Crazy, Beautiful World*.

21   For example, 'Outside there's a whole world changing / We can't stand here, trapped inside' (Johnny Clegg & Savuka, 'These Days', on *Heat, Dust and Dreams* [album, Sandton: EMI, CDEMCJ (WF) 5499, 1993]); 'You've gotta roll with the punches and change with the times' (Clegg, 'Gumba Gumba Jive', on *Third World Child*).

22   For example, 'A victim of history or just a sign of the times' (Johnny Clegg & Savuka, 'Woman Be My Country', on *Cruel, Crazy, Beautiful World*).

23   For example, 'I saw a dream whose time has come / In the best of times and in the worst of times / Oh, your time will come' (Johnny Clegg & Savuka, 'Your Time Will Come', on *Heat, Dust and Dreams*).

24   For example, 'Dance across the centuries / Dance across the sea of time' (Johnny Clegg & Savuka, 'Dance Across the Centuries', on *Shadow Man*).

25   For example, 'Hunting my tomorrow on the edge of time' (Johnny Clegg & Savuka, 'African Shadow Man', on *Shadow Man*).

26   For example, 'Just a child lost in time' (Johnny Clegg & Savuka, 'The Promise', on *Heat, Dust and Dreams*).

27   For example, 'It's killing time' (Johnny Clegg & Savuka, 'These Days', on *Heat, Dust and Dreams*).

28   For example, 'We are fetching our future, grabbing our tomorrow' (Johnny Clegg & Savuka, '*Siyayilanda*', on *Shadow Man*); 'The shape of his own future, now in his own hands' (Johnny Clegg & Savuka, 'One (Hu)'Man One Vote', on *Cruel, Crazy, Beautiful World*); 'Foreign nights are filled with future dreams kept on hold' (Johnny Clegg &

Savuka, 'Foreign Nights', on *Heat, Dust and Dreams*); 'Far below, we leave forever / Dreams of what we were' (Johnny Clegg & Savuka, 'Scatterlings of Africa' on *Third World Child*).
29 Clegg, 'Third World Child' on *Third World Child*.
30 Johnny Clegg & Savuka, 'Human Rainbow', on *Shadow Man*.
31 Johnny Clegg & Savuka, 'Warsaw 1943', on *Cruel, Crazy, Beautiful World*.
32 Johnny Clegg & Savuka, 'When the System Has Fallen', on *Heat, Dust and Dreams*.
33 Johnny Clegg & Savuka, 'Tough Enough', on *Heat, Dust and Dreams*.
34 Clegg, 'Africa Rising', on *New World Survivor* (album, Pretoria: Value Music, CDVM (WFL) 45, 2002).
35 Clegg, 'All Is Not Lost', on *Third World Child*.
36 Johnny Clegg, 'Jongosi', on *One Life* (album, Johannesburg: Sting Music, STIDCD 106, 2006).
37 For example, 'There's a new day coming ... Against yesterday's tide' (Clegg, 'Africa Rising', on *New World Survivor*).
38 Clegg, 'The Revolution Will Eat Its Children', on *One Life*.
39 Johnny Clegg, 'Witness', on *King of Time* (album, Johannesburg: Universal Music, UMGCD 145, 2017).
40 Johnny Clegg, 'Manqoba', on *Human* (album, Johannesburg: Sting Music, STIDCD(WA) 182, 2010).
41 Clegg, 'King of Time', on *King of Time*.
42 Various Artists, *Power of One: The Songs Of Johnny Clegg*. Album. Los Angeles: Rhythm Safari, RSFCD 1046 (174), 2008.
43 Johnny Clegg & Savuka, 'Cruel, Crazy, Beautiful World', on *Cruel, Crazy, Beautiful World*.
44 Johnny Clegg, *My Favourite Zulu Street Guitar Songs* (DVD, Sydney: Scatterlings Pty Ltd and Rhythm Dog Music, 2010).
45 Estelle Sinkins, 'Johnny Clegg', *The Witness*, 2010, accessed 14 May 2025, https://witness.co.za/archive/2010/06/12/johnny-clegg-20150430/.
46 Johnny Clegg, 'Golden Country' (on soundtrack, Duncan MacNeillie, dir., *Jock the Hero Dog*, [Johannesburg: Jock Animation, 2011]); Clegg, *Human*; Ella Terri et al., *A Country Imagined* (Johannesburg: SABC2/ Curious Pictures, 2010).
47 Johnny Clegg, 'MANDELA', *Facebook*, 12 December 2013, https://www.facebook.com/johnnycleggsa/posts/10151893957889811/.
48 British High Commission Pretoria, 'Her Majesty Queen Elizabeth II Birthday Honours 2015: South Africa', 13 June 2015, accessed 11 April 2025, https://www.gov.uk/government/news/her-majesty-queen-elizabeth-ii-birthday-honours-2015-south-africa.
49 Jane Dutton, 'Tonight with Jane Dutton: Johnny Clegg Special,' *eNCA*, 18 December 2018, YouTube video, 22:56, accessed 11 April 2025, https://www.youtube.com/watch?v=d7Futvwgyuk&t=157s.
50 Johnny Clegg, 'The Importance of Ending on the Off-Beat in Umzantsi and Isishameni Dancing', in *Papers Presented at the Symposium on Ethnomusicology, Number 18, 2004*, ed. Andrew Tracey, 30–31. Grahamstown: International Library of African Music, Rhodes University.
51 Clegg, 'Importance of Ending', 31.
52 'Family Postscript', in Clegg, *Scatterling*, 300–301.
53 Jessica Levitt, 'I Feel Like I Can Keep Going Forever, But I Know It's an Illusion: Johnny Clegg in His Own Words', *TimesLive*, 17 July 2019, accessed 11 April 2025,

54   https://www.timeslive.co.za/tshisa-live/tshisa-live/2019-07-17-i-feel-like-i-can-keep-going-forever-but-i-know-its-an-illusion-johnny-clegg-in-his-own-words/.
54   Perlman, 'Final Journey Part 1'.
55   Clegg, *Scatterling*, 3–4.
56   Clegg, 'King of Time', on *King of Time*.
57   Clegg, *Scatterling*, 5.
58   Clegg, 'King of Time', on *King of Time*.
59   Perlman, 'Final Journey Part 1'.
60   Clegg, 'Touch the Sun', on *One Life*.
61   Juluka, *'Impi'*, on *African Litany*; Clegg, 'Touch the Sun', on *One Life*.
62   John Perlman, '#UnderTheSkin: Johnny Clegg: Final Journey Part 2,' *eNCA*, 28 February 2019, YouTube video, 14:09, accessed 11 April 2025, https://www.youtube.com/watch?v=ltTArxpzag8.
63   Clegg, *Scatterling*, 293.
64   Perlman, 'Final Journey Part 1'.
65   Perlman, 'Final Journey Part 1'.
66   The 'Final Journey Tour' began in Cape Town on 30 June 2017 and ended on 13 October 2018 in Mauritius.
67   D.H. Lawrence quoted in Clegg, *Scatterling*, xix.
68   Clegg, *Scatterling*, 2.
69   David Zeitlyn, *An Anthropological Toolkit: Sixty Useful Concepts* (New York: Berghahn, 2022).
70   Clegg, 'Touch the Sun', on *One Life*.
71   Clegg, *Scatterling*, 2.
72   Roddy Quin, 'Foreword', in *Scatterling of Africa: My Early Years*, by Johnny Clegg, ix–xviii (Johannesburg: Pan Macmillan, 2021).
73   Both of these phenomena had an impact on Clegg's personal and professional missions, most obviously his engagement with the communities in migrant hostels, and, less known, his involvement in the campaigns for tuberculosis treatment organised by the Treatment Action Campaign.
74   Clegg played a leadership role in SAMA, according to the book on David Webster by Julie Frederikse, *They Fought for Freedom: David Webster* (Cape Town: Maskew Miller Longman, 2000). See also chapter 7 in this book by Michael Drewett.
75   The 1987 Johnny Clegg & Savuka song 'Missing', on *Third World Child*, is said to have been inspired by Webster's activism, particularly his work regarding the death squads and detention centres that were responsible for thousands of people going missing.
76   David Webster quoted in a tribute by Eddie Webster, 'F11_David Webster_0.pdf', *South African History Online*, accessed 13 April 2025, https://www.sahistory.org.za/people/david-joseph-webster.
77   Frederikse, *David Webster*.
78   Johnny Clegg & Savuka, 'Human Rainbow', on *Shadow Man*.
79   Samuel G. Freedman, 'Johnny Clegg's War on Apartheid,' *Rolling Stone*, 22 March 1990, accessed 13 April 2025, https://www.rollingstone.com/music/music-features/johnny-clegg-south-africa-apartheid-samuel-freedman-860888/.
80   Freedman, 'Johnny Clegg's War on Apartheid'.
81   Freedman, 'Johnny Clegg's War on Apartheid'. The album cover of *Cruel, Crazy, Beautiful World* features a young Jesse sitting atop his father's shoulders.

82 Webster's assassin had been identified as an apartheid hitman working for the state, Ferdi Barnard. He was sentenced to life imprisonment in 1999 and released on parole in 2019.
83 John Avildsen, dir., *The Power of One* (Burbank: Warner Bros Pictures, 1992). The book, *The Power of One* (New York: Random House, 1989), had been written by South African-born Australian author Bryce Courtenay, published in 1989 and set in the author's childhood during the Second World War.
84 Clegg, 'All Is Not Lost', on *Third World Child*; Hans Zimmer, 'Southland Concerto' (soundtrack, John Avildsen, dir. *The Power of One* [Burbank: Warner Bros Pictures, 1992]), YouTube video, 02:27, accessed 14 May 2025, https://www.youtube.com/watch?v=gUh0IMQ99kg.
85 Thandeka Tembe, conversation with the author, November 2023.
86 There is controversy and speculation around Ndlovu's death. See Jeremy Simmonds, 'Dudu Zulu', in *The Encyclopedia of Dead Rock Stars: Heroin, Handguns, and Ham Sandwiches* (2nd edition, Chicago: Chicago Review Press, 2012), 287.
87 Johnny Clegg & Savuka, 'The Crossing (*Osiyeza*)', on *Heat, Dust, and Dreams*.
88 Johnny Clegg & Juluka, 'Johnny Clegg & Juluka Rockpalast,' 1997, YouTube video, 1:45:00, accessed 13 April 2025, https://www.youtube.com/watch?v=PhAOR-z3igI&t=127s.
89 Juluka, 'Sky People', performed at the 'Free People's Concert', University of the Witwatersrand, 16 February 1974. Digitised reel-to-reel tape, hymap-dm-reel-free-peoples-concert-1974-001, Hidden Years Music Archive, Documentation Centre for Music, Stellenbosch University.
90 Juluka, '*Ubaba Akalele*' ('The Father Is Not at Peace'), on *Crocodile Love*.
91 Clegg, 'Gumba Gumba Jive', on *Third World Child*.
92 Johnny Clegg & Savuka, 'Dance Across the Centuries', on *Shadow Man*.
93 Johnny Clegg & Savuka, 'Cruel, Crazy, Beautiful World', on *Cruel, Crazy, Beautiful World*.
94 Johnny Clegg & Savuka, 'Dela', on *Cruel, Crazy, Beautiful World*.
95 Johnny Clegg & Savuka, 'Warsaw 1943', on *Cruel, Crazy, Beautiful World*.
96 Johnny Clegg & Savuka, 'I Can Never Be (What You Want Me to Be)', on *Heat, Dust and Dreams*.
97 Dutton, 'Johnny Clegg Special'.
98 Clegg, 'Hooked on Tragedy', on *Third World Child*.
99 Clegg, '*Thamela*', on *One Life*.
100 Clegg, '*Asilazi*', on *One Life*.
101 Clegg, 'Hidden Away Down', on *Human*.
102 Perlman, 'Final Journey Part 2'.
103 Friends of Johnny Clegg, 'The Crossing', 6 December 2018, YouTube video, 06:42, accessed 13 April 2025, https://www.youtube.com/watch?v=WKWEEpA0HkY.
104 Johnny Clegg & Savuka, 'The Crossing (*Osiyeza*)', on *Heat, Dust and Dreams*.
105 Mandela Day is a South African public holiday held annually on 18 July, Mandela's birthday, to honour his life and legacy.
106 Johnny Clegg & Savuka, '*Asimbonanga*', on *Third World Child*. See chapter 12 in this book by Nicol Hammond for a discussion of the meanings and resonances of this song.
107 Ndlovu Youth Choir, 'A Tribute to Johnny Clegg', YouTube video, 01:29, accessed 14 May 2025, https://www.youtube.com/watch?v=jns5qY4R87c.

108   Harry Belafonte quoted in Clegg, *Scatterling*, v.
109   The first time I met Qoma was in 2007, when I was in high school, attending one of Clegg's gigs. Early on in my anthropology degree at Wits I would accompany Qoma to Kwa Mai Mai Market and to the dance events on Sundays near Jeppe Hostel – partly to conduct fieldwork, but mostly to experience the world expressed in Clegg's songs and stories.
110   Thandeka Tembe, translation in conversation with the author, November 2023.
111   SABC News, '[LIVE] Johnny Clegg Public Memorial Service', YouTube video, 01:35:02, accessed 14 May 2025, https://www.youtube.com/watch?v=ZyXslBDVrTo.
112   Marguerite Coetzee, 'Johnny Clegg Memorial: Laying Down Our Troubles', *SA People*, 26 July 2019, accessed 13 April 2025, https://www.sapeople.com/fab-south-african-stuff/johnny-clegg-memorial-laying-down-our-troubles/.
113   John Perlman, '#UnderTheSkin: Johnny Clegg: Final Journey Part 4', *eNCA*, 28 February 2019, YouTube video, 16:25, accessed 13 April 2025, https://www.youtube.com/watch?v=CrQPsJboTNs&t=140s. Clegg did not recall the name of the author of *Black Dogs*; however it is plausible that the author is Ian McEwan.
114   'I've Been Looking' by Jesse Clegg was included on the *King of Time* album and was performed on the 'Final Journey Tour'; Jaron Clegg, 'Johnny Clegg & Savuka – Take My Heart Away (High Society Remix)', 30 June 2016, YouTube video, 04:52, accessed 13 April 2025, https://youtu.be/lL4_flXbHhs?feature=shared; Johnny Clegg, 'Johnny Clegg – King Of Time', 26 January 2018, YouTube video, 03:15, accessed 13 April 2025, https://youtu.be/Q7ssXuvNf9k?feature=shared; Perlman, ' Final Journey Part 2'.
115   Tembe, conversation with the author, November 2023.
116   Filmmaker, music producer and owner of Shifty Records Lloyd Ross recorded the dance tribute by Clegg's George Gogh team (Lloyd Ross, 'Johnny Clegg Tribute Dance', 1 September 2019, Vimeo video, 02:17, accessed 13 April 2025, https://vimeo.com/357503285?share=copy). In a caption to the video, Ross described this celebration of Clegg's 'unique life' as a 'stark contrast to the looting and burning marauders down the road. Respect and love for Johnny were thick in the air'.
117   *Impepho* is a dried plant that is burned in order to communicate with ancestors or the deceased.
118   Johnny Clegg speaking in the video 'Johnny Clegg & Juluka Rockpalast'.
119   Real Concerts, 'Johnny Clegg's traditional Zulu crossing', 25 February 2020, YouTube video, 01:23, accessed 13 April 2025, https://youtu.be/j9Bwaqizbvc?feature=shared. '*Ukubuyisa isidumbu*' means 'bringing back the body'. This was the topic of a paper Clegg wrote in 1979 that was presented at an African Studies seminar: Johnny Clegg, '"*Ukubyisa Isidumbu* – Bringing Back the Body": An Examination into the Ideology of Vengeance in the Msinga and Mpofana Rural Locations, 1882–1944', in *Working Papers in Southern African Studies*, vol. 2, ed. Philip Bonner, 165–181 (Johannesburg: Ravan Press, 1981). In the paper he examines the ideology of vengeance: a logic that legitimises the act of feuding.
120   Tembe, conversation with the author, November 2023.
121   Perlman, 'Final Journey Part 2'.
122   SABC News, '[LIVE] Johnny Clegg Public Memorial Service'.
123   Clegg, *Scatterling*.
124   Jesse Clegg, 'Jesse Clegg – Waiting on the Outcome (Official Video)', 8 December 2021, YouTube video, 03:56, accessed 13 April 2025, https://youtu.be/UvEKVYz77Ew?feature=shared; Jesse Clegg and Msaki, 'Friday Guest: 'Johnny [*sic*]

Clegg, Msaki' Perform 'Hoping for a Miracle'", *eNCA,* YouTube video, 03:11, accessed 14 May 2025, https://www.youtube.com/watch?v=SHBsFNJHNeU.
125 The concert is described in chapter 2 of this book by Lizabé Lamprechts and Pakama Ncume.
126 'Free People's Concert', 16 February 1974.
127 Johnny Clegg & Savuka, 'Tough Enough', on *Heat, Dust and Dreams*.
128 These are the words of Andrew Grant Innes in chapter 3 of this book.
129 Shelley TSivia Rabinovitch, 'Tikun Olam', *Facebook,* 20 July 2019. https://www.facebook.com/groups/155466707851840/?hoisted_section_header_type=recently_seen&multi_permalinks=2422953197769835. Westpark Cemetery in Johannesburg, close to Emmarentia Dam where Clegg had performed several times, contains Christian, Jewish, Muslim and Chinese burial areas.
130 Clegg, 'Hidden Away Down', on *Human*.
131 Clegg, *Scatterling*, 3. This is perhaps a reference to anthropologist Clifford Geertz's statement that 'man is an animal suspended in webs of significance he himself has spun' (Clifford Geertz, *The Interpretation of Cultures* [New York: Basic Books, 1973]).
132 Walk the Moon, 'Fire in Your House (Official Video) ft. Johnny Clegg, Jesse Clegg', 12 September 2021, YouTube video, 05:00, accessed 13 April 2025, https://youtu.be/swCYGfqoxK4?feature=shared; Walk the Moon (featuring Johnny Clegg and Jesse Clegg), 'Fire in Your House', on Heights (album, New York: RCA Records, 19439-91277-2, 2021).
133 This explanation was provided at Jesse Clegg's concert at Montecasino in Johannesburg in November 2023, called 'Songs and Memories'.
134 Friends of Johnny Clegg, 'The Crossing'; Walk the Moon (featuring Johnny Clegg and Jesse Clegg), 'Fire in Your House'.
135 Walk the Moon (featuring Johnny Clegg and Jesse Clegg), 'Fire in Your House'; Tembe, translation in conversation with the author, September 2021.
136 Johnny Clegg & Savuka, 'Woman Be My Country', on *Cruel, Crazy, Beautiful World*. The image of the house may – intentionally or otherwise – be related to Carl Jung's interpretation of the house as a representation of the human psyche: an interaction between a facade and an interior that corresponds with an integrated public life and a private self (Carl G. Jung, *Memories, Dreams, Reflections,* trs. Richard Winston and Clara Winston [New York: Pantheon Books, 1961]).
137 Clegg, '*Utshani Obulele*' on *One Life,* 2006, which features the isiZulu saying '*Utshani Obulele, buvuswa wumlilo*' ('The dry, dead grass is made new and fresh again by fire').
138 Clegg, 'Wishing Well,' on *King of Time*.
139 Clegg, *Scatterling*, 293.
140 The name 'Skeyi' given to Johnny Clegg is explained by Sipho Mchunu and Andrew Grant Innes in chapter 6 of this book.

REFERENCES

Avildsen, John, dir. *The Power of One*. Film. Burbank: Warner Bros Pictures, 1992.
British High Commission Pretoria. 'Her Majesty Queen Elizabeth II Birthday Honours 2015 – South Africa'. 2015. Accessed 13 April 2025. https://www.gov.uk/government/news/her-majesty-queen-elizabeth-ii-birthday-honours-2015-south-africa.

Clegg, Jaron. 'Johnny Clegg & Savuka – Take My Heart Away (High Society Remix)', 30 June 2016. YouTube video, 04:52. Accessed 13 April 2025. https://youtu.be/lL4_flXbHhs?feature=shared.

Clegg, Jesse. 'Jesse Clegg – Waiting on the Outcome (Official Video)', 8 December 2021. YouTube video, 03:56. Accessed 13 April 2025. https://youtu.be/UvEKVYz77Ew?feature=shared.

Clegg, Jesse and Msaki, 'Friday Guest | 'Johnny [sic] Clegg, Msaki' Perform 'Hoping for a Miracle''. *eNCA*. YouTube video, 03:11. Accessed 14 May 2025. https://www.youtube.com/watch?v=SHBsFNJHNeU.

Clegg, Johnny. 'Johnny Clegg – King Of Time', 26 January 2018. YouTube video, 03:15. Accessed 13 April 2025. https://youtu.be/Q7ssXuvNf9k?feature=shared.

Clegg, Johnny. 'The Importance of Ending on the Off-Beat in Umzantsi and Isishameni Dancing'. In *Papers Presented at the Symposium on Ethnomusicology, Number 18, 2004*, edited by Andrew Tracey, 30–31. Grahamstown: International Library of African Music, Rhodes University.

Clegg, Johnny. *Scatterling of Africa: My Early Years*. Johannesburg: Pan Macmillan, 2021.

Clegg, Johnny. '"*Ukubyisa Isidumbu* – Bringing Back the Body": An Examination into the Ideology of Vengeance in the Msinga and Mpofana Rural Locations, 1882–1944'. In *Working Papers in Southern African Studies*, vol. 2, edited by Philip Bonner, 165–181. Johannesburg: Ravan Press, 1981.

Coetzee, Marguerite. 'Johnny Clegg Memorial: Laying Down Our Troubles'. *SA People*, 26 July 2019. Accessed 13 April 2025. https://www.sapeople.com/fab-south-african-stuff/johnny-clegg-memorial-laying-down-our-troubles/.

Courtenay, Bryce. *The Power of One*. New York: Random House, 1989.

Dutton, Jane. 'Tonight with Jane Dutton: Johnny Clegg Special'. *eNCA*, 18 December 2018. YouTube video, 22:56. Accessed 13 April 2025. https://www.YouTubevideo.com/watch?v=d7Futvwgyuk&t=157s.

'Free People's Concert'. University of the Witwatersrand, 16 February 1974. Digitised reel-to-reel tape, hymap-dm-reel-free-peoples-concert-1974-001. Hidden Years Music Archive, Documentation Centre for Music, Stellenbosch University.

Frederikse, Julie. *They Fought for Freedom: David Webster*. Cape Town: Maskew Miller Longman, 2000.

Freedman, Samuel G. 'Johnny Clegg's War on Apartheid'. *Rolling Stone*, 22 March 1990. Accessed 13 April 2025. https://www.rollingstone.com/music/music-features/johnny-clegg-south-africa-Apartheid-samuel-freedman-860888/.

Friends of Johnny Clegg. 'The Crossing', 6 December 2018. YouTube video, 06:42. Accessed 13 April 2025. https://www.YouTube video.com/watch?v=WKWEEpA0HkY.

Geertz, Clifford. *The Interpretation of Cultures*. New York: Basic Books, 1973.

Johnny Clegg & Juluka. 'Johnny Clegg & Juluka Rockpalast', 1997. YouTube video, 1:45:00. Accessed 13 April 2025. https://www.youtube.com/watch?v=PhAOR-z3igI.

Jung, Carl G. *Memories, Dreams, Reflections*. Translated by Richard Winston and Clara Winston. New York: Pantheon Books, 1961.

Levitt, Jessica. 'I Feel Like I Can Keep Going Forever, but I Know It's an Illusion: Johnny Clegg in His Own Words'. *TimesLive*, 17 July 2019. Accessed 13 April 2025. https://www.timeslive.co.za/tshisa-live/tshisa-live/2019-07-17-i-feel-like-i-can-keep-going-forever-but-i-know-its-an-illusion-johnny-clegg-in-his-own-words/.

MacNeillie, Duncan, dir. *Jock the Hero Dog*. Film. Johannesburg: Jock Animation, 2011.

Ndlovu Youth Choir. 'A Tribute to Johnny Clegg'. YouTube video, 01:29. Accessed 14 May 2025. https://www.youtube.com/watch?v=jns5qY4R87c.

Perlman, John. '#UnderTheSkin: Johnny Clegg: Final Journey Part 1'. *eNCA*, 28 February 2019. YouTube video, 14:09. Accessed 13 April 2025. https://www.youtube.com/watch?v=yOLRnIYlQtI.
Perlman, John. '#UnderTheSkin: Johnny Clegg: Final Journey Part 2'. *eNCA*, 28 February 2019. YouTube video, 12:23. Accessed 13 April 2025. https://www.youtube.com/watch?v=ltTArxpzag8.
Perlman, John. '#UnderTheSkin: Johnny Clegg: Final Journey Part 4'. *eNCA*, 28 February 2019. YouTube video, 16:25. Accessed 13 April 2025. https://www.youtube.com/watch?v=CrQPsJboTNs.
Quin, Roddy. 'Foreword'. In *Scatterling of Africa: My Early Years*, by Johnny Clegg, ix–xviii. Johannesburg: Pan Macmillan, 2021.
Real Concerts. 'Johnny Clegg's Traditional Zulu Crossing', 25 February 2020. YouTube video, 01:23. Accessed 13 April 2025. https://youtu.be/j9Bwaqizbvc?feature=shared.
Ross, Lloyd. 'Johnny Clegg Tribute Dance'. 1 September 2019. Vimeo video, 02:17. Accessed 13 April 2025. https://vimeo.com/357503285?share=copy.
SABC News. '[LIVE] Johnny Clegg Public Memorial Service'. YouTube video, 01:35:02. Accessed 14 May 2025. https://www.youtube.com/watch?v=ZyXslBDVrTo.
Simmonds, Jeremy. 'Dudu Zulu'. In *The Encyclopedia of Dead Rock Stars: Heroin, Handguns, and Ham Sandwiches*. 2nd edition, 287. Chicago: Chicago Review Press, 2012.
Sinkins, Estelle. 'Johnny Clegg'. *The Witness*, 12 June 2010. Accessed 14 May 2025. https://witness.co.za/archive/2010/06/12/johnny-clegg-20150430/.
Terri, Ella, Liza Key, Feizel Mamdoo, Vincent Moloi, Guy Spiller and John Trengove, dirs. *A Country Imagined*. Television series. Season 1, presented by Johnny Clegg. Johannesburg: SABC/ Curious Pictures, 2010.
Walk the Moon. 'Fire in Your House' (Official Video) ft. Johnny Clegg, Jesse Clegg, 12 September 2021. YouTube video, 05:00. Accessed 13 April 2025. https://youtu.be/swCYGfqoxK4?feature=shared.
Webster, Eddie. 'F11_David Webster_0.pdf'. *South African History Online*. Accessed 13 April 2025. https://www.sahistory.org.za/people/david-joseph-webster.
Zeitlyn, David. *An Anthropological Toolkit: Sixty Useful Concepts*. New York: Berghahn, 2022.
Zimmer, Hans. 'Southland Concerto'. On soundtrack of *The Power of One*. United States: Elektra Entertainment, 1992. YouTube video, 02:27. Accessed 14 May 2025. https://www.youtube.com/watch?v=gUh0IMQ99kg.

DISCOGRAPHY

Clegg, Johnny. 'Golden Country'. On soundtrack, Duncan MacNeillie, dir. *Jock the Hero Dog*. Film. Johannesburg: Jock Animation, 2011.
Clegg, Johnny. *Human*. Album. Johannesburg: Sting Music, STIDCD(WA) 182, 2010.
Clegg, Johnny. *King of Time*. Album. Johannesburg: Universal Music, UMGCD 145, 2017.
Clegg, Johnny. *My Favourite Zulu Street Guitar Songs*. DVD. Sydney: Scatterlings Pty Ltd and Rhythm Dog Music, 2010.
Clegg, Johnny. *New World Survivor*. Album. Pretoria: Value Music, CDVM (WFL) 45, 2002.
Clegg, Johnny. *One Life*. Album. Johannesburg: Sting Music, STIDCD 106, 2006.
Clegg, Johnny. *Third World Child*. Album. Johannesburg: MINC, MINC (L) – 1140, 1985.
Johnny Clegg & Savuka. *Cruel, Crazy, Beautiful World*. Album. Sandton: EMI, EMCJ (E) – 7934461, 1989.

Johnny Clegg & Savuka. *Heat, Dust and Dreams*. Album. Sandton: EMI, CDEMCJ (WF) 5499, 1993.

Johnny Clegg & Savuka. *Shadow Man*. Album. Sandton: EMI, EMCJ (D) – 7904111, 1988.

Johnny Clegg & Savuka. *Third World Child*. Album. Sandton: EMI, EMCJ (D) – 2407331, 1987.

Juluka. *African Litany*. Album. Johannesburg: MINC, MINC – (L) 1020, 1981.

Juluka. *Crocodile Love*. Album. International: HR BV Music/One World Music/CNR Music, 3032202, 1997.

Juluka. *Scatterlings*. Album. Johannesburg: MINC, MINC – (L) 1040, 1982.

Juluka. *Stand Your Ground*. Album. Burbank: Warner Bros Records, 925 155-1, 1984.

Juluka. *Universal Men*. Album. Johannesburg: Gramophone Records Co./CBS Records, CBS – DNW 2429, 1979.

Juluka. *Work For All*. Album. Johannesburg: MINC, MINC (L) 1070, 1983.

Various Artists. *Power of One: The Songs Of Johnny Clegg*. Album. Los Angeles: Rhythm Safari, RSFCD 1046 (174), 2008.

Walk the Moon (featuring Johnny Clegg and Jesse Clegg). *Heights*. Album. New York: RCA Records, 19439-91277-2, 2021.

CONTRIBUTORS

Marguerite de Villiers Coetzee is an anthropologist, artist and futurist from South Africa, born at a time when the country was transitioning to democracy. Music is the language with which she senses and makes sense of the time and space in which she exists, and of those that came before and are yet to be. Johnny Clegg shaped her life trajectory and it is through his contribution to the world that she now conducts research, formulates strategies and tells stories across past, present and future horizons. She is currently studying for her PhD at the University of Oxford.

Michael Drewett is a professor in the Department of Sociology at Rhodes University. He is the co-editor (with Martin Cloonan) of *Popular Music Censorship in Africa* (2006) and (with Sarah Hill and Kimi Kärki) of *Peter Gabriel: From Genesis to Growing Up* (2010), and is currently working on a book about popular music censorship in South Africa. He produced the documentary film *Stopping the Music* (2002) about an instance of South African music censorship. He is the coordinator of the Cutting Grooves Censorship of Popular Music in South Africa Archive, and in this capacity has worked with Shifty Records on two CD compilations, organised an exhibition on the censorship of music during apartheid at the National Arts Festival in Grahamstown (now Makhanda) and worked with the Museum of World Culture in Gothenberg, Sweden, setting up a sub-exhibition of censored music during the apartheid era. He is a collaborator on the South African music archival project *Mixtapes ZA*.

Andrew Friedland is the Richard and Jane Pearl Professor Emeritus in the Environmental Studies Department at Dartmouth (University) College in Hanover, New Hampshire, USA. Professor Friedland has researched ecosystem science in montane regions of the northeastern US and has taught environmental science and energy courses. He holds a PhD in earth and environmental science from the University of Pennsylvania. In 2015, he was inducted as a fellow into the American Association for the Advancement of Science.

Nicol Hammond is an associate professor of cultural musicology at the University of California, Santa Cruz. She holds a PhD in ethnomusicology from New York University and a BMus from the University of the Witwatersrand. Her research explores music performance and listening practices in contexts of transformation, including the new South Africa, queerness, transnational pageantry, trauma and education.

Brett Houston-Lock is a former South African musician and journalist who now lives in the UK and works as a media consultant. Before leaving South Africa he worked in the Rhodes University Department of Journalism and Media Studies. He is a co-producer of the popular podcast about South African music, 'Tune Me What?', and a collaborator on the South African music archival project *Mixtapes ZA*. He is the author of the innovative AI-themed book *Man/Verses/Machine* (2023).

Andrew Grant Innes (Andy Innes) is the former guitarist, vocalist and music director of the Johnny Clegg Band, and worked with Clegg in the studio and on stage from 1992 until 2019. He has worked in various facets of the music industry as a performer, producer, artist manager, innovator and non-profit organisation director. He has co-authored a paper on Johnny Clegg's impact on culture and anthropology with Lucilla Spini for the *International Journal of Anthropology*, and was involved in the transcription of historical South African guitar styles together with Billy Monama for the Indigenous African Music Transcription Project. He currently works in music composition and production, live performance and artist management. He also sits on the board of the South African Music Performance Rights Association and is a PhD candidate at Stellenbosch Business School, conducting research on the relationship between culture and psychological contract.

Lizabé Lambrechts is an extraordinary associate professor at the Africa Open Institute for Music, Research and Innovation at Stellenbosch University. Over the past decade she has collected, archived and preserved the Hidden Years Music Archive, one of the biggest popular music archives in South Africa. She is the research director of the project 'Decay without Mourning: Future Thinking Heritage Practices', as well as the CEO of Nuuseum, a non-profit organisation dedicated to preserving and sharing cultural heritage. As an archivist, curator and academic, her research and publications focus on archive, power, heritage and memory.

Chris Letcher is a South African film composer, songwriter and senior lecturer in screen music composition at the University of Edinburgh. He has recently composed a score for the feature film *Don't Let's Go to the Dogs Tonight* (Sony Pictures Classics, 2025). He has published essays on issues of process in screen music creation and on musical representation in African cinema in *Music, Sound, and the Moving Image*, *The Journal of Film Music* and *Ethnomusicology Forum*. He has written a chapter on Cristóbal Tapia de Veer's score for *The White Lotus* (2021–2025) for the forthcoming publication *Sonic Production Practices in Contemporary Film, TV and Short-Form Media*.

Sipho Mchunu is a musician and farmer. He met Johnny Clegg in the early 1970s and the two began to play music together, soon performing at folk gatherings as Johnny and Sipho before changing their name to Juluka in 1979. In 1985 he left Juluka in order to focus on his family and his farm. In 1989 he recorded the solo album *Yithi Esavimba*, released in France, and followed that in 1990 with the album *Umhlaba Uzobuya* produced by 3rd Ear Music in Durban. He continued to perform with Johnny Clegg as Juluka from time to time; they brought out a further Juluka album, *Crocodile Love*, in 1997, and he joined Clegg as a guest artist for some of his final shows. In 2018 the Durban University of Technology awarded him an honorary doctorate of philosophy in visual and performing arts. In 2021 he released the album *Iselula*.

Caleb Mutch is a research scientist at the Max Planck Institute for Empirical Aesthetics. He has been a post-doctoral research fellow and visiting assistant professor at Indiana University, and prior to that he served as a lecturer at Columbia University, where he also completed a PhD in music theory. He studies topics including the history of music theory from antiquity to the romantic era, formal analysis of baroque and classical music, and South African popular music. His research has been published in journals including *Music Theory Spectrum*, *The Journal of Mathematics and Music*, *Popular Music* and *The Journal of Music Theory*.

Pakama Ncume is a sound archivist and librarian at Stellenbosch University Library and Information Services. From 2017 to 2021 she was responsible for digitising the reel-to-reel and cassette tapes in the Hidden Years Music Archive. Her master's degree focused on the Market Theatre Café, documenting the music and musicians who performed in this alternative music space.

Richard Pithouse is a distinguished research fellow at the Global Centre for Advanced Studies in Dublin and New York, an international research scholar in the Department of Philosophy at the University of Connecticut, an extraordinary professor in the Department of Language Education at the University of the Western Cape, a columnist for the *Mail & Guardian* and the Africa Coordinator of the Progressive International. He is the former editor of *New Frame*, described by Achille Mbembe as 'one of the most exciting political, intellectual and cultural projects to emerge in Africa'. He is also the founder of The Commune, a radical bookstore, and The Forge, a space for public discussions, performances and exhibitions, both located in Johannesburg. As the founding editor of Inkani Books, he commissioned the recently published isiZulu translation of Frantz Fanon's *The Wretched of the Earth*.

Lucilla Spini a bio-anthropologist and sustainability expert. She has held various positions within the United Nations System (for example, the United Nations Educational, Scientific and Cultural Organization) and non-governmental organisations, and has contributed to international negotiations on environmental challenges and sustainable development, managed sustainability projects and programmes, and contributed to scientific publications and UN reports. She has also served as an adjunct assistant professor in anthropology at the University of Waterloo and as an adjunct professor in the School of Geography and Earth Sciences at McMaster University. She has been a Giorgio Ruffolo research fellow in sustainability science at Harvard University's John F. Kennedy School of Government, a policy leader fellow at the School of Transnational Governance of the European University Institute, and is currently senior research fellow with the Italian National Research Council's Institute for Heritage Science (Istituto di Scienze del Patrimonio Culturale del Consiglio Nazionale delle Ricerche). She received a BA (Honours) in anthropology from New York University in 1997, an MSc in human biology in 1998 and DPhil in biological anthropology in 2005 from the University of Oxford, and a *Laurea* in foreign languages and literature from the University of Florence in 2019, with a thesis on J.M. Coetzee. In 2020 she published the book *Of Scatterlings and Stakeholders: Diversity, Inclusion and Transnational Governance for Sustainable Development* in memory of Johnny Clegg. She has considered herself as a Scatterling since 1986.

Martina Viljoen is a research fellow at the Odeion School of Music, University of the Free State. She publishes on topics concerning cultural musicology, critical musicology and the aesthetics of music. She was the guest editor of a volume on critical theory and musicology for *The International Review of the Aesthetics and Sociology of Music* in 2005. She has participated in an international research project on South African kwaito music, published in *The World of Music* (2008). She contributed to the first international reader on hip hop and religion, *Religion and Hip Hop* (2014), and was the editor of *Musics of the Free State: Reflections on a Musical Past, Present, and Future*, published in the series *Musicology Without Borders* (2015). She is also the editor of the book *A Passage of Nostalgia: The Life and Work of Jacobus Kloppers* (2020). Her most recent work focuses on ethno- and Afrophobia in South African protest songs.

INDEX

Page numbers in *italics* indicate photographs.

A
Abdullah Ibrahim 26, 259
Actuel 62, 148
Africa, Mervyn 33, 89
African Litany (Juluka) 88
   'African Sky Blue' 7, 47, 94, 96, 119
   'Impi' 3, 53–55, 94, 96, 119, 132, 253
   'Mama Shabalala' 94, 271
African National Congress (ANC) 93, 136, 157
Aggett, Neil 67, 84, 89, 97, 233, 243n16
Anderson, Muff 64, 243n14
anthropology 269
   Clegg's background in 1–2, 4, 10, 184, 186, 190, 252, 255, 270–271, 282–283, 294
   see also Clegg's musical identity: impact of anthropology background on
anti-apartheid/anti-racist movements in Europe 148, 154, 156–158
   see also British Anti-Apartheid Movement; France; United States of America: anti-apartheid movement in
apartheid culture-power construct 43
   censorship as weapon in 2, 6, 29, 37n52, 46, 62, 64, 252, 261
   Clegg's countercultural resistance to 13, 47, 55, 63–65, 68–70, 75, 83–84
   continuing effects of 54–55
apartheid era 5
   assassinations/death squads 67, 69, 86, 157, 177, 186, 252, 283–284, 300n75, 301n75, 302n82
   harassment and repression of Clegg in 61–62, 84, 98, 252
   homeland (Bantustan) system 43, 242n5
   multiracial events in 24, 26, 29–30, 64, 252
   restrictive realities of 2–3, 5, 26, 43
   see also racial segregation in South Africa; Webster's assassination
Artists Against Apartheid 138, 158, 163n46
'*Asimbonanga*' 6, 33, 103, 105, 150, 153
   Joan Baez recording of 186, 231, 238
   interwoven call and response structures of 229–235, 240, 242n12
   overt message of resistance in 38n69, 67–68, 71–72, 74–75, 83, 89
   Zulu protest origins of 12, 88, 231
   see also Mandela, Nelson: *Asimbonanga* as tribute to
'*Asimbonanga*', shifting meanings of 241
   iconic celebratory version with Mandela 12, 78n35, 230, 234–236, 249–250
   Savuka version 231, 243n16
   Snotkop and Karen Zoid medley 78n41, 230, 238–241
   Soweto Gospel Choir renditions 13, 78n41, 230, 235–237

B
Baez, Joan 186, 231, 238
Belafonte, Harry 134, 157, 260, 265n37, 286
Berger, John
   A Seventh Man 91, 93, 105–106
Berklee College of Music 11, 195

Biko, Steve 67, 86, 89, 233 *see also* Gabriel, Peter: 'Biko'
black trade union movement 97
  Clegg's involvement in 86–87, 98
  1973 strike 86
Blundell, Keith 20, 25n8
Braudo, Muriel (Clegg's mother) 2, 21
Bright Blue 127, 259
British Anti-Apartheid Movement (AAM) 140
  link between BMU and 138–139, 141
  position on cultural boycott 9, 125–128, 130, 132–136, 138–139, 142n8, 259
British Musicians' Union (BMU)
  Clegg's confrontations with 9, 125, 130–133
  Clegg's expulsion from 9, 135–138, 158, 259
  resolution on cultural boycott 126
Brock University, Ontario 189–190
Brutus, Dennis 157, 187
Butler, Jonathan 128, 134
Butler, Judith
  idea of performativity 63, 66, 73

C

Career Opportunities (John Hughes) 10
  schizophonic placement of 'Cruel, Crazy, Beautiful World' in 169–170, 176–177, *177*, 178, 179n3, 181n27
Celluloid, Paris 147–148
City University of New York (CUNY)
  Clegg as guest lecturer at 11, 185
  Clegg's honorary doctorate from 4, 11, 190–191
Clegg, Jaron 42, 288, *289*, 292
Clegg, Jesse 42, 178, 272, *273*, *274*, *279*, 284, 288, *289*, 292, *292*, 294, *294*, 295, *295*, 300n81, 302n114
Clegg, Johnny *270*, *296*
  birth of 2, 21
  legacy of 4–5, 13, 102, 251, 260
  see also death of Johnny Clegg
Clegg, Mylah Thandolwethu (grandchild) 288
Clegg's activism
  anti-apartheid 1–3, 49, 84–85, 197, 252
  in France 147, 151, 154, 157–8, 160
  intertwining of cultural and 1, 55, 62, 67, 151, 177, 183, 190–191, 193, 196 *see also* black trade union movement: Clegg's involvement in
Clegg's deep connection with Zulu culture 2, 7–8, 11, 13, 21, 23–24, 31, 260
  and concepts of masculinity 73–74, 85, 90, 94, 96, 98, 104, 191
  initiation into *iNala* age regiment 52–53–54
  Ukwamukelwa Ekhaya ceremonies 51–52, 54, 58n39&40
  through use of Zulu guitar and dance styles 12, 21–23, 25, 29–30, 33–34, 62, 64–5, 88–89
  see also cultural appropriation critiques of Clegg; maskanda; *ngoma* dancing; Zulu identity: Clegg's forging of
Clegg's lyrics 63–64
  allegory of 'the journey' and of belonging in 3, 66, 71–73, 78n31, 173
  concepts of displacement, loss and repression in 71–72, 74, 76, 173
  death and metaphorical associations as theme of 284–286
  'dream' of reconciliation as recurring theme in 69, 71–72, 74
  Marxist understanding of labour in 7, 90
  poetic power of 90–91, 105
  recurrent migrant labour theme in 7–8, 90–93, 98, 104–5
  references to political uprising in 70–71
  time and space as recurring theme in 13, 270–271, 280–281
  transgressive mixing of cultural symbolism in 12, 14, 31, 62, 65–66, 68, 74–75, 191, 271
Clegg's musical identity
  African humanist 6, 61, 72, 75, 190
  artistic evolution of 5, 12, 34–35
  entwining of race and class in 6–7, 26, 64, 84, 95, 106
  influence of anthropology background on 6, 13–14, 61–62, 75, 183, 185, 199
  performative subversive artistic expression of 63, 66, 72–76, 252
  polycultural 6–7, 19–20, 26, 33–34, 62, 71
Clingman, Paul 20, 28
  Father to the Child 29, 87–88
  crossover with Clegg and Mchunu 29–30, 32, 87–88

Cologne Zulu Festival, Germany 88, 128, 142n20
Conrath, Phillipe 153, 158
Coplan, David 64, 67, 184, 189
Count Wellington Judge 24, 26
Craig, John 129, 131, 135
Cruel Crazy Beautiful World
   as song dedicated to first son Jesse 178
   'One (Hu)'Man One Vote' 7, 63, 69–72, 76, 79n46&47, 104, 249
   see also Career Opportunities: schizophonic placement of 'Cruel, Crazy, Beautiful World' in; Italy: *Cruel Crazy Beautiful World* tour of; Webster, David: dedication of 'One (Hu)'Man One Vote' to
cultural appropriation critiques of Clegg 13, 45, 250
   on *Deep Cut* podcast 251–253, 255, 259
   definition of term 263n7
   and denial of artistic collaboration 252, 257–258, 260–263
   far left opinions on 262
   and international reviewers' prejudices 253–254
   Mabe Thobejane's views on 261–262
   Mchunu's views on 258
   Nhlanhla, Ngcobo on 254
   North American perspective of 13, 250–251, 258–259
   world music purists' views on 253, 257
   see also apartheid culture-power construct: Clegg's countercultural resistance to; Clegg's deep connection with Zulu culture
cultural boycott 126, 185
   Clegg's attempts to navigate 9, 125, 131–136, 138–139, 259
   different applications of 185
   impact on South African musicians 127
   see also British Musicians' Union: support of cultural boycott; UN resolution on academic and cultural boycott

D
Dammers, Jerry 138, 232
Dartmouth (University) College
   Clegg's honorary doctorate from 4, 11, 192, *193*

Clegg's lectures at 188–189, 191–192, *194*, 196–198
Montgomery fellowship award 11, 192–195, 203n57, 204n67
death of Johnny Clegg 41, 84, 160, 272, 293
   Emmarentia Dam tribute concert (2022) 292, *292*, *293*
   how he confronted it 14, 276, *276*, 278, 280–283, 293–295
   Mchunu's eulogy on 41–42, 119, 256
   newspaper tributes to 250, 260
   public memorial service 287, *287*, 288
   tribute Zulu dance event 288, *289*, *290*, *291*, *292*, 302n116
   ukubuyisa at Mchunu's home 290
   see also Johnny Clegg Band: Final Journey Tour; *King of Time*
Dibango, Manu 153, 155
Dlanga, Mandisa 192, 230, 234
Durban University of Technology 4, 11

E
End Conscription Campaign 98, 239

F
Fanon, Frantz 85–86
February, Judith 67, 74–75
Fédération Mondiale des Villes Jumelées 148, 161n4
'Festival Jazz et Musiques Métisses', Angoulême 9, 148–149, 155, 158, 160, 161n3
folk music scene
   Clegg's feelings about 23–24
France
   anti-fascist and anti-racist counterculture in 156–157
   Chevalier de l'Ordre des Arts et des Lettres award 3–4, 10, 154
   Clegg's engagement with French culture and language in 158–160
   support for anti-apartheid struggle in 9–10, 154, 156
France, Johnny Clegg Band in 9, 65, 128–129, 147, 150–151, *152*, 153 163n36
   In My African Dream website 158
   performances at Angoulême festival 9, 148–149, 158, 160, 161n3

France, Johnny Clegg Band in (*continued*)
    see also '*Festival Jazz et Musiques Métisses*'; '*Le Zoulou Blanc*'; Renaud; *Shadow Man* documentary
'Free People's Concerts' 5, 20–21, 24, 26–27, 27, *28*, *28*, 86, 292
    as platform for counterculture movement 29
    see also 'Tribal Blues Concerts'
Freedman, Samuel 178, 219
Freedom's Children 20, 26

G

Gabriel, Peter 134, 162n17, 219
    'Biko' 78n37, 232, 235, 237–238, 243n16, 244n22
Gordimer, Nadine 157, 187
Group Areas Act *see under* racial segregation in South Africa
Gumede, Sipho 33, 89

H

Hammond-Tooke, David 184–185, 200
Heat, Dust and Dreams (Savuka) 83, 154, 253–254
    'The Crossing' 7, 104–105, 285–286, 295, 303n136
Hidden Years Music Archive 5, *20*, *27*, *28*, 242n6
    digitisation project 19–21, 30, 35n1, 231
    see also Marks, David
Hollywood cinema, use of Clegg's music in 10, 169–170, 173, 178–179, 179n2, 181n25 *see also Career Opportunities*; *Rain Man*
Hotline 251, 259

I

Idir 154–155
Innes, Andy (Andrew Grant) 62, 192
International Tracks (Juluka) 225n25
    'Akanaki Nokunaka' 48, 101–102
Isandlwana, Battle of 53, 94
Italy 75, 129, 157
    Cruel Crazy Beautiful World tour of 154, 158
izibongo see Pooley, Thomas: on *izibongo*; praise names in Zulu culture

J

Jansen, Robbie 33, 89
Japan 127, 129
Jarre, Jean-Michel 157
Johannesburg Democratic Action Committee (JODAC) 136–137, 139
Johnny Clegg Band 158–159
    death of band member Bongani Masuku 275
    Final Journey Tour 141, 195, 249, 282, *289*, *296*
    Human Tour 188–190
    Lebanon Opera House concerts 192, 194, 202n43
    see also France, Johnny Clegg Band in; Innes, Andy
Johnny Clegg & Savuka *see* Savuka
Juluka 2–3, 5–6, 63, 169
    disbanding of 49–50, 102–103
    early focus on Zulu culture and social issues 47–48, 84
    impact of cultural boycott on 125, 128–132, 140–141
    international exposure of 5, 8–9, 49, 63, 100–101, 143n42, 147, 158
    unique South African sound of 30, 33, 62–64, 88–89, 94, 143n42, 209, 222
    use of verse-chorus form by 214–215, 218, 223, 230
Juluka Live (*The Good Hope Concerts*) 103, 215, 218

K

Keuzenkamp, Carike 238–239
Kidjo, Angélique 254–254
King Sunny Adé 49, 130, 155
King of Time 280–281
    'I've Been Looking' 302n114
    'King of Time' 281
    'Oceanearth' 159–160

L

Ladysmith Black Mambazo 88, 93, 128, 254
Lang, Jack 154, 156, 163n43
'Le Zoulou Blanc' ('The White Zulu') 9, 62, 148, 153, 160
Lindberg, Des and Dawn 22, 35n8, 44–45

M

Mackay, Ramsay
  Orang-Outang 24, 26
Mahlathini and the Mahotella Queens 93, 134, 254
Makeba, Miriam 134, 148, 259
Makhabeleni (Sipho Mchunu's home) 44, 50–51, *51*, *53*, 87, 118
Malombo 20, 24, 26, 93
Mandela, Nelson
  Asimbonanga as tribute to 12, 38n69, 63, 67–68, 78n40, 89, 231
  death of 235, 275
  release from prison of 9, 12, 89, 140–141, 154, 186, 234
  Savuka's exclusion from 70th birthday concert of 9, 125, 134–135, 137, 144n72, 243n22, 259
Mango Groove 251
Marikana massacre 106, 251
Market Theatre 30, 88
  Clegg and Mchunu at Market Café 5, 19, *20*, 21, 28, 30–32, 231
Marks, David 5, 20–22, 30
  3rd Ear Music Company 20, 24, 26
  see also Hidden Years Music Archive
Masekela, Hugh 134, 259
maskanda 12, 22–23, 29, 30, 32–34, 35n5, 84–85, 104, 225n26, 253, 256, 262
  Clegg's unique crossover style of 62, 65, 68, 88–89, 94, 101, 220, 231, 242n9, 243n14
  guitar and dance styles 21
  walking songs 25, 27–28, 31, 191
Matanzima, Kaiser 12, 38n69, 88–89, 231, 242n5
mbaqanga 12, 62, 65, 67–68, 95, 101, 220, 222–223, 226n30 *see also* township jive
McDonald, David 63, 72–74
Mchunu, Sipho 2
  core Zulu traditions and beliefs of 49–50, 52, 58n38
  efforts to foster non-racialism by 13
  existential challenges faced by 6, 43
  honorary doctorate (Durban University of Technology) 4
  Mchunu's bond with Clegg 2, 6, 30–31, 42–45, 118
    teenage friendship 21, 84, 256–257
    through musical collaboration 4–7, 9, 24–25, 32–34, 65, 84, 87, 128, 249, 256–257
    see also 'Free People's Concerts'; Juluka
  Mchunu's solo projects
    Iselula 103
    Umhlaba Uzobuya 103–104
    Yithi Esavimba 103
Meintjes, Louise 65, 219, 222
migrant workers 2, 31, 106
  cosmology of 92
  see also Berger, John: *A Seventh Man*
migrant workers, Clegg's empathy with life-world of 47, 84, 87, 91, 105–106
  through formative encounters in hostels 7–8, 21, 24, 44, 115–119, 300n73
  see also Clegg's lyrics: recurrent migrant labour theme in
Mousset, Christian 148–149, 154, 161n7
Mthethwa, Nathi 287, 292
Musa Ukungilandela (Juluka) 105
  'Akanaki Nokunaka' 47, 101–102
  'Woza Moya' 48
Mutwa, Credo 21–22
Mxenge, Victoria 67, 78n36, 89, 233, 243n16
Mzila, Charles (Charlie) *114*, *290*, 297
  Clegg's early teacher and mentor 2, 21, 84–85, 114, 118, 197

N

'National Folk Song Festival' 21–22, 24
  Clegg's performance at 22–23, 34
Ndlovu, Dudu 2, 104, 116, 118
  impact of his death on Johnny 283, 285–286
N'Dour, Youssou 219, 254
Neruda, Pablo 61, 72, 76n3, 90, 99, 108n24
ngoma dancing 25, 36n24, 65, 85, 90, 94, 276, 278
Niederlander, Edi 20, 22, 28

O

One Life 162n24
  'Touch the Sun' 281
Oppenheimer, Harry 44–45

P

praise names of Johnny Clegg 8, 41, 56n2, 114–115
    Clegg's explanation of 116–118
    see also Zulu poetic narrative: bestowal of praise names in
Pooley, Thomas 62, 64–65, 69, 74, 76
    on *izibongo* 24
Pratley, Colin 24, 33, 89

Q

Qoma, Bafezane 2, 55, *114*, 286, 302n109

R

racial segregation in South Africa 13, 26, 37n52, 43–44, 63, 66, 232
    Group Areas Act 43, 197, 203n62
    pass laws 6, 26, 63, 66
Radio Zulu 37n52, 46
Rain Man (Barry Levinson) 171
    recontextualisation of 'Scatterlings of Africa' in 169–170, 172–173, 174, *174*, 175–176, 178, 179n3, 180n17, 186
    see also Zimmer, Hans: score of *Rain Man*
rainbow nation ideology 42, 83, 89
Rand Daily Mail 131–132
Record Business 129–130
Renaud 9, 149, *150*, 154, 156, 162n24
    'Jonathan' 151
    lifelong friendship with Clegg 151
    'Miss Maggie' 150
Rhodes University 276
Rocard, Michel 9, 153
Rolling Stone 178, 253
Rosenthal, Hilton 2, 89, 98, 129, 141, 186
    on production of Johnny's songs for films 169–171, 174–175, 177, 180n10, 181n25
    Plus 4 Studio, Los Angeles 187, 201n23
    on reworking of 'Scatterlings of Africa' 215, 217–218

S

Safari Records 129, 131
Samudzi Zoé 250, 255
Savuka 3, 5, 48
    cultivation of Pan-African/world music sound 170n6, 209–210, 212, 219–220
    impact of cultural boycott on 9, 125, 132–136, 138–139
    international reception of 103–104, 169–170
    introduction of two-step drum pattern 210, 212–214, 216–218, 222–223, 224n14
    transition from Juluka to 7, 11, 49–50, 103
Scatterling of Africa: My Early Years (Clegg's autobiography) 3, 23, 34, 46, 85, 160, 199, 222, 260, 269, 278, 282–283, 292, 295, 297
    Belafonte's message in 286
Scatterlings (Juluka) 103, 130, 132, 153
    'Ijwanesbeki' 96–98
    move away from political allegory in 96–97
    'Scatterlings of Africa' 3, 6, 8–9, 63, 65–67, 71, 75, 129,
    'Siyayilanda' 12, 97, 150, 210, 224n12
    see also Shadow Man: reworking of 'Siyayilanda' in
Séchan, Renaud *see* Renaud
Serote, Mangane Wally 148, 157
Shadow Man (Savuka) 151, 162n12, 253
    'I Call Your Name' 12, 119, 153, 210, 219–220, *221*, 222–223, 226n31
    reworking of 'Siyayilanda' in 12, 150, 209–215, 217, 222, 224n5, 7&12
    'Talk to the People' 7, 63, 69, 71–72
Shadow Man documentary 149–151, 162n17
Shamley, Colin 20, 22, 28
Shore, Larry 11, 185
Simon, Paul
    accusations of cultural appropriation against 260
    Graceland 171, 186, 255, 259
Six, Claude 9, 141, 148–149, 151, *152*, 154, 159–161
South African Broadcasting Corporation 29, 62
South African Musicians' Alliance (SAMA)
    Clegg's role in 3, 140, 187, 300n74
    David Webster as founder of SAMA 283–284
    position on cultural boycott 134–135, 139
Soweto uprising (1976) 87, 93

Spini, Lucilla 50, 62, 66
Springsteen, Bruce 96, 108n23, 253
   'Sun City' 101, 109n61
Stellenbosch University 21, 35n1
Stand Your Ground (Juluka) 48, 100, 101
Stoddard, Jack 135–136, 138

T

Tambo, Dali 138, 163n46
Taylor, Timothy 65, 243n16
Third World Child 65, 67, 103, 133, 150, 172, 186, 213, 224n8, 225n25, 284
   'Missing' 300n75
   'Scatterlings of Africa' (reinterpretation of) 10, 12, 62–63, 71, 75, 184, 186, 209, 215–219, 222, 225n20
   see also *Rain Man*: recontextualisation of 'Scatterlings of Africa' in
Tholet, Clem 22, 28
township jive 62, 67–68, 95, 101, 253
Touré Kunda 148, 155
'Tribal Blues Concerts' 20–21, 24–26, 34 36n26 *see also* 'Free People's Concerts'
The Troubadour 21, 35n8&9
tuberculosis 62, 283
   Clegg's involvement in TAC campaigns 195, 300n73

U

Ubuhle Bemvelo (Juluka) 95, 101, 128–129, 147, 220
ubuntu 190, 199, 229, 236, 241n4
umhube bow (mouthbow) 30–31, 38n58, 47, 57n28, 88–89, 92
UN resolution on academic and cultural boycott 184
   and effective blacklist 126–127, 141
   symposia on 3, 11, 139, 164n53
   see also cultural boycott
United Democratic Front (UDF) 78n41, 79n44, 89
   Clegg's connections with 68, 98, 101–103
   conflict between Inkatha and 102–103
   position on cultural boycott 136, 139
United Kingdom (UK) 2, 96, 125
   presentation of OBE to Clegg (2015) 4, 275–276
   Thatcher government 127, 130, 133, 150

United States (US) 49
   anti-apartheid movement in 185, 187
   Clegg's engagement with academic institutions in 10–11, 183, 187–188, 199
   music tours in 133, 186, 188–190
   see also City University of New York; Dartmouth College, New Hampshire
Universal Men (Juluka) 33, 88, 105
   'Africa' 1–2, 32–33, 92
   'Deliwe' 33, 90, 93–94, 271
   '*Inkunzi ayihlabi ngokumisa*' 47, 92–93
   'Old Eyes' 91–92, 94
   'Sky People' 91–92, 271, 285
   '*Thula 'Mtanami*' 31, 33, 92
   see also Clegg's lyrics: recurrent migrant labour theme in
University of KwaZulu-Natal 4, 11, 184, 190, 192, 196, 198
University of Natal *see* University of KwaZulu-Natal
University of Witwatersrand *see* Wits University

V

van der Merwe, Schalk 239, 244n26
van Zandt, Steven 101, 109n61
Verwoerd, Hendrik 260, 263
Via Afrika 127, 259

W

Wa Madhlebe *indlamu* dance group 24, 27, 28, 36n35
   '*Emadlozini*' 27–28
'Walk the Moon' 294, *295*
Washington Post 49, 250, 255
Webster, David
   assassination of 69–70, 177–178, 186, 252, 283–284, 302n82
   as mentor and friend of Clegg 2, 70, 79n44, 86, 177–178, 186, 252, 283–284, 300n75
   dedication of 'One (Hu)'Man One Vote' to 69, 284
Wits University 2, 85
   Clegg as junior anthropology lecturer at 2, 10, 79n44, 184–185, 199–200

Wits University (*continued*)
    Clegg and Mchunu performances on campus of 24–26, *27*, *28*, 86
    Clegg's honorary doctorate from 4, 188
    Clegg's student years at 2, 29, 61–62, 85–87
    see also 'Free People's Concerts'
Work for All (Juluka)
    'Bullets for Bafazane' 2, 98
    'Baba Nango' 7, 98
    'December African Rain' 98, 271, 282
    '*Mana Lapho*' 98–99
    'Mdantsane (Mud Coloured Dusty Blood)' 99–100
world music 171–172, 219
    France as fulcrum for 9, 147–149, 153–156
Woza Friday 7, 29–30, 87–88
    banning from airplay of 29–30, 37n52, 46, 243n13, 255
    workers' song 95–96

Z

Zimmer, Hans
    score of *Rain Man* 171–173, 175, 180n10
Zulu cultural traditions and philosophies
    isiphandla 51–52
    stick fighting 21, 25, 32–33, 36n24, 115–116, 149, 191
    universal themes of death and loss 14, 28, 50, 66, 285
Zulu, Dudu Ndlovu *see* Ndlovu, Dudu
Zulu homestead
    isibaya as gravitational centre of 51–54
Zulu identity 24, 107n4
    Clegg's forging of 2, 8, 11, 14, 73–74, 119, 197, 199
Zulu poetic narrative
    bestowal of praise names (*izibongo*) in 8, 113
    see also praise names of Johnny Clegg

www.ingramcontent.com/pod-product-compliance
Lightning Source LLC
Chambersburg PA
CBHW020516080526
44583CB00013B/625